THE NEW WORLD
OF TRAVEL 1989

THE NEW WORLD OF TRAVEL 1989

BY ARTHUR FROMMER

A FROMMER BOOK ✦ PUBLISHED BY PRENTICE HALL TRADE DIVISION ✦ NEW YORK ✦

Published by Prentice Hall Trade Division
A Division of Simon & Schuster, Inc.
Gulf + Western Building
One Gulf + Western Plaza
New York, NY 10023

Book Design by Gates Studio

Research Assistance
by Andi Vayda

Photo Research
by Gillian Theis

ISBN 0-13-617408-6
ISSN 0893-1895

Manufactured in the United States of America

Contents

Preface to Arthur Frommer's New World of Travel 1989

Nel mezzo del cammin di nostra vita"—At a midpoint in the path of my life, to crib from Dante, I felt a sharp malaise about the state of American travel, and with my own role in it.

After 30 years of writing standard guidebooks, I began to see that most of the vacation journeys undertaken by Americans were trivial and bland, devoid of important content, cheaply commercial, and unworthy of our better instincts and ideals.

And overpriced, even in the budget realm.

Those travels, for most Americans, consist almost entirely of "sight-seeing"—an activity as vapid as the words imply. We rove the world, in most cases, to look at lifeless physical structures of the sort already familiar from a thousand picture books and films. We gaze at the Eiffel Tower or the Golden Gate Bridge, enjoy a brief thrill of recognition, return home, and think we have travelled.

Only later do we ask: to what end did I travel? With what lasting rewards?

And these disappointments are not always reduced or affected by the decision to travel cheaply—as I once largely believed. Though the use of budget-priced facilities will *usually* result in a more meaningful trip—because they bring us closer to the realities of the countries through which we pass—they do not guarantee that condition. Even people staying in guesthouses and pensions can pass their days in senseless "sight-seeing," trudging like robots to Trafalgar Square and various Changings of the Guard.

No. To me today, travel in all price ranges is scarcely worth the effort unless it is associated with people, with learning and ideas. To have meaning at all, travel must involve an encounter with new and different outlooks and beliefs. It must broaden our horizons, provide comparative lessons, show us how those in other communities are responding to their social and industrial problems. At its best, travel should challenge our preconceptions and most cherished views, cause us to rethink our assumptions, shake us a bit, make us broader-minded and more understanding.

It is toward achieving that kind of travel—that infinitely more memorable form of travel—that this yearly book hopes to contribute. Its method is to turn a spotlight on a host of little-known travel programs and organizations that surface each year, usually to benefit only the smallest portion of our population.

All over the world, and at home as well, a tiny segment of the travel industry is laboring to add valuable content to the travel experience:

• These are the people who operate ambitious study trips, and scientific tours; they offer challenging, politically oriented journeys, and excursions into the Third World.

• Their aim is to change your life. They experiment with new lifestyles and spiritual quests at yoga retreats and utopian communities, at tented Caribbean resorts and macrobiotic farms, at personal growth centers and adult summer camps.

• They sail the smallest of cruise ships into tiny ports and fishing villages unsullied by mass tourism.

• They practice "integrated tourism," using local facilities, and broadcast appeals for ethical tourism and tourism for the poor.

• They go on treks into the Himalayas or bicycle tours into the Dordogne.

• They enable Americans to study foreign languages at overseas schools, stay as guests in the homes of private families abroad, share the life and rhythm of Australian sheep farms, study 16th-century art with a connoisseur in the Belgian Ardennes.

• They promote homestays among people of accomplishment in Britain, or volunteer workcamps on the coasts of four continents.

But they are fledgling travel companies without funds to properly advertise their new approach; their trips, in consequence, are confined to the barest few.

In this book, hopefully, they will find their voice. Each new edition will atempt to introduce the best of them, and especially those with novel travel ideas: new themes of travel, new travel methods, new programs, new vacation possibilities, new and better ways of visiting old destinations, new destinations. Out of the welter of obscure new travel organizations emerging each year, surely one will lead to at least one new vacation activity for each of our readers.

One, did I say? Why not two or three? Travel should be no occasional fling, but a normal and frequent, integral part of one's life. To have that requires that you learn to cut transportation costs. And so the second theme of this yearly book will be the many new methods of traveling cheaply—from air fare bucket shops to travel rebators and distress merchants, from freighters, charters, and standby fares to air courier services and discount cruise agents—all the myriad travel bargains that surface each year to permit the most alert of our fellow citizens to travel frequently. All this will be discussed not as an end in itself, but simply as a means of reaping the pleasures and rewards of frequent, far-ranging foreign travels.

Our ability to engage in that sort of travel is nothing short of a miracle. We are the first generation in human history to fly to other continents as easily as people once boarded a train to the next town. We are the first generation in human history for whom travel is not restricted to an affluent few, but is available to many.

We should not squander our opportunity. Travel, for too long, has been trivialized in the popular press and by the promoters of popular tours; it deserves better. It is an enduring subject of human concern, the essential requisite for a civilized life, perhaps the most effective tool for reducing foolish national pride and promoting a world view.

It is too important a subject to be left to the commercial megaliths of the travel industry.

Hence, this book.

See you next year.

ARTHUR FROMMER
January 1989

A Request for Comments: The best of books is a collaboration between author and reader. In subsequent editions of this book, we hope to supplement our own recommendations with yours. If you know of additional travel organizations or programs of the sort we've cited, or if you have comments of any sort relating to our text, won't you let us know of them?

Send your comments and/or selections to Arthur Frommer, c/o Prentice Hall Trade Division, One Gulf + Western Plaza, New York, NY 10023.

Introduction to a New Form of Vacation

To Americans of taste and intelligence, the standard holiday trip has frequently become, at best, a crushing bore, at worst a horror, a nightmare. All over the world, small-minded entrepreneurs, urged by profit, have nullified the charm, complexity, and distinctive qualities of numerous leading destinations.

And if this seems an exaggerated complaint, then let me cite several typical experiences familiar to every person who has recently traveled.

• You succumb to the ads for a winter charter program going to a once-quaint fishing village on Mexico's Pacific Coast. You arrive at a mini-metropolis thronged with crowds and lined with gaudy shops displaying mountains of earrings and mass-produced rugs. At the doors to restaurants, the wait for tables is three-quarters of an hour. In the lobbies of hotels, massed ranks of viewers watch U.S. football on satellite TV. Escaping to the beach, you are besieged by hawkers, assaulted by teenagers dropping from the skies in parasails, deafened by the motors of waterski boats.

• You join the strolling crowds in Spain's Toledo, heading for the church that displays El Greco's "Death and Burial of Count Orgaz." Arriving at the site, you jostle with 200 other clamoring visitors for a fleeting glimpse of the glass-protected painting, distanced by a crush of human bodies. You experience the same mob scenes at the Sistine Chapel, the Louvre, the Church of St. Bavo, the Nikko Shrine.

• You visit a medieval cathedral on the castle hill of Prague, and find yourself surrounded by a dozen clusters of tourists straining intently to hear the burst of commentary emerging from their suffering guides. As you seek to concentrate on the art and mood of the High Gothic era, you hear instead the distracting mini-lectures of a dozen touring companies, delivered in French and Russian, Japanese and German, broken English and distorted Danish.

• You arrive, ten minutes before curtain time, in the red-velvet-and-gilt setting of a Parisian music hall, where not a single other person is yet in sight. Suddenly the tour buses appear and the hall is instantly awash with foreigners carrying cameras and guidebooks. Tired dance numbers slouch onto the stage, their music canned, their theme without the slightest reference to even the popular culture of France. Broadly exaggerated imitations of French music hall variety ensue, done without finesse or talent—and hardly rehearsed. Totally contrived for the tourist, simple-minded, and infuriating.

Why are these scenes so frequently encountered?

• Because certain areas of the world are simply being visited by too many.

• Because tour buses, charter flights, and crowds of frantic, camera-toting visitors are spilling over from celebrated plazas, squares, beaches, and airports in the more popular, standard cities or islands.

• Because key attractions are besieged by throngs.

• Because, in response to the numbers, multinational chains have thrown up massive, towering hotels that soon preempt the field, but only serve to separate their guests from the life and atmosphere surrounding them.

• Because large tour companies, intent on the bottom line, follow the course of least resistance, take you only to the famous and familiar, seek to simplify the travel experience, and make it as dumbly comforting, both mentally and physically, as possible.

How, under these circumstances, can a self-respecting, intellectually curious, spirited individual continue to travel?

The answer lies in a new approach, to new destinations, using new modes of travel and lodging, in search of learning. That "New World of Travel" is broadly available to any reasonably energetic person, at lower costs than the standard form of vacation travel, and it is invigorating beyond compare, producing all the rewards (and more) that travel brought before the world became homogenized and mobbed. No matter what your age or resources, once you have taken a nonstandard trip, you will never again return willingly to the hackneyed variety.

The key objective is to experience events, lifestyles, attitudes, cultures, political outlooks, and theological views utterly different from what you ordinarily encounter at home. Unless that happens, why travel? Why endure the fatigue of transportation, and its associated burdens, just to reach a replica of your familiar surroundings? Unless vacation travel is a learning experience, unless it leaves you a bit different from what you were when you began, it is, in my view, a pointless physical exercise.

In seeking these rewards of nonstandard travel, you are now assisted by a growing multitude of small, alternative-travel companies or resorts—more than 1,200 described in this book—of which only a handful existed as recently as ten years ago. The all-but-unnoticed emergence of this new segment of the travel industry—new tour operators, new facilities, new programs, new forms of lodging—is a major phenomenon. It reflects a massive dissatisfaction by large numbers of Americans with the simplistic travels offered by established travel firms and facilities. In effect, tens of thousands of our fellow citizens have opted for adventures of the mind when they travel, a New World of Travel.

Some, for want of assistance, have relied on do-it-yourself methods to enter the New World, and those, too, are described in this book. Essentially, the effort is to stay ahead of the crowds, attempting always to select new destinations and unvisited areas for vacation travel. In each yearly edition of this book, I shall be searching for the as-yet-undiscovered: the places that deserve to be visited, but which for one reason or another—lack of government publicity, difficulty of access—have not to date become the subject of mass-volume, commercial travel. And these, I suggest, are always the sites of memorable vacations.

But usually the process of alternative travel requires an organization: it often involves booking a program or facility that pursues themes or beliefs outside one's normal ken: New Age therapies or Eastern theologies, holistic healing or macrobiotics, utopian living or rebellious politics, Nicaragua or abstract art.

One engages in these novel travel pursuits not necessarily out of a sympathy for such credos, but to be fully alive, open to all thought, constantly questing. I happen to be, in my own beliefs, very much a rationalist, agnostic, suspicious of spiritual claims or sudden panaceas. And yet the most rewarding travels of my life have been those when I exposed myself to diametrically opposing beliefs, in a residential setting, among adherents to those other beliefs, and with an open mind.

Such is the classic travel experience, exhilarating and enlarging; the rest is mere tourism, and painfully dull. Not to have heard alternative viewpoints in the places where they prevail, not to have visited countries of the Third World or nations of Eastern Europe, not to have met the people of other cultures in a nontouristic setting, is not to have lived in this century.

Which brings me to the final, key ingredient of productive, rewarding travel: people. We all know that the encounter with foreign people, on a human scale, away from hotels and tour buses, is the single most memorable event of any trip. Yet most of us pursue that goal of meeting people in an unplanned, helter-skelter fashion, simply hoping that lightning will strike.

The new approach to travel brings careful deliberation, even organization, to such meetings:

• First, by utilizing lodgings that are not standard hotels, but accommodations indigenous to their surroundings, operated by people representative of their respective cultures, and patronized by the world's most interesting tourists—dynamic, spirited, free-thinking people from around the world who disdain the normal channels of commercial tourism and gravitate to such alternative lodgings.

• Second, by choosing tour operators who expose you to the realities of life at each destination, and not simply to sights gussied up or contrived for the visitor. That, too, is a major theme of this book, and the subject of considerable discussion.

• And finally, by utilizing those many nonprofit programs that actually place you in the home of a foreign family, or at least arrange for a social encounter, over tea or at meals.

A wise man once said that Hell consists of being condemned to stay at a different Holiday Inn every night unto eternity.

No such fate awaits our readers. With joy and enthusiasm, let's embark now for the "New World of Travel."

To Pauline
from her proud father

I ≠ VACATION "RESORTS" THAT STRETCH YOUR MIND AND CHANGE YOUR LIFE

Vacationing at a "Personal Growth Center": Esalen and Others

Their Aim Is to Fulfill the Human Potential, to Expand Consciousness and Improve Personal Relationships

Workshop at Omega Institute

Jam session at Omega

On a broad lawn leading to a steep cliff, above the rocky surf and sea lions of the Pacific Ocean, couples hugged or stroked each other's arms. Occasionally they reached out to pat the cheek of a passing stranger.

Others raged in response to a trivial slight. Some of them arm-wrestled, grimly, to settle a dispute.

In scenes such as this, flung across the covers of *Life* and *Look*, the Esalen Institute of Big Sur, California, introduced America in the 1960s to "encounter therapy" and related offshoots of the "human potential movement." Drunk with the vision that they could lead humankind into a new era of heightened insight, sensitivity, and understanding, the personalities associated with Esalen—Michael Murphy, Fritz Perls, Ida Rolf, Abraham Maslow, Will Shutz, Virginia Satir, Rollo May, Gregory Bateson—converted that isolated stretch of seafront heights into a place of unfettered experimentation in psychology, and fired the thought of millions, while offending or frightening legions of others.

Esalen Now

What has happened to Esalen in the ensuing years? Though no longer in the news, it perseveres, even thrives, but at a more measured pace, thoughtful and cautious. And it has spawned over a dozen imitators: residential retreats where hundreds of Americans devote their vacations to exploring a range of psychological subjects so broad as to require college-like catalogs to list them all. Encounter therapy—that almost-instant process of shedding inhibitions and responding to every repressed emotion—is now only one of numerous treatments under study at America's personal growth centers.

For one thing, the early leader of the encounter movement—Michael Murphy, co-founder of Esalen—is no longer certain of the long-term benefits of the art. It is, he believes, only a start—this stripping away of defenses through encounter techniques—which must be succeeded by longer-lasting and less dramatic work. Others have concluded that encounter therapy can be positively dangerous, exposing serious underlying pathologies without providing a trained therapist to deal with what's exposed.

And so the core curriculum of the centers is currently devoted to such multiple emerging sciences as gestalt therapy, psychosynthesis, Ericksonian hypnosis, shamanic healing, neurolinguistics, Feldenkrais, and Rolfing. From these basic inquiries emerge, at some centers, more popular discussions: "Intimate Relationships: Keeping the Spark Alive," "Burn-out: Causes and Cures," "Letting Go—Moving On," "Building Community: A Learning Circle," "Agenda for the 21st Century." All are aimed at expanding human potential, tapping into energies and abilities as yet unknown.

At Esalen, instruction is through seminars or workshops extending over a weekend ($295, including room and board) or five-day midweek ($575). Many first-timers select the orientation workshop simply known as "Experiencing Esalen" (sensory awareness, group process, guided fantasy, meditation, massage), or the somewhat similar "Gestalt Practice"; others choose from more than 100 other widely varied subjects taught throughout the year.

Studies are combined with exquisite relaxation, in a lush oasis of gardens, birds, and natural hot springs; the latter bring 110° sulfurous water into bathhouses where residents can soak for hours while watching the sun or moon set into the ocean below. Rooms are comfortable and pleasantly decorated, but must be shared with others (usually), and lack telephones, TV sets, or radios; a retreat atmosphere is maintained. Meals are served in a dining hall where dress and décor are casual but the cuisine is gourmet. The Esalen gardens and nearby farm supply the majority of the many options in the daily salad and vegetables bar.

When the 100 guest beds are not fully booked (which is common during the winter season and sometimes happens during midweek in summer), it is possible simply to stay at Esalen without enrolling in a seminar. The cost of this varies, but falls into the $70 to $80 range for a night and a day, including dinner, breakfast, and lunch. Often people come to Esalen simply for a bout of quiet writing, or during a time of life transition. As workshops and bed spaces fill up

early (especially in summer), it is important to plan a trip to Esalen well in advance. You may either phone for a catalog or to reserve a workshop on your credit card (call 408/667-3000), but the preferred method is to write c/o **Reservations, Esalen Institute, Big Sur, CA 93920.** The location is 300 miles north of Los Angeles, 175 miles south of San Francisco, between the spectacular coastal highway and the 100-foot cliffs overlooking crashing waves below.

And how do people respond to that setting? I can best report the reaction of a middle-aged couple from Santa Barbara who come here for a semi-annual "fix," to "feel alive and revitalized." Apart from their interest in Aikido movement/meditation (subject of their workshop), they feel that Esalen "has the nicest piece of real estate in the world—beach, rocks, surf, sea, air, mountains, hot tubs, good food, and loving people—who could ask for anything more?"

And Farther Afield

Though Esalen was the first, it is now but one of a dozen such "personal growth" retreats on both coasts of the United States and in between.

Their goal? It is again to fulfill the "human potential," to expand consciousness and improve personal relationships, to tap into the same mysterious sources of energy and spirit that enable mystics in other lands and on other levels to enjoy trances and visions, to walk on nails or fast for days.

Their method? Workshops of a week's or a weekend's duration, attended by vacationing members of the public, who offer up their own psyches to these new therapies or to classroom training.

Unlisted in any directory of which I am aware, and marketed through severely limited mailings or classified ads in magazines of small circulation, they are nonetheless open to all and worthy of far broader dissemination.

East Coast

Omega Institute, Lake Drive (R.D. 2, Box 377), Rhinebeck, NY 12572 (phone 914/338-6030 from September 15 to May 15 and 914/

At Big Sur, on the California coast: the model for a dozen other, quite remarkable, "resorts."

Carl Rogers, teaching at Esalen

An Esalen seminar

Esalen garden

266-4301 from May 15 to September 15), is—apart from Esalen—the lodestone; it attracts up to 400 people a week during its summer operating period from mid-June to mid-September. On a broad lake flanked by extensive, hilly grounds of forest and clearings, in a joyful atmosphere of kindness and smiles, it presents weekend and weeklong workshops ranging from the clearly lighthearted ("Vocal Joy," "Delicious Movement") to the softly therapeutic ("Working with Dreams," "The Fear of Losing Control," "Choosing to Connect") to the arcane and abstruse ("Oriental Diagnosis," "Interfacing Psychology and Spirituality," "The Tibetan Path of Love and Compassion"); many of the most famous figures in the human potential movement—Ram Dass and Ashley Montagu, Ilana Rubenfeld and Per Vilayat Inayat Khan—make an appearance. Tuition averages $50 a day; housing and meals (vegetarian) add $27 or $35 in campsites or dorms, up to $40 and $60 in private cabins. You can contact Omega directly for a copy of their 72-page catalog.

Camp Lenox, Rte. 8, Lee, MA 01238 (phone 413/243-2223): In the southern Berkshires, on 250 hillside acres overlooking a lake, it accepts adults in June and September only, in facilities otherwise operated as a children's summer camp in July and August. Seminars are on weekends only, cost $140 to $215 per person including full board (gourmet vegetarian), and pursue such themes as "Living in the Spirit," "An Invitation to Radical Aliveness," and "The New Sacred Psychology."

Aegis, The Abode, R.D. 1, Box 1030D, New Lebanon, NY 12125 (phone 518/794-8095): On three-day weekends from June through September, supplemented by five-day midweek sessions in June and July, and occasional workshops in other seasons, outsiders come to study on this mountain in the Berkshires with a permanent community of "Sufis"—the gentlest of people who have made an eclectic choice from the prophetic messages of all religions, both Western and Eastern. Faculty includes a Benedictine monk, a rabbi, an American Indian. Sample workshops: "Optimal Functioning in Daily Life," "Healing and Wholeness in Psychotherapy," "The Shared Heart," "Buddhist Meditation," "Homeopathic Medicine"; there is much meditation. To weekend tuition costs averaging $100, add room and board charges of about $30 a day in a dorm or cabin, $20 a day in a campsite.

Wainwright House, 260 Stuyvesant Ave., Rye, NY 10580 (phone 914/967-6080): A stately mansion on elegant grounds, just north of New York City, it offers year-round daily workshops—some for only a day in duration—in Jungian studies, spiritual disciplines, "health and wholeness," other topics of psychology. Themes are far-ranging—"Depth Psychology," "Spiritual Development," "Global Issues," "Sonic Meditation," "The Psychology of Illness"—but from a relatively traditional, even Christian, viewpoint. One-day tuition ranges from free to $50, and overnight accommodations run from $25 (dorm) to $35 (per person, double room). Meals are offered in the dining room at additional cost. And a catalog of courses is free for the asking.

West Coast

Naropa Institute, 2130 Arapahoe, Boulder, CO 80302 (phone 303/444-0202): Summer only. In a partly urban setting, but on the slopes of the Rockies, it is serious and intellectual, but with a heavy emphasis on innovative, psychological approaches to music, theater, dance, and creative writing. Nevertheless, workshops also include "The Intimate Relationship as a Practice and Path," "Nurturing," "Contemplative Psychotherapy," "Christian or Buddhist Meditation." Most short-term guests (less than a month) use nearby University of Colorado housing for room and board costs of about $150 a week, to which average tuition fees of about $250 should be added.

Feathered Pipe Ranch, P.O. Box 1682, Helena, MT 59624 (phone 406/442-8196): Open in spring and summer only, using log-and-stone ranchhouse accommodations in a stunning Rocky Mountain location bordered by a national forest. The program consists of "holistic life seminars," heavily spiritual, but also including standard yoga workshops, studies in

holistic health, male/female relationships. Ilana Rubenfeld presented her widely acclaimed five-day "synergy" workshop (gestalt therapy combined with Feldenkrais and other forms of "body work") at Feathered Pipe recently. Charges average $700 a week for instruction, meals, and dorm-style lodging.

Ojai Foundation, P.O. Box 1620, Ojai, CA 93023 (phone 805/646-8343): Workshops with intensely spiritual themes are conducted throughout much of the year on these 40 acres of semi-wilderness land two hours north of Los Angeles. "Ritual Geomancy and Celebration," "Engaged Buddhism," "The I-Ching," and "Taoist Yoga" are among the studies pursued. Tuition (including lunch) is $110 to $125 (depending on the course) for a weekend, $175 for four days, $275 for a week; campsite use, breakfast, lunch, and dinner are $20 a day more.

Hollyhock Farm, P.O. Box 127, Manson's Landing, Cortes Island, B.C., Canada V0P 1K0 (phone 604/935-6465): One hundred miles north of Vancouver, in the Strait of Georgia, this is a warm-weather-only (May through October) facility on an expanse of beach and 23 acres of gardens, orchards, and forest. Workshops are generally five days in duration, average $525 (and less) for tuition, room, and board, and explore such subjects as "Tibetan Buddhism," "Exploring the World of Alternative Medicine," "Vipassana Meditation," and "Tai-Chi Chu'an."

Each center issues catalogs or other descriptive literature, to be carefully perused before enrolling. From personal experience, I can assure that a stay will cause you to discover, at the very least, important new aspects of your inner life and relations with others. ≈

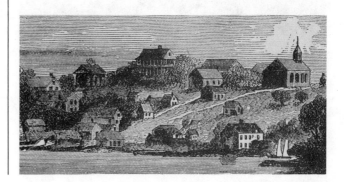

A Summer in the New Age

On a Rising Tide of Public Interest Spurred by the Works of Shirley MacLaine, Consciousness-Exploring Resorts and Retreats Have Emerged All Over the Nation

Redwoods of Shenoa Retreat Center

When Shirley MacLaine first revealed in a spate of best-selling paperbacks that she had lived past lives, gained strength from crystals, and experienced other cosmic phenomena, she did more than simply popularize a set of beliefs—she all but created a new segment of the travel industry. Because her writings had swayed a mass audience, other enthusiasts of the "New Age" were able to open holiday resorts and vacation villages to explore the subject in weekend and weeklong seminars, workshops, and "retreats." Today, on a rising tide of success, and in more locations than many suppose, the countryside centers they founded are busily erecting new log cabins, more communal dining halls, additional meditation tents, and extra dormitory *yurts* (quaint, dome-topped lodges) to house a growing clientele.

But unlike their star performer, most New Age resorts want nothing to do with magic crystals, channeling, and past-life regression. Rather, they are peopled for the most part with fairly sober types—including eminent academic figures—whose most extreme belief is to suspect that humankind is poised on the brink of a major, evolutionary expansion of consciousness, whose frontiers they wish to explore. Or else they search for a single, universal force that may animate all living things on earth, holding out hope for eventual communication between species (animals, plants) and a growing closeness with nature. Or else they simply attempt to create a more caring, nurturing society through attention to spiritual concerns of a nondivisive sort.

A vacation at a New Age resort is therefore infinitely less exotic than most assume. It is, according to numerous reports, and based on my own one experience, relaxed and unpressured, nonjudgmental, but intellectually invigorating, and spent among a great many open-minded people. Certainly it can do you no harm, and the advantages are considerable: an open-air vacation in which all the standard recreations are available to supplement or substitute for the seminars, and all at costs that are among the lowest in the vacation field.

Five Major Resorts

Shenoa Retreat Center, P.O. Box 43, Philo, CA 95466 (phone 707/895-3156): Like most of the New Age resorts, it occupies a glorious physical setting, adjoining a virgin redwood forest and state park, above a 60-acre meadow bordered by three bubbling streams. You are in Mendocino County north of San Francisco (but warmer than that sometimes-chilly city), a half hour from the Pacific, in a facility of several rustic buildings (dining lodge, cabins), pleasant swimming pool, and tennis courts. The remarkable cost? $40 a day per adult in cabins, $22 camping, including all three meals (another $5 on weekends); plus a quite reasonable but varying sum (as little as $40 for three full days) for attendance and instruction at purely optional workshops and seminars in core subjects of the New Age: "Intuitional Work and Dream Process," "Consciousness Healing," "Community Building," "Using Mental Images to Resolve Issues," a "Course in Miracles," or "The Manifestation of Spirit in the Life of the Planet at This Time." Some guests skip the seminars, savor the setting, and pay only $40 daily for everything else. Founded by alumnae of the famous Findhorn community in northern Scotland—first of the classic New Age retreats (1962)—Shenoa attempts to emulate Findhorn in its broad and tolerant approach, and permits proponents of every sort of spiritual belief to appear at its rostrum. Studies occupy half the day, after which guests can, in the center's words, "read, play, dream, swim, go for long walks in the forests or along the river, become renewed, refreshed, and inspired in this special place with like-minded, like-hearted people."

Chinook Learning Center, P.O. Box 57, Clinton, WA 98236 (phone 206/321-1884): On a stunning 64 acres of evergreen forest and meadowland, with a view of the Olympic Mountains, and close access (three miles) to the beaches of Puget Sound, the 17-year-old Chinook has a main house and scattered cabins housing 20 or so guests, but accommodates the bulk of its visitors (130 more) on campsites serviced by a central dining hall. Because of the camping emphasis, fees can run as low as $95, but generally average $175,

Most New Agers believe that humankind is poised on the brink of a major, evolutionary expansion of consciousness.

Group at Shenoa

Shenoa crafts

7

But unlike their star performer, most New Age resorts want nothing to do with magic crystals, channeling, and past-life regression.

Games at High Wind Farm

High Wind seminar

Greeting the dawn at High Wind

for a long-weekend, three-night "program" of accommodations, all meals, and instruction on such themes (in 1988) as "An Inquiry into 'Gaia'" (theory that all the earth is a single, living organism), "Spirit and Soul," "Guiding Myths for Men and Women," "Holding Your Dreams in Community," and "Bonding with the Earth Through Meditation and Ritual." Other summer sessions run from four days to a full week or more, and some include workshops in various arts and crafts. A major fundraising program, now in progress, should shortly increase the number of indoor accommodations at this important New Age establishment.

High Wind Farm, Rte. 2, Plymouth, WI 53073 (phone 414/528-7212): Primarily a permanent ecological community pursuing a wide variety of researches into energy conservation, organic gardening, and cooperative living. But a strong spiritual tone underlies the rational practices, and every summer—late June to early August—High Wind invites a number of New Age groups and speakers to present workshops for transient guests in such topics as "Our Role in a Holistic Universe," "Wonders of the Inner Mind," "Accelerating Human Consciousness," "Social/Global Transformation," or "The Well-Being of Body, Mind, and Spirit." One such summer program, a full eight days and eight nights in length, costs a total of $325 per person, including room, all three meals, and all instruction. At most other times of the year, guests are invited simply to observe and share the experience of High Wind Farm for $30 to $35 per person per day, including accommodations and all meals. On such latter stays, as the group explains, you can "walk in the woods and fields, retreat, study, chat with available staff, lend a hand with cooking if you like." The farm complex, with its numerous, separate structures and homes, Community Center, "bioshelter," greenhouses, and big, red barn, occupies 128 verdant acres of rolling hills. Request, in particular, the 24-page tabloid newspaper of High Wind, called *Windwatch*.

Joy Lake Mountain Seminar Center, P.O. Box 1328, Reno, NV 89504 (phone 702/323-0378): A large, 48-page catalog is required to list and describe the dizzying array of New Age topics and therapies taught in more than 80 three- to seven-day workshops, from May through September, at this forested, mountainside setting overlooking Joy Lake in the eastern Sierra Nevadas, a half hour's drive from Reno. Courses range from such highly arguable themes (to put it mildly) as "The Therapeutic Use of Crystals," "Past Life Recall Through Memo Therapy," and "Herbal Wisdom," to a host of utterly respectable, well-supported disciplines. The latter category includes lectures by such eminent authorities as Dr. Fritjof Capra, author of the widely acclaimed *The Tao of Physics*. Some of the workshops are taught outdoors—on the meadow, under Ponderosa pines, amid wildflowers and the chirping of pheasants in the Joy Lake aviaries. Afternoons, participants can simply relax "in a hammock listening to the creek bubble," says one brochure. For all this, room and board totals only $40 per person per day, with accommodations provided in either cabins or four-person *yurts* (with nomadic-style domes). You then add tuition costs, which average $150 for a three-day workshop, but vary widely.

The Center of the Light, P.O. Box 540, Great Barrington, MA 01230 (phone 413/229-2396): A strange amalgam of New Age beliefs and broad Christian doctrines, the center is administratively staffed, in large part, by ministers of the "Church of Christ Consciousness" (which claims to be wholly nondenominational), but teachers include students of the Kabbalah, holistic health practitioners, body awareness specialists, faith healers, researchers in paranormal experiences, and neurolinguistic educators. The curriculum is eclectic, to say the least. The summer program consists of two- to five-day workshops costing $90 to $150, to which you add $35 a day for room and board, using rustic dormitory cabins (bring your own sheets and blankets) segregated by sex; a limited number of "doubles" cabins, for couples, are available at the same $35-per-person charge. If guests wish, they can stay at the center in summer without taking a workshop, simply for the daily $35 charge. The prospect is tempting: you are in the western Berkshires, near Tanglewood and Jacob's Pillow, surrounded by

orchards, lawns, gardens, fields, woods, and lakes. Facilities include a pool, tennis court, ball fields, and hiking trails. And the natural-foods cuisine, primarily vegetarian, is tasty and abundant.

Some critics charge that New Age beliefs are a substitute for political or social commitment, or a flight from serious, practical concerns, and a part of me shares those doubts. Nevertheless, while acknowledging my own preference for the rational over the mystical, and therefore a prejudice against the New Age, I have to admit the importance of these speculations and the reasonable possibility that they may be on the right track (although centuries away from corroborating their instincts). As a vacation activity, these pleasant mental exercises are among the more agreeable of all available options—certainly they're superior to the stressful programs of most resorts—and enjoyed in the company of kind and gentle people. Why not give them a try? ≈

Arriving at Shenoa

Vista of Shenoa

A Visit to Famous Findhorn

Thousands Enjoy an "Experience Week" at the World's Most Celebrated "New Age" Community

Gates to Universal Hall, Findhorn

Fired from his job as a hotel manager, a restless Peter Caddy moved with his wife, three children, and a family friend to a car-trailer parked on a bleak stretch of sandy seacoast in northeastern Scotland, near a village named Findhorn.

And there, in 1962, he grew cabbages weighing 42 pounds. Claiming to tap into a life force that animates the universe, using meditation and "attunement" to feel at one with nature, this rather conventional Englishman created a garden so fertile as to cause dozens of others to join him in building a New Age community on the surrounding site. Its aim: to expand the human consciousness, and thus change the world.

Today the cabbages are no more. Residents of the Findhorn Foundation joke about the phenomenon that brought them worldwide attention. "And anyway," said one to a recent guest, "why should anyone want to eat cabbage for a month?"

But what survives is an impressive, sprawling, residential-and-classroom complex of 180 permanent members, another hundred or so visitors pursuing successive, one-week courses of instruction—and a potent tourist attraction. By the thousands each year, adherents of a dozen, radically differing theories of the human potential, joined by others who are simply curious, flock to what has by now become the single most famous utopian community on earth.

The Evolution in Its Function

But Findhorn today is more a learning center than a community. Though the cultivation of its famous garden (books have been written about it) continues to be a major activity, Findhorn is far from self-sufficient in food or other products, and only a handful of its members work at life-sustaining tasks. Rather, the bulk of its population are administrators, publicists, or teachers, or loyal volunteers at housekeeping (kitchen, transport, maintenance, accounts). Through those labors they keep the area alive with periodic workshops, seminars, and conferences exploring the spiritual bases of life. And these are attended by guests from around the world.

The goal is a breathtaking one, massively ambitious. "We believe humanity is on the verge of a major evolutionary leap," says one explanatory leaflet, "an expansion of consciousness" creating "new patterns of civilization and a . . . culture infused with spiritual values. . . . We seek [to discover that] new awareness in our own daily lives."

The steps toward the goal are more modest, and pursued in a highly reasonable manner. Findhorn teaches no single creed, explores the principles of all spiritual outlooks, grants total freedom of expression, and tends to ignore exotic dogmas. In its directory of workshop topics, not a single one deals with Shirley MacLaine–type speculations into reincarnation, channeling, or magic crystals. Rather, it is the subconscious and the intuitive, the impact of mind upon body, the potential of human imagination, that form the core of discussions listed under such headings as "Meditation as a Way of Life," "Reawakening the Metaphoric Mind," "Dreams and the Spiritual Path," "Learning to Love," "Coming Alive," "A Working Retreat for Managers," "Holistic Healing"—in short, the entire range of the more defensible forms of New Age thinking.

Workshops average £175 ($298) a week, including room and full board, and most are one week in duration.

The Experience Week

The strict prerequisite for attending a workshop, however, is prior participation in an "Experience Week" offered Saturday to Saturday throughout the year, and costing £165 ($281) for all-inclusive arrangements; that weekly sojourn is the major means for visiting Findhorn on a touristic or temporary basis.

"Experience Week" guests stay for seven nights in two- to six-bedded rooms of Findhorn's Cluny College, a large, old (but well-maintained) former hotel overlooking a golf course; there they also take their meals (vegetarian, fresh, delicious). Throughout the week they tour every part of the Findhorn Foundation, including its work "departments," hear lectures by staff and celebrated theorists, engage in "sharings"

Its aim: to expand the human consciousness, and thus change the world.

Dance-in-progress, Findhorn

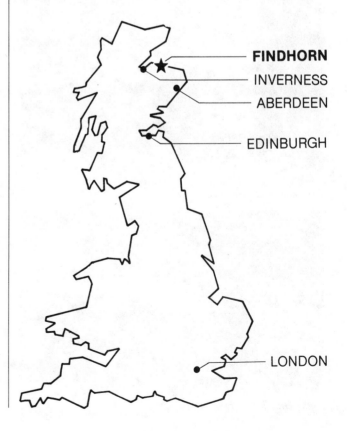

FINDHORN
INVERNESS
ABERDEEN

EDINBURGH

LONDON

Findhorn teaches no single creed, grants total freedom of expression, and tends to ignore exotic dogmas.

Guests of Findhorn

Universal Hall, Findhorn

Cluny Hill Center, Findhorn

(communal social gatherings), "sacred dancing," and innovative games designed to strip away repressions and wasteful defenses. They talk endlessly and lovingly with fellow guests about personal problems and goals. For each of five weekdays they also work for four hours in Findhorn's garden or kitchens, because work is regarded as a "cement" that brings community members together spiritually, a caring gesture more than a task.

Before each work period, members and guests hold hands in a brief meditation to "attune" to each other and the project ahead. They talk with one another as the work proceeds, express mutual affection, become a close-knit group. Numerous observers (including my college-age daughter, Pauline, who visited Findhorn on my behalf this past summer) have commented on the energy and enthusiasm that go into such projects, and their impact on Findhorn, where grounds and structures are remarkably well kept and clean. In the kitchen, she reports, "work was done quickly and efficiently, and was more enjoyable than burdensome."

Although Findhorn's "Experience Weeks" have a large capacity, they are always heavily booked, especially in summer, when applications six to nine months ahead are advisable. Write for application forms, and further information, to **Accommodations Secretary, Findhorn Foundation, Cluny Hill College, Forres, Scotland IV 36 ORD (phone 309-73655).** Another Findhorn number for more general information is 309-72288.

Visiting children are not accepted, and have little role at Findhorn, except during occasional "Family Weeks."

Alternative Possibilities

For would-be visitors unable to spend a full week at Findhorn, three lesser and last-minute alternatives are available.

First, you can simply wander through Cullerne, the main gardening area of the foundation, open to the public from sun-up to sundown. Some casual visitors have been known to work in that garden; in a large barn on the site, a downstairs coatroom provides raincoats and galoshes to poorly equipped, impromptu volunteers.

Or you can take a guided, but free, two-hour tour of the foundation's grounds, starting daily at 2 p.m. in spring, summer, and fall, but on Tuesday and Saturday only in winter. Tours set out from the Phoenix Shop (a combination bookstore and health-food purveyor) in The Park, which is the large area of trailers where Peter and Eileen Caddy first placed their home. The epochal, small green trailer is still there, but used as an office, and found directly across from the guest reception center. Nearby is the Universal Hall, Findhorn's showplace for conferences and performances; the Sanctuary (for meditation); the Apothecary Shop (herbal medicines prescribed by holistic physicians who have seen the light); a Community Center with food service; craft studios; pottery and weaving barns; a graphic design shop; a printing plant; and more.

Perhaps the best alternative visit is an unplanned, three-day stay as a "short-term guest." Here, you generally arrange your own accommodations (either pitching a tent or using one of the many £9-a-night B&Bs or guest-accepting farmhouses in the vicinity), but present yourself daily to Findhorn for three hours of work (in your choice of departments, morning or afternoon), supplemented by participation in various gatherings and evening fests to which you'll then be invited. You simply show up unannounced at the reception center in the Park, or better, write or phone ahead to the **Findhorn Foundation (Short Term Guests), The Park, Forres, Scotland IV 36 OTZ (phone 309-30311),** in which latter case you'll sometimes—but rarely—receive a bed in Cluny College.

Despite your daily, three-hour stint of work, you'll pay a "short-term charge" of £10 ($17) a day, or whatever you are able to afford (my backpacking daughter offered, and paid, £6), plus £2 ($3.40) for every meal taken. Unlike Experience Week guests who are often bused from place to place on the extensive grounds of Findhorn, short-term guests make their own way to and from, and are probably best advised to have a car.

Bear in mind that the Findhorn Foundation is wholly distinct from the adjoining, tiny village of Findhorn—the latter a former fishing town, today a resort whose docks berth pleasure craft. In walking distance from the village's center is a long and lovely beach known as the "Riviera of Scotland" (but normally too cold for swimming).

The nearest, larger village is Forres, about five miles away, and nationally acclaimed for its own gardens. In the vicinity is the well-preserved Cawdor Castle, full of armor, traditional furniture, and portraits of the Cawdors.

A larger nearby city is Inverness, 30 minutes by car from Findhorn, and proud possessor of a major airport. But trains stopping at Forres can also bring you to Findhorn.

Elsewhere in this book, I've written about an easily visited rationalist community in Britain, the Centre for Alternative Technology near Machynlleth, Wales, where residents apply logic, science, and egalitarian principles to the conduct of community life. In Findhorn, you have the contrasting spiritual approach to many of the same concerns, and both communities provide the basis for a profoundly important, endlessly fascinating, vacation trip to the U.K. ≈

On the Road to Utopia

At "Intentional Communities" Across the U.S.A., Short Stays and Visits Are a Mind-Expanding Experience

Raising a barn at Sirius

Sunrise Ranch Community

Show me a utopian community, and I'm soon walking on air. The very thought of people uprooting themselves and reassembling to lead a rational life brings goosepimples to my flesh, awakens youthful dreams of a better world.

Well, wonder of wonders, our nation harbors a hundred and more utopian communities, and some of them accept short-term visitors. Can you think of a more rewarding weekend or weeklong stay than at a modern Walden, an Erewhon, a Shangri-La?

None of them, of course, would be so bold as to style themselves by those long-hallowed names. Rather, they are simply "intentional communities"—the modern term for those who have gathered onto a rural or small-town site to pursue a carefully planned life of cooperation and sharing.

Some are simply working farms occupied by three or four families, and obviously unsuitable for visiting tourists. Others, a growing number, are elaborate villages, with 60 to 100 residents, that encourage visitors and maintain overnight lodgings for them. From there they take you to classrooms, tour you through the site, lecture and prod you to reexamine your own harshly competitive life.

If all this seems threatening, or against your political grain, you might pause to consider that throughout history, similar intentional communities—both here and abroad—have introduced approaches to life, and forms of social organization, that later became commonplace.

The communal homes of a Denver or Washington, D.C., in which young single people share costs, are outgrowths of the experience of intentional communities. So are the ever-more-frequent platonic households of two singles of the opposite sex sharing an apartment.

The very same intentional communities first launched to a broader audience the current, widespread consumption of health foods, the growing practice of holistic medicine, protection of the environment, energy conservation and the use of nonfossil fuels, the soaring interest in Eastern philosophies and religions (zen, tao, yoga), humane attitudes toward animals.

"We are like laboratories for research into the future," said a member of one community in the course of my own visit. "We are testing the methods that people a hundred years from now will use to improve their lives."

Their Visitor Programs

Care to observe? The most rewarding vacations I know are spent as a guest (or working guest) on the grounds of a hundred such villages that avidly encourage visitors as a means of spreading their utopian views. They house and feed you for the most nominal charge, because their goal (to put it bluntly) is to change your life—and the life of this planet.

Yet though they proselytize, they do not brainwash. The mildest of people, they fully expect you to recoil initially from such community concepts as "trans-species interaction" (communication with animals, insects, and plants)—and they take no offense at your own disbelief. They are just as accustomed to resistance when first they introduce you to "communal childcare," "planetary citizenship," or "extended families." Instead of arguing, they return calmly to work while you, in dazed confusion, ponder upon an unsettling eruption of new ideas.

And ponder them you will. Just wait until you encounter "variable labor credits" or "flexible work weeks"! Your mind will almost audibly stretch as you learn, at some communities, that members performing desirable work (like childcare) receive fewer hours of credit than members performing undesirable work (like cleaning latrines). By opting for the latter, aspiring artists and writers can reduce their communal labors to two or three days a week—and isn't that sensible?

Among the communities that take visitors are these prominent examples (rich opportunities for your next holiday trip):

Twin Oaks, Virginia

Twin Oaks, near Louisa, Virginia: Nearly 100 people live in this 21-year-old collection of farm buildings on 400 acres of woods, creeks, hilly pastures,

Can you think of a more rewarding weekend or weeklong stay than at a modern Walden, an Erewhon, a Shangri-La?

Sauna at Breitenbush

Foundation for Feedback Learning

and meadows—their goal an eventual community of 200 to 300. To promote both membership and viewpoints, visits are permitted, but only on most (not all) Saturday afternoons from 1 to 4 p.m. (no food is served), for $3 per adult, and only through prior arrangement by phone. Those more seriously interested in joining are then allowed to make a three-week visit, for $2 a day, using self-supplied sleeping bags on the floor of several visitors' rooms.

Heavily influenced by the utopian novel of the Harvard psychologist B. F. Skinner (*Walden Two*), the community attempts to be a "model social system" through rational approaches to life that avoid the spiritual emphasis of several other communities. Political solutions are stressed, logic is the tool, and all forms of modern media—books, records, tapes, and magazines, everything except television (because it promotes "those values and products that we are trying to avoid")—are amply available on site.

At Twin Oaks, all labor, property, and resources are held in common, but personal privacy is fiercely protected. Children are raised as in an Israeli kibbutz, occupying their own residence and raised by all adult members. Supervision of economic life is by numerous planner-managers elected to short terms, and the community is self-sufficient through the manufacture of handcrafted hammocks and chairs, other small industries, the cultivation of extensive organic gardens serving a mostly vegetarian table.

Twin Oaks is easily reached by bus or car from Washington, D.C., but is even closer to Richmond, Charlottesville, or Culpeper. For literature, or to schedule a visit (even the afternoon visit must be booked in advance), contact **Visitor Program, Twin Oaks Community, Louisa, VA 23093 (phone 703/894-5126)**.

East Wind, Missouri

East Wind, near Tecumseh, Missouri, in the Ozark hills, is another, kibbutz-like, B. F. Skinner–influenced community of 50 or so members pursuing a "peaceful, cooperative, and egalitarian" life free of "racist, sexist, and competitive behavior." Constantly experimental,

open-minded, and diverse, it places a music practice space next to a dairy barn, a trailer-library alongside the inevitable shops for producing hammocks, sandals, and—a proud specialty—"nut butter." Members, each with a full vote, have substantial labor or production quotas, but enjoy weekend rest, plus three weeks of vacation a year, and can earn additional vacation by producing "overquota." Children are raised by "metas"—members who have chosen child-care as their work—but have at least three other "primary people" in their lives: their parents, and one or two others chosen by the parents.

Because East Wind is anxious to expand, it encourages visits (costing only $2 a day) for up to three weeks by people who then work the same number of hours as members and spend only the amount of money on site as would equal a member's allowance. Any fears of a Spartan life that these rules may evoke are soon overcome by the idyllic natural setting of the site, an area renowned for its swimming, canoeing, hiking, and other outdoor recreation.

Write ahead for reservations (and don't simply drop in) to **East Wind Community, P.O. Box FB5, Tecumseh, MO 65760 (phone 417/679-4682)**.

Sirius, Massachusetts

Sirius, near Amherst, Massachusetts, emphasizes spirituality to the same or even greater extent than its political notions of cooperation and sharing; indeed, it differs from numerous other communities by encouraging members to earn their own incomes, sometimes at jobs in neighboring towns. But most of the members purchase food jointly, take most meals communally, own the 86 acres of their site jointly, reach community decisions by consensus—and meditate until all members acquiesce in the "rightness" of the decisions taken.

Like Thoreau, the Sirius participants have built their homes "in the woods," and there they engage in organic gardening, holistic health practices, and solar building. But it is personal growth to which most attention is paid. Though members are free to pursue varying spiritual disciplines, they believe in the God within each human being and the "interconnectedness" of all nature (animals, plants, humans). Several prominent members are alumni of the famous Findhorn Community in Scotland (we've already visited that magical place in a previous essay) and apply the same loving care to gardens and forests that Findhorn regards as a moral imperative.

Personal growth, so claims the Sirius group, results from the demands of harmonious group living. Members rid themselves of old patterns, become "agents of change," build for themselves and others "a more peaceful, loving world."

Visits by outsiders can be made for several days or up to several weeks. Less intensive, free open houses are held on the first and third Sundays of every month, starting with a "New Age Sunday Service" at 11 a.m., meditation at 12:30 p.m., a "potluck lunch" (you either bring your own or make a small donation) at 1 p.m., and then a tour of the community at 2:30 p.m. On overnight stays of any duration, guests either join in community work or spend the time in quiet contemplation; accommodations fees are on a sliding scale according to the guest's income, include all three meals daily, and range from $25 to $45 a day. Guests are always asked (even for attendance at a free Sunday open house) to phone first for instructions and to let Sirius members know that they are coming.

Though Sirius is located on Baker Road in Shutesbury, its mailing address is **Sirius Community, P.O. Box 388, Amherst, MA 01004 (phone 413/259-1251)**.

Sunrise Ranch, Colorado

Sunrise Ranch, near Loveland, Colorado: One of the oldest (1940s) and most successful (150 residents) of the alternative communities, its emphasis is almost entirely on personal, spiritual growth, and not on communal, social, or economic practices. Still, a major activity is organic gardening (supplying most of the ranch's foodstuffs), followed closely in the use of personnel by clerical functions supporting the worldwide activities of the Society of Emissaries, the sponsoring organization. The latter's doctrines are a mild, broad, and initially hard-to-comprehend philos-

Some are elaborate villages, with 60 to 100 residents, that encourage visitors and maintain overnight lodgings for them.

Mealtime at the Foundation for Feedback Learning

A room at the Foundation

Throughout history, similar "intentional communities" have introduced approaches to life, and forms of social organization, that later became commonplace.

Baking bread at Sirius

An "Equinox meeting" at Sirius

ophy of "quality living" through "alignment with the rhythms and cycles of life." "Manipulation," says Sunrise teacher Nick Giglio, "as well as hidden agendas and tools of persuasion are unnecessary excess baggage."

Visiting facilities are extensive, cost only $25 a day (the suggested "donation"), including all three meals, and should be reserved in advance by writing to **Sunrise Ranch, 5569 No. County Rd. 29, Loveland, CO 80537 (phone 303/679-4200 or 667-4222).** Loveland is 50 miles north of Denver, and the ranch is seven miles from Loveland.

Stelle, Illinois

Stelle, 90 miles south of Chicago: At the opposite political spectrum from the communal societies described above, Stelle is a small (125 members), planned village (like a miniature Columbia, Md., or Reston, Va.) in which homes are privately owned and incomes privately earned. But various cooperative (not communal) institutions bind the residents together, including bulk purchases of food, joint operation of a local telephone exchange, periodic "celebrations," and a town hall form of pure democratic government. Residents consider themselves an extended family.

The village is most productively visited not for contacts with its residents (here, occasionally difficult to arrange), but for exposure to the library, publications, and audio-visual presentations of its quarterly, *Communities Magazine,* dealing with subjects that affect the operation of intentional communities. You do this either on a day trip, or overnight for $18 single, $25 double, including breakfast, at any of about 20 bed-and-breakfast houses. Write or phone in advance to **Communities, 105 Sun St., Stelle, IL 60919 (phone 815/256-2200).**

Five More Communities

Appletree, near Eugene, Oregon: A tiny, rural commune of rational, egalitarian practices. Overnight or weeklong visitors pay $4 and three hours of work a day, and are asked to apply by writing at least two weeks in advance. Persons staying in nearby towns can visit for part of a day by simply phoning at least a day ahead. Write **Appletree, P.O. Box 5, Cottage Grove, OR 97424 (phone 503/942-4372).**

Mettanokit, in southern New Hampshire: An income-sharing, decision-sharing group of 20 individuals seeking to create a society (in their words) of "loving, cooperative, zestful, intelligent, creative human beings." They work by consensus, apportion all household and cleaning tasks equally, and enjoy receiving a constant flow of prenotified visitors who pay $10 a day for room and board on visits of several days (visitors share in the work and social activities of the community). Contact **Mettanokit, Another Place, Rte. 123, Greenville, NH 03048 (phone 603/878-9883 or 878-3117).**

The Foundation for Feedback Learning, on Staten Island, New York: Minutes from the towers of downtown Manhattan, a 40-member group inhabits seven large houses in which they pursue researches so eclectic as to defy generalization: language training, psychodrama, biofeedback, and furniture repair. Visitors to New York may stay with them for one-month periods, for $350 per person in double rooms, including all meals. Contact the **Foundation for Feedback Learning, 135 Corson Ave., Staten Island, NY 10301 (phone 718/720-5378).**

Breitenbush Retreat, 60 miles from Salem, Oregon: Here are 30 adults (with 9 children) of widely divergent political and spiritual views, but all with a fierce urge to enjoy a life in nature, and warm, caring relationships. At a 3,000-foot elevation in the Cascade Mountains, they found and restored this isolated warm-springs resort, where they provide guests with vegetarian meals, holistic health care, meditation, and other such "therapies" for only $30 a night ($35 on Friday, $40 on Saturday), with full board. Those more seriously interested in the communal practices of Breitenbush may stay for a week entirely free on a Volunteer Work Program involving 40 hours of moderate duties and full opportunity to attend all meetings and discussions. Contact **Breitenbush Community, P.O. Box 578, Detroit, OR 97342 (phone 503/854-3314 or 854-3315).**

Green Pastures Estates, in Epping, New Hampshire: A spiritual community in a small New England village; the 80 or so members aged 10 to 84 occupy a compound of period structures clustered around a central dining room where meals (both vegetarian and non-) are taken communally. Some members "live in" but "work out" at jobs in neighboring towns, and then pay Green Pastures for their room and board. Others work the adjoining 160-acre farm. All pursue a goal of spiritual growth or maturity that stresses the responsibility of each individual for his/her own emotional state. By attaining that growth (taught, among other topics, at four evening "services" each week), members aid the community to become a joyful, creative, smoothly interacting group. Visitors wishing to participate for a short stay will receive room and board for only $25 a day (a suggested donation) by writing in advance to **Green Pastures Estates, Ladd's Lane, Epping, NH 03042 (phone 603/679-8149).** Epping is between Portsmouth and Manchester, about seven miles from Exeter.

And Still Others

Since most intentional communities receive frequent visits by like-minded members of other such communities, members are usually aware of the distinctive features, pros and cons, of several. They share this knowledge with visitors, networking in open, unabashed fashion. Soon you become aware of both the nationwide and international ramifications of the "intentional communities" movement, enriching your knowledge of the contemporary world, and perhaps learning of how people will live in future years.

The current-day community members total as many as 200,000 people. In hundreds of small farm settlements or tiny villages, or more frequently in thousands of urban communal households, they have rejected the current forms of society and sought Utopia: a life of cooperation not competition, of sharing not owning, of full equality and democracy, without direction or domination from above. ≈

America on $25 a Day, Via the Yoga Route

Remarkable Vacations, Rewarding and Cheap, at Ashrams Clustered Near Both Coasts

Asanas at the White Lotus Foundation

I am not a yogi. And considering my feverish lifestyle, horrendous eating habits, and stubborn rationalism, that's the understatement of the year.

But yogi or not, some of my happiest holidays have been spent at yoga retreats. When it comes to inducing sheer serenity, restoring vigor, flushing toxins from both mind and body, nothing beats these mystical *ashrams* (schools, places of learning) with their vegetarian meals and quiet hillside settings, their twice-daily *asanas* (languid stretching exercises) and moments of meditation, their gentle people.

And when it comes to cost, nothing else in the vacation field even remotely compares. At a score of residential, countryside ashrams clustered near both coasts, the charge for room and all three meals amounts—if you can believe it—to $25, $35, and $40 a day.

Why so cheap? Because the meals are vegetarian, the sites are often donated, and the staff works for free, performing karma yoga (selfless service).

Why, then, aren't they inundated with guests? Because the public, in general, recoils from Eastern thought, equating all such teachings with those of Sun Myung Moon, assuming dreadful acts of brainwashing or abandoned conduct, as at the turbulent Rajneeshpuram in Oregon or the doomed Guyanese community of mad Jim Jones.

As applied to the yoga movement, nothing could be further from the truth. A philosophy of life, not a religion; a questing science, not a dogma—yoga is the most tolerant of creeds, its practitioners good-humored, broad-minded, and modest, non-authoritarian. At the U.S. ashrams, nothing is mandatory other than attendance at the asanas (physical exercises or postures) and silent meditations—and that, only to screen out persons who are simply seeking a cheap crashpad for their vacations.

Apart from those two limited daily sessions, no one cares about what you do or where you go, or whether you even attend lectures of the guru. He or she is regarded with affection, called *guruji* or *swamiji* (dear little guru, dear little swami), but treated as fallible, and certainly not as a Godhead. Some instructors at the ashrams—even a director or two—will stress their distance from Hindu theology and their pursuit of yoga primarily for its physical and calming benefits.

Though the residential ashrams in North America number far more than a score, not all have guaranteed staying-power. Those that do, include:

The Sivananda Retreat

On Paradise Island, the Bahamas: You've heard of Club Med; now meet Club Meditation (at a fifth the price). The ashram that's a 150-bed tropical resort, it sits next to sugary-white sands, across the bay from Nassau on four beachfront acres donated to the Sivananda Vedanta movement by an admirer; the popular, other-worldly complex is now in its 22nd year. You arise at dawn to meditate on the beach, proceed immediately (and before breakfast) to a two-hour exercise class (asana), partake at last of a mammoth vegetarian brunch, and are then allowed to do nothing at all (except swim, snorkel, and sun) until 4 p.m., when a second round of asanas is followed by supper at 6 p.m., meditation at sunset, and bed. Accommodations range from airy dorms in a colonial building ($40 per person per night, including meals and exercise classes) to double rooms in modern cabins ($45) to "meditation huts" ($55) overlooking the sea. Contact **Sivananda Ashram Yoga Retreat, P.O. Box N7550, Nassau, Bahamas (phone 809/326-2902)**, for reservations or literature, or you can speak with the New York office: **Sivananda Yoga Center, 243 W. 24th St., New York, NY 10011 (phone 212/255-4560)**.

Kripalu Center

Near Lenox, Massachusetts: In the many wings and 400 rooms of a former Jesuit monastery, on a hillside overlooking Lake Mahkeenac in the Berkshire Mountains of western Massachusetts, Kripalu is one of the largest of all ashrams, with one of the most varied programs—its brochure resembles a college catalog crammed with courses and options. Soothed by the ministrations of a largely unpaid staff of volunteers, you

exercise, meditate, wander, and soak, attend lively seminars and yet dine in complete silence at thrice-daily vegetarian buffets, hear lectures by the impressive Yogi Amrit Desai (*gurudev*—beloved teacher). Accommodations are comfortable, in spacious dorms (10 to 22 people) of wide-frame, wooden double-deckers, or in pleasant private rooms, and yet the all-inclusive charge—for housing and all three meals, exercise classes, and most other activities—is only $45 per person in the dormitories, $55 per person in a standard double room. Write or phone **Kripalu Center, P.O. Box 793, Lenox, MA 01240 (phone 413/637-3280)**. A smaller branch (up to 50 guests) pursuing similar policies is maintained on a wooded site outside Philadelphia: **Kripalu Yoga Ashram, 7 Walters Rd. (P.O. Box 250), Sumneytown, PA 18084 (phone 215/234-4568)**. The latter charges $45 per person for a shared room, $50 single, including all meals and programs.

Two in New York State

The Yoga Ranch, at Woodbourne, New York: About two hours by bus from New York City, it occupies a stunning setting atop a wooded hill, looking down into a valley and up onto another hill, the mountains of the Catskills receding into the distance. Dotted about are open areas devoted to organic farming or used by grazing deer. On the extensive grounds, a one-acre pond is deep enough for swimming, while nearby stands a stone-faced sauna, wood-fired, rock-heated, and steamed by pure, mountain spring water—one-of-a-kind. "You'll be doing good for a lot of people if you recommend us," said the co-director at the end of our talk. "They come here with jangled nerves, and then leave completely restored." The charge for that revival is an astonishing $25 per person per day (half price for children under 15, free for children under 5), including yoga asanas (exercises), meditation, accommodation in twin or triple rooms, and two vegetarian meals. Write or phone **Sivananda Ashram Yoga Ranch, P.O. Box 195, Woodbourne, NY 12788 (phone 914/434-9242)**.

Ananda Ashram, near Monroe, New York: Despite

When it comes to inducing sheer serenity, nothing beats these mystical retreats with their vegetarian meals and quiet hillside settings, their twice-daily *asanas* (languid stretching exercises) and moments of meditation.

White Lotus seminar

Lunch at the Yoga Ranch

its resident guru (a soft-spoken, self-effacing, former physician, now Shri Sarasvati) and classic activities (which include lessons in the much-stressed science of pranayama—breath control), the 25-year-old Ananda Ashram has a far-less-pronounced Eastern orientation than some others: it schedules meditation for as late as 9 a.m. on weekends, invites guest teachers from all religious disciplines, and presents classes in creative music, drama, dance, and visual arts. Less than 90 minutes by bus from New York City, at the base of the Catskill Mountains, it occupies 100 wooded acres, including a large private lake, and houses 60 visitors in several guesthouses, for an all-inclusive room-and-meals charge (on seven-night stays) of $200 per week. Lesser stays are $35 per day in mid-week for room and meals, per person; $40 per day on weekends. Contact the **Ananda Yoga Retreat, R.D. 3, Box 141, Monroe, NY 10950 (phone 914/782-5575).**

Three in California

The Yoga Farm, at Grass Valley, California: Cheapest of the residential ashrams ($25 a night, mainly in triple rooms, including vegetarian meals), but the smallest also, with space for just 30 guests, the farm is the personal favorite of the eminent Swami Vishnu Devananda, head of the Sivananda movement. Like thousands of others over the years who have driven up the 50 or so miles from Sacramento and then followed dirt roads to the isolated setting, he values the special simplicity and quiet of this rustic, two-building resort, with its changeless routine of meditation/exercises/free time. In the latter period, as you hike to the top of an adjoining hill and lie daydreaming on its crest, you see the majestic Sierras spread out before you. A very special place. Write or phone **Sivananda Ashram Vrindavan Yoga Farm, 14651 Ballantree Lane, Grass Valley, CA 95949 (phone 916/272-9322).**

The White Lotus Foundation, in elegant Santa Barbara, California: Some 1,800 feet up the mountains just behind the city, overlooking the Pacific Ocean and the Channel Islands, and founded in 1967 and currently directed by guru Ganga White, author of the book *Double Yoga*, its principal emphasis is on yoga and related disciplines (bodywork, shiatsu, acupuncture, acupressure), conveyed to guests through workshops, seminars, and classes throughout the year. A 5,000-square-foot central building provides some of the accommodations, but most guests stay in three- to four-person yurts scattered about the 40 acres of grounds. Personal retreats and classes in yoga can be pursued at any time of the year, at a $30-per-day charge which does not include meals (participants buy and cook their own food in a central kitchen), but more elaborate one-week and 16-day "intensives" are scheduled at frequent intervals throughout the spring, summer, and fall, and these include meals prepared by two noted vegetarian chefs, as well as morning-till-night classes (in-depth yoga training) at a cost of $675 to $750 for the one-week sessions, $1,250 for the 16-day "intensives." Since the weather of Santa Barbara is mild even in the winter (daytime temperatures in the upper 60s or low 70s), yoga-inclined travelers might schedule a personal visit at that time of year, at the $30-a-day tariff. To reach this very contemporary, eclectic yoga center, contact: **The White Lotus Foundation, 2500 San Marcos Pass, Santa Barbara, CA 93105 (phone 805/964-1944).**

The Expanding Light, near Nevada City, California: A strange amalgam of faiths, this is the yoga ashram located on the grounds of a larger utopian Christian community known as the Ananda World Brotherhood Village. The "town," 1,000 acres in size, was formed in 1967 by 250 devout people who are also practitioners of yoga, and regard it as complementary to the other faith. Today, at the Brotherhood Inn and other scattered structures and (in summer) tents, 125 visitors can engage in a retreat of classic yoga practices—early-morning and late-afternoon asanas and meditations —supplemented by classes and workshops on both Christian and yogic themes. For weeklong stays, the daily charge is $25 for campers bringing their own tents, $35 per person in a double room, $50 for a private single room, including all three vegetarian meals and classes. Guests volunteering for a "work exchange" program, doing some cooking or cleaning, pay only $18 a day. Ananda is 15 miles from Nevada City; the latter is 70 miles north of Sacramento. Contact **The Expanding Light, c/o Ananda World Brotherhood Village, 14618 Tyler Foote, Nevada City, CA 95959 (phone 916/292-3494 or toll free 800/346-5350).**

Still Other Possibilities

I have not described the important 2,000-bed Muktananda Center in South Fallsburg, New York (phone 914/434-2000), because of its heavy (and somewhat atypical) theological emphasis, which stresses chanting and meditation to a far greater extent than hatha (physical) yoga and exercises. But you should know that Muktananda charges only $35 a night for bed and all three meals in its dormitory rooms housing four to six people apiece. You can cut that cost to $25 a night by using housing farther away from the main facility, and not quite as comfortable.

Nor have I mentioned large retreats in Canada and Baja California.

To find other residential ashrams, phone the in-city centers listed under "Yoga Instruction" in the *Yellow Pages,* and ask the personnel to name the countryside location, if any, to which they go for an occasional retreat. I'd be grateful if you'd also pass on the information to me, at the address listed in the Introduction; and in gratitude, I press my hands together beneath my lips, and intone: "Jai Bhagwan" ("I honor the spirit within you"). ≈

Ananda Ashram, Monroe, New York

II ≠ POLITICAL TRAVEL, TO SEE FOR YOURSELF, TO WIDEN YOUR VIEW

Meet the Political Travel Agent, a New Breed

Their Trips and Tours Are Sharply Different from the Usual Variety—Profound and Stimulating

In the heart of Central America

Nicaraguan schoolchildren

They are fed up and furious with the Changing of the Guard, the beach at Copacabana, the Golden Gate Bridge.

Though they are travel professionals, they are grieved by the often-trivial content of their profession. Unlike the usual travel agent—who tends to be a rather conservative retail merchant, glued to the bottom line—they are passionate idealists out to change the world.

Travel, they believe—properly conducted and serious in content—can change the consciousness of the traveler, and thereby alter the United States. Whether to the right, left, or center, and in however small a way, they feel they can make a difference.

Meet five examples of the "political travel agent" or "public affairs travel agent":

The Travellers' Society

Open-minded, inquisitive, idealistic, and a little left of center is this increasingly well-known agency of four female partners (all unsalaried) and several hired hands. They emerged in unlikely fashion from the liberal wing of the Republican Party in Minnesota (now extinct), and once staged a counter-rally to the pro–Vietnam War appearance in Minneapolis of then-Gov. Ronald Reagan of California. Pushed from Republican ranks by these and other stands, they purchased an old-line travel agency and quickly proceeded to make the Travellers' Society into a major source of public-interest tours booked by people from all over the country.

Though the Society occasionally favors its middle-income clientele with the chic and glittering trip—accompanying the Minneapolis Symphony Orchestra to Hong Kong, or traipsing through vineyards and wineries in Australia—those are atypical lapses from a preoccupation with serious contemporary issues. Almost monthly they send groups to Central America (Costa Rica or Nicaragua), or to compare Third World problems in Jamaica and the Dominican Republic (where they eschew the beaches and meet with activists of all views), or to view an altogether different form of

political ferment in the Soviet Union and China (where the tours are carefully planned to skip the standard sights and focus on realities). Trips are preceded by predeparture seminars; groups are led by acknowledged experts in the destination; resource people are contacted in advance to schedule interviews and lectures at the site of travel.

Efficient to a fault, adept at modern marketing, the Society's staff never forgets its larger goal. "If we could only persuade our senior senator to join our Nicaraguan tour," one Society's partner wished aloud, "if he would go, as we go, to visit that nine-year-old crippled by a Contra landmine, and look into her eyes, he'd change his vote." For literature, contact **The Travellers' Society, P.O. Box 2846, Loop Station, Minneapolis, MN 55402 (phone 612/342-2788).**

GATE (Global Awareness Through Experience)

Here is the reflection in travel of the surging "Liberation Theology" movement in the Catholic church. Determined to expose a wider public to the realities and sufferings of Third World nations, nuns of the Sisters of Charity founded the odd travel agency called GATE in Mount St. Joseph, Ohio, seven years ago, then moved its offices in 1986 to Harlingen, Texas, near Brownsville and the Mexican border, to be closer to their population of concern. From Harlingen each month, photocopies of typewritten travel brochures—like none you've ever seen—go cascading forth to every part of the country, advertising GATE-led tours to Nicaragua and the barrios of Peru, or to "base communities" in Mexico. In place of "today we journey to the famous waterfall," GATE's literature talks of "dialogues with ministers, professors, and the poor," attendance at "meetings of popular movements . . . supporting their search and struggle for freedom in their country." Tour rates (and amenities) are moderate in level; participation is ecumenical and increasingly promoted also by Protestant groups; tour leaders and destination representatives (some of them on-the-spot missionaries) are opinionated but noncontrolling. Some tours go to countries of Eastern Europe.

But the emphasis is nonetheless on themes of Liberation Theology. As defined by Sister Patricia McNally, the U.S. GATE coordinator, it is "a theology in which we are all brothers and sisters, achieving equality, freeing and then empowering the oppressed to achieve their full dignity, enabling them not always to be dominated by some white-faced person. . . ." For literature, send a stamped, self-addressed envelope to **GATE, P.O. Box 3042, Harlingen, TX 78551.**

People to People International

This is the "centrist" of the political travel agencies, more heavily involved in broad public affairs than in special-interest advocacy or politics, and so prestigious as to be frequently mistaken for a U.S. government agency.

It once was. President Dwight D. Eisenhower founded it in 1956 out of a belief that people-to-people contacts across national boundaries were as vital as government efforts to maintain world peace. He initially made the organization a part of the U.S. Information Agency, then in 1961 persuaded his friend, Joyce Hall, of Hallmark Cards in Kansas City, to fund the transition to a private, nonprofit corporation for which the then-former President Eisenhower was the first chairman of the board. Today, in addition to its several Student Ambassador Programs sending teenagers abroad, and American-homestay plans for foreign visitors to the U.S., PTP organizes trips by several thousands of adult Americans each year to visit with their counterparts abroad: lawyers with lawyers, teachers with teachers, scientists with other scientists in their field. The goal: to "unleash the common interests among citizens of all countries and avoid the difference of national self-interest." More than 180 overseas chapters in 34 countries make the arrangements for personal contacts; several prestigious U.S. tour operators handle the technical arrangements. Because itineraries involve an intricate schedule of meetings, briefings, speeches, and seminars, the trips aren't cheap. Contact **People to People International, 501 E. Armour Blvd., Kansas City, MO 64109 (phone 816/531-4701).**

Others, Center and Left

Friendship Tours, of Modesto, California: Another "centrist" approach to political touring, non-ideological but people-to-people in its orientation. To a broad variety of standard trips (China, Russia, Africa), Friendship Tours attaches university lecturers or noted journalists, then works to schedule meetings and interviews with relevant individuals at the destination. For information, contact **Jo Taylor, Friendship Tours, 1508 Coffee Rd., Suite H, Modesto, CA 95355 (phone 209/576-7775).**

Anniversary Tours, of New York City: The most leftward-leaning of all the groups, Anniversary Tours is almost in the category of a solidarity tour operator bringing preconvinced people to express their support of the Eastern European countries, to which its trips primarily go. Yet, surprisingly, some participants have reported open-minded exchanges of views and searching inquiries, even on the "Marxist Scholar Tour" to the Soviet Union, the "Friendship May Day Tour" to Russia and Prague, the "Bulgarian Youth Folk Dance Tour," the "Parents & Children's Tour to the German Democratic Republic." Tours cover a multitude of special interests, and are carefully designed to go leagues beyond the standard sights. On a "Comparative Economics Tour," you visit with noted academicians, factory workers, and officials of the Foreign Trade Ministry in Budapest, Tashkent, and Moscow. On a "Moscow Marathon Tour," you visit an Olympics training camp, speak with athletes, participate in an easy ten-kilometer race. For the rest of your life, when friends boast of having traveled "off the beaten track," you can respond with the broadest of arrogant grins. For literature, contact **Anniversary Tours, 330 Seventh Ave., Suite 1700, New York, NY 10001 (phone 212/465-1200, or toll free 800/223-1337 outside New York State).**

Although the bulk of the new "political travel agents" send their clients to all parts of the world, a number focus solely on problems of the Third World. Because the latter approach is somewhat different, I've split off the Third World specialists from the preceding discussion and dealt with them mainly in the very next essay. Please read on. ≈

Though they occasionally favor their clientele with the chic and glittering trip, those are atypical lapses from a preoccupation with serious contemporary issues.

Reality Tours to the Third World

On "Travel Seminars," in Nations with Three-quarters of the World's Population, Americans Are Exploring the Most Important Issues of Our Time

How many "worlds" do you know? To how many "worlds" have you traveled? Apart from a periodic jaunt to Mexico or the Caribbean, have you traveled to the "Third World"? And can those beach vacations at a Club Med in Cancún, or a casino-resort in Curaçao, really be regarded as trips to the Third World?

Five organizations outside the bounds of the normal travel industry have set about operating "reality tours" to the true Third World. Their aim is enlightenment rather than recreation or rest. Their area of activity is the poorest part of what is also called the "developing world": most of Central and South America, most of Africa, much of Asia. Their method is to stress contact with ordinary people of the Third World, to expose tour passengers to conditions experienced by residents of that "world" (who make up three-quarters of the population of the earth). And their search is for solutions: to poverty and debt, domestic instability and disease, the unequal allocation of income and resources.

So is the trip a chore, an exercise in self-flagellation? Far from it, say the backers of these odd travel ventures. For this, it is claimed, is "transformational travel" that irrevocably broadens the mind and liberates the spirit of those who engage in it, makes them clear-headed and emphatic in their public judgments, enhances their love for humankind, gives them goals and purpose. And some concessions are made to personal comfort: the use of modest hotels in place of mud huts, an occasional stay in modern dormitories or pleasant private homes.

Largest of All

The Center for Global Education, Augsburg College, 731 21st Ave. South, Minneapolis, MN 55454 (phone 612/330-1159), is the largest of the Third World tour operators. Though its base is that of a small Lutheran school with limited funds, it successfully sends out more than 40 groups a year—often a departure a week—to countries of Central America for the most part, but occasionally to the Philippines and islands of the Caribbean, and rarer still, to the Middle East. Most tours are planned to visit combinations of two and three countries—say, Guatemala and El Salvador, or Mexico, Honduras, and Nicaragua—for 10 to 14 days, at total tour costs of $1,300 to $1,800 per person, including air fare, accommodations, and all meals.

Trips here are called travel seminars, and seminars they most emphatically are: discussions from morning till night with a multitude of individuals and groups. In recent brochures, participants are scheduled to meet, on the one hand, with officials of the U.S. embassy in each capital, and with members of the U.S. business community there, for one viewpoint, but also with contrary-thinking clergy from "base Christian communities" in each nation. And then, to inject still more "voices" into the talk:

In Honduras: "Dialogue with officials of the Honduran government . . . with peasants and labor union leaders. . . . Visit to U.N. refugee camps . . . to a Honduran military base and discussion with U.S. military personnel. . . . Dialogue with religious and human rights organizations. . . . Visits to development projects in rural Honduras."

In El Salvador: "Discussion of foreign policy issues with Salvadoran government officials. . . . Dialogue with mothers of disappeared persons. . . . Visit to church-sponsored refugee camps. . . . Dialogue with representatives of the church."

In Mexico: "Visit to a squatter settlement in Cuernavaca and discussion with residents about their situation. . . . Visit to a rural village and discussion with peasants."

Heavily influenced by the Brazilian educator Paulo Freire, the center's officials take pains to emphasize their use of his theories: that "experiential education" (here, a short-term immersion in travel) is the most potent form of self-education; that dialogue, in which people critically assess their own situation, can liberate them from prejudice and lead to beneficial social action; that even the illiterate can gain from such dialogue; and that communication can be achieved between the poor and nonpoor, greatly benefiting both.

Accordingly, the center stresses advance preparation for travel, which "helps people recognize their biases and provides them with tools to discern the truth in the voices they will hear." En route, it exposes passengers to "a variety of political points of view so that they can reflect more critically on all the voices they hear." And though it seeks to meet with leaders and decision-makers in the countries it visits, it "places emphasis on learning from the victims of poverty and oppression—those who do not often have an opportunity to speak."

Accommodations in most nations are in modest hotels, or in the organization's own dormitory-style residences in Mexico and Nicaragua. For literature, contact the center at the address above.

Towards "Transformative Education"

Plowshares Institute, P.O. Box 243, Simsbury, CT 06070 (phone 203/651-4303), operates a similar if smaller program, but to a broader array of geographical areas—Africa, Asia, India, South America—and with a particular emphasis on critical issues of U.S. foreign policy toward the Third World, debt and apartheid among them. The organization was founded in 1982 by a Protestant minister, the Rev. Robert Evans, whose life and outlook were profoundly changed by a stint as visiting professor in the African nation of Uganda; he resolved soon after to use travel as a means of "transformative education," and has since co-authored an important book often cited by others in the field, *Pedagogies for the Non-Poor* (Maryknoll, N.Y.: Orbis Books, 1987; $13.95).

The strategy of Plowshares is to visit areas and organizations of the Third World where active solutions are afoot to the area's classic problems; the group apparently feels it is nonproductive simply to dwell upon festering conditions or to feel rage without hope. Once at the destination, according to program director Hugh McLean, "we find articulate voices on all sides of each issue; the goal is to listen to as many voices as possible." On a recent visit to Mexico, Plowshares travelers met with officials of IBM, but then with landless peasants; with members of "PRI" (Mexico's ruling political party), but then with social workers and "base Christian communities in the barrios"; they lived in a dormitory of the Lutheran Theological

Their search is for solutions: to poverty and debt, domestic instability and disease, the unequal allocation of income and resources.

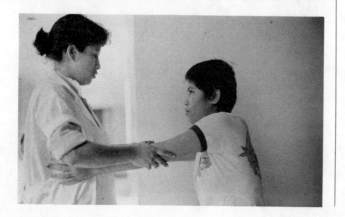

Seminary in Mexico City, but then traveled to the poor and rural province of Hildalgo in the north to visit creative development projects.

Tours are frequently co-sponsored by a variety of other religious organizations, including New York's Union Theological Seminary, but also by a host organization at the destination; in upcoming months, for instance, Plowshares will go to the Union of South Africa to "dialogue" with the South African Council of Churches as well as senior members of the government (an 18-day trip for $2,950, including air fare, meals, and all else). As they did in past years, they will visit the black ghetto of Soweto, and some participants will stay overnight in Soweto homes, in addition to visiting Afrikaaner families in Pretoria.

Plowshares passengers sign a "covenant": that they will engage in considerable preparation for the trip, live "at the level" of their hosts (dormitories, government rest houses, private homes), and tell of their experiences to others, in both formal and informal talks, for at least a year following the trip. For brochures, write to the address above (enclosing a stamped, self-addressed envelope).

Other Important Groups

Food First, 145 9th St., San Francisco, CA 94103 (phone 415/864-8555), is primarily an educator and publisher on the root causes of world hunger: why it occurs, what can be done. In 1986, with sponsorship of a first tour to Haiti and the Dominican Republic, it decided to use travel experiences in agricultural communities as a "window" (their term) onto broader structural issues: how a society deals with its social and political problems. Soon it was offering several tours a year, primarily to rural villages abroad, meeting with both government officials and private persons, in places as diverse as Honduras, the Philippines, and Nicaragua. Participants stay in private homes or very modest hotels, which brings costs down to a low $1,850, for instance, for a two-week trip to the Philippines from the West Coast, air fare and all else included. There, after meetings and briefings in Manila, the Bataan export processing zone, and the Subic naval base, tours split into groups of as few as three people to visit the sugar-producing province of Negros (where malnutrition is rampant), or to meet with land-seeking peasants in the province of Cagayan de Oro. Write for literature to the organization's "reality tours" department, but this time enclose $2 for postage and handling.

Our Developing World, 13004 Paseo Presada, Saratoga, CA 95070 (phone 408/379-4431), is another, secular, West Coast heavyweight in the Third World field. A nonprofit group whose directors are mainly educators and researchers from cities in northern California, it schedules its departures primarily from Los Angeles and San Francisco, but also permits participants to join up in Miami or Mexico City on those of its tours that go to Central America, and uses New York as its gateway to Africa. A major focus is on problems of development in southern Africa (Zimbabwe and Mozambique); a frequent practice is to "theme" each tour to concentrate on one particular subject matter per destination: "Women's Role in Development," "Appropriate Technology," "Education and Health Care," and so on. Except for the occasional one-month trip to Africa from New York (costing a high $4,000, all inclusive), trips are two to three weeks in duration, usually range from $1,639 (for two weeks) to $2,399 (for three weeks), using West Coast departure points, are also totally all inclusive, and (in the words of co-director Vic Ulmer) "bring the realities of the Third World into the consciousness of North Americans through direct contact with the people of those areas." Thus a three-week summer tour to study "Human Services in Honduras and Nicaragua" will meet with peasants, social workers, church leaders, "members of Christian base communities," trade unionists, and government officials, and will visit facilities ranging from medical clinics to day-care centers. U.S. participants are particularly sought from among teachers, social workers, and health-care professionals; but any concerned member of the public can come.

The Church Coalition for Human Rights in the Philippines, 110 Maryland Ave. NE (P.O. Box 70), Washington, DC 20002 (phone 202/543-1094), supplies information on numerous locally sponsored, church-endorsed "travel seminars" to the Philippines in 1989–1990, when that nation has been designated by the National Coalition of Churches as the geographical focus of their study tours program. Costs are in the low to mid $2,000s, all inclusive, and while preference is given to members of the sponsoring denomination, places are open to all.

Finally, **G.A.T.E. (Global Awareness Through Experience), P.O. Box 3042, Harlingen, TX 78551 (phone 512/428-0836),** is a small group of Catholic nuns who operate tours to Third World areas where other Catholic clergy are engaged in "liberation theology," a struggle to empower the poor. Assisted by resident priests and other church workers at the destination, tour participants look and listen, debate and discuss, while occupying lodgings so modest that G.A.T.E.'s tours are among the cheapest in the field: $400 plus air fare for ten all-inclusive days in Mexico, $1,100 plus air fare for two such weeks in Peru, $1,000 plus air fare for 11 days in Nicaragua. Enclose postage in requesting their largely typewritten literature.

The Third World. Our understanding of the human condition is stunted so long as we delete it from our travel plans. Thanks to the efforts of five unusual "tour operators," that needn't be the case. ≈

The Bold, New World of the Feminist Tour Operator

Organized Travel for Women Only

Womanship

Should women travel only with other women? Should they do so on occasion?

If the trip is one of outdoor adventure, involving physical challenge, should they travel only with other women? Should they agree to include men on a group tour only if the group is led by a woman?

Because so many women are responding to one or more of the above questions with a resounding "Yes," a sizable new segment of the travel industry has emerged to serve their wants. As surprising as it may seem, more than 50 tour companies in a dozen major states are now openly feminist in their orientation, and limit their clients or leadership to women only.

The reason is unrelated to sexual proclivities or the lack of them. From a review of their literature, not one of the 50 new firms seems operated for homosexuals, and most stand carefully apart from a wholly separate group of tour companies openly appealing to gay men or gay women.

The Premise of Feminist Travel

Rather, the move to feminist travel seems motivated by a combined goal of consciousness-raising and female solidarity, and by the belief that women enjoy a holiday change of pace, stress-free, relaxing, when they travel only with other women. Though the philosophy is rarely articulated in the feminists' tour brochures, and is obtained with difficulty even in conversations with feminist tour operators (I've now spoken with several), the gist of it seems as follows:

When women travel with men, and especially on outdoor trips, both they and the men, say the feminists, tend to fall into predetermined gender roles: the men do the heavy work, the women putter about and cook. Traveling only with other women, women accept greater challenges, court greater responsibility, acquire new skills, gain confidence and a heightened sense of worth.

Male travelers are conditioned by society to be excessively goal-oriented: they must conquer this or that mountain, show prowess and strength, domineer. Most women, by contrast, enjoy the mere experience of

A sizable, new segment of the travel industry has emerged to serve the feminist cause.

A Womanship group

Womanship training

About to embark

travel, the joy of encountering nature, all without stressful competition or expectations. They have less need to boast and strut; they lack the male's inner urge (from early upbringing) to seem always skillful, strong, serene, and protecting. "I don't want to be protected on vacation," say many women; "I want to be myself."

In the presence of the other sex, so goes the argument, both sexes find it difficult to "let down their hair." On a tour limited to women, say the feminists, these tensions subside. Women spend less time on personal appearance and grooming, dispense with sexual role-playing, care only for themselves.

"And why should men feel threatened by that need?" asks one prominent female tour operator. "Why should an all-female tour be the subject of sneers? Men have been going off to hike or fish 'with the boys' for centuries."

Practical considerations: Since everyone on a woman-only trip is "single," participants pay no single supplement, but instead share rooms and costs. Since some male spouses don't care for outdoor trips, feminist tours often provide the only vacation outlet for women who genuinely enjoy the attractions of nature. Then, too, women who are recently widowed or divorced are enabled by such tours to meet others in the same situation; the experience is healing, restorative. But mainly, the women "take charge" of their holiday, free from the customary domination of men.

Hub of the Movement

The largest (65 departures a year) and oldest (12 years) of the feminist tour operators, and a clearinghouse for all the rest, is Woodswomen, of Minneapolis. Nonprofit, and eager to promote the offerings even of its competitors, its twice-yearly publication, *Woodswomen News,* is replete with the ads of dozens of widely scattered feminist travel firms. Most of the latter are engaged in purely local operations.

While Woodswomen is also heavily oriented toward its own state of Minnesota (and the nearby Northwest), it supplements that emphasis with expeditions to California, Alaska, Ireland (for biking), the Swiss Alps (for hiking), and Nepal (for trekking, an organized walk along the lower slopes of the Himalayas). Send either $2 (for postage and handling) for a copy of the organization's 20-page *Woodswomen News,* or else $15 for a year's membership (including all publications and related services), to **Woodswomen, 25 W. Diamond Lake Rd., Minneapolis, MN 55404 (phone 612/822-3809).**

Active and Thriving

Runners-up to the leader? Marion Stoddart's Outdoor Vacations for Women Over 40, of Groton, Massachusetts, and Bonnie Bordas's Womantrek, of Seattle, Washington, vie for the No. 2 spot. The first is active mainly in the northeastern states; the second (Womantrek) ranges far afield to China and Nova Scotia (on bicycle tours), Peru, Nepal, Crete, and northern India (for trekking), Thailand, Tibet, the Galápagos, Africa, and Baja California (the latter for sea kayaking, open to "absolute beginners"). Contact **Outdoor Vacations, P.O. Box 200, Groton, MA 01450 (phone 617/448-3331),** or **Womantrek, 1411 E. Olive Way (P.O. Box 20643), Seattle, WA 98102 (phone 206/325-4772),** requesting literature on the areas that interest you.

Still another relatively large firm is Womanship, of Annapolis, Maryland, offering a learn-to-sail program in a field of sport heavily dominated by men. Because (according to founder Suzanne Pogell) men tend to handle the main tasks on sailing expeditions, women are rarely able to do more than prepare the sandwiches; certainly they never "take charge" of the vessel. With Womanship, they do, gaining confidence, achieving independence. Weekend, weekday, and weeklong cruises are offered for beginners aged 20 to 70, in locations ranging from Chesapeake Bay, Long Island Sound, the west coast of Florida, and the Pacific Northwest (San Juan and the Gulf Islands) to the U.S. and British Virgin Islands. Contact **Womanship, Inc., 137 Conduit Street, Annapolis, MD 21401 (phone 301/269-0784 or 301/267-6661).**

Other major feminist tour operators include **New Dawn Adventures, 518 Washington St., Glouces-** ter, MA 01930 (phone 508/283-8717), heavily emphasizing camping retreats on the island of Vieques, Puerto Rico; **Mariah Wilderness Expeditions, P.O. Box 248, Point Richmond, CA 94807 (phone 415/233-2303); Adventures for Women, P.O. Box 515, Montvale, NJ 06745 (phone 201/930-0557),** centering on New Jersey and New York; **Alaska Women of the Wilderness, P.O. Box 775226, Eagle River, AK 99577 (phone 907/688-2226),** which has thus far provided confidence-building programs to more than 1,000 women (highly recommended); **Earthwise, 23 Mt. Nebo Rd., Newtown, CT 06470 (phone 203/426-6092);** and **New Routes, Inc., R.R. 5, Box 2030, Brunswick, ME 04011 (phone 207/729-7900).** ≈

Outdoor Vacations for Women

A Womanship skipper

A Visit to the World of "Small Is Beautiful"

At the Centre for Alternative Technology in Wales, the Most Basic Assumptions of the Industrial West Are Attacked and Derided

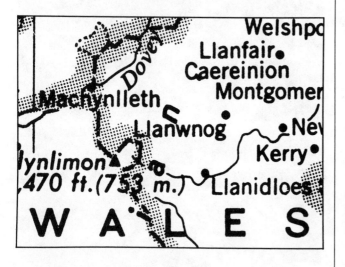

What do we really seek on a holiday abroad? Should we travel simply to feel pleasure? Or should we travel sometimes to get mad? I opt for the brand of travel that disturbs mental calm, compels you to think, challenges your most cherished beliefs, supplies new ideas and comparative lessons, leaves you a bit different from when you began.

In the alpine-like center of Wales, near the dreamy little town of Machynlleth (pronounced "mah-hun-lith"), Britain's Centre for Alternative Technology does just that. It disputes the very need for industrial development, rejects all arguments for large-scale commercial growth, condemns the activities to which the greater number of Americans have devoted their lives. In so doing, it acts as the cutting edge for an ideological movement that has won the loyalty of millions of Europeans, and even achieved a semblance of political power in Germany. To the "Greens" of Europe, the extreme ecologists, the fierce, anti-nuclear-power activists, the advocates of "Small Is Beautiful," to similar groups in 21 European nations, the Centre has become a secular Mecca to which more than 50,000 people make visits each year. No one understands contemporary Europe who does not understand the movement it represents.

You reach Machynlleth by British Rail in four comfortable hours from London's Euston Station, changing at Shrewsbury (pronounced "shroze-berry") and proceeding from there through the "harp-shaped hills" of Wales (Dylan Thomas's phrase) into one of the least populated areas of the British Isles—a scene of rocky heights dotted with patches of dark-green outcroppings. At Machynlleth, a three-mile ride by taxi or bus takes you to the bottom of a soaring but thoroughly exhausted slate quarry where signs advise you, in Dante-esque fashion, to abandon your car and ascend the steep hill on foot.

You are leaving behind civilization as we know it. The Centre—a tiny, working village—is unconnected to the electric grid of Britain, or to water mains. It provides its own power from wind, solar, or hydro sources; produces much of its own food from organic gardens, fish ponds, and poultry yards on the site; replaces worn-out machinery with parts forged by its own blacksmith. Within its bounds, nothing is wasted: organic refuse is recycled into compost-created fertilizers; metal is fired down and reused; sludge is collected from septic tanks and placed into methane digesters for the production of combustible gas and fertilizer by-products; homes are insulated to an extraordinary degree; even human urine is preserved for soil fertilization via amusing, odorless "pee collectors" discreetly placed at convenience stops. On the grounds, past a forest of solar panels, near a grove of modern metal windmills of every shape and size, runs an electric truck recharged by on-site water turbines powered by rushing streams. Using and displaying such "alternative technology," a utopian community enters its 15th year in mid-1989, locked in combat with the enemies that its chief theorist, the late E. F. Schumacher, succinctly ticked off as "urbanization, industrialization, centralization, efficiency, quantity, speed."

The combatants in this awesome battle, permanent residents of the Centre, are a slowly changing group of 32 young Britons whose average tenure here is about four years. A highly attractive lot, neatly if simply dressed in work clothes, well educated and articulate, they defy the stereotyped image of the "eco-freak," and emerge from a broad mix of schools and skills. Two are Ph.D.s in electrical and mechanical engineering; three are registered architects. All receive the same subsistence-level salary, except those with dependent children, to whom a "need-related" supplement is given. They eat communally (of a largely vegetarian diet), govern themselves by consensus reached at fortnightly meetings, confront daily decisions in 15-or-so, four-member "topic groups" each dealing with specialized work areas. They receive no major government support, and are a nonprofit organization subsisting almost entirely on admission and study-course fees paid by members of the public.

Going Beyond Conservation

Why have they come together at the Centre to lead lives that, to the outsider, seem so harsh and confined?

It is a working city meant to be visited and observed by a steady stream of tourists—a teaching device as much as a laboratory.

Harnessing wind at the Centre

The Centre disputes the very need for industrial development, rejects all arguments for large-scale commercial growth, condemns the activities to which the greater number of Americans have devoted their lives.

Solar panels at the Centre

It is because they share a common vision that goes far beyond the well-publicized conservationist goals of preserving natural beauty and reducing harmful pollution. To the European ecological movement, simple technology and decentralized economic organization are part of a happier, healthier approach to life, as well as a moral imperative. By using renewable sources of energy present in nature, by keeping technology simple and small, one preserves meaningful work opportunities for more and more people, they argue; one spreads the activity of production over broad rural areas, slows the movement to cities and the creation of inhumanly large industrial complexes, keeps nations democratic and people healthy, promotes nonviolence in all spheres of life, teaches personal responsibility, and—most important—shares the dwindling supply of finite fossil resources more equitably among all the people of the earth.

To these ends, all 32 of "The People," as the Centre styles its staff, are researchers relying for their daily existence almost entirely on small machines and devices that make use of wind, sun, water, and biomass for their energizing forces. Though the technology itself emerges from universities and laboratories around the world, it is the Centre's task, they believe, to "live with" the machines, discovering the necessary modifications and improvements that only actual experience can provide.

School and Laboratory

Are they, then, simply a test-tube community? They are more. Though officials of the Walt Disney organization would blanch at the comparison, they are perhaps a tiny version of what the late Walt Disney once envisioned as his EPCOT Center in Orlando, Florida: an actual working city that would, at the same time, be visited and observed by a steady stream of tourists—a teaching device as much as a laboratory. While Disney obviously failed to pull off the feat of combining two such antagonistic functions, the Centre quite demonstrably does.

It teaches. Its staff supplies a running commentary as they go about their tasks. You compliment a chef on the bean-sprout salad served in the Centre's superb vegetarian restaurant and he runs into the kitchen to extract a large bell jar in which the sprouts are grown, explaining how you, too, can enjoy such daily treats from the moistened seeds of simple alfalfa. You gaze over the shoulder of an engineer adjusting a "biomass gasifier" and she hastily explains how a renewable supply of wood, burned in a near-vacuum, will result in a combustible gas capable of powering an electric generator. Everywhere are colorful, cartoon-illustrated explanations and exhortations: "Use Less / Build to Last / Reuse / Repair / Recycle." "What good is efficiency if it puts people out of work and uses up resources?" "Gross product per head measures only the quantity of our wealth, not the quality of our lives. Are we happier?"

The Centre's staff heatedly deny that their work is of exclusive relevance to the Third World, responding to a frequent comment. It is morally and politically indefensible, they affirm, that the advanced West should make such a lavish disproportionate use of the world's resources, especially fossil fuels (America, with 6% of the earth's population, uses 40% of the world's primary resources). And there are insufficient such resources for the entire world to follow the wasteful, indulgent course of the West; consequently, that course must change—in all areas.

They also deny that the current glut in oil is at all significant; it is a brief lull in the crisis, a fool's paradise. Even were those supplies sufficient, their use exacts too high a human toll in acid rain, pollution, industrial blight, ruined lives; and fossil sources can, in any event, be put to better use than as energy. So goes the argument of Wales's Centre for Alternative Technology, in seminar presentations, group discussions, gardenside chats, quiet admonitions from engineers tinkering with a solar roof, a waterless toilet, a compost heap, or an "aerogenerator" manufactured at the Centre and sent around the world.

Planning a Visit

Two days set aside from the normal routines of a British vacation, or added to it, suffice for a thorough visit to the Centre. After traveling there by train from London (£28, approximately $48, round trip), most visitors base themselves in Machynlleth (where the Wynnstay Hotel, phone 2289, is your best bet, followed in distant second place by the Glyndwr, phone 2082) or in Corris, two miles from the Centre (Hotel Braich Goch, phone 73/229), or in several guesthouses in the area.

The Centre is open to visitors every day of the year except Christmas, for an admission charge of £2.30 ($3.90) for adults, less for seniors, students, and children. Two weekends a month from October to June it offers two-day courses in which you pursue one topic per weekend: blacksmithing, low-energy buildings, solar collectors and systems, organic gardening, wind power, etc. Free time involves explorations of Machynlleth, mid-Wales, and the Cambrian Coast. For specific dates, subjects, and application forms, contact the **Courses Coordinator, Centre for Alternative Technology, Machynlleth, Powys, Wales, U.K. SY20 9AZ (phone 06/54-2400).**

Visits of lesser duration are best followed by self-drive tours through awesome Wales, perhaps starting at the nearby small (but active) seaside town of Aberystwyth, heading north from there to Snowdon, highest mountain in Wales, visiting abandoned lead mines en route. Richard Llewellyn's Welsh classic, *How Green Was My Valley,* is your best preparatory reading.

But now it is dusk, at the end of a day of "alternative technology," and you are coming down from the mountain, perhaps jarred and disquieted, perhaps exhilarated, always alive with new ideas. This new approach—this confrontational approach—to travel has converted a routine British vacation into a memorable one, of lasting value. ≈

III ✻ CEREBRAL VACATIONS, IN THE SUMMERTIME

Summer Camps for Adults

Audubon Camps, Sierra Camps, Unitarian Camps, and Political Camps Use "Sleepaway Camps" for Grownup Needs

Sierra Club expedition

You approached it through a forest, on a dirt road, beneath a canopy of leafy boughs. You slept there in a rustic cabin or a lean-to made of logs. You ate in a wooden mess hall, at long, communal tables; swam in a lake; sat around an open fire at night.

And paid very little.

Sleepaway camp. Was there ever a better vacation? A more treasured time of childhood? And can those joyful, vibrant, inexpensive holidays be reexperienced at a later time, as an adult?

The answer is a limited yes. Provided you apply soon enough—say, by early spring, before the rolls are filled and closed—you can stay at one of nearly 50 widely scattered camps that operate for people of all ages, 18 to 80, in a setting almost identical to those cherished memories of youth.

Audubon Ecology Camps

These have existed for 53 years. On a thickly wooded 300-acre island off the mid-coast of Maine, at a lofty ranch in the Wind River Mountains of northwestern Wyoming, and in a large nature sanctuary near Greenwich, Connecticut, the National Audubon Society has enabled adults from all over the nation to enjoy an intense, camp-style experience, for one or two summer weeks, with all forms of plant and animal life: birds and marine mammals, insects, herbs and wildflowers, mink, beaver, otter, and eagles. You go birding or canoeing at 7 a.m., take leisurely hikes through open meadows or on mountain trails, make field trips to a hemlock gorge, and alternate all the outdoor activity with attendance at classroom lectures by expert naturalists. The simple aim is to reintroduce you to nature and its delicate balancing act; to show how all life is interdependent, and what you can do to protect it.

In the undeveloped, wilderness settings of all three camps, you quickly forget all urban concerns, but enjoy a reasonable standard of comfort at the same time: original homestead cabins in Wyoming (mostly dormitory in style, but with some facilities for couples), wood-frame dormitories and a restored 19th-century farmhouse on Hog Island in Maine, slightly more modern facilities and private rooms in Connecticut. Hearty meals are served buffet style, three times a day.

Connecticut camp sessions, from late June to mid-August 1989, are run for one week and cost a flat $425 per person, including all instruction, room and board, all field trips and recreation.

Wyoming's camp is also operated from late June through the middle of August 1989, and consists of both one-week and two-week sessions in "field ecology," costing $425 for one week, a remarkable $650 for two weeks, again all inclusive.

The camp in Maine runs from early July to early September 1989, and consists of one- and two-week sessions in "field ecology" ($495 for one week, $695 for two weeks, all inclusive) and one-week sessions in "field ornithology" (for $525, all inclusive).

There's not another cent to pay (except your transportation to the camp), nowhere at all to spend additional money, and no supplement for single persons traveling alone.

Who attends the Audubon camps? People of all ages and backgrounds: an accountant from Atlanta alongside a professional educator from San Francisco, college students, firemen, and retired senior citizens—their common tie, the urge for a vacation "with more substance to it than sitting on a beach," in the words of Philip Schaefer, Audubon's director of camps and summer programs. Returning to nature, he adds, is an "emotional as well as a learning experience," and at the final campfire, "there isn't a dry eye."

For extensive, colorful literature and application forms relating to all three camps, contact the **National Audubon Society, Audubon Camps and Workshops, 613 Riversville Rd., Greenwich, CT 06831 (phone 203/869-2017).**

Sierra Club "Base Camps"

Here's an even older program of adult summer camps, a small part of the much-broader year-round schedule of "outings" operated since 1901 by the fierce and powerful (450,000 members) environmentalist club called Sierra. In "wild places" of the United States, at least a dozen times each summer, experienced Sierra volunteers establish "base camps" at small cabins or lodges, or at tented camp areas, to which other participants then usually hike in from a road several miles away. Once established at the base camp, to which supplies have been brought by mule, vehicle, or porters, campers make day hikes into the surrounding countryside, or simply enjoy the outdoor pleasures of their wilderness base. Most of the base camps are in California or the Sierra Mountains of California/Nevada; a few are in Arizona, Oregon, New Mexico, West Virginia, and the Great Smoky Mountain Park of Tennessee/North Carolina.

With a minor exception or two, charges are remarkably low, even though all inclusive: as little as $205, $280, and $290 for some one-week stays; an average of $335 and $390 for other one-weekers; a usual top of $475. The occasional two-week trip is priced, in 1989, at an astonishing $490. That's because all campers pitch in to perform camp tasks, including cooking, supervised by the camp staff.

Sample base camp stays planned for 1989: in the Tahoe Forest of California/Nevada, near early Indian habitats, abandoned mines, and ghost towns; near the Donner Pass amid majestic rock cathedrals and trout-stocked lakes; on a Navajo reservation near Canyon de Chelly National Monument of Arizona; in a nationally protected area of fossil beds in Oregon; in the densely wooded Monongahela Forest of West Virginia. Though the accent throughout is on fun—the sheer pleasure of removing oneself for a week or two to an untouched, untrammeled wilderness—participants (of all ages, and including families) have the added opportunity to "network" with other kindred sorts, the dedicated environmentalists of our nation.

The full list of base camps appears in a larger directory of club outings bound each year into the January/February edition of *Sierra,* the club's magazine. For a copy, send $2.50 to **Sierra Club, 730 Polk St., San Francisco, CA 94109;** and for other specific information or longer leaflets on individual base camps, contact the **Sierra Club Outing Department, 730 Polk St., San Francisco, CA 94109 (phone 415/**

776-2211). Since base camps are open only to Sierra members or "applicants for membership," you'll later need to include your membership application and fee ($15 for seniors, students, and people of limited income, $33 for all others) with your reservation request.

Unitarian Camps

And then you have the often more comfortable and more numerous adult summer camps of the merged Unitarian/Universalist church, each one of which is open—as a matter of firm church policy—to Americans of all religious persuasions and of none. Acting from the same tolerant impulses that led them to found the American Red Cross, the ASPCA, and much of the public school movement, Unitarian/Universalists have here created a major travel/vacation resource, yet one that is unknown to much of the traveling public.

Why do they invite people of all religious persuasions to make use of their summer camps? Certainly not to proselytize or seek converts—they don't believe in that. Rather, as it's been explained to me, because they seek to discover common bonds among all humankind, and common spiritual truths; because their creed is without dogma and broadly compatible with all other faiths. What better place to experience such unity, they theorize, than at a summer gathering, in a pleasant, unstressed, cooperative camp?

Because some of the Unitarian/Universalist camps fill up by summer, you'd be well advised to apply quickly to one of the following:

Star Island Camp, New Hampshire: A rustic, rocky, sea-enclosed marsh connected to the mainland by a single radiotelephone (for emergency use only), Star Island is one of the historic "Isles of Shoals" off the New England coast (reached by ferry from Portsmouth, N.H.). A naturalist's dream, a photographer's vision, it has been owned by the Unitarians since 1915, and used as an adult summer camp (swimming, boating, fishing, hiking, tennis, softball) open to all, but mainly patronized by Unitarian/Universalists. From mid-June to early September, singles, couples, and families can opt for "theme weeks" focused on the arts, natural history, international affairs, psychology, and the like. They stay either in a wooden main building or a number of cottages (comfortable but not modern) at charges averaging $250 per adult per week for room, full board, and all activities. Prior to summer, contact **Star Island Corporation, 110 Arlington St., Boston, MA 02116 (phone 617/ 426-7988)**; thereafter, **P.O. Box 178, Portsmouth, NH 03801**.

De Benneville Pines Camp, near Angelus Oaks, California: Half an hour from the better-known town of Redland on the mid-Pacific coast, in a heavily wooded area laced with hiking trails, its Unitarian programs—again, open to all—consist primarily of a "family week" in late July and a "theme week" (which was chamber music in 1988) in late June. Family week is devoted to classic summer recreations, with the Unitarian theme largely limited to evening campfire discussions of broad ethical themes. Accommodation is in cabins; meals, according to staff, are "honest-to-goodness homemade—i.e., bread done from scratch"; all-inclusive weekly charges average $200 per adult for family weeks, much less for children, under $300 per adult for the theme-week session. Contact **De Benneville Pines, HC–01, Box 13, Angelus Oaks, CA 92305 (phone 714/794-2928)**.

Mountain Highlands Camp of North Carolina: This consists of cabins and lodges atop Mount Little Scaly (4,200 feet), overlooking the Blue Valley of the Blue Ridge Mountains. "Our camp," says guest relations coordinator Louis Bregger, "is completely surrounded by national forest and thus affords us beautiful, unthreatened vistas." Except for a single week reserved for training Unitarian leaders (mid-July), all other summer weeks (early June through August) are open to persons of all religious backgrounds and of any age. Themes, which supplement a daily routine of swimming (in a small, spring-fed lake), hiking, arts and crafts, include "Singles Week," "River-Rafting," "Folklore and the Truth," "Life's Purposes," "Adventures for All Ages," and "Dare to Explore." Cabin accommodations, high-quality meals—figure from $280 to $400 per adult per week for everything.

Contact **Mountain Highlands Camp, 841 Hwy. 106, Highlands, NC 28741 (phone 704/526-5838).**

Unirondack Camp, of upstate New York: On a peninsula jutting into Beaver Lake, near the western edge of Adirondack Park, this one is surrounded by thousands of acres of "forever wild" forest preserve, rugged hills, and abundant wildlife. Though most of its summer program is devoted to young people, two one-week sessions are reserved for "intergenerational families" and also accept adults without children in tow. In early July it's music-related activities for all ages; in early August, a "creative" week of singing, folk dancing, arts and crafts—all in addition to the usual hiking, canoeing, sailing, and swimming. Totally absent: religious pressures. "We respect different traditions," says one of its Unitarian administrators. "Our themes are simply participatory democracy, a reverence for the natural world, a search for excellence and personal growth." Accommodations are cabins or a log-style dorm with hot and cold running water, all near a large shower house. Adult prices average $175 a week for room, board, and activities; children pay $80 to $150, according to age. Contact the **Administrator, Unirondack, 320 Rockingham St., Rochester, NY 14620 (phone 716/271-6434).**

Aurora Institute, Alberta, Canada: In the awesome foothills of the Canadian Rockies, this one-week Unitarian camp (the second week of August in 1989) makes use of cedar-log buildings on the grounds of the Goldeye Center, a private camp operated by Canadian co-op associations. It is definitely open to U.S. citizens and to people of all faiths, "who will not feel uncomfortable," says Katie Sather, director of the institute. "We are very much *not* evangelical." Normal camp activities (lake canoeing, nature walks, choir, and crafts) alternate with a broad range of multiple workshops (purely optional): "Beyond War (Peace Consciousness)," "Essentials of Worship," "Clarifying Your Relationships with Money," "Gay-Straight Dialogues," "Tarot," "Family Puzzles," "Readers' Theater," among others. Fees are remarkably cheap: as little as $200 per adult for the entire week, meals included,

You are in a setting almost identical to those cherished memories of youth.

Sierra Club outing

Star Island Camp

In undeveloped wilderness, campers quickly forget all urban concerns.

American Hiking Society project

A.H.S. volunteers

if you stay in the dorm; about $100 more in smaller log guesthouses. Write **Aurora Institute, P.O. Box 1794, Lacombe, Alberta T0C 1S0, Canada.**

The Hersey Retreat, on Penobscot Bay, Maine: A small "resort" off the mid-coast of Maine, this shingle-style lodge (built in 1909) and adjoining farmhouse are owned by the Universalist church, but open to all—including families—in the month of August. "In keeping with our liberal tradition," says the group's brochure, "we invite others to share our facility in summer." Afternoons make use of broad recreational opportunities in a superb, beach-lined setting; mornings are given over to discussion of the following 1989 themes: "Religious Education: Children in Crisis" (early August), "Some Things Considered: Mid-Life Decisions" (mid-August), and "Music Week" (late August). August sessions are known as "family camps" and average $150 per adult, $80 for children 6 to 18, $45 for children 5 and under. Prior to summer, write **Hersey Retreat, P.O. Box 1125, Bangor, ME 04401;** thereafter, **P.O. Box 1183, Stockton Springs, ME 04981.** Or phone the director of Hersey, David Greeley (207/722-3405).

Ferry Beach Camp, on the coast of Maine: For its summer-long, ten-week program of adult activities, open to all without question, Ferry Beach makes use of 30 woodland acres on Saco Bay, and adjoining sand dunes and pine groves, with access to bike paths and walking trails in a state park. Though participants are free to romp and relax, they can also attend weeklong conferences from the end of June through the Labor Day weekend. Conference themes will be in the spirit of these from the 1988 season: "Exploring the Maine Coast," "Creative Leisure," "Alternative Lifestyles to Retirement," "Single-Parent Families," "Tai-Chi and Fine Arts." Expect to pay about $300 per adult for a week's room, board, registration, and activities, slightly less for children, much less for those occupying tented campsites. Contact **Ferry Beach Park Association, 5 Morris Ave., Saco, ME 04072** (phone 207/282-4489).

Camp UniStar, in northern Minnesota: A Unitarian camp maintained, this time, exclusively for adults and families through all of June, July, and August. On the northeast tip of isolated Star Island in Cass Lake, accessible only by pontoon boat, Unitarians and "like-minded individuals" occupy cabins and lodges of a simple nature, but all with private facilities. They take meals communally in a nearby dining hall from which smoking has been banished. While the key aim is relaxation, pursued in unstructured fashion, lecture/discussions are had from 10 a.m. to noon daily on such weekly themes as "Writing and Reading Fiction," "Family Reconstruction," "Israeli/Palestinian Tensions," "Philosophy and Fishing," "An Examination of American Identity." Charges run to approximately $175 per adult for the week (including the boat over and back), as little as $90 per child. Prior to June 1, contact **Judy Burtis, 7325 Fremont Ave. South, Richfield, MN 55423 (phone 612/866-8248);** thereafter, **Camp UniStar, Star Island Water Rte. 51, Cass Lake, MN 56633 (phone 218/335-2692).**

Rowe Camp, in the Berkshires of northwest Massachusetts: A Unitarian children's camp for much of the summer, Rowe largely replaces the youngsters with adults during two warm-weather periods: for a week in July ("Women's Week") and a week in early August ("Liberation Camp"); the former is a consciousness-raising program for females only, while the latter attempts to free all participants—singles, couples, families—"from whatever confines their spirits." In both, daily workshops deal with growth in the physical, emotional, spiritual, and political realms; and all is combined with swimming, dancing, canoeing, silkscreening, weaving, and picnics—a joyful, dynamic, but intensely spiritual atmosphere. Scattered wooden cabins and main lodges resemble the camps of your own youth. The all-inclusive cost for a week averages $290 per adult, $200 to $220 per accompanying child, depending on age. Contact **Rowe Camp, Kings Highway Road, Rowe, MA 01367 (phone 413/339-4216).**

A Political Summer Camp

Finally, a group of proud and unrepentant, happy and defiant liberals from all over the nation (of all ages, families and singles) converges each summer on the World Fellowship Center in the White Mountains of New Hampshire for a special vacation.

With its 300 acres of forest, mile-long Whitton Pond for swimming and boating, cookouts, campsites and rustic lodge buildings, WFC would seem at first to be a standard resort for standard, warm-weather relaxation.

But from mid-June to early September, every week of the summer there is devoted to such atypical, even unsettling, "resort" themes as "Care for the Poor," "Central America—Witness to War," "Cracks in the System," "Bretton Woods Revisited," "Peace Priorities." Noted lecturers take to the stump on each week's topics; and twice-daily discussions, at 10:30 a.m. and after dinner at 8 p.m., alternate with lighthearted blueberry-picking, exercise sessions, and swimming.

All three meals are included in the room rates, and yet those charges amounted last season to only $185 or $225 per person per week (depending on room category) or to only $135 per week for people bringing a tent. At those price levels, space fills up fast.

For information and application forms, contact **World Fellowship Center, RR2, Birch Street, Box 53, North Conway, NH 03860 (phone 603/447-2280).** (The group's special summer address and number is: **World Fellowship Center, RD Box 136, Conway, NH 03818 (phone 603/356-5208).** ≈

Museum and chapel at Star Island Camp

Campus Vacations

Like the TV Hosts of "Fantasy Island," They Enable You to Briefly Re-experience the "Shortest, Gladdest Years of Life"

At a college gallery

Class at Penn State

Remember them? Those wondrous years? You lived in a dorm, next door to a dining hall. Your days stretched on without limit, it seemed, and there was time for everything: discussions lasting hour after hour, a movie at night, the stillness of library and lab, your mind pulsing with new ideas and challenging thoughts.

"Bright college years"—through a wise use of vacation time, you can touch them again, feel the glow, recharge the spirit. At scattered colleges and universities, a number of short-term summer programs enable adults of all ages to briefly re-experience "the shortest, gladdest years of life."

There are, by my reckoning, 14 such schools. For a week in summer, when the campus blooms, they open their residences, dining halls, and classrooms to every sort of student from around the nation, without conducting tests or issuing grades, and at wonderfully low costs. Few other short vacations offer so much pleasure, and yet such mental growth.

And how do these programs differ from the "learning vacations"—an exotic cruise, an archeological dig—that we, as alumni, are so often offered in the mails? First, because they are offered to alumni and non-alumni alike. Second, because they are operated by the university itself, on a nonprofit basis, and not by a commercial tour operator or professor-turned-entrepreneur. Third, because they take place on campus. Fourth, because, unlike other classier, costlier seminars conducted on campus, these place you not in nearby hotels but in simple college dorms, from which you take your meals in adjacent student cafeterias, exactly as you did at the ages of 19, 20, and 21. And last, because, unlike the somewhat similar Elderhostel programs, they are available to youngsters in their 30s, 40s, and 50s as well.

14 Campus Choices

Cornell's Adult University is the most ambitious of the lot, four one-week sessions beginning July 2, 1989. At least 300 people attend each week, enjoying comfortable student lodgings and highly regarded food, eminent professors, bright fellow "students," the verdant surroundings of Cornell's famous hillside campus ("high above Cayuga's waters"), and sensible prices: $540 to $610 per week per adult, including tuition and full room and board; $180 to $295 per child, depending on age. Most adults opt for a single one-week topic, taught in daily sessions (they let out in mid-afternoon) throughout the week: "Frontiers of Technology," "Louis XIV and Versailles," "The Physics of Everyday Things," "Poets and Prophets: The Heritage of the Greeks and Hebrews," "Modern England," and "The Jurisprudence of the Holocaust" are highly illustrative samples from last year's and this year's (1989) curricula. The quality of instruction, and convivial afternoon and evening recreation, create a setting so compelling that some guests need almost to be evicted after their week in "Brigadoon"; though the literature doesn't say so, guests are encouraged to stay for only a single week (but may add another), and early applications are advisable. Contact **Cornell's Adult University, 626 Thurston Ave., Ithaca, NY 14850 (phone 607/255-6260).**

Brown's "Summer College" invites both alumni and "friends" of the university to enjoy a remarkable week (mid- to late July) of high-quality lectures and discussions by eminent Ivy League professors. Each year's program pursues one common topic in morning sessions throughout the week, which are then followed by one's choice of varying afternoon subjects. 1987's theme was the pre-Columbian civilization of the Aztecs, Maya, and Incas; 1988's program explored the difficult task of American secondary education in building both competence and character, both "cleverness" and "goodness"; 1989's theme hasn't been chosen as we go to press. Brown University, along with Dartmouth (discussed below), was the grandparent of continuing education in America and one of the earliest operators of short-term, residential, summer courses for adults. With room, board, and tuition included, expect to pay $440 to $600 per person. Contact **Brown's Continuing College, P.O. Box 1920, Providence, RI 02906 (phone 401/863-2474).**

"Summer of '89" at the College of Wooster, Ohio,

Unlike other classier, costlier seminars, these place you not in nearby hotels but in simple dorms.

The Asimov Seminar, Rensselaerville, New York

Summer scholars at Indiana University

consists of lectures from 8:30 a.m. to noon, followed by buffet luncheons and afternoon excursions to attractions in the area, followed by films or light opera (*H.M.S. Pinafore, Wiener Blut*) at night, and gala dinners consisting occasionally of barbecues in a giant tent. All this occurs from June 11 to 17, 1989, with academic matters pursued for six straight days, through noon of Saturday. 1988's theme topic was "The Presidency of the United States," as presented by eminent faculty members; 1989's topic is as yet unchosen as we go to press. Although organized by the Office of Alumni Relations, its staff members assure me that mere "friends" of the college are admitted to the program and to use the near-pastoral setting of a 300-acre campus and its many recreational facilities. Room, full board, and tuition total $341 per person for the entire week, using university dorms and the Lowry Center Dining Hall. Contact **Summer of '89, Office of Alumni Relations, The College of Wooster, Wooster, OH 44691 (phone 216/263-2263).**

The Vacation College of Slippery Rock University, Pennsylvania, occupies a 600-acre campus 50 miles north of Pittsburgh, in the rolling, tree-lined hills of western Pennsylvania. This is a far less academically intense program of such courses as "Word Processing," "Stained Glass," "Tombstone Geography," and "The Power of Laughter," all interspersed with golf, tennis, swimming, excursions, and organized evening events. You can schedule attendance at as many as three topics in your one-week stay, which runs from June 18 to 23 of 1989. As at all the other schools, you face no examinations, receive no grades, stay in university residence halls (here, with separate bathroom facilities for men and women on each floor). "Early-bird" registrants (applying before May 16) pay only $245 per person for a full week's room, board, and tuition; otherwise, $295. Participants are adults only, without their children, most in their early 40s, some in their 70s. Contact **Vacation College, Office of Continuing Education, Lowry Center, Slippery Rock, PA 16057 (phone 412/794-7551).**

"The Mini University" of Indiana University is from June 18 to 23, 1989, and consists of 112 lectures on 112 separate subjects delivered by 114 faculty members of the great Hoosier center of learning; you are encouraged to attend as many as you can manage in the course of a six-day, five-night stay in Halls of Residence costing $245 per adult for a week's room, board, tuition, and registration. Children coming along are sent to a day camp at nearby Shawnee Bluffs, but then stay with their parents at an average cost of $123 per week, including registration and all meals. Costs are kept low by the fact that all profs donate their services free, as they speak on topics clustered under such headings as "Humanities," "Sciences," "International Affairs," "Arts," "Business," "Domestic Issues," "Health, Fitness, and Leisure." Contact **Mini University '89, Indiana Memorial Union M-17, Bloomington, IN 47405 (phone 812/335-6120).**

The Asimov Seminar at the Rensselaerville Institute, Rensselaerville, New York, presents, as its discussion leader, none other than Isaac Asimov, famed science fiction writer, futurist, and college professor. The setting: a rural "think tank" and conference center in upstate New York, which occupies 100 acres of meadows, woods, flower gardens, and varied recreational areas. Each summer for the past 17 years (and in late July of 1989) Asimov has been conducting a provocative seminar on developing technologies and issues of the future (artificial intelligence, organ transplants, space colonization), using a unique "simulation" approach to cast students as "role players" in the resolution of numerous hypothetical, brain-stretching problems. Though not on a college campus, the experience is remarkably akin to a "campus vacation" and costs $450 for each of two people staying together, $550 single—private room, all meals, and tuition. Contact **The Rensselaerville Institute, Rensselaerville, NY 12147, Attn: Mary Ann Ronconi (phone 518/797-3783).**

Grace Graham Vacation College, at the University of Oregon in Eugene, takes place in mid-August, and last year featured a thorough, full-week discussion (morning, afternoon, and evening) of "Ethical Dilemmas: Issues in Law, Politics, Medicine, Business, and the Press" (1989's subject matter hasn't been announced as we go to press in late 1988). Lectures and seminars are delivered or led by a multidisciplinary faculty from the Law School, School of Journalism, and Department of Philosophy, and are impressive, indeed, in their depth and serious approach; but no tests follow the brainy debates! Students of all ages—but mostly middle-aged—stay in a high-rise residence located between the campus and downtown Eugene, take their meals in university dining rooms, and pay $400 per person in double rooms, $450 single. Contact **Grace Graham Vacation College, University Housing, University of Oregon, Eugene OR 97403 (phone 503/686-4277).**

The Vacation College of the University of North Carolina at Chapel Hill draws its faculty from the several noted universities in the area (including Duke), a resource so rich that two separate weeks are offered and two alternative subjects per week are taught throughout the day. From June 25 to July 1, 1989: topics akin to last year's "The World of the Old Testament" and "German Culture from Bismarck to the Nazis." From July 23 to July 29, 1989: topics akin to last year's "Art and Civilization" and "Victorian England." Musical programs or appropriate films are the relaxing evening activity. Tuition for the week is $250 per person, but meals and lodging in campus dormitories are billed separately, at a yet-to-be-determined (but moderate) charge. Contact **Humanities Program, CB# 3420, 209 Abernethy Hall, University of North Carolina, Chapel Hill, NC 27599 (phone 919/962-1106).**

The Johns Hopkins Alumni College, which readily admits non-alumni to its sessions, will probably move its 1989 site to the Wintergreen Resort near Charlottesville, Virginia, because of ongoing dorm renovations at its normal location. The use of deluxe condominiums at that elegant mountain center causes prices per person to be a high $590 for the week, including tuition and accommodations, but only three dinners. Four noted historians chair the one-week session in July of 1989, discussing changing conceptions of mankind's nature and place in the universe. In true Johns Hopkins tradition, the talk is on a lofty plane, and

They are operated by the university itself, on a nonprofit basis.

"Hands-on" learning, Indiana University

Children's program at Penn State

Time off at Indiana U.

Lectures are impressive in their depth and serious approach, but no tests follow the brainy debates.

Field seminar at Cornell's Adult University

Outdoor class at Indiana University

ranges from Greek philosophies to present-day notions of genetic engineering and artificial intelligence. Evenings involve slide shows of pagan and early Christian art as a "change of pace." "This is always the best week of my whole summer," wrote one enthusiastic participant after 1988's session. Contact the **Johns Hopkins Alumni College, 3211 N. Charles St., Baltimore, MD 21218 (phone 301/338-7963).**

Smith College Adult Sports and Fitness Camp, for both men and women, is a highly active week of classroom instruction in fitness, nutrition, and stress management, alternating with active participation in yoga, cycling, hiking, swimming, canoeing, badminton, squash, tennis, and other forms of aerobics. The college's facilities for all this are among the best in the nation, and applications (from adults of all ages) are so heavy that two separate sessions have been scheduled for 1989: the second and third weeks of June. A single fee of $550 per person covers sports, instruction, and room and board (single or double rooms) from dinner Sunday through breakfast the following Saturday. Contact **Jim Johnson, Adult Sports and Fitness Camp, Scott Gymnasium, Smith College, Northampton, MA 01063 (phone 413/584-2700, ext. 3975).**

The Dartmouth Alumni College, in Hanover, New Hampshire, operating for 12 consecutive days from July 9 through July 20 of 1989, is among the oldest and most serious of summer campus sessions for adults, and assures me it is open to non-alumni. Each morning of the nearly two-week period, two lectures are followed by small-group discussions with faculty, but afternoons are left mostly free for tennis or golf on campus, boating, or hiking in the White Mountains. Evenings are devoted to films, special lectures, concerts, or plays related to that summer's theme, which in 1989 will be "China: Old and New." Professor of Religion Robert Henricks will oversee a program of "major national names" as guest speakers, in addition to eminent faculty members from all departments of the college, including even the physical sciences. Participants pay $910 for the two weeks (that's per person, double occupancy, for those out of college for more than ten years; younger grads get a discount of about $250 per person), including accommodation in Dartmouth dorms, books, instruction, and all meals (of which two are festive banquets). Contact **Dartmouth Alumni College, Dartmouth Continuing Education, 308 Blunt Alumni Center, Hanover, NH 03755 (phone 603/646-2454).**

The Alumni College of Penn State is yet another of those mistitled programs meant mainly for alumni, but firmly open to all. It is also somewhat less of an academically rigorous program than a partly recreational week for the entire family. In 1988 classroom time included such lectures as "Weather Forecasting on Television," "What's So Natural in the Food You Eat?" "International Law in the Reagan Years," "Human Aging: Fact and Fiction," and "Massage Techniques for the Home." Oxford it's not, but rather a type of "cruise with faculty," according to one staff member. A fee of approximately $65 a day covers your accommodation in university residence halls (bath down the corridor), all meals, and all tuition. Dates are July 9–15, 1989, and you can contact **Rick Dorman, Penn State Alumni Association, 105 Old Main, University Park, PA 16802 (phone 814/865-6516).**

Skidmore College's Summer Special Programs, near Saratoga Springs, New York, invites several different groups to use its campus in summer for residential adult study programs, and some of the latter are open to the public at large. I'm particularly impressed by the two- to four-week creative-writing course of the New York State Writers' Institute (mid-July of 1989; $900 for two weeks, $1,560 for four weeks, all inclusive), by the nine-day conference and workshops of the International Women's Writing Guild (late July of 1989; approximately $568 for tuition, room, and board), and by the open-to-everyone Alumni/Parent Seminars of Skidmore itself (early to mid-August of 1989; $455 for a week's tuition, room, and board to pursue studies in history, literature, psychology, or art). Contact, respectively, **Prof. R. Boyers, N.Y. State Summer Writers Institute, Skidmore College, Saratoga Springs, NY 12866; International Women's Writing Guild, P.O. Box 810, Gracie Station, New York, NY 10028; or Office of the Dean of Special Programs, Skidmore College, Saratoga Springs, NY 12866 (phone 518/584-5000, ext. 2264).**

Finally, Colby College of Waterville, Maine, plays host each August to the Great Books Summer Institute, an intensive discussion and analysis of four outstanding books that participants (up to 250 of them) have already read and pondered prior to arriving for their one-week stay. This year's dates are August 6–12, 1989; this year's fee is $315 to $330, either single or double occupancy, including all lodging in college residence halls, all meals, and all tuition, as well as the four books sent to you via U.P.S., about a month in advance. During the session attended several years back by a friend of mine, books for discussion included Thomas Mann's *The Magic Mountain,* Fritjhof Capra's *The Tao of Physics,* and William Barrett's *Irrational Man;* participants discussed the interrelationship of the books and their themes, in a week that was described to me as quite remarkably stimulating and satisfying. Scheduled for 1989: *The Aquarian Conspiracy, Wholeness and the Implicate Order, The Universe Is a Green Dragon,* and Thornton Wilder's *The Skin of Our Teeth.* One note: Discussions are led by a lay "moderator," not a professor, whose role is to elicit student comments and not to hand down scholarly judgments from above. For information, contact **Great Books Summer Institute, 680 Elton Ave., Riverhead, NY 11901, Attn: Dan Kohn (phone 516/727-8600).**

At all such schools: When the week is over, and "students" depart, what usually is their appraisal of the experience? "It was a stimulating relief from my day-to-day office routine that I do not find lying on a beach," said one. "It was good to talk ideas with my spouse," said another, "and know both of our heads were still very much alive." ≈

Vacationing at a Cultural Folk Dance Camp

With an Intensity That Must Be Seen to Be Believed, Some Americans Devote Their Holidays to Exploring the Folkways of Ethnic Cultures

At the Country Dance and Song Society

On winter evenings in deserted gyms, they dance to the music of a dozen cultures, learning the steps as they go along, helping their partners, uncritical of the efforts of a sheer beginner.

Summers, from late June to early September, they repair to wooded settings near lakes or mountains to dance the entire day and evening. For a full week, or at least a long weekend, residential, rural folkdance camps provide an increasingly popular holiday/vacation alternative to tens of thousands of Americans.

Their atmosphere is among the most democratic of all our holiday institutions. Participants are wholly intergenerational and range from college sophomores to dynamic seniors in their 70s—some bearded, some in bold gypsy skirts or country dirndls. Without introduction, they take your hand to start a dance, then hand you off without skipping a beat to the next in a circle or line of whirling, or foot-stomping, or waltzing, dancers. There are no awkward social barriers, no inquiries into background or tastes, no attention paid to beauty or dress.

The music to which you dance, and the steps, are those that descend not from a paid composer or choreographer, but from the people, mainly poor people, and are then handed down from decade to decade by oral tradition or direct demonstration. It is intensely ethnic music and dance, and usually jumps from country American to Balkan to Greek and Israeli in the course of a single set.

It is also soul-stirring, insistent, pulsating music and dance that makes you joyous to be alive, and exercises every faculty of mind and limb. If you've never been to a folkdance camp or even folkdancing, you might think of taking the plunge, because the steps are easily learned and sheer beginners are accepted at virtually every camp.

The major camps—as best I've been able to determine—are the following:

On Both Coasts

Pinewoods Camp, near historic Plymouth, Massachusetts: Here is perhaps the most extensive of the residential, folkdance programs, a series of eight one-week sessions running from early July to early September. But all are focused on English, Scottish, and American forms of the art, without the enlivening digressions (in my opinion) into the Balkan or Mexican varieties that mark so many other camps. Still, for lovers of those familiar steps, here are several hours daily of dancing paradise, in spacious and airy wood pavilions scattered over 24 acres of pine groves. Housing, almost always double occupancy, is in rustic, screened cabins located among the trees, but none far from two clear-water lakes for swimming and boating. Seven of the weeks are sponsored by the Country Dance and Song Society, cost $350 a week (in all but one instance) for room, full board, and dancing, and inquiries should be sent, prior to around June 30, to **CDSS, 17 New South St., Northampton, MA 01060 (phone 413/584-9913),** and thereafter to **CDSS, Pinewoods Camp, Off West Long Pond Road, Plymouth, MA 02360 (phone 508/224-4858).** One session (early July, and usually $350, all inclusive) is sponsored by the Royal Scottish Country Dance Society, and features the three or so basic steps of Scottish folkdancing in endless combinations. A bagpiper wakes you in the morning! Contact **RSCDS, c/o Ken Launie, 15 Salem St., Cambridge, MA 02139 (phone 617/491-6855).**

Centrum Foundation, Port Townsend, Washington: A nonprofit arts-and-education group sponsoring summer music, theater, and writing conferences at a 100-year-old former army base called Fort Worden; participants stay in single or double rooms carved out of barracks now owned by the State Parks Department. The site overlooks the awesome Cascade and Olympic Mountains on one side, the Strait of Juan de Fuca, with its long, sandy beach, on the other. August 20–27, 1989, there is "International Folk Dance and Music Week," teaching and practicing four different types of international dances. Tuition, room, and board run $285 per person. Contact **Centrum Foundation, P.O. Box 1158, Port Townsend, WA 98368 (phone 206/385-3102).** A second week of "Mazurka Dancing," under different auspices (see below), some-

times takes place at Fort Worden in the week before the Labor Day weekend. Mazurkas—a Polish couples' dance—swept the world in the 19th century, and influenced other dances right through the ragtime era. Common is the feeling of exhilaration it inspires. The dance is intricate, and provokes a sensation "akin to flying or riding horseback." Tuition, room, and board are $300 for the week. This time, contact **Flying Cloud Academy of Vintage Dance, c/o Richard Powers, 3623 Herschel Ave., Cincinnati, OH 45208 (phone 513/321-4878).**

Stockton Folk Dance Camp, in Stockton, California: One of the nation's oldest, in its 42nd year, it always takes place the last week of July and the first week of August, Sunday through Saturday. With several two-hour classes running simultaneously, it isn't possible to sample everything, and many people therefore go for both weeks. According to one teacher, Stockton is not well suited for beginners, but is rather a skilled "work camp" for learning new dances. Accommodation is in University of the Pacific dorms, and fees for tuition, room, and board run about $400 per week. Contact **Stockton Folk Dance Camp, c/o Bruce Mitchell, Director, University of the Pacific, Stockton, CA 95211 (phone 916/488-7637).**

Maine Folk Dance Camp, near Bridgton, Maine: Another highly important one, it consists of nine weeklong sessions held from July 1 through the Labor Day weekend, at a 37-acre, lakeside camp setting about an hour to the northwest of Portland, Maine. Housing is in individual cabins sleeping two people. Each day features the dance repertoire of a different nation: you wake one morning, let's say, to Mexican music, eat Mexican food, learn Mexican dances, and have a fiesta at night. Some participants claim the regimen to be better than actual international travel, since they experience "real" aspects of a culture, not tourist ones. Room, board, classes, and festivals cost under $400 a week, depending on the accommodation. Prior to early June (by which time much space is booked), contact **Maine Folk Dance Camp, P.O. Box 2305, North Babylon, NY 11703 (phone 516/661-3866);** thereafter, **Maine Folk Dance**

Camp, P.O. Box 100, Bridgton, ME 04009 (phone 207/647-3424).

And Elsewhere

Lady of the Lake, of northern Idaho: In the popular resort area of Lake Coeur d'Alene, an hour from Spokane, Washington, this is an almost frantically intense week (the last full week of June) of folkdancing that starts at 9 a.m. each day and roars on till 11 p.m. You do "contras," squares, clogging, and "vintage" (turn-of-the-century) dancing, aided by accomplished instructors and musicians, all for the remarkably low weekly charge of $275, including meals and accommodations in rustic cabins housing six to ten people. Children aren't encouraged to come. Contact **Lady of the Lake, c/o Penn Fix, W. 703 Shoshone, Spokane, WA 99203 (phone 509/838-2160).**

Buffalo Gap Camp, near Capon Bridge, West Virginia: A 2½-hour drive from Washington, D.C., Buffalo Gap Camp (on a spring-fed, clear-water lake) becomes an international dance camp on the three-day Memorial Day and Labor Day weekends, charging $200 per weekend for dancing, ethnic meals, and lodging in dorm-style cabins. Teachers are brought in from around the world to supervise exotic, foreign folkdances from 9 a.m. to 5 p.m. (repeated at evening dance parties), and yet total beginners are invited to the camp. In between the opening and closing dates for summer the camp is rented to outside groups for weeklong sessions of specialized dancing ("Scandinavian Week," "Balkan Week"). For information on the full summer program, contact **Buffalo Gap Camp, c/o Mel Diamond, 2414 E. Gate Dr., Silver Spring, MD 20906 (phone 301/589-9212 during office hours, 301/871-8788 evenings and weekends).**

Mendocino Country Dance Camp, in northern California: Living in small cabins sleeping from five to six people, in a natural redwood grove of magnificent mammoth trees, you dance English and American squares and "contras" from 9 a.m. to 5 p.m., enjoy a short break, and then continue at an evening dance party that starts at 8 p.m. and officially ends at 11

p.m.—but frequently continues for most of the night! Beginners are very much encouraged and supported. Dates are July 15–22, 1989, and the approximate cost is $350 for housing, meals, and instruction. Contact **Mendocino Country Dance Camp, c/o Fred Perner, 3234 Ramona St., Palo Alto, CA 94306 (phone 415/856-3038).**

Kentucky Summer Dance School, at Berea College in Berea, Kentucky: Always the last week in June, it's in a sylvan place—a historic, small town set in the foothills of the western Appalachians, and at a college noted for its support of the folk arts. Instruction ranges from traditional American dances to the most esoteric of the British and Scottish steps, and much of the classroom music is live. Charges average $250 for adults, $220 for teenagers, $175 for children 6 to 12 (who pursue a separate program), for meals, tuition, and lodging in college dorms. Contact **Kentucky Summer Dance School, c/o Don Coffey, 1581 Bond's Mill Rd., Lawrenceburg, KY 40342 (phone 502/839-6220).**

Augusta Heritage Arts Workshops, at Davis & Elkins College, West Virginia: In the context of a much broader, summer-long program delving into every conceivable folk art and craft, specialized dance weeks take place in late July (for Irish, English, and French-Canadian "step dances" only) and in early August (for southern squares, contras, swing dances, Cajun dances, clogging, and callers' workshops). Work is intense but open to all levels of expertise; lodging is in college residence halls, on the hilly, 170-acre campus of Davis & Elkins in the highlands (2,000 feet) of central West Virginia. Cost for a week: just over $300 for tuition, meals, and semiprivate room. Contact **Augusta Heritage Center, Davis & Elkins College, 100 Sycamore St., Elkins, WV 26241 (phone 304/636-1903).**

John C. Campbell Folk School of Brasstown, North Carolina: "Dance Weeks" at this noted, 61-year-old school for folk arts and crafts take place on scattered dates throughout the year, and are almost wholly devoted to steps and formations of the home-grown variety, thoroughly American. Grounds are a 365-acre campus nestled between the Smokies and the Blue Ridge Mountains, a 2- to 2½-hour drive from such cities as Atlanta, Chattanooga, Knoxville, Asheville, and Greenville. Meals, as you'd expect, are southern, home style, and accompanied by home-baked bread. And weekly charges average only $300 in dorms, slightly more per person in double rooms, for tuition, meals, and lodging. Contact **The Registrar, John C. Campbell Folk School, Brasstown, NC 28902 (phone 704/837-2775 or 837-7329).**

Fiddle and Dance Workshops, in the Catskill Mountains of New York State: The camp is Ashokan, along a lake at the base of heavily forested hills, 2½ hours north of New York City by car. And there, for three consecutive weeks in August 1989, dedicated folkdancers (including beginners) attend either the "Northern Week" (squares, contras, and couple dances of New England, Britain, France, Sweden, and Canada), the "Southern Week" (Appalachian, Cajun, and "oldtime," plus buckdancing, clogging, and "flat-footing"), the "Celtic Week" (Irish, Scottish, and Northumbrian), or the "Western and Swing Week" (country, western, cowboy, Texas two-step, jitterbug, and lindy). Just $325 a week covers tuition, meals, and lodging in bunkhouse dorms, 15–20 people per room. Contact **Fiddle and Dance, R.D. 1, Box 489, West Hurley, NY 12491 (phone 914/338-2996).**

Flying Cloud Academy of Cincinnati, Ohio: Every year in the third week of June, it sponsors a "Vintage Dance Week" for instruction in 19th-century and ragtime-era social and couple dances. "This is what our great-great-grandparents did," says director Richard Powers, "with original orchestrations, taught by the best teachers. Beginners need not fear; we'll instruct them." Tuition charge is only $145, and housing expenses vary from either nothing at all (in the homes of "friends of the Academy") to the standard rates of motels, B&B houses, and college dorms in the area; a committee assists with lodging. Contact **Richard Powers, 3623 Herschel Ave., Cincinnati, OH 45208 (phone 513/321-4878).**

Oglebay Dance Camp of Wheeling, West Virginia: This dance camp, the oldest in the country, schedules three-day/two-night camps each year for the Memorial Day and Labor Day weekends in a 1,400-acre park outside the city limits, on the landscaped grounds of a former farm set in rolling hills. Participants sleep in bunk beds like those of a children's summer camp, and spend their days and evenings in ethnic-dance classes supervised by three specialist instructors. Total cost: $125, including meals, lodging, and instruction. Contact **Oglebay Dance Camp, 1330 National Rd., Wheeling, WV 26003 (phone 304/242-7700).**

But Are You Up to It?

A word of warning before you enroll in any program: Be sure you can take the pace. Sessions involve as many as nine hours of movement per day—the most protracted "aerobic exercise" in America—beginning with up to six hours daily of workshops, followed frequently by three hours of "partying" (continual dancing) at night. And be sure you can move in rhythm to music. Some retirees looking for a new vacation experience, but physically awkward or unable to last on the floor for more than an hour, have had a miserable time at dance camps. Try looking up a local teacher before you leave.

Despite this caution, most dance camps are open to sheer beginners, although some are more attuned to them than others. Mendocino has been mentioned to me by several people as particularly suitable for duffers, but Stockton isn't.

Finally, bear in mind that the world of folk life and art, represented in part by the folkdance movement, is a vast one, yet largely "underground" and little known. Though I've mentioned the major camps, dozens of smaller ones were necessarily overlooked. Once you tap into the rich folk-life culture, you'll quickly discover many other such opportunities, and add new dimensions to your life. ≈

IV ≈ VOLUNTEER VACATIONS, FOR FREE OR ALMOST-FOR-FREE

Volunteer Vacations for Vital Adults

At Locations Ranging from Wilderness Lands in the U.S. to Collective Farms in Israel, the Donation of Your Labors Can Result in a Free or Almost-Free Stay

La Sabranenque in the south of France

Archeological Institute of America volunteers

Some of us devote our vacations to frantic aerobics—jogging, jumping, straining, pulling, and clamping on Sony Walkmen to ease the crushing boredom of the aimless sport.

Other, more enlightened sorts gain the very same aerobic benefits—and personal fulfillment of the highest order—by engaging in voluntary physical labor at a socially useful project, in mountains and deserts, forests and farms. Though most such "workcamp" activity is designed for the vacations of young people, a number of other major programs are intended for adults of all ages, or—in some instances—for adults up to the age of 40.

A Hundred Holiday "Digs"

All over the world, but at home as well, archeological excavations utilize volunteer labor by adults with no previous experience in the art. In many cases the projects pick up all expenses of your stay (other than transportation to the site); in some instances they also pay you a small salary; in most, they charge a fairly nominal fee for your Spartan room and board.

And though the work is often limited to the painfully slow removal of earth from fragile fossils—with a toothbrush, no less, delicately, as you crouch over a slit trench in the baking summer sun—it leaves you full of fatigue, drenched with sweat, and pounds lighter, at the end of each day's stint. Who needs the Golden Door?

Minimum stays range from three days to the entire summer. Examples? In Arizona, California, and Oregon, in the warm-weather months, a government-sponsored archeological survey will use summer-long volunteers to "identify and record prehistoric and historic sites . . . in rough terrain. . . . Volunteers will receive partial insurance coverage, on-the-job transportation, training, room, and board." At the east Karnak site of Luxor, Egypt, volunteers for six weeks are needed in May and June of each year to unearth building blocks used for the sun temples of the Pharaoh Akhenaten; "lodging and meals on site are provided without charge, except on Fridays (the day off)." In York, England, volunteers throughout the year pay $100 a week for the expense of participating for as little or long as they like in excavating stratified Roman, Anglo-Saxon, Viking, and medieval ruins of that historic city. Near Pisa, Italy, two-week volunteers are currently being sought this summer for excavations of 12th- to 15th-century structures in the Ripafratta area; volunteers pay $110 a week for room and board.

The chief source of information is the 80-page *Archeological Fieldwork Opportunities Bulletin,* listing a hundred domestic and foreign "digs," issued each January by the Archeological Institute of America. (Some listings, you should be warned, are of "field schools" rather than "fieldwork," and involve substantial tuition charges.) Send $8 for a copy to **A.I.A., 675 Commonwealth Ave., Boston, MA 02215 (phone 617/353-9361),** and add $2.50 more if you wish it sent by first-class mail.

A Stint as a Stone Mason

La Sabranenque is the strange but melodious source of this next volunteer vacation; it sends you to labor in the summer months in what many consider to be the most attractive areas in all of Europe: southern France and northern Italy. Nonprofit, and international, its goal is to restore a host of decaying, crumbled, medieval villages at hillside locations throughout the historic area. It did so first in the early 1970s, with spectacular success, in the village of St-Victor-la-Coste, France, returning to their original form the 14th- and 15th-century stone farm buildings, chapels, and other community structures that had become heaps of rubble in the ensuing centuries. So favorable was the reaction of historians (and the French government), and so improved was the life of the village, that several other French and Italian villages immediately invited the group to attempt similar reconstructions of their own medieval ruins. Today, a half dozen such projects are pursued each summer, all utilizing international volunteers to set the stones and trowel the mortar for fences and walls.

Because the ancient structures of a European rural village are rarely more than two stories high, the work

requires no special construction or engineering skills; stone-laying is quickly taught at the start of each two-week or three-week session. Charges to the volunteers for housing, full board, and all activities are $380 for two weeks (spent in France only, at St-Victor-la-Coste), and $710 for three weeks (spent in both France and Italy; round-trip transportation between France and Italy is included). For more detailed information, contact **La Sabranenque Restoration Projects, c/o John K. Simon, 217 High Park Blvd., Buffalo, NY 14226 (phone 716/836-8698).**

Maintaining the "Wild Lands"

You achieve this next worthy end by participating in a Sierra Club Service Trip operated in nearly 20 U.S. states by the mighty conservationist organization called Sierra, now 450,000 members strong. Because many of the trips are subsidized by corporate donations, fees are low: as little as $150 for all the expenses of a ten-day tour of duty, except for transportation to the site—and that's a fairly average charge for the 50-some-odd service trips offered from April through late September; one-week trips cost even less, $90 in many cases.

You perform your "service" in some of the most enchanting places in all of America, not the standard, popular national and state parks, but the remote and less accessible ones, like the Gila Wilderness of New Mexico, the Washakie Wilderness of Wyoming, the Adirondack Forest Preserve of New York. Though most of the work is related to trail maintenance—by encouraging visitors to use well-marked trails, and limit their wanderings to them, Sierra protects the delicate ecosystems of the park—projects extend to numerous other matters. "Workdays," says one description of a Sierra project, "will be divided between cleaning up nearby abandoned mining towns and reconstructing part of the Brown Basin Trail." Says another: "We will re-vegetate campsites." Or "our work will include cleanup and maintenance in and around the most imposing prehistoric ruins of the Southwest"; "we will cut and clear downed trees and underbrush from . . . around Chub Pond north of Old Forge."

Half the days of every trip are devoted to simple enjoyment of the wilderness; half are workdays. Lodging is in rustic cabins, lodges, or tents; cooking is cooperatively done by all participants; companionship is provided by vital, dynamic Americans of all ages. Complete descriptions of each service trip are set forth annually in the January/February edition of *Sierra,* official magazine of the club. For a copy of that listing, send a $2 check to **Sierra Club Information Services, 730 Polk St., San Francisco, CA 94109.**

Preserving the Trails

Slightly different in character is the even more extensive program of volunteer work projects in national and state parks, and national forests, for which the American Hiking Society serves as clearinghouse. Each year it lists several hundred such opportunities, for which food and lodging costs are either nil or nominal; volunteers provide the open-air parks with services that tight budgets will not allow the government agencies themselves to supply. Thus, for two to six weeks people act as unpaid, or nominally paid, "hosts" of campgrounds, build suspension bridges in Yellowstone National Park, weed out nonnative plants from Haleakala National Park in Hawaii, spot and record the movements of bald eagles, act as deputy forest rangers or fire lookouts, even help out in the on-site offices of parks and forests. But mainly, in keeping with the core function of the nation's major hiking club, they maintain forest trails—and what "aerobics" that entails! "We clear brush, grub out stumps, trim vegetation, remove downed trees, repair erosion damage, and generally keep trails open . . . using hand tools like shovel, pick, pulaski, and saw. . . . It's strenuous," says an A.H.S. publication.

For information, write for a copy of *Helping Out in the Outdoors: Volunteer Opportunities on Public Lands,* to the **American Hiking Society, 1015 31st St. NW, Washington, DC 20007,** enclosing $3 to cover costs.

Replacing a Reservist

Far less traditional, but fully as vital, is an unusual three-week stint of voluntary effort in the state of Israel, at any time of the year, and free of expense except for air fare (which, on this subsidized program, costs as little as $508 for a student traveling to Israel in off-season, $658 for adults in other months).

But once there, "they" take care of everything else: room and board, even a set of boots and khaki fatigues.

"They" are the Israeli army. As a "Volunteer for Israel"—aged 18 to 65, male or female, Jew or gentile—you're housed at an Israeli military base, working at light, unskilled chores for 5½ days a week (for three weeks) to free up Israeli reservists for actual military training.

At an armored camp near Ashkelon, you grease or paint tanks, tighten the screws on howitzers, make careful inventories of spare parts. At an infantry bivouac in the Negev, you cook for the troops or serve in the mess hall. At a supply depot near Jerusalem, you sort uniforms, pack kit bags, clean rifles, or cut grass.

The working day is from 8 a.m. to 4 p.m. In the evenings, there's a "rec room" and subtitled movies or an Israeli professor (doing reserve duty) happy to deliver a lecture (in English) on the Dead Sea Scrolls or the current Mideast conflict.

You sleep in barracks segregated by sex, but take your meals with both male and female soldiers, enjoying mammoth Israeli breakfasts of yogurt and fresh vegetable salads, eggs, bread, and black coffee.

If, following your stint, you wish to stay on for extra weeks in Israel (this time, at your expense), your air ticket is easily extended for up to 180 days.

Some Americans devote every one of their yearly vacations to the work I've just described—and then can't wait to return. Some older Americans go several times a year.

"It can be tedious," wrote one volunteer-grandmother in her 60s, in a newsletter for alumni of the program. "I packaged coffee beans for distribution to the troops. But I was happy to do it.

"Some grandmothers take their grandchildren to the park—and some grandmothers volunteer for the Israeli army."

(Incidentally, though you assist that army, you do not join it or otherwise endanger your U.S. citizenship.)

Groups depart on three-week programs as often as eight times a month in the busy summer season, four times a month in the winter. Participants apply either to the New York office of Volunteers for Israel or to volunteer representatives. Recently, the organization has begun offering civilian projects as well (such as three weeks of voluntary effort in an Israeli geriatrics center), about which you might inquire when you write or phone.

Contact **Volunteers for Israel, 40 Worth St., Room 710, New York, NY 10013 (phone 212/608-4848).**

Alleviating World Poverty

You perform this next voluntary deed with a highly impressive group. Like the fictitious priest who lived among the lepers, beggars, and cart-pullers of *The City of Joy*—that massive bestseller found on all the newsstands—so permanent members of the Fourth World Movement share the actual lives of the most abject poor in shantytown communities all over the world. Without making quite the same commitment, nonpermanent "volunteers" spend two weeks each summer in workcamps at the movement's international headquarters in Pierrelaye, France, held late June to mid-July, mid-July to early August, and early to late September. No knowledge of French is needed; total cost for the two-week stay is 350 francs (around $60); work includes carpentry, painting, masonry, cooking, followed by evening discussions and readings, until recently with the movement's much-revered founder, the late Fr. Josef Wresinski.

Other volunteers devote three months, at any time of the year, to an internship at the movement's New York headquarters, again working with families living in extreme poverty on projects designed to draw them back into society: street libraries, literacy and computer programs, family vacations. Interns share housing (free) and housing duties with permanent Fourth World members, but are asked to make a small contribution to food costs during the first month only.

Because the movement is painfully strapped for funds, be sure to enclose an already-stamped, self-addressed envelope (and perhaps a contribution too) when requesting further information and literature: **Fourth World Movement, 172 First Ave., New York, NY 10009 (phone 212/228-1339).**

Working on a Kibbutz

Finally, a 30-day overseas opportunity for young adults (up to 32 or 40 years of age; see below). That's the minimum stay required to share the life of an Israeli kibbutz, one of the communal societies that contain only 3% of the Israeli population, but produce 50% of its food and none of its crime. A type of collective farm in which property is held in common and children raised as a group, the kibbutz has long held a strong fascination for Americans, both Jewish and gentile. Responding to a heavy demand, the kibbutz movement currently permits young Americans (18 to 32) of any religion to join their ranks for a one-month (or longer) "workcamp vacation" for a fee of only $65, plus air fare to Israel. Or they accept a slightly older group (18 to 40) on a five-week "Kibbutz/Discovery" program consisting of only three weeks at the kibbutz, one week of archeological digs, and one week on tour in Israel, for a total of $1,750 per person, this time including round-trip air fare to Israel. Workcampers labor in the fields for six hours a day, six days a week, receive all meals daily, and live with a kibbutz family. Other plans requiring longer stays involve language instruction (Ulpan), even university courses. And all are sponsored and operated by the strangely named **Kibbutz Aliya Desk** (desk of what?), **27 W. 20th St., New York, NY 10011 (phone 212/255-1338)**, which represents an impressive 280 kibbutzim (the plural of kibbutz). Other Kibbutz Aliya Desks (check the phone books) are in Chicago, Los Angeles, San Francisco, Houston, Atlanta, Miami, Denver, Pittsburgh, New Orleans, Cleveland, St. Louis, Boston, Milwaukee, and Philadelphia; write or call them for literature. ≈

Send Your Child to an International Workcamp!

They Bear No Resemblance to the "Gulag," But Rather to the Best Form of Residential Education, Among Other Young People from Around the World

At the Zaporozne Camp, the Ukraine

Opposite page, upper photo: *Building a shelter in Vermont* lower photo: *Trail maintenance in the Black Forest of West Germany*

This summer, many thousands of American teen-agers will be hurtling through Europe by escorted motorcoach, isolated from the life of that continent by the steel-and-glass enclosure of their buses. They will socialize with one another, speak and hear English throughout, eat in segregated portions of hotel dining rooms, and regard themselves—subconsciously but firmly—as a privileged elite.

A better-informed segment of our youth will be sent by their parents, out of motives of the purest love, to international workcamps. Several hundred such places are found in countries of both Western and Eastern Europe.

There they will perform socially useful projects in the full midst of the European population. They will mix with other international young people, attempt foreign languages, make lifelong friendships, enjoy the satisfaction of contributing to worthy efforts, gain an appreciation for the realities of life abroad, and feel their minds stretch and grow.

And having paid only their air fare to reach the workcamp, they will receive free room and board once there.

Workcamp—Really a Misnomer

"International workcamps"—a horrid term un-related to the happy atmosphere of the sites—were first formed at the end of World War I. A Swiss pacifist, Pierre Ceresole, conceived of projects in which youth of the former combatants—France and Germany—would work together to clear the wreckage of war. Fittingly, he chose the battlefield of Verdun for the first voluntary "workcamp."

In the several decades since, many hundreds of communities have sponsored similar efforts at other sites in Europe or, in a few instances, in North America. People in each locality propose a socially significant task to be performed by international volunteers, and raise the funds to pay for the modest local lodgings and meals required by the participants. Then, by various means of publicity, for which UNESCO has been the most effective channel in recent

There they will enjoy the satisfaction of worthy efforts, gain an appreciation for the realities of life abroad, and feel their minds stretch and grow.

A teenage work gang

times, they invite young people of the world to travel at their own expense to the workcamp site. Once there, on stays averaging three weeks, the volunteers receive free room and board (and sometimes a bit of pocket money) in exchange for a few hours of enthusiastic effort each day.

While no one would denigrate their ensuing accomplishments, it becomes clear that the camaraderie of shared work, and the international understanding it brings about, is as important as the structures they build or the services they render.

What do the young volunteers do? In the midlands of England, they take underprivileged children on summer excursions to the sea. On the outskirts of Paris, they fill in for vacationing orderlies at centers for the aged. In the national parks of Germany, they restore hiking trails or clear away debris. And in the slums of Boston, they help to refurbish low-cost housing for the poor.

As many as 1,500 workcamps are operated throughout the year, although the great bulk take place in the summer months.

The Major Sources

Here in the United States, the two major clearinghouses for information on nearly 1,000 international workcamps (they will also book you into them) are: **Service Civil International (SCI/USA), c/o Innisfree Village, Rte. 2, Box 506, Crozet, VA 22932 (phone 804/823-1826); and Volunteers for Peace International Workcamps (VFP), Tiffany Road, Belmont, VT 05730 (phone 802/259-2759).** SCI requires its overseas volunteers to be at least 18 years of age, and will accept 16- and 17-year-olds only into its several domestic workcamps scattered around the country. VFP will accept 16- and 17-year-olds at more than 100 workcamps in France and Germany, in addition to its U.S. workcamps, and enforces an 18-year-old minimum only for the remainder of them.

SCI, with branches ranging from the U.S. to India, is the more strongly ideological of the two; many of its workcamps stress liberal political values or ecological concerns. Recent workcamps have included construction of energy-efficient "hogans" (dwellings) and aid to elderly people on Navajo reservations in the Far West; renovations to facilities at the Fort Apache Youth Center in the Bronx, New York; staffing of various European refugee centers for displaced Tamils from Sri Lanka; garage work in Hamburg, Germany, converting trucks into ambulances for the SWAPO movement in Angola.

VFP is less political in its approach. "We believe that any opportunity to come into contact with other cultures is worthwhile," says its co-director, Penny Coldwell. Sample activities include digging water trenches for remote Turkish villages, creation of a community center for newly settled-down gypsies in England, or replanting a park devastated by construction in Greenland.

Interestingly, both programs include numerous camps in Eastern Europe (gardening in Czechoslovakia, forestry in Hungary, repairing the Lidice concentration camp memorial in Poland); and VFP is particularly proud of its nine-year record of sending youthful American participants to several different workcamps in the Soviet Union. For two- and three-week periods of summer 1989, international volunteers will join an equal number of Soviet youngsters in cultivating apricot trees at a co-op farm in the Ukraine, working in a nature reserve at the Puschino Biological Center near Moscow, or attending another larger (300 participants) "service camp" in Moscow itself. Work fills half a day, discussions and debates the other half, but no proselytizing occurs, claims VFP, and U.S. kids do more than hold their own in the lively afternoon discussions. Unlike other European workcamps, those in the USSR require a $250 payment by foreign participants.

What does it all amount to? Listen to the returning, three-week volunteers. "It was wonderful," said a youngster from Michigan, "to see people working toward a common goal, not as 'Americans' or 'Czechs' or 'Germans' or 'Catholics' or 'Protestants' or 'Jews,' but as people." "I felt so lucky to have befriended people from around the world and across the political spectrum," said another. "There were 60 of us, from 14 nations, and after work we would sit around a campfire. What followed were conversations and arguments, some dancing, and also some people sitting quietly, reflecting. It was during those informal times that I learned the most."

Both the SCI and VFP directories for the coming summer are published in April. SCI's costs $2; VFP's, $10 (but the latter charge also includes subscription to a newsletter and is deducted from any later registration fee). After perusing the several hundred descriptions of workcamps, applicants pay (to SCI) $25 for a U.S. workcamp assignment, $50 for one abroad; and (to VFP) $75 per workcamp in Western Europe, $90 per workcamp in Eastern Europe. Some youngsters attend multiple workcamps in the course of an active summer.

A Similar Program

A similar, but much smaller, workcamp program is offered by the official U.S. student travel organization, the **Council on International Educational Exchange (C.I.E.E.), 205 E. 42nd St., New York, NY 10017 (phone 212/661-1414).** Here the literature is free, but a later application costs $100. ≈

Co-workers from the area

Selfless Vacations, the Jimmy Carter Way

The Rewards of Undertaking an Uncommon Series of "Outer-Directed" Trips

Volunteer in Honduras

A Korean guest of the Friendship Force

His life—comparatively speaking—was in ruins. He had been defeated for reelection to the presidency. His family business was in debt. Prematurely retired, shaken and adrift, he faced a mid-life crisis more intense than most, but similar in essence to that confronting millions of middle-aged Americans.

And so he and his wife traveled. But in a different way. What restored the spirits of Jimmy and Rosalynn Carter, among several major steps, was an uncommon series of selfless, "outer-directed" trips. For them, travel was undertaken to discover new world issues and social needs, and—equally important—to be involved in curing the ills that travel revealed.

The vacation challenge, writes the former president, "lies in figuring out how to combine further education with the pleasures of traveling in distant places, and, on occasion, helping to make the lives of the people you visit a little better." Having done both, the Carters leave little doubt that the activity has launched them on a second, rewarding phase of life.

In a remarkable book recently published by Random House—*Everything to Gain: Making the Most of the Rest of Your Life*—Jimmy and Rosalynn Carter tell, among other things, of the several life-enhancing travel or travel-related organizations with which they have associated their names, or which they recommend to others. These are: the Friendship Force, Habitat for Humanity, GATE (Global Awareness Through Experience), the Citizen Exchange Council, and the International Executive Service Corps.

The Friendship Force

This is already known to many Americans. It is the 11-year-old nonprofit Atlanta-based organization founded by the Carters and the Rev. Wayne Smith, which each year sends thousands of adult travelers ("citizen ambassadors") to live for one or two weeks in foreign homes found in 45 countries, including the Soviet Union. Subsequently, the foreign hosts come here to live in American homes. Since the stay in each case is basically without charge (except for transportation and administration), the cost of a Friendship Force holiday is considerably less than for standard trips to the same destination, and upward of 400,000 people have thus far participated. Upon returning, they continue to exchange correspondence or privately arranged visits with the families they have met. In this way, writes Rosalynn Carter, "friendships are . . . made that can only lead to a more peaceful world."

For information on membership in the Friendship Force, and on the 1989–1990 exchanges planned from dozens of U.S. cities, write **Friendship Force, Suite 575, South Tower, One CNN Center, Atlanta, GA 30303 (phone 404/522-9490).**

Habitat for Humanity

This is a less obvious travel resource. Based in Americus, Georgia, near the Carter household in Plains, it was created 12 years ago (before the Carters' involvement in it) to work for the elimination of poverty housing (namely, shacks) from the U.S. and the world. Its founder, a fierce Christian crusader named Millard Fuller, enlisted the assistance of Jimmy Carter in the period immediately following Carter's defeat for reelection.

At Fuller's urging, the Carters traveled by bus to Manhattan, lived in a spartan, church-operated hostel, and worked each day for a week as carpenters in the rehabilitation of a 19-unit slum tenement in New York's poverty-ridden Lower East Side. The worldwide publicity from that volunteer effort made Habitat into a powerful organization that built more than 2,000 houses in 1988 (and a projected 2,500 homes in 1989) in 280 locations in the United States and Canada, and in 25 Third World nations overseas.

Jimmy and Rosalynn Carter continue to travel periodically to workcamps at these locations.

Though others may recoil from the suggestion that arduous, physical labor on a construction site can be a "vacation" activity, hundreds of Habitat volunteers disagree. To cast their lot with the poor is, for them, many times more refreshing than lazing at a tropical resort. If they have one to three weeks off, they travel to work at scores of Habitat locations in the U.S. and Canada, paying for their own transportation and food,

and often receiving accommodations—rather basic —at the site. No prior construction experience is required.

When volunteers do possess special qualifications, and have several months to give, they can occasionally go to the overseas projects of Habitat (managed by three-year volunteers), again paying their own way. There, they work side by side with the very Zaireans, Ugandans, Peruvians, and South Sea islanders who will eventually occupy the homes under construction.

For information on how you can devote your vacations to building a "habitat for humanity," or for application forms, contact **Habitat for Humanity, Habitat and Church Streets, Americus, GA 31709 (phone 912/924-6935).**

G.A.T.E., C.E.C., and I.E.S.C.

Other Carter-approved travel programs include the **International Executive Service Corps, P.O. Box 10005, Stamford, CT 06904 (phone 203/967-6000),** arranging trips by retired business executives to lend their expertise to would-be entrepreneurs in developing nations; **Citizen Exchange Council, 18 E. 41st St., New York, NY 10017 (phone 212/889-7960),** offering group trips to engage in exchange of views with counterpart organizations in the Soviet Union; and **GATE (Global Awareness Through Experience), P.O. Box 3042, Harlingen, TX 78551 (phone 512/428-0836),** with tours to experience the realities of Third World life, as operated by an order of Catholic nuns, the Sisters of Charity.

For the Carters, as for so many Americans, simply to lie on a beach, or otherwise turn off the mind, is no longer the sole—or even the wisest—approach to vacationing. Using the mind is a far happier leisure activity. Seeking challenge and new ideas is the way to travel pleasure. A change can help us, in Allan Fromme's words, "become more alive again."

And when the changes achieved through travel are combined with selfless activity—work designed to help others or advance world understanding—then what results is not a mere vacation, but some of the most rewarding interludes of life. ≈

V — NEW AND CHEAPER LODGINGS, FOR PEOPLE WEARY OF STANDARD HOTELS

Removing the "Youth" from "Youth Hostels"

A Revolution Has Altered the Character of These Inexpensive Lodgings, Making Them Available to Mature Adventurers of Every Age

Open to all in Washington, D.C.

It was a mixed-up scene, to say the least. But strangely affecting. In a corner of the lounge, a middle-aged pianist sat rifling off a Schubert cadenza while a teenage music-lover turned the pages of her sheet music. At a chessboard nearby, two college students stared at their rooks and knights while a white-haired senior offered occasional advice. And at an overstuffed couch under a notice-filled bulletin board, several eager young people sought travel advice from a couple in their 40s.

If you were now to learn that this jumbling of the generations—young with old, newly retired with newly wed—was occurring not in a school, but in a youth hostel, you'd probably be startled. Unknown as yet to the vast majority of American travelers, every youth hostel organization in the world (other than in the German state of Bavaria) has eliminated the maximum-age limitation on youth-hostel membership or the right to use youth-hostel facilities. A small but growing population of every age and condition—married and single, elderly, middle-aged, baby boomer, yuppie, and preppie—are today flocking to make use of the cheapest lodgings and most dynamic travel facilities on earth.

What Is a Youth Hostel?

And what are these structures that now accept "young people of all ages"—to use a newly coined slogan of the hostels? They range from ancient castles to modern farmhouses, from Buddhist temples to converted water mills, from rambling Victorian mansions to four-masted sailing ships to glass-walled high-rises in the center of great cities—some 5,000 hostels in all (in 74 different countries), of which 240 are here in the United States. While the beds they offer are often double-decker cots in privacy-lacking dormitories (but segregated by sex, with men in one wing, women in another), their facilities are otherwise comfortable and clean, closely supervised by "hostel parents," social, cheery, priced in pennies—and now multigenerational in clientele, as I was recently able quite personally to confirm.

The scene that began this essay was one I witnessed recently in the public areas of the Washington, D.C., youth hostel short blocks from the White House. I had arrived in Washington on a Friday afternoon, without reservations, never dreaming that every hotel in town would be sold out. They were. Shaken and dismayed, but vaguely aware of the revolution in youth-hostel policies, I rushed from the Capitol Hilton (where I had just been turned down) to the Capitol Hostel, if it could be called that. And moments later I was ensconced in a quite decent (if somewhat dreary) single room at the grand rate of $29 a night, tax included. I could have stayed in the dorms for only $10 a night.

If the locale had been Europe, Mexico, or the Far East instead of Washington, D.C., I could have enjoyed similar facilities for as little as $6, $7, or $8 a night, sometimes with breakfast included. Only in the United States, and only in the nation's capital at that, do youth-hostel prices rise to the princely levels I encountered that night. Almost everywhere else they amount to a near-negligible expense, permitting seniors to enjoy a major extension of their time spent on travels.

Prior to retirement most of those seniors had money but no time. Now they have time but less money. The ability to use $6-per-person hostels instead of $50-per-person hotels suddenly enables mature citizens—even those on Social Security—to enjoy the same three-month stays abroad that many younger Americans experience on their summer vacations. How many retired Americans could undertake trips of that length if they were compelled to pay normal hotel rates on each and every night?

The "Senior" Revolution

What brought about this revolution? Some hostelers point to the laws against age discrimination enacted in numerous enlightened countries. Some mention the growing realization by youth-hostel organizations of their need for income and patronage in those non-summer months of the year when young people are in school and unable to use hostels. Still others suggest that the lowering of age bars, occurring gradually in different countries, came about when hostel-loving

They range from ancient castles to modern farmhouses, from Buddhist temples to converted water mills, from rambling Victorian mansions to four-masted sailing ships.

Oldest U.S. hostel, Bowmansville, Pennsylvania

Marquette House Hostel, New Orleans

Whether married or single, elderly, middle-aged, baby-boomer, yuppie or preppie, you may now make use of the cheapest accommodations on earth.

Boston International Hostel

Ft. Lauderdale hostel

"baby boomers" approached their middle years and insisted on the right to continue using hostel accommodations. "Hosteling gets into your blood and you can't get rid of it," say Hal and Glenda Wennberg of central Maryland, who met at a hostel in 1946 and soon were husband and wife. Though the American youth-hostel organization has always, in theory, been open to people of all ages (unlike its European counterparts), it is only recently that youth hostels have openly advertised the right of seniors to join and participate. In Europe, formal decisions were required, and taken, to accomplish the same goal.

"The reason we use hostels," says an elderly hosteler and former college lecturer from Nebraska, Jane Holden, "is because hosteling is an attitude, not simply a source of cheap accommodations for penniless young people. That attitude never changes. To me, the finest moments of life are in meeting people from different countries and backgrounds, and extending friendship to them. Even if it means trading off a bit of comfort and privacy."

Do mature hostelers find it difficult to mix with members 40 years younger than they? "Not at all," say Edwin and Jeanne Erlanger, hostelers since the mid-1950s. "Once people work together in the kitchen or begin discussing that day's news, the barriers just fade away. Wherever it is—Japan, Austria, Mexico—the generations have far more in common than you'd think." One prominent San Francisco member of Golden Gate Youth Hostels, the sassy, 72-year-old Miriam Blaustein, is also a leading activist in the highly political Grey Panthers. "I am still as youthful mentally as I ever was!" she states. "But I know my limits. I will not exceed them, nor will I impede what the younger people are doing. My work in youth hostels is part of a broader effort against 'ageism.'"

When seniors first began using youth hostels in heavy numbers, some youth-hostel "parents" (managers) persisted in giving preference in reservations to young members; that's now ended, says an official of American Youth Hostels, Inc., and he has never received a single complaint of age discrimination. Other mature guests were a bit nonplussed by the dormitories assigned to them, although many soon found that hostel managements were at pains to provide them with such private rooms as existed. Still another AYH executive points out that the trend in youth-hostel construction around the world is to rooms housing no more than four or five persons, and occasionally to the standard twin-bedded or single-room variety.

An often-heard proposal is to formally eliminate the word "youth" from the organization's title. Though that idea was rejected by the organization's board of directors, individual hostels have taken steps to do just that. In the Washington, D.C., structure, the word "Youth" in a large neon sign has been replaced by the word "International"—Washington International Hostel—and staff members inside patiently explain that the "youth" in the title of their sponsoring organization means "young in spirit" or "young in outlook," and not in chronological terms of age. As if the dream of Ponce de León were finally at hand, today's mature citizens find "eternal youth" in a youth hostel.

Enter Elderhostel

But now a caution. This newly acquired ability by mature and senior citizens to make use of youth hostels should not be confused with a wholly separate program of study tours called Elderhostel. Limited to people over the age of 60 (but open as well to their spouses of any age), "Elderhostel weeks" are conducted by the Elderhostel organization of Boston, Massachusetts, at more than 1,000 universities and other educational institutions in the U.S. and abroad. Domestically, Elderhostel programs last for one week and cost $215 to $250 per person, plus air fare. Internationally, Elderhostel programs are usually of three weeks' duration—a week apiece in each of three foreign centers—and average $1,780 per person, including air fare. In each case participants stay in unused or temporarily vacated university residence halls or youth hostels, receive all three meals each day, and attend at least 4½ hours a day of classroom instruction.

What sort of instruction? The courses range from "Modern Italian History" to theories of Albert Einstein to "The Architecture of Jerusalem"—to any topic at all, in fact, so long as that subject does not deal with problems of aging or other issues uniquely affecting senior citizens. The goal of Elderhostel is to permit senior citizens to remain vital and alive to current concerns, and the formula has proved immensely popular. Reacting to course announcements in Elderhostel's thrice-yearly free catalog (supplemented by intermittent newsletters), nearly 200,000 people over age 60 will pursue such instruction in 1989. That catalog is today stocked in most public libraries, but can also be obtained by contacting: **Elderhostel, 80 Boylston St., Suite 400, Boston, MA 02116 (phone 617/426-7788).**

Meanwhile, to simply stay at youth hostels regardless of your age, get a youth-hostel membership card from **American Youth Hostels, National Administrative Offices, P.O. Box 37613, Washington, DC 20013 (phone 202/783-6161),** or a local youth hostel council in your own city, if one exists. Enclose $10 (plus $1 for postage and handling) if you are 17 and under, or age 55 and older; $20 (plus another dollar) if you are age 18 to 54; $30 for family membership. You'll receive the card, and a manual listing youth-hostel facilities of the United States. For an additional $8.95 (plus $2 for postage and handling), you'll receive a similar but more extensive handbook of youth hostels in Europe and the Mediterranean area, and still another $8.95 (plus another $2 for postage and handling) will bring you the same for Africa, Asia, Australia, and New Zealand. And suddenly a brave new world of remarkably inexpensive lodgings becomes available to you, permitting almost constant travel—month after month—for an outlay that would barely secure two or three nights at the average hotel! ≈

The Rise of the "Private" Hostel

A Hundred Converted Hotels Now Sell Lodgings by the Bed, Not the Room, to Respectable Adults

Colonial Inn Hostel, Huntington Beach, California

Like a shadowy presence, without ads or flashy signs, a hundred "private hostels" charging $10 to $15 a night have quietly emerged in America's largest cities. And while their amenities are not of the level of the nation's similarly priced budget motels—Red Roof Inns, Econotels, Motel 6s, and the like—they are not, like the latter, on the outskirts of town, along deadening highways, but in the very center: in the heart of San Francisco or New York, in downtown Los Angeles or near the Chicago Loop, at the harbor of Seattle or a block from the Greyhound Station in Tucson.

They emerged in apparent response to the lodging needs of cost-conscious European and Asian tourists now flooding into the United States. Sensing a profit, or simply wanting to be of aid, an unlikely mix of entrepreneurs and idealists began adopting one of three time-honored approaches toward solving a shortage of transient housing. They bought or leased bankrupt, shabby hotels, and quickly touched them up. They leased a floor or two of a standard modest hotel, and proclaimed the space a "hostel." Or they converted residential or specialized buildings—a winery, a rambling Victorian home—into public accommodations use. Into the rooms of each such establishment they brought multiple beds (three or four beds per room in most cases, small dormitories of double-decker cots in others), for such is the key to hostel operation, and the secret of their ability to charge less. More beds are packed into a given space than in normal hotels, maintaining income while slashing rates.

When you stay at a "private hostel," just as at an official "youth hostel" you pay by the bed, not by the room. You stay, in the usual case, in a room with strangers of all ages (but of the same sex). Although, if you're traveling as a couple or group, you often occupy the room with people chosen only by yourself, that isn't guaranteed, and the opposite situation is often lauded by the visionary founders of some hostels. "We bring the traveler a new socio-cultural experience," I was told by one hostel owner. "Sharing a room with tourists of other nations is a means of breaking down barriers."

I first learned of the new "private hostels" in the

Yellow Pages. Looking for a hotel, I chanced upon a category called "hostels"; and as goosepimples slowly spread upon my arms, I awoke to the fact that the establishments listed were not the standard "youth hostels," but a new breed of budget lodgings. "Then felt I like some watcher of the skies," in Keats's phrase, "when a new planet swims into his ken."

I have now seen a half dozen private hostels and interviewed (by phone) the managers of others, and here is how they differ from the more familiar youth hostels:

Although both the youth hostels and the new private hostels accept people of all ages—the term "youth" in the title of the former is an increasing misnomer and anachronism—the private hostels tend to attract an older average age range and get fewer actual youths. The private hostels also have smaller rooms and fewer large dormitories, and place no more than three or four beds in their private rooms. That contrasts with the "pack-'em-in," dormitory-oriented philosophy of the youth hostels. "Our guests value the camaraderie of our public rooms and lounges," says one private hostel manager, "but they place a greater emphasis on privacy in their sleeping arrangements." Also, since most private hostels are in former hotels, their rooms are usually equipped with private baths— "private," that is, for the three or four people in that room—with fewer of the larger communal facilities found in youth hostels.

And since the age of the average guest in the private hostels is higher, the latter have fewer of the distinctive, youth-oriented operating policies of the youth hostels: fewer curfews and other forms of strict supervision.

The hundred or so private hostels consist of about 55 fully independent properties and two "chains": the **International Travelers Club,** headquartered at **25 Windward Ave., Venice, CA 90291 (phone 213/ 399-7649),** and the **American Association of International Hostels (A.A.I.H.),** headquartered at the **New York City International Hostel, 255 W. 43rd St., New York, NY 10036 (phone 212/354-7900).**

A.A.I.H. is a loose marketing organization of 35

Unlike the budget motels, they're found not on the outskirts, along deadening highways, but in the very center.

Rec room, Venice Beach hostel, California

More beds are packed into a given space, maintaining income while slashing rates.

Outside the hostel of Venice Beach

Montara Lighthouse Hostel, California

Venice Beach "Cotel"

independently owned hostels in roughly that many major cities, all using the term "international" in their titles—New Orleans International Hostel, Denver International Hostel, Miami Beach International Hostel—despite the fact that most guests aren't "international" at all, but simply cost-conscious American travelers. The group is headed by Ron Mitchell, a 20-year veteran of American Youth Hostels, who left that organization after acrimonious policy disputes. His new "international hostels" charge a youth hostel–like average of $8 to $10 per person for their occasional dormitories, up to $15 per person per night for their more numerous double, triple, or four-bedded rooms, and perpetuate a great many other youth hostel traditions: guests are "requested" (but not required) to perform a few light chores each day (making their own beds, sweeping up), rooms and floors are segregated by sex, and bus station–type lockers are frequently used for luggage and valuables.

Outstanding hostels in the A.A.I.H. chain: Orlando, Denver, Santa Fe, and (especially) Huntington Beach, California, the last 40 minutes south of Los Angeles. Guests seem to feel less enthusiastic about the branches in downtown Los Angeles, San Francisco, and Portland (Oregon).

The "Ritz-Carltons" of the private hostels are those of the International Travelers Club. Indeed, some of these $12-a-night (on average) lodgings are so well-endowed that they are classified by their sponsors not as "hostels" at all, but as "cotels"—"community hotels" —in which few rooms contain more than three beds. Yet like the others they normally rent by the bed, not the room, and go for $10 to $15 per person per night.

The unique creation of two, young, international businessmen—Urs Jakob and Klaus Stölting—who had tired of traditional commerce, they are staffed by international volunteers, decorated in wild, eclectic fashion (wall murals, fishermen's nets, giant plants) to create a "sense of place," occupy period buildings in a number of instances, and adhere to highly liberal policies that encourage constant socializing and parties, that make them—in the words of one guest—"a cross between a YMCA and a Club Med." The "club" currently consists of ten structures in the United States and Canada, and another six in Australia, New Zealand, and Nouméa, New Guinea. Their ideal guest, according to Urs Jakob, is an around-the-world traveler taking six months or so for the trip. A former emphasis on West Coast locations (Los Angeles, San Francisco, Hawaii) has recently been balanced by the decision to open two branches in New York City, of which one occupies the top floor of the large and recently refurbished Carter Hotel on West 43rd Street off Times Square.

The "cotels," with their notice-packed bulletin boards, paperback libraries, and eager amateur managers—each encouraged to let imagination soar—are all radically different in appearance. The International Travelers Club Cotel in Venice Beach, California, is the old (1901) St. Charles Hotel, a national landmark building that once hosted Charlie Chaplin. Musicians in its café were playing lively folk songs in the course of my own recent visit. The International Travelers Club Cotel Globe in San Francisco is a mix of hostel rooms (two double-decker beds, $10 per person) and hotel rooms ($15 per person double, $25 single), all with private bath and floors with green shag rugs and artfully done oil trims spattered by a volunteer on skateboard. In the less private International Travelers Club Hostel Waikiki, lobby furniture is from a Japanese sushi bar and ceilings are covered by bamboo shoots and beach mats.

At each of the club's hostels or cotels, and in sharp contrast to the "early-to-bed, early-to-rise" atmosphere of the official youth hostels, curfews are unknown and conversations go on late into the night. "People here are adults," says Jakob, "and expected to behave reasonably. We don't treat them as in an institution." Nor is the performance of house chores expected of guests. Perhaps because of that, a great many guests are in their 40s and 50s (though most are 20 to 35), some European, some American, all seeking budget lodgings, but with a social atmosphere.

For a list of leading A.A.I.H. or International Travelers Club hostels or cotels, see the Appendix to this book, which contains a rather extensive description of them (including an enumeration of which hostels offer private room accommodations as well, in which you do not rent by the bed). For the others, look in the *Yellow Pages* under "Hostels," keeping in mind that these "Poor Man's Hiltons" come and go with dizzying rapidity. Last year's Manhattan *Yellow Pages* contained such listings, while this year's edition—inexplicably—doesn't, despite the thriving current operation of several. Persevere. ≈

Private hostel, Orlando, Florida

In a Housekeeping Van: The Art of "Gypsying"

On No More Than Their Social Security Income, Some Americans Are Able to Keep Constantly Traveling

To all the standard forms of travel, add a new one: gypsying. It consists of staying constantly on the move—year after year, exploring multiple countries—but living on almost nothing (or at best, on Social Security income).

And if that seems a pipedream, adolescent and unreal, hold on, reserve judgment. Unending travel, by normal people, is the passionate theme of what may well become a minor travel classic, published last year by John Muir of Santa Fe, and distributed by W. W. Norton.

The book is *Gypsying After 40.* Its author, Robert W. Harris, is a middle-aged Seattle architect who discovered 11 years ago that he had unfinished goals, a passion to view the world, a yearning to return to fundamentals, and a deep concern about the pressured, money-focused nature of his life.

So he became a "gypsy."

Though he and his wife had few resources, their savings sufficed to buy a housekeeping van from a used-car dealer in London. In it, they learned that people can greatly control the level of their material needs (and thus their travel costs), reducing those wants in a drastic degree by simply making psychological adjustments. Living in sturdy but simple clothes, preparing their own meals in the van from foodstuffs purchased en route, using the same unpretentious vehicle for both accommodations and transportation, they learned to live as travelers for a fraction of the sum that others spend as tourists.

And were thus able to travel without cease.

Today they are in their 11th year of continual, "long-term" travel, crisscrossing nation after nation, month after month, on costs that average (independent of the earlier purchase price of the van) a remarkable $800 a month—the sum that many retired couples enjoy from Social Security alone. And the resulting character of their life, they believe, makes pitiful the structured, earthbound, higher-spending existence of the rest of us.

Apart from continual spiritual experiences that Harris lyrically describes—"When travel took command of my life, extraordinary events shook the core of my being"—he relearned as a "gypsy" to savor the most ordinary values, patterns, and events of life.

"Poetry and beauty became infinitely more important to us than security. . . . The arrival of dawn, the goings-on around us—insects moving, animals grazing, farmers harvesting—became spectacles. . . . Rich curiosity and heightened awareness increased."

No more for them the tourist throngs and standard attractions: "The strong personal character and dignity of people as they live day-to-day became the focus of our travels. . . . The gypsy life afforded time to cavort with nature, dive into deep wells of reading, warm the fires of friendship, wrestle with meditations."

Most wondrous of all, he discovered, too, that multitudes of others were "gypsying" along the byways of Europe and North Africa, Mexico and the Far West: "Thousands of people make long-term travel their main mode of existence and awake each morning as if it were the shining first day of their lives."

How is it done? How, on a small retirement income, can one travel without let-up? *Gypsying After 40* prescribes a few simple rules:

• The modest van: Self-transportation is the key, not a resplendent, gas-guzzling motorhome, but a van converted inexpensively into living space, cheap to run, and so unpretentious as to offer no target to vandals or thieves. (In some cases, a live-in boat does the job.)
• "Free camping": You eschew, to the extent possible, the organized, pay-to-enter campgrounds, and simply park the van at night in legally permitted places: village greens, churchyards, even gravesites, public areas for pasturing sheep, on farms (after permission has been obtained), castle grounds, in city parks, at well-secured freight trucking areas in port cities, alongside marinas or historic ruins (where you tip the guards or invite them for a drink in the van).

"If you free-camp," writes Harris, "you do not need to have a specific destination in mind, nor a campground to reach before dark. You amble along, unhurried. . . . You savor each moment."

You also meet a better class of people, he implies, "a woman camping alone at interesting, scenic ruins, busily sketching . . . a large family stopping where they could swim, sun, and fish."

• Rural settings: You stay mainly in small towns or in farm locations, where you live for a quarter the usual price; you dart daily into the big cities from your rural base, and return there at night.
• Warm-weather countries: You of course avoid the colder climes. You traverse the sights of northern Europe only in summer, the Mediterranean countries in spring and fall, North Africa (Morocco, especially) or Mexico in winter.
• You slow down: You avoid expense by careful deliberation, and by patience in securing the right air or sea fares.
• And finally: You avoid hotels, restaurants, and high-season tourist locations like the plague.

There is, of course, far more to gypsying than this; it is set forth in 250 closely reasoned pages, available today in most bookstores.

I met Robert Harris and his wife, Megan, at a television talk show on travel. He is a white-haired, white-bearded, ebullient elf of a man, glowing with life and vigor; she, a still-attractive matron-turned-gypsy, blessed with a glamour undimmed by life in a van.

And what were they confiding to each other in the moments before the broadcast?

Their desire to return to the road. ≈

At Home on the Road: The RV Life

The Range of Motorhome Options Has Greatly Increased Your Ability to Enjoy Meaningful, Low-Cost Vacations in the U.S.A.

Colorado road scene

Five-bedded Spirit
Opposite page: *Six-bedded Winnebago motor home*

It's the opposite of chic, somewhat rustic and rough. Yet the fastest-growing means for vacationing in America is the recreational vehicle. And though I be drummed from high society for saying so, the people using them are the finest travelers our country has.

You meet them with increasing frequency. They can be your best friends who have just returned from a three-month trip through the national parks—in a shiny new motorhome—and claim it's the best thing they've ever done. They are your neighbors who have bought a trailer they're going to use to "winter" in a luxury RV resort of Florida. They are images of yourself as you daydream about getting away from it all, buying a recreational vehicle, and taking off to see the great outdoors, the sights of the Southwest, the scattered grandchildren across the land.

But how do you get started? Buying a recreational vehicle—an RV—is a major investment that can even go over the six-figure mark. Is it worth the outlay? Will you enjoy the lifestyle of the semi-nomad? Will you get restless and claustrophobic, or will you have the travel experience of a lifetime? A bit of analysis is in order:

The Vehicles Themselves

"RVs"—a generic term for a conveyance that combines transportation with living quarters—come in two varieties. They can be motorized (like motorhomes or van conversions) or towable units (like travel trailers, truck campers, and folding camp trailers).

The motorhomes, most popular among retired Americans, are built on or as part of a self-propelled vehicle chassis, with kitchen, sleeping, bathroom, and dining facilities all easily accessible to the driver's cab from the inside. They range from 18 to 33 feet in length, can sleep from two to eight people, and cost from $22,000 for "compacts" to $48,000 for larger types, with luxury-status models going way up, to $150,000 and more.

Conversions are cheaper (but smaller). These are vans, originally manufactured by an automaker, that have been modified for recreation purposes through the installation of side windows, carpeting, paneling, cus-

tom seats and sofas, and assorted accessories. They can sleep from two to four people, and sell for an average of $19,000.

Travel trailers are hard-sided units designed to be towed by an auto, van, or pickup truck, and can be unhitched from the tow vehicle. They sleep four to eight people, and provide such comforts as kitchen, toilet, sleeping, dining, and living facilities, electric and water systems, and modern appliances. Models range from $5,000 to $36,000, depending on size and features.

Truck campers are camping units that are loaded onto the bed or chassis of a pickup truck. Many have kitchen and bathroom facilities. They sleep two to six, and go for $2,000 to $10,000.

Folding camping trailers are units with collapsible sides that fold for lightweight towing by a motorized vehicle. Set up, they provide kitchen, dining, and sleeping facilities for four to eight people, and sell for between $1,500 and $8,000.

The Advantages

In an RV, you follow your own totally flexible time schedule, without fixed reservations anywhere, without depending on others (hotels, trains, planes). You don't constantly pack and unpack; in fact, you carry no luggage. You cook when you like, eat out only when you wish, say good-bye to greasy spoons, and usually enjoy home-prepared food.

You can have your pets with you. You can visit friends or relatives anywhere in the country without imposing on them: your RV, parked in their driveway, becomes your own private guest cottage—as well as your summer beach house, your winter chalet.

You make friends easily upon arriving at a camping ground or RV resort. RV-ers are, in general, enthusiasts who love their lifestyle and like sharing it with new people. They are constantly attending rallies, caravans, campouts, meeting with other RV-ers to share common interests.

"It's difficult to be lonely in a campground," one confirmed RV-er told me. "Our luxury RV resort in Florida ($15 a night) was constantly holding social

events. Between dinners and galas, folk dances and exercise classes, meeting new people was not only simple—it was unavoidable."

And RV travel is economical. You can purchase fresh local produce on the road and cook your own meals. Your stay at campgrounds is usually nominal ($5 to $15 a night is typical). And there's no one to tip. A recent study showed that an RV vacation cost about half the expense of a car/hotel vacation, one-third the cost of a bus/hotel or train/hotel holiday, and one-fourth the cost of an air/hotel vacation.

The Drawbacks

But RV travel is not for everyone—it may not be for you. A Philadelphia couple I know who recently spent four months traveling across country in a motorhome issued the following caveats: "Be sure," they said, "you feel extremely comfortable with whomever you will be traveling with; you're going to spend long periods of time in close quarters. Be sure you're an expert driver and enjoy spending long periods on the road. Above all, don't take this kind of trip unless you're extremely flexible, elastic, and able to cope with new situations, which happen all the time. Mechanical breakdowns are not uncommon and you have to be able to handle them without getting upset."

Renting Before Buying

Like many first-time RV-ers, my informants began by renting a motorhome, got used to driving a large vehicle and used to spending a great deal of driving time together. Now they're so enthusiastic, they're planning to sell their large suburban home, move into a small apartment, buy an RV, and spend at least six months on the road each year. "The excitement and variety of life cannot be compared with any travel experience we've ever had—and we're experienced foreign travelers," they say. "It's a new kind of life, a brand-new world we never saw before."

The Rental Process

First step is to look in your local telephone directory under the category "Recreation Vehicles—Renting and

Leasing." Or you can call one of the two major national companies that have toll-free 800 numbers: **Cruise America (phone 800/327-7778)** and **U-Haul International, RV Rental Division (phone 800/821-2712)**. A third major firm, Altman's America, has only a local number (818/960-1884), but you can write to them: **Altman's America, 6323 Sepulveda Blvd., Van Nuys, CA 91411.** It's also useful to obtain the book called *Who's Who in RV Rentals,* listing the names and rates of more than a hundred other dealers; it's $5 from the **Recreational Vehicle Rental Association, 3251 Old Lee Hwy., Fairfax, VA 22030.**

Rental costs vary considerably, depending on type of vehicle, when and for how long you want it, season, and other variables. From the U-Haul company, I secured a quote (cheapest of all) of $30 a day, $180 a week, for a small, 13-foot camper trailer that will sleep two adults and one child; their 16-foot vacation trailer (available at present only on the West Coast) sleeps two adults and two children, and rents for an average of $40 a day, and $225 a week. One of their "grander" motorhomes—either a 26-foot Alumalite by Holiday Rambler or a 27-foot Southwester by Fleetwood—will average $600 to $700 a week, plus mileage (19¢ per mile). But that's for a vehicle that can sleep six people and is fully self-contained, with such added features as a microwave oven, roof air conditioning, its own generator and propane tank (so that a hookup is not necessary), power steering, and almost everything else you can name.

It is usually cheaper to rent from a private individual, but then you must be aware of the risk you take if a breakdown should occur; a private owner can usually do little for you, while with a major company, repairs are either handled on the spot or you are given a new vehicle and put back on the road within 24 hours. Rental dealers may also apply the cost of a rental to a future purchase. They can provide you with broad forms of insurance. Some will arrange tour packages if you're traveling to popular state or national parks or historic landmarks. Others offer orientation sessions and packages which include linens and cookware.

The most important step is advance study and comparison shopping before you rent. Make sure you understand the terms of the agreement; take your vehicle out for a test spin; and reserve as far in advance as possible. Indeed, the "RV life" is becoming so popular that a reservation several months in advance might not be a bad idea. ≈

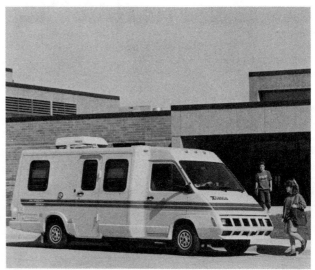

Four-bedded Itasca

Four-bedded LeSharo

Cottages, a New Weapon in the Arsenal of Budget Travel

Costing Far Less Than a Villa or Apartment Rental, They Also House You in Areas Unaffected by Mass Tourism

In Hartest, Suffolk, England

To guesthouses and student dorms, hostels and pensions, to third-class hotels with bathless rooms, and private homes with rooms for rent—to all such havens for the budget-minded transatlantic tourist, you can now add a new form of low-cost lodging: the European "cottage." For some of us, those tiny dwellings full of charm can prove the cheapest of all accommodations—and the single best introduction to life in the Old World.

But it's important to know what they are and what they're not.

What Is a Cottage?

First, a European cottage is very different in location and appearance from a vacation home. The latter is generally in jam-packed resort areas, near seashores or mountains, in world-famous locations publicized for years. To rent one, you contact an international real-estate broker—like Blanding's, of Washington, D.C., or Villas International, of New York City—and pore over glossy, four-color photos of designer interiors and pastel throw-cushions. You pay a rather hefty price for your two- to four-week rental—about the same as you'd spend here at home—and fly to the remoter airports, like Nice or Rome, to claim your impressive hideaway.

A cottage, by contrast, is almost never in a resort area—else it would have been grabbed up long ago, restyled and refurbished, and thus transformed into a vacation home. Rather, a European cottage is in purely rural locations, near prosaic villages or small towns. Most are in walking distance—true—of pubs, shops, or cafés, but often at least a mile or two away.

They also come from another age, and are the sort of structure rarely built today: of stone, small and box-like, in period designs with tiny windows, sometimes topped by a thatched roof or ancient tiles.

But they are charming and idyllic, full of repose, a refuge from modern pressures. And however basic they may appear, they are today equipped with the simple essentials: private bath or shower, gas or electric stoves, flip-a-switch heating.

Most important, they're cheap. When occupied by four to six people (in a minimum of two bedrooms, but often with three), they rent for as little as $250 a week in winter, $300 in spring, $350 in summer, even at current exchange rates. Because of that, they're rarely (or only reluctantly) handled by traditional brokers, or by the trendy travel agencies that deal in Mediterranean villas and Swiss chalets. But more and more Americans have ferreted them out, and at least a half dozen U.S.-based organizations have emerged in recent years to facilitate the process of booking them.

Organizations and Sources of Information

Cottages and Castles, of Elkton, Virginia, is the leading source of British cottage rentals, despite having been in business for only two years. It is a venture launched by the publishers of the prestigious monthly *British Travel Report,* who are a bit bewildered—from several indications—by the explosive response to their initial cottage offerings. Currently the fledgling organization represents from 35 to 40 British brokers with 7,000 cottages to rent. And these—in locations all over England, Scotland, and Wales—can usually be had for a week, and also for two weeks, but rarely for longer than that because of heavy demand. To beat the rental limitations, some avid Anglophiles move from cottage to cottage, spending a week at each.

The average cost? Remarkably low. Some lucky renters pay only $250 a week in low season (November through March), $325 a week in mid-season (April, May, September, and October), $375 a week in high season (June through August)—and those are the total rates for four to six people. Although the charges go higher in upgraded categories, the three cheapest categories (A, B, and C) are hugely popular and highly praised by people who have actually stayed in them.

Consider, for example, the timbered Churn Cottage near Siddington, Gloucestershire, in the bucolic Cotswolds. Set on a 750-acre farm, but close to the city of Cirencester, its facilities include three bedrooms (for five people), large kitchen and dining room, bathroom, color TV, and garage, in a setting for quiet walks along

These tiny dwellings full of charm can prove the cheapest of all introductions to life in the Old World.

In Cadgwith, Cornwall, England

A European cottage is radically different in location and appearance from a "vacation home."

Semi-detached English cottage

the River Churn and fishing for local trout, with village shops and pub nearby. Though this one is two categories higher than the A level, it rents for only $375 a week in low season, $425 a week in mid-season, and $475 a week in high season. The latter rate works out to barely more than $13 per person per night.

Or try the B-level, thatch-roofed Medieval Cottage in the tiny village of Wrangaton, Devon, 12 miles from the coast at the edge of the Dartmoor National Park, with Torquay and other delightful towns nearby. It offers two bedrooms for four people, a kitchen, lounge, bathroom, color TV, and parking, for approximately $300 a week in low season, $350 per week in mid-season, and $400 a week in high season—$15 per person per day in the latter instance.

For a catalog that pictures and describes 65 representative examples of the 7,000 cottages available to you, send $2 to **Cottages and Castles, c/o British Travel Associates, P.O. Box 299, Elkton, VA 22827 (phone 703/289-6514, or toll free 800/327-6097 outside Virginia)**, and state your preferences, the dates you need, and the kind of group you are. Within 24 hours Cottages and Castles will propose a specific cottage rental suiting your needs, and everything proceeds from there.

For comparative purposes, you might also send for the programs of three similar organizations: **Heart of England Cottages, P.O. Box 261, Westwood, MA 02090**, enclosing $3.50 for an assortment of cottage brochures, including some for Ireland as well (the $3.50 will be deducted from the cost of any subsequent bookings, which average $240 a week); for residents of North and South Carolina, Tennessee, Florida, Georgia, Alabama, Mississippi, Arkansas, Louisiana, Oklahoma, and Texas, **Heart of England Cottages, P.O. Box 888, Eufaula, AL 36027 (phone 205/687-9800)**, which will send free literature depicting 200 to 300 cottages available for one, two, three, and four weeks; and **Eastone Overseas Accommodations, 6682 141st Lane North, Palm Beach Gardens, FL 33418 (phone 407/622-0777)**, specifying the location you prefer, and they'll send you photocopies of lengthy listings in the area (no fee is required).

The Gîtes of France

In France, the cottages are 20,000 in number, similarly priced or even lower in cost than the British variety (which is to say, remarkably cheap), and known as *gîtes* (pronounced "zheet"), an antiquated medieval term for "abode" or "lodging." Again they're found mainly in countryside locations, but nowhere near resorts, among populations whose warmth and generosity toward visitors are the very opposite of some Parisian attitudes. From your *gîte,* by bike or rented car, you'll drive to shop in nearby French villages, explore historic sights, enjoy ravishing landscapes, practice your French, and conserve your cash. *Gîtes* rent for as little as $200 a week (for a minimum of four people, remember); a usual high of $450 a week, in a long high season of April through October (though they can run higher in August); and for less than that—say, $170 a week—in March or October. Rentals can be had for a single week, except in July and August, when a two-week stay is required.

Why are the *gîtes* so cheap? Because they're rent-controlled. In the immediate postwar years, when thousands of the French abandoned their ancient residences to move to cities or more modern homes, the French government offered subsidies to preserve and maintain the *gîtes,* on condition that they be offered for vacation rentals at low prices. Today the gîtes of France remain a largely governmental institution administered by the 95 *départements* of France, and marketed by the government-sponsored Fédération de Gîtes. With typical French flair, each *gîte* is awarded a symbol of either one, two, or three ears of corn, to rate its comparative quality.

I'm looking at several photographs of *gîtes* as I write these words. One, a charming, shuttered cottage with coral-tile roof, as in a Van Gogh painting, is 37 miles from the Riviera Coast, in Regusse, the *département* of Var. It's rated three ears of corn, can sleep up to six people, and costs only $314 a week in any month other than July or August (when the charge is $427 a week).

Another, a large and ancient, stone-walled structure in St. Germain sur Vienne, in the *département* known as Indre et Loire, eight miles from the renowned Chinon (site of the castle), is still another three-ears-of-corn winner that can house up to five people and yet rents for only $250 a week in April, May, October, and November, $310 a week in June and September, $365 a week in July and August. Those dollar prices are calculated at the very latest exchange rates.

The chief U.S.-based source of *gîtes* is **The French Experience, Inc., 171 Madison Ave., New York, NY 10016 (phone 212/683-2443).** Write for their catalog called "France Beyond Clichés," which contains additional information and application forms. And don't confuse the rental of an entire *gîte,* for one to four weeks, with a system for obtaining bed-and-breakfast in private French homes; the latter are called *gîtes de chambres* or *gîtes d'étape,* and I'll have more on those in next year's edition of this book.

In the meantime, picture yourself living like a resident, not a tourist, in France, ensconced in your own private *gîte.* Wandering to a French village market, where luscious vegetables and exquisitely presented cuts of meat are arrayed before you. Standing with your spatula and a *Larousse Gastronomique* in a French kitchen, attempting to out-do Julia Child. Savoring the taste of that fresh macon or beaujolais as you pour it from a pitcher into a cool stone mug. Ooh-la-la! ≈

Cottages on an English road

Camping in the Caribbean

On Six Major Islands or Locales, Supervised Sites Await Your Tent—for as Little as $2.50 a Night

Esperanza Beach, Vieques, Puerto Rico

Public beach of Tobago

Opposite page: *Humacao Beach, Puerto Rico*

I f you're like me, then on your first trip to the sultry Caribbean, you have at some point asked: "Why am I staying in a hotel? With heat so intense, and nights so balmy, why must I pay a king's ransom for space in a high-rise tower? Why can't I simply sleep on a beach, under canvas, for peanuts?"

Well, glory be, the very same thought has now occurred to a growing legion of open-air entrepreneurs. And today, commercial campsites await your tent in multiple, major Caribbean locations. And I'm referring to organized and supervised sites, attended at night, with showers, toilets, and—often—electricity.

Though some tropical islands forbid camping (snooty Bermuda is one, except for organized Scout groups and the like) and others discourage it (Antigua), while still others permit it but then provide no organized facilities for it (Trinidad/Tobago, Dominican Republic, Grenada), six enlightened locales have made the activity into a major tourist resource:

Puerto Rico

Puerto Rico is one such place, although it burdens the sport with a touch of bureaucracy, a required permit obtained in the manner explained below. Yet fully seven public beaches (*balnearios*), renowned for their swimming, now possess supervised campsites, of which the best endowed (electricity, showers) are at Luquillo and Cerro Gordo. Luquillo, with 52 sites renting for $8 per site per night, $12 with roof, is in eastern Puerto Rico (Rte. 3, km marker 35.4) on a full mile of white sand shaded by majestic coconut palms. Cerro Gordo, with 58 tentsites renting for the same, is in northern Puerto Rico (Rte. 690, near Vega Alta), on a beach almost as grand. More Spartan sites lacking electricity (you use lanterns) and showers are: Añasco, in western Puerto Rico (Rte. 3, km 77; $5 per campsite, $20 per cabin); Punta Guilarte, in southeastern Puerto Rico (Rte. 3, km 128, near Arroyo; tentsites for $5, cabins for $20); Seven Seas Beach, near the marina area of Fajardo in eastern Puerto Rico (Rte. 987 connects Fajardo to Seven Seas Beach, where tentsites are $5 a night); and finally, the rapidly developing

island of Vieques, off the eastern coast of Puerto Rico (where campsites rent for $5 nightly on Sun Bay—"Sombe"—off Rte. 997, looking out onto the eerie glow of Phosphorous bay).

Elsewhere in Vieques, at the feminist retreat called New Dawn, for women only, tents can be pitched on platform sites (limit of three people per site) for $10 a night, $60 weekly, with breakfast and dinner available in the adjoining main house for an extra $15 per person daily. For feminist tenting, write **New Dawn Adventures, 518 Washington St., Gloucester, MA 01930 (phone 617/283-8717), or P.O. Box 1512, Vieques, PR 00765 (phone 809/741-8614).** For all other Puerto Rican camping locations, write for an application form (resulting in a permit) and reservations to **Departamento de Recreación y Deportes, Compañía de Fomento y Recreativo, Oficina de Reservaciones para Centros Vaccacionales, Apartado 3207, San Juan, PR (phone 809/722-1771 or 809/721-2800, ext. 275).**

British Virgin Islands

The British Virgin Islands are a second renters' heaven. On the islands of Jost van Dyke and Tortola, facilities aren't simply in the form of bare sites for pitching your own tent, but include already-erected, two-person tents on elevated wooden platforms, with cot beds, lanterns, linen, and even cooking utensils. Such elaborate canvas lodgings rent to two people for $16 a night ($2.50 for a third person) at Brewers Bay Campground in Tortola, and for $25 a night ($5 for a third person) at Tula's N&N Campground on Jost van Dyke. Cost-conscious as I may be, I'd still choose the more expensive Tula's on enchanting Jost van Dyke (whose population is all of 130 people), which provides campers with coal or wood for cooking, two restaurants in the area, a grocery store next door, and several rope hammocks along the beach (a bare campsite at Tula's is $15 for up to three people). The smaller Brewers Bay Campgrounds has freshwater showers (as does Tula's), a beach bar and tiny restaurant, and a beachfront location about three miles from Road Town, with its 1,000 inhabitants, overly urbanized by my standards.

For reservations or information, contact: **Tula's N&N Campground, Little Harbour, Jost van Dyke, British Virgin Islands (phone 809/77-40774 or 77-53073); or Brewers Bay Campgrounds, P.O. Box 185, Road Town, Tortola, British Virgin Islands (phone 809/49-43463).**

U.S. Virgin Islands

The U.S. Virgin Islands offer superlative camping on the stunning, white-sand beaches of the island of St. John, two-thirds of which is a national park. Cinnamon Bay Campground, operated for the U.S. Park Service by the elegant Rockresorts organization, is the standout. Its bare campsites (for erecting your own tent) are less than a two-minute walk from the sea; are serviced by a cafeteria, convenience store, lavatories, and shower in separate buildings; and rent for only $10 a day for two people throughout the year, $2 per third or fourth person. Park naturalists attached to the camp lead you on all-day hikes or provide snorkeling instruction. Not within my own definition of low-cost camping, but popular, is a separate section of 56 already-erected 10-by-14-foot tents on wooden floors, and with cot beds, stove, ice chest, and utensils; the latter rent to two people for $27 a day from September 1 to December 19, $50 a day from December 20 to March 31, and $40 a day from April 1 to August 31, with third and fourth persons paying $6 extra. For bare sites, book directly with the local manager at **Cinnamon Bay Campground, Cruz Bay, St. John, U.S. Virgin Islands 00830 (phone 809/776-6330).** But for those furnished, luxury tents, contact **Rockresorts Reservations, 30 Rockefeller Plaza, Suite 5400, New York, NY 10112 (phone toll free 800/223-7637).** Down the coast on the same island, the well-known Maho Bay Camps rents furnished, kitchen-equipped, canvas-sided, hillside cottages for $45 (off-season) or $67 (high season) per cottage per night, but those (in my view) can't qualify for low-cost camping status either. Still, if you're interested, write **Maho Bay Camps, 17-A E. 73rd St., New York, NY 10021 (phone 212/472-9453, or toll free 800/392-9004 outside New York State).**

Belize

Belize (not an island, but a Central American country in the Caribbean) provides camping on its popular *cayes*—thin, water-surrounded, beach-lined strips of land just off its coast. Three of the closely grouped cayes are called the Bluefield Range, and there, at a working, lobster-and-fishing camp known as Ricardo's, sites for erecting your tent are rented for $2.50 a night; you're then right alongside a group of only slightly more expensive beach huts on stilts in the water, with budget-priced restaurant and constantly staffed office to aid you. Write or phone for information and reservations to: **Personalized Services, 91 N. Front St. (P.O. Box 1158), Belize City, Belize (phone 011/501-77593).** Elsewhere among the cayes, the ultra-budget Caye Caulker has several wooden beachfront "hotels" whose proprietors, I am told by several recent visitors, will permit you to pitch your tent in back for the same $2.50 a night. Here, you simply appear on the spot and ask.

Jamaica

Jamaica offers supervised camping, with electricity and running water, in all three of its major tourist areas, but for more than most others charge. Near Montego Bay, Damali Beach Village rents sites for $8 per person (not per site) per night, and will also rent you a tent (if you haven't brought your own) for $4 extra per night. A restaurant, bar, and water sports are all nearby. Contact **Damali Beach Village, P.O. Box 61, Montego Bay, Jamaica (phone 809/953-2387).** At Ocho Rios, Hummingbird Haven charges $7 per person per night for a bare site, but has no tents for rent. Contact **Hummingbird Haven, P.O. Box 95, Ocho Rios, Jamaica (phone 809/974-5188).** Near Negril Beach, on those cliffs with steps descending into the sea, Lighthouse Park offers tent spaces for $8 per person per night; and nearby, for a younger crowd, Roots Bamboo on the beach charges only $4 per person, and also rents tents for $4 more. Contact **Lighthouse Park, West End, Negril, Jamaica (phone 809/957-4346); or Roots Bamboo, Negril Beach, Negril, Jamaica (phone 809/957-4479).**

For organized camping in the Blue Mountains of central Jamaica, contact **Jamaica Alternative Tourism, P.O. Box 216, Kingston 7, Jamaica (phone 809/927-2097),** whose president, the dynamic Peter Bentley, is a source for all manner of Jamaica adventure tours.

Since campsites are also used by the local population, they afford you a rare and rewarding chance to meet the Caribbean people on an equal footing, not tourist-to-bellman or tourist-to-chambermaid. And they place you in the open air, among settings of awesome natural beauty. ≈

Maho Bay Camp, St. John, U.S. Virgin Islands

Caribbean waters

The Village Apartment, Your Base for an "Untour"

A Former University Professor Sends Thousands Each Year to Experience the Typical Life of Hamlets Bypassed by Commerce and Tourism

Swiss festival

Opposite page: *Kaub, West Germany*

Housed in a hotel, taking meals in a restaurant, all in the commercial center of a large city, how could one hope to experience the culture and lifestyle of a foreign people?

That was the basic flaw in traditional tourism, as it appeared to a university professor named Harold Taussig, who lived in a suburb of Philadelphia.

So in 1976, he took the usual step of forming a travel company named Idyll Ltd. to provide "Untours" for "Untourists." These consist of three-week stays in housekeeping apartments located in isolated villages of Austria, Switzerland, Germany, Wales, and Scotland.

Now you probably haven't heard of Idyll, or Untours, or Untourists, because Professor Taussig doesn't advertise and never has, but relies solely on "word-of-mouth" for his bookings. Nor does he market his Untours through travel agents. In that way, he saves a 10% commission and keeps prices low.

But from a total of six clients in 1976, his Untours were sold to more than 2,000 customers in 1988, virtually all from personal recommendations. Current bookings indicate an even larger, geometric increase in 1989, despite the sharp decline of the U.S. dollar in Europe.

What's Different About Untours?

How do "Untours" differ from the villa rentals of international real-estate brokers? The latter assign you to trendy vacation homes in popular seaside or mountain resorts, intended for and inundated by tourists.

Untours, by contrast, take you to towns of which tourists have never heard, to such unlikely locations as Meiringen, Switzerland (pop. 4,000) or to the dozing, dreaming St. Goar, Germany (pop. 2,000).

There you live—usually—in a two-family house, enjoying separate quarters and entrances, but close proximity to foreign, small-town neighbors, downstairs. You shop at the local butcher or grocer, wander to the tiny post office and chat with its one-person staff, share the daily cycles and rhythms of village life.

To an extent currently unknown in the United States, Taussig says, village life remains vibrant and

"BERLITZ...BOTH PRACTICAL AND PLEASURABLE." *TRAVEL & LEISURE*

BASED IN THE HEART OF EUROPE, IN LAUSANNE, SWITZERLAND, BERLITZ GUIDES HAS BEEN A LEADER IN INTERNATIONAL TRAVEL AND LANGUAGE PUBLISHING FOR NEARLY 20 YEARS. WITH FOUR MILLION COPIES SOLD ANNUALLY, THE BERLITZ IMPRINT SYMBOLIZES QUALITY AND RELIABILITY FOR TRAVELERS WORLDWIDE.

PUBLISHERS OF:

TRAVEL GUIDES

PHRASE BOOKS

DICTIONARIES

CASSETTEPAKS

SKI GUIDES

BERLITZ BLUEPRINTS

DELUXE GUIDES

CRUISE GUIDES

COUNTRY GUIDES

ITEMS FOR FOREIGN VISITORS

MORE FOR THE $ COUPON BOOKS

SELF-STUDY LANGUAGE COURSES

BERLITZ GUIDES

EASY GOING
1400 SHATTUCK AVE.
BERKELEY, CA 94709

They take you to towns of which tourists have never heard.

Castel Pfalz, West Germany

Welsh accommodations

viable in Europe. Governments there subsidize their agriculture and agricultural communities to a far greater degree than here, and villagers need not commute to jobs in larger towns or otherwise forsake their village roots. Accordingly, he claims, the Untourist is able to experience the highlights of a rural culture that has hardly changed in hundreds of years.

Among the villages of Europe, he chooses the untouristy for his untourists, rejecting such well-known, postcard-pretty hamlets as Gstaad or Oberammergau, Zermatt or Velden. "Have you ever wondered," he writes in a 60-page newsletter sent to past and potential untourists, "what these alleged paradises were like before everybody else discovered them?"

They were like Breconshire, he says, the current Welsh location for his "untours" in Britain; there an Idyll representative, cooking an evening meal of roast lamb for her American guests, sends "her little girl running down the hedgerow to a neighbor's garden to borrow some mint for the sauce. . . . She has mint in her own garden but it's not exactly the right sort for mint sauce, and she particularly likes the mint picked just minutes before she uses it."

In preparation for their stays at these idyllic Edens, untourists receive a heavy packet of typewritten booklets providing them with hints and rules of conduct, hand-drawn diagrams ("unmaps") of their airport arrivals and village locations, inked overlays enabling them to decipher European railroad timetables, handy foreign phrases, suggestions for walks and hikes outside each particular village, thumbnail sketches of village personalities, other carefully tested tidbits of information, written as if in a letter to a friend.

Upon arrival, they are met by members of Idyll's staff, who escort them to the village destination, get them settled, and remain accessible throughout the summer in a nearby town for problem-solving and advice.

As if in a co-op, all staff of Idyll Ltd. receive the same salary as Taussig, participate in all decisions on an equal basis with him, and set the profit markup on Idyll's prices at just the level needed to provide each of them with a living wage. Such is Taussig's vision of a "just world," according to him. That policy, and the zero cost of advertising, probably account for Idyll's low prices, which are remarkable indeed in this expensive travel year.

The Destinations

Idyll's 1989 "Untours" to Germany (three weeks in length, running from early May to late September) include round-trip air on Lufthansa between New York and Frankfurt, an unlimited-mileage German railpass for each person, two half-day excursions, and the fully equipped apartment, and cost as little as $1,051 for each of four people traveling together, $1,114 for each of three, $1,248 for each of two.

Idyll's 1989 Untours to Switzerland, its most popular program, are also for three weeks, departing on Swissair from New York or Boston at various intervals from early May to late September. They include round-trip air, transfers, excursions, assistance, a "Swiss Holiday Pass" for unlimited transportation (bus or train) throughout Switzerland, and the apartment for 21 nights, and cost as little as $1,146 for each of four people traveling together, $1,185 for each of three, $1,274 for each of two.

Idyll's 1989 Untours to Austria are on Lufthansa to Salzburg (via Frankfurt) from early May to mid-September, and last three weeks; they include transatlantic air, transfers, car or train with unlimited mileage throughout, and the apartment. Rates are $1,328 for each of four people staying together, $1,329 for each of three, $1,380 for each of two. Add-ons are available from other Lufthansa departure cities in the U.S.

Idyll's 1989 Untours to Britain, using British Airways, deviate from the normal pattern. Here, you spend either two weeks in a London apartment and then a week in your choice of a village in either Scotland or Wales, or one week in London and two in Scotland or Wales. Including round-trip air to London from New York, Boston, Philadelphia, or Washington, D.C., three weeks' accommodations, a transportation pass for London and one- or two-week BritRailpass for the trip to and within Scotland or Wales, and several other features, the price is as little as $1,494 for each of

four people traveling and staying together, $1,594 for each of three, $1,791 for each of two. Departures on this combined "town and country" untour are from late April to late September.

Two totally new Untours for 1989 are the "Glasnost" Untour to Vienna and Budapest (a week in each), costing $1,340 for each of four people, $1,450 for each of three, and $1,470 for each of two; and a three-week Untour to New Zealand, costing $1,970 for each of four people, $2,100 for each of three, and $2,500 for each of two people traveling together.

For brochures, schedules, ratesheets, and bulky newsletters, contact Untours, at **Idyll Ltd., P.O. Box 405, Media, PA 19063 (phone 215/565-5242).** ≈

Cafe Sacher, Vienna

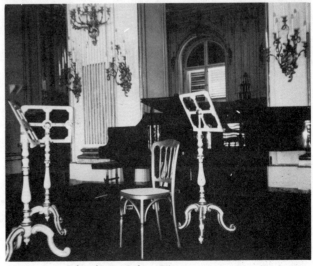

Music room, Schoenbrunn Palace, Vienna

Budget Motels, America's Greatest Travel Achievement

The Advent of Quality Inns Into the Under-$30-a-Night Category of Double Rooms, Brings Major New Savings to the Vacationing Motorist

Sample room of a Sleep Inn

Within the room is a remote-controlled color television set with a built-in VCR; a video vending machine in the lobby supplies first-run movies for the glistening screen. Along the wall stands a mini-bar. On the ledge by a queen-size bed is a pushbutton telephone with speed-dial capabilities for fast phoning—it connects you in a flash, for instance, with a pizza-delivery firm—while an ultramodern GE reverse-cycle air-pump unit heats or cools the room at an instant's touch.

And how much for all these amenities, similar to those in the most deluxe of international hotels?

Just $28 a night, for two people, at the height of the travel season. Per *room,* not per person.

Meet "Sleep Inns," the cheapest of motels, yet equipped, if you can believe it, in the fashion described above. The newest creation of Quality Inns—third-largest hotel chain in the world—Sleep Inns are about to sprout by the dozens, by the scores, and eventually by the hundreds along the highways of America, setting off a titanic battle with the hitherto reigning champion of the low-priced inns: Motel 6.

And we, the public, can only be the winner.

The budget motel is the single greatest achievement of the American travel industry. Modern, and nearly as comfortable as the standard hotel, yet renting for peanuts, it has no major counterpart in any major nation outside the U.S. Abroad, in most large countries, an expenditure of $30 to $40 a night will now barely suffice to rent a pension room for two people in an ancient structure or converted residence, without private bath, and usually without air conditioning, TV, or telephone. Here, the same expenditure at a budget motel places two people in a new facility custom-designed for hotel use, in an air-conditioned room with private bath and TV, with all or most of the other facilities of higher-priced establishments, and often even with swimming pool. What they lack are only large lobbies, conference rooms, elaborate eating places, and items of décor. The difference is often a psychological one, nothing more.

The budget motel was born in Santa Barbara,

California, in 1962, with the construction of the first Motel 6, charging, as its name revealed, as little as $6 a night per room. The product was such an "overnight" success that dozens of others soon emulated it. A study by the accounting firm of Laventhol & Horwath identified as many as 50 nationwide chains in the "U.S. economy/limited-service lodging industry," of which 19 chains consisted of more than 50 properties apiece.

What's Budget and What's Economy?

But one chain's conception of "economy" doesn't always mesh with another's. Though the initial effort, by Days Inns and others, was to compete with the radically low rates of Motel 6, participants soon began charging a wide range of prices, usually higher ones, and total price confusion reigns today. Some "economy motels" charge in the mid-$20s for a double room, others in the mid-$30s, still others in the mid-$40s, and some, which call themselves economy-style chains, are today building motels to rent in the low $50s per double room.

Nor can one discern the price range of a budget motel from its name. Ha'Penny Inns and Super 8 sound awfully cheap, but aren't at all in the ranks of the truly cheapest.

To make things worse, some budget chains charge a wide variety of rates in a single motel, or charge widely differing rates in differing locations and properties, or increase their rates in peak-season periods, or constantly shift the rates, on even a daily basis, to match the competition. When the *Consumer Reports Travel Letter* of the prestigious Consumers Union tried to assist its members in gauging the costs of budget motels in its February 1988 issue, it was forced to print such double-room spreads as "$26 to $115" for Rodeway Inns, "$33 to $100" for Ha'Penny Inns, "$23 to $75" for Budget Hosts. Some help!

On a far less scientific basis, I recently wrote for the directories of the 20 largest budget chains (more than 50 properties apiece), and then riffled through the pages to spot the price that most frequently appears for a double room. My survey results in the following groupings:

In the "super-budget" area of motels consistently charging under $30 for a double room, for most of their properties and most of the time, are four large chains: Motel 6, Scottish Inns, Sixpence Inns, and All Star Inns, with Sleep Inns about to make a breathless appearance. One should note that Scottish Inns and All Star Inns are not entirely consistent in quality or design, as some are formerly independent properties built for "momma-and-papa" operations, and only later acquired or franchised by the larger chains.

Hovering at the very outer edge of the "super-budget" category, just before the next price level, are Budgetels, averaging almost exactly $30 for a double room. They're a growing, aggressive chain.

In what we might next call the "standard budget" category of motels consistently charging under $40, but over $30, for a double room, are at least Super 8 Motels, Regal 8, Shoney's, and Knights Inns. Add to the lower end of this category National 9 Inns, which sometimes charges even below $30, but also above $30, for a double room. And at the upper end, add such "hybrids" as Susse Chalet, Red Roof, Econo Lodge, and Rodeway, charging from the $30s to the $40s for a double room.

(Interestingly enough, the mammoth Marriott Hotels Corporation was recently poised to enter the "standard budget" field with its new chain of low-priced Fairfield Inns, striking terror into the psyches of the companies listed above. But more recent price announcements for the first of the new Fairfields have led me to conclude that they will be, at best, upper-range "hybrids," charging from the high $30s to the mid-$40s for a double room. Apparently, you've got to have budget principles in your very soul to create miracle rates of the Super 8 or Sixpence variety.)

The remainder of the big players among the budget chains are those that invariably charge in the $40s for a double room: La Quinta and Friendship Inns are among them. The much-publicized new budget operations of the giant Holiday Inns chain (called Hampton Inns) and Quality Inns (Comfort Inns were their cheap variety, before Sleep Inns) are only barely within economy limits: most double rooms rent for the

"Sleep Inns" are about to sprout by the hundreds along the nation's highways, setting off a titanic struggle with Motel 6.

Desk at a Sleep Inn

The size of a Sleep Inn room

mid-$40s, and even into the $50s, at Hampton and Comfort.

But once the price structure is understood, where are the budget motels found? Alongside highways, mainly in Sunbelt states, and only recently, and to a lesser extent, in colder climes. That latter phenomenon once caused critics to conclude that flimsy construction, suitable for the South, and lack of expensive heating facilities were the basis of their low charges. Not so, say the several chain presidents with whom I've spoken; the early Sunbelt locations were chosen to track the most popular vacation movements of Americans throughout the year. Now, with greater experience and momentum, the Northeast, Midwest, and Pacific Northwest are beginning to get their "budget motels."

The chief factor determining where they will be built is the cost of land: a usual, necessary maximum of $7,000 to $10,000 per room, which usually relegates the budget motels to roadside locations on the outer peripheries of cities. Since in-city land costs several times that much (except, say, in Butte, Montana), it isn't likely that we'll be seeing these $20-a-night and $30-a-night rooms in urban centers.

The cost of actually constructing and furnishing a room must then be kept to about $20,000 in order to charge rates in the upper $20s per room per night. The belief that they can do so, and nevertheless create a superior room, is what has led the executives of Quality Inns to announce the imminent creation of as many as 300 Sleep Inns.

The New "Sleeps" Challenge Motel 6

From their campus-like headquarters outside Washington, D.C., equipped with laboratories and testing machines, sample rooms and architects' tables, Quality Inns has designed an absolutely standard, off-the-shelf, but radically different form of hotel room for Sleep Inns, which franchisees must then construct "as is," under master construction contracts negotiated by Quality Inns. Rooms will be 70% the size of standard rooms—the key factor in keeping costs low—but so artfully designed, with curving walls for a portion of the bathroom, as to create the appearance of greater space. Acrylic stall showers will substitute for bathtubs.

Only one type of bed has been ordered for Sleep Inns, of the queen-size variety, and only one such bed will be in each room. Travelers seeking twin beds will either need to go elsewhere or rent adjoining rooms. By using such approaches, executives of Quality Inns believe they will be able to equip the rooms with elegant space-age amenities—VCRs and the like—and yet hold rates to the $24-to-$29 range, competitive with Motel 6 and other super-budget chains.

The first Sleep Inn, it is claimed, will be open by early 1989 (using prefabrication and other advanced techniques, a 100-unit Sleep Inn can be built in six months). About 65 more will join the chain by the end of the year, and hundreds thereafter. Contracts are presently being let for the first Sleep Inns, in locations ranging from Pennsylvania to Utah. Inquiries about foreign Sleep Inns have been received from England, Australia, Brazil, and the islands of Tahiti.

And how are they reacting at Motel 6? With 439 dirt-cheap but modern motels presently in operation, all company owned, the pioneering budget hotelier is currently and calmly adding 30 to 40 more Motel 6s each year, and plans to continue doing so on into the foreseeable future. Many new such "6s" are especially planned for the Atlantic seaboard, from which the chain has been conspicuously absent in the past.

"But aren't you concerned about Sleep Inns?" I pressed a succession of Motel 6 executives. "They can say they'll be charging $24 to $29 a room," said one, "but they're a franchised operation; how will they keep their franchisees in line? What's to stop a Sleep Inn from succumbing to temptation and raising the rate when the area is jammed?"

"Do you know what our average room rate will be in 1989?" he continued, with mounting excitement, rising from his chair, and beginning to shout:

"Twenty-four dollars and fifty-four cents!"

Such is the crowning glory of the American travel industry, the one domain in which no one beats us, not even the Japanese.

Obtaining the Directories

If you're to expand your travel horizons, you'll want to seek out the cheapest of the budget motels for your own next trip. Write for directories to **Motel 6,** 14651 Dallas Pkwy., Dallas, TX 75240; "**Sleep Inns,**" c/o Quality Inns, 10750 Columbia Pike, Silver Spring, MD 20901; **Scottish Inns,** c/o Hospitality International, Inc., 1152 Spring St., Atlanta, GA 30309; **All Star Inns, Inc.,** 2020 De La Vina St. (P.O. Box 3070), Santa Barbara, CA 93130; **Econo Lodge,** 6135 Park Rd., Charlotte, NC 28210; **Budgetel Inns,** 212 W. Wisconsin Ave., Milwaukee, WI 53203; **Super 8 Motels, Inc.,** 1910 Eighth Ave. NE, Aberdeen, SD 57401; **Knights Inns,** 6561 E. Livingstone Ave., Reynoldsburg, OH 43068; **Regal 8 Inns,** 800 S. 45th St., Mount Vernon, IL 62864; **Susse Chalet Inns,** Chalet Drive, Wilton, NH 03086; **La Quinta Inns,** P.O. Box 790064, San Antonio, TX 78279; **Rodeway Inns,** 3838 E. Van Buren, Phoenix, AZ 85008; **Hampton Inns,** 6799 Great Oaks Rd., Memphis, TN 38138; **Shoney's, Inc.,** 1727 Elm Hill Pike (P.O. Box 1260), Nashville, TN 37202; **Sixpence Inns of America, Inc.,** 1751 E. Garry Ave., Santa Ana, CA 92705; or **National 9 Inns,** 9010 Soquel Dr., Aptos, CA 95003. ≈

Fairfield Inn by Marriott

Bed and Breakfast in a Private Home

The Use of "RSOs" Has Now Become the Key to Finding a Proper "B&B"

A Connecticut B&B

The bedroom upstairs

Clint Eastwood's Carmel, California, has banned them altogether. So has trendy Santa Fe. The once-burgeoning bed-and-breakfast industry—a source of livelihood for more than 20,000 American households—is currently beleaguered with threats from zoning officials, angry hoteliers, and frightened neighbors of the B&B proprietors.

To make things worse, numerous Americans are bad-mouthing these unpretentious, overnight lodgings, claiming them to be more expensive, on occasion, than comparable hotels.

What has happened to the B&B movement? In my view, simple growing pains, basic misunderstandings, and nothing more. An activity less than ten years old (for all practical purposes) is moving into maturity, achieving importance and setting off understandable—if flawed—reactions.

The B&B Boom

Although people from time immemorial have been renting spare rooms in their homes to transient visitors, the activity came of age in the United States only with the creation of large-scale "reservations service organizations" (RSOs) in the late 1970s. Such RSOs as Bed-and-Breakfast Rocky Mountains, Bed-and-Breakfast Nebraska, Bed-and-Breakfast Philadelphia, and scores more, provided the marketing efforts and all-day telephone confirmations in their respective cities, states, or regions that no individual B&B house could afford to supply on its own.

An explosion in the use of B&Bs soon followed. The cost-conscious public, on arrival in a large city, had only to look under "B" in the telephone book to find the area-wide reservations service that could recommend any number of B&Bs and then confirm space at them.

To aid matters more, various telephone companies soon created a "bed-and-breakfast" category in the *Yellow Pages,* enabling travelers to find those few ornery RSO services whose names did not begin with "B": Sweet Dreams and Toast, Urban Ventures, Pinellas County Bed-and-Breakfast, etc.

Suddenly, the public had a sure-fire means of always uncovering a nearby B&B. But more important, they were able at last to deal only with homes that had been prescreened for suitability by a larger organization.

The single greatest dread of the traveler—arriving at an improper lodging, to be met by an unshaven and bleary-eyed proprietor—was overcome, and Americans by the tens of thousands began flocking to guest-accepting homes confirmed and vouched-for by a regional "reservations service organization."

The Negative Reaction

And then the reaction set in.

First from the hotel industry. Whether America's commercial innkeepers are behind the banning of B&Bs in Carmel and Santa Fe is hard to determine. But there are suspicions of their part in drafting fire regulations that impose unreasonable burdens (in my opinion) on the bed-and-breakfast industry. A recently enacted New York State fire ordinance (admittedly, the nation's most stringent) requires elaborate sprinklers, expensive extra stairs, special fire doors, of any establishment housing more than four paying visitors on a habitual basis. The application of such rules to an easily evacuated, one-story ranch house or simple two-story home seems a bit much.

Other attempts to put B&Bs out of business have focused on residential zoning laws that forbid the taking of "boarders." But most courts have responded that the boarder ban was meant to refer to guests who were full-time residents of the city, not transient visitors, and that other significant differences also made the rules inapplicable.

Such zoning fights—the disputed interpretation of various vague prohibitions against commercial activity—are obviously the result of fears that a steady stream of B&B visitors will cheapen a residential neighborhood, attracting motor vans, backpackers, impecunious wanderers, and the like to an area of quiet homes.

As sensitive as we all might be to such concerns, there seems no evidence at all to support the prediction. B&B houses have no signs outside, nor are they open to

Confusing a B&B inn with a B&B house, disgruntled guests have proceeded to damn the entire movement.

B&B, New England

Your room in a New York brownstone

In a B&B home, the family does not derive its entire income from that activity.

Breakfast in a Connecticut B&B

B & B, Dingle, Ireland

walk-in members of the public—as in a hotel—but only to specific individuals who have made reservations in advance. Far from harming a community, experience shows a thriving bed-and-breakfast industry attracts the best sort of additional tourism: from sensitive and reasonably well-financed travelers who prefer the charm of a private home to an impersonal hotel or flashy motel. It brings considerable extra income, even prosperity, to the areas in which those homes are located.

Why You're Not Seeking a B&B Inn

A problem of equal weight has been the adverse reactions of some travelers to the rates charged by B&B "inns," which are frequently higher than in a hotel. Confusing a B&B inn with a B&B house, such disgruntled guests have proceeded to damn the entire movement. It is important that, somehow, both the B&B proprietors and the writers of B&B guidebooks adopt a proper, semantic distinction between B&Bs that are inns rather than homes.

A B&B inn is a multiroom structure wholly devoted to transient visitors. It is often a place of exquisite décor, down comforters, punctilious attentions, and cinnamon croissants (or strawberry-flavored quiche) for breakfast. Its prices are, often justifiably, higher than those of hotels.

By contrast, a B&B home is that of a normal, private family that has simply decided to supplement its income by setting aside one or two spare rooms—rarely more—for occasional paying guests. The family does not derive its entire income from that activity, but simply an extra $3,000 to $6,000 a year—the average earnings cited by most reports on the B&B industry (supplemented by the family's frequent ability to write off a portion of their home expenses or home purchase price on their taxes).

Places that are B&B houses as opposed to B&B inns continue to charge from 40% to 50% less than comparable hotels all over the country. Yet because they are confused with B&B inns, they are suspected of gouging. The industry needs different names for different categories.

Becoming a B&B Host

What should someone do who is tempted to enter the bed-and-breakfast field? If you, for instance, should have a spare room or two in your attractive and well-located home, should you simply phone up the nearest "reservations service organization" forthwith (they're listed in the *Yellow Pages* under "Bed and Breakfast Accommodations") and ask them to list you? (The RSO fee is usually 20% to 30% of the sums they generate for you.)

Greater deliberation is called for. If you live in a large city, check first to learn whether a local "urban independent night school" (a Learning Annex, Discovery Center, Open University, or some such) is offering a one-night course in "How to Start a Bed-and-Breakfast Business." There you'll learn of additional pitfalls in addition to prospects.

Or else order a copy of one of the several books on the subject, such as *Open Your Own Bed & Breakfast* by Barbara Notarius and Gail Brewer (John Wiley & Sons, New York; $10.95). Its chapters ("Is It for You?" "Financial Considerations," "Advertising," "Working with a Reservations Service," etc.) deal with just about every question you may have.

Ms. Notarius, herself a successful B&B host, has recently formed a consulting service that operates periodic one-day seminars around the country ($150) for would-be hosts of B&Bs, and also provides personal, one-on-one advice to persons contemplating the more serious step of opening a multiroom B&B inn. Contact **Barbara Notarius, INNsider's Expertise, Inc., 129 Grand St., Croton-on-Hudson, NY 10520 (phone 914/271-2922).**

Or for a more intensive look at B&B inns, not homes, order *So . . . You Want to Be an Innkeeper* ($12.95 through the mails from **101 Productions, 834 Mission St., San Francisco, CA 94103**). The several authors of this book also issue an innkeeping newsletter and operate three-day workshops ($375) twice a year for people aspiring to enter the field. For information on both, write **Innkeepers, 1333 Bath St., Santa Barbara, CA 93101.**

A wise man once said that Hell consisted of being condemned to stay, each night into eternity, in a different Holiday Inn. Through the judicious use of B&Bs, that need not be your fate.

They provide us with a refreshing and cheaper alternative to the stale and increasingly standard hotel. ≈

B&B bedroom, Riverside Drive, New York

B & B, Bunratty, Co. Clare, Ireland

Learn to Bargain in the Marketplace of Hotels

By Ridding Yourself of Pompous Dignity, You Can Save Thousands in the Years Ahead

If the class—ahem!—will come to order, we shall discuss the single most important skill in all the world of travel: how to "bargain down" the price of hotel rooms. That talent can save you thousands in the years ahead.

Start from the premise that nothing in this life is more "perishable" than a hotel room. If such a room should go unrented on a particular night, its value for that night can never again be recouped by the owner of that hotel.

Accordingly, it behooves that owner to rent the room for almost any price rather than leave it unoccupied. Why? Because the cost of placing a guest in the room, as opposed to keeping it empty, is measured in terms of a dollar or two: a change of towels and sheets, a bit of electricity, a cake of soap. A reduced (but still a reasonable) amount of room income is therefore better than no income at all.

Such reasoning has led smart hoteliers the world over to authorize their front-desk clerks to respond favorably to requests for discounts, if that should be what's needed to fill rooms on a slow night. And every nationality of traveler the world over is aware of their willingness to do so, and therefore bargains—except the American.

Bargaining with Dignity

Why not Americans? Because to most of us the very act of bargaining is vulgar and degrading.

No one else regards it as such. If you will stand in the lobby of a large Venetian hotel on a November afternoon, when 60% of the rooms in Venice are empty, chances are that you'll soon spot a well-dressed English tourist or an affluent German tourist or a French one approaching the desk and politely stating: "I am looking for a room that costs no more than 50,000 lire" (nearly $40).

This tourist knows full well that there is no such thing here as a room for 50,000 lire. He is bargaining. He is saying, in effect: "If you will rent me a room for 50,000 lire, I will stay in your hotel. Otherwise, I will stroll down the street and seek another hotel."

To bargain over hotel rates does not require that you act like a hysterical fishwife or a tobacco auctioneer.

In other words, to bargain over hotel rates does not require that you comport yourself like a hysterical fishwife or a tobacco auctioneer. It can be done—as in the above example—with dignity, by indirection.

Often it requires only that you use a "code word" to convey to the desk clerk that you are "shopping." How many times have you heard a traveler inquire as to whether the hotel grants a "corporate rate" or a "commercial rate"—thus bargaining, and usually successfully, for a reduced rate?

What's to prevent you from doing the same? Why can't you name the corporation or firm for which you work and then speculate: "I'm sure we must have a special rate at this hotel." If the hotel is empty and you appear disposed to leave the hotel unless a discount is granted, will anyone challenge the statement? Does anyone really care whether your company has made such arrangements? Or are they anxious to fill their hotel?

Or else you name your occupation and ask for a reduction based on that. You ask for a "teacher's rate" or for a "student's rate." You request a "civil servant's rate" or a "minister's rate" (that always works). You might as well ask for a "stenographer's rate" or for a "dentist's rate." What matters is that you are subtly (and politely) communicating the message that you will stay at the hotel only if they grant you a discount.

When I was a travel agent, I used to phone from the airport, announce that I was seeking a room, but only if I could have a "travel agent's rate." And in that fashion I was usually able to cut my hotel costs in half.

It just so happened that I was telling the truth—I *was* a travel agent. Yet in 20 years of using the tactic, not once was I ever asked to prove it. For, in reality, the hotels didn't care. If the night was a slow one and they needed the business, they were quite happy to accept any assertion of status as an excuse for cutting the rate and keeping the guest.

Recently I phoned two professors at the prestigious Cornell University School of Hotel Administration to confirm these hotel policies, and although both pleaded to remain nameless, they instantly did.

What Not to Do

Why, then, I asked, do some hotel guests encounter rejections of their requests for reductions?

It is primarily because, they replied, most people phone nationwide toll-free "800" numbers to seek reservations and rates. The minions who man the phones at central reservations headquarters of the large hotel chains have no authority to cut rates. Rather, one should place the call directly to the hotel and speak to someone more entrepreneurially inclined. If those local, and directly interested, people are made to know that you will stay at the hotel only if a lower rate is found, they'll often find that rate.

All hotels quote from "the top down," added one professor. "When you tell them the rate is unsatisfactory, they'll quite frequently find a lower one."

The second frequent mistake, say my informants, is to make the request—tired and burdened with luggage—in the lobby of the hotel. Once at the front desk, you are presumed by most hotel personnel to be in no position to walk out if discounts aren't given. A better course, they say, is to phone from the airport or train terminal, and announce from there that you are seeking a room that costs "no more than $—." Such a call is obviously from a "shopper," and the desk clerk will take pains to do what's necessary to make the sale—provided, of course, that the night is a slow one.

Best of all is to write ahead. In scheduling a vacation trip to Barbados or Jamaica in the dead month of June, for instance, you advise the hotel: "I am planning a stay, but only if I can secure a room for no more than $40 a night." "It so happens we have such a room" will come the instant reply.

"Ask and it shall be given," says the Bible.

The final error, say my academic friends, is to bargain at the wrong time of year. Obviously, bargaining will not work during peak hotel seasons, when hotels are confident they will fill up. But all hotels have slow weeks or months, or slow "down cycles" during a week. Hotels in business centers like New York, Chicago, or Philadelphia are packed to capacity from Monday through Thursday, then empty and hurting from Friday through Sunday. The traveler who pays full rate—who fails to bargain—on weekend nights is a chump. That traveler is simply subsidizing the weekend stays of package tourists enjoying rooms at half the rate.

Conversely, in resort locations like Atlantic City or Las Vegas, hotels are full on Friday and Saturday nights but often quiet at other times. If you're a Monday arrival at Harrah's or the Golden Nugget, bargain!

In a country that currently deifies the "free market" and worships the likes of Adam Smith and Milton Friedman, isn't it surprising that we as individuals should be reluctant to bargain over the price of a hotel room? Who decrees that hotel rates are fixed in stone? Who denies us the right as free consumers to flex our economic muscle?

Travelers of all nations, unite! You have nothing to lose but your pomposity! You have savings to win! ≈

VI ⚎ NEW MODES
OF TRAVEL

Cooperative Camping with 14 Others in a Fully Equipped Van

It Is a Sensible Travel Method for People Reluctant to Transport Camping Equipment and Vehicle to Areas Overseas or Far Away

"When I use a word, it means just what I choose it to mean—neither more nor less."

Those were the sentiments of Humpty Dumpty in Lewis Carroll's *Through the Looking Glass*. They could have applied to the antics of travel brochure writers in describing the activity of cooperative camping. By refusing to use the term—substituting instead a dozen or so contrived titles which only they understand—the pamphlet authors have so confused matters as to conceal this marvelous travel mode from 80% of the people who could have benefited from it.

Cooperative camping (the name they won't use) is a cheap and sensible travel method for people who haven't the energy, funds, or commitment to buy and then transport their own camping equipment and/or camping vehicle to regions overseas or far away.

The operators of cooperative camping tours print literature in which they describe dozens of potential itineraries throughout the United States, Mexico, and Europe. They schedule departures for each itinerary, take bookings from widely scattered individuals, and ultimately assemble a group of about 14 for each departure.

When the group of 14 reaches the jumping-off point (London, Mexico City, Los Angeles, or New York), they board a 15-person van furnished by the operator and driven by a professional guide—the only paid employee on the trip. The vehicle is already supplied with up to eight state-of-the-art tents, elaborate camping utensils, and (sometimes) sleeping bags —although most companies require that you provide the latter. Except for that last item, passengers avoid all the expense and burden of outfitting themselves for camping.

On the first day of the trip, participants vote to establish a "food kitty," fixing the sum they will collectively spend each day for campfire meals. Members of the group, in rotation, shop for groceries along the way, and then rotate the cooking and cleaning chores. They each pitch their own tent each night and pack it away in the morning. The driver drives. Since the group carries its own accommodations (the tents) and needn't adhere to hotel reservations, they are able either to follow the preplanned itinerary or make broad deviations from it. They are also able to travel through areas where standard hotels aren't found.

The entire trip is unstructured and fun, close to nature and informal, adventurous, instructive—and cheap. The average cooperative camping tour costs around $35 a day, plus air fare, and plus about $4 per person per day in contributions to the food kitty.

The Major Companies

So why haven't you heard of it? Blame the following: TrekAmerica, of Gardena, California, is the largest U.S. operator of cooperative camping tours, but ought to be spanked for semantic inexactness. A "trek" isn't what they do; in holiday travel, a "trek" is an organized walk along the lower slopes of the Himalayas, Andes, or Swiss Alps, in which porters or pack animals carry your gear. Such adventure travel companies as Himalayan Travel, Mountain Travel, and Journeys, operate treks. Cooperative camping tours of the sort organized by TrekAmerica are often to distinctly unadventurous places—Yellowstone, Salt Lake City, Yosemite—but are accomplished through the delightful, semi-adventurous mode of camping.

Despite my quibbles, the company is a superb source of cooperative camping: 20 itineraries through North America, from two to nine weeks in length, with up to two dozen yearly departures per itinerary, at daily costs of $30 to $45, plus air fare, and plus a food kitty of about $30 a week. But passengers are limited to the age group of 18 to 35. Write for colorful catalogs to: **TrekAmerica, P.O. Box 1338, Gardena, CA 90249 (phone 213/321-0734, or toll free 800/ 221-0596 outside California).**

Toucan Adventure Tours, of Manhattan Beach, California, offers cooperative camping to offbeat locations in Mexico, and makes them available to people of all ages, encouraging even oldsters to come along. But how does their literature describe the tours? As a "Mexico Toucan Adventure." Only within the text do you occasionally learn that "many nights we will camp along secluded beaches where we only have to step from

The vehicle is already supplied with up to eight state-of-the-art tents and elaborate camping gear.

Participants vote to establish a "food kitty," fixing the sum they will spend each day for campfire meals.

our tents to reach the sea. . . . We'll take time to climb a volcano, camp along beautiful mountain lakes, and visit villages where artisans craft fine works."

Toucan studiously avoids "tourist Mexico." Acapulco appears on no itinerary. Rather, from Mexico City you head south into the highlands, to Oaxaca and Tuxtla Gutierrez, or to enchanting San Cristobal de las Casas and Palenque. Or else you travel the length of Baja California, to Santa Inez and Guerrero Negro, to La Paz and Cabo San Lucas.

Itineraries are usually three weeks in length (but can range from ten days to eight weeks), cost as little as $345 for ten days (plus air fare and food kitty), $495 to $565 for two weeks, $720 to $825 for three weeks, and are scheduled throughout the year. Phone or write: **Toucan Adventure Tours, Inc., 1142 Manhattan Ave., CP #416, Manhattan Beach, CA 90266 (phone 213/546-1196).**

Tracks, of London, England (now there's a trendy name describing nothing), raises the formal age limit to 38, but also explains that "travellers who are not in this age range are welcome, so long as they understand that our tours are designed for the 18–38's." Its vehicles (all supplied with camping equipment) traverse every standard European itinerary ("Ten Countries in 23 Days," "Eighteen Countries in 70 Days"), and even branch out to Eastern Europe and Russia, where it warns that "campsites . . . and camping conditions are not equal to those of Central Europe." Unlike the other companies I've surveyed, it frequently assembles larger groups than the standard 14 or so, and reserves the right to use 40-passenger motorcoaches for transportation between camping sites. But the gathering of larger groups makes for generally lower prices than the others: as little as $28 and $30 a day on the longer itineraries. To confuse matters even more, its U.S. representative is a "trekking" organization: **Himalayan Travel, Inc., P.O. Box 481, Greenwich, CT 06836 (phone 203/622-6777, or toll free 800/ 225-2380 outside Connecticut),** from which four-color brochures are available.

Pioneer Travel Service, of Cambridge, Massachusetts, runs perhaps the most unusual tour of all:

cooperative camping and driving through the Soviet Union, on two lengthy itineraries (six weeks for $2,990 including air fare, nine weeks for $3,490 including air fare), ranging from Leningrad to the Black Sea on one route, into Central Asia on another. It imposes no age limit whatever, and attracts half of its participants from non-college-age adults, the other half from its largely Harvard and MIT base. (Families with children are, however, discouraged.) Surprisingly, the program is now in its 23rd consecutive year, receives full cooperation from Intourist, the Soviet travel agency, and yet allows its participants maximum exposure (on campgrounds, in shops, in smaller towns) to Soviet citizens and ordinary institutions of Soviet life. Rave comments from several recent participants lead me to believe that these are among the most rewarding trips around. Contact **Pioneer Travel Service, 203 Allston St., Cambridge, MA 02139 (phone 617/547-1127).**

Finally, American Adventures, of Cambridge, Massachusetts, operates camping tours along nine far-ranging itineraries within the United States and Canada, for up to 13 passengers apiece, most for ages 18 to 38 but some for all ages also, traveling cooperatively. Trips are two to six weeks in length, average $35 a day (plus $5 daily for the food kitty), but require that you make your own way to the starting points, either New York or Los Angeles. Wonder of wonders, the company places the words "Camping Trips" (in small type) on the front cover of their catalog, and may even go to the title "Tenting Trips" in 1989. Progress! Write to: **American Adventures, Inc., 650 Cambridge St., Cambridge, MA 02141 (phone 617/499-2730).**

A Last Example

Cooperative camping is also the solution to a shortage of tourist housing in Alaska. Already notoriously short of peak-season accommodations, the 50th state is best visited in any event on excursions into its parks and uninhabited wilderness, where few or no lodgings exist. The company that enables you to do so: CampAlaska Tours for tourists of all ages, and for families.

You supply the sleeping bag, they provide all else:

14-passenger vehicle with driver, state-of-the-art tents, other camping gear and cooking equipment (in the classic fashion of "cooperative camping" tours). Tours average $70 a day (plus a food kitty contribution of $6 a day), last 7 to 48 days (but average 12), depart from early June to mid-September, and transport no more than 12 individuals booking each departure (of which more than such departures are available). They leave mainly from Anchorage, and include all overland and ferry transportation, entrance to national parks and campgrounds, services of CampAlaska's guide, and use of their camping equipment. You visit the continent's most spectacular natural wonders, breathe exhilarating air, go fishing, climbing, trekking, and rafting.

For irresistible literature, contact: **CampAlaska Tours, P.O. Box 872247, Wasilla, AK 99687 (phone 907/376-9438).** ≈

"Overlanding," the Last Great Travel Adventure

In Self-sufficient "Expedition Trucks," Modern-Day Tourists Travel for 7 to 42 Weeks Across Asia, Africa, or South America

Preparing lunch for a stop en route

An overlanding group
Opposite page: *Setting up camp*

When Marco Polo traveled in the 13th century from Venice to the Chinese court of Kublai Khan, he became the first person to use "overlanding" as a method of tourism. He made scarcely any use of sea routes or even river transport, went for great distances where there were no roads, and slept every night in cloth tents, not inns.

That's "overlanding." And amazingly enough, today thousands of tourists are using much the same methods, as offered by several overland tour companies of Britain, to accomplish journeys almost as long (7 to 42 weeks), just as exotic (trans-Asia, trans-Africa), and nearly as full of insight, learning, and satisfaction.

Overlanding is the closest modern approach to the experience of the great explorers. Although it uses several familiar practices of "cooperative camping" (people become participants in the mechanics of their own trip, sharing the cooking and pitching the tents), it differs in radical respects from the far tamer activities of the cooperative camping tour operators. The latter take you to commercial campsites near large cities or well-visited attractions, and travel from place to place on modern highways, or at least paved ones.

The overlanding companies go on dirt roads, or backroads, or where there are no roads at all, in underdeveloped areas of untouched fascination, the largely uncharted. Their journeys are through the rawest countryside, not near cities, in circumstances that afford them the closest contact with rural people of Asia, Africa, and South America, their three principal destinations.

Overlanders offer travel adventure and unpredictability (though almost complete safety). On such a trip, you encounter, let's say, a washed-out bridge and must shift routes. You find that sand dunes have shifted and obliterated tracks through the Sahara, and again you improvise. In Zaire, you take out batteries from your own vehicle to start the stilled motor of a ferry that must take you across a raging stream. In Cameroon, you discover that the border to Nigeria has been closed for political reasons, and again you and your group make decisions about where to go next.

Their journeys are through the rawest countryside, in close contact with rural people.

Overlanding in Zaire

An "expedition truck"

Riding High Above the Ground

The key to overlanding is the "expedition truck," usually an open-sided 20-passenger British-made Bedford with extremely high ground clearance. This permits the vehicle to drive along a riverbed if the roads have been washed out, to come on and off primitive ferries, to negotiate a boulder-strewn path.

The vehicle has so much storage capacity as to be virtually self-sufficient. It carries 200 gallons of fuel (for a 2,000-mile range), 100 gallons of drinking water, oil enough for 12,000 miles, gas stoves, and a huge supply of food. Do these provisions seem excessive? Well, one particularly important route for overlanders, bringing them to the very heart of the Dark Continent, is from Tamanrasset, Algeria, to Gao, Mali. The distance is 1,000 miles on a soft sand track—up to ten days of driving—unaided by a single filling station, a single store, or a single house, with no wood for a fire and no food nearby. Overlanders value the capacity of their Bedford truck.

The development of such vehicles in the early 1960s gave overlanding its start, on a route much favored by the English and Australian adventurers who make up half the audience for it: from London to central India. For nearly 20 years, until conditions in Iran and Afghanistan became unstable, overlanding companies in Britain sent out many dozens of departures each year on a four-month journey somewhat similar to that of Marco Polo: from Europe to and through Turkey into Persia (Iran) and through what is now Afghanistan to India.

The overlanding companies continue to operate that four-month route to this day (for $3,145), though they skirt through only the barest part of Iran (completely away from Teheran) and substitute the Baluchistan Desert of southern Pakistan for the former route through Afghanistan. Even so, most American participants ask to overfly Iran (and do so), leaving the group in Turkey and then awaiting arrival of the truck in Pakistan. Unfortunately, too, the new Pakistan-for-Afghanistan routing has eliminated much of the former dramatic encounter with tribespeople and colorful cultures along the way.

Therefore, in recent years, trans-Africa trips have overtaken the trans-Asian jaunts in popularity. People sign up many months ahead for the 16- to 18-week trip from London to Dover and Europe, and then through North and Central Africa to Nairobi in East Africa. Or they opt for a longer, 21-week journey that includes West Africa as well.

More recently, a number of one-month to six-month trips through South America—seeking out the unusual and the out-of-the-way—have begun to enjoy heavy bookings. And overland operators have now begun to operate shorter, three-week and four-week varieties as well, such as a three-weeker in Africa called "Gorillas, Volcanoes, and Pygmies," that starts and ends in Rwanda, but also takes in Zaire and Uganda.

Companies and Costs

Astonishingly, most long-term (one month and more) overlanding tours cost only $30 to $40 per person per day, including meals, but plus air fare to the jumping-off point (which is London in most instances). Participants come equipped with only their clothing and a sleeping bag; the overlanding company provides everything else: vehicle, fuel, food, tents, cooking equipment, a driver/leader. One such firm—Guerba Expeditions—provides three paid personnel per truck (a driver/leader, assistant, and a cook), yet charges only $2 to $3 a day more than the others. While all members of a Guerba expedition continue to participate in chores and cooking, they do so to a slightly lesser extent than is usual.

Guerba, from its base in London, takes participants aged 18 through 65 on all their overland itineraries. Another major company, Encounter Overland, of London, limits its passengers to those aged 18 through 40. Though nearly a dozen other companies in Britain offer overlanding tours of differing durations and destinations, and their number is joined by one or two companies in Holland, I am reliably told that Guerba (with 20 expedition trucks) and Encounter Overland (with 40 such vehicles) account for more than 80% of the market. Of each 20 people who board one of their trucks for this supreme adventure, four or five are

generally British, four or five Australian, three from the U.S., three Canadian, two from New Zealand, and two or so are English-speaking northern Europeans.

Both companies are represented in the United States by Adventure Center of Oakland, California, which makes their yearly catalogs available free of charge, and then accepts bookings on their overland programs. And both publications are so colorful, well written, and compelling as to awaken the Marco Polo in each of us. Contact **Adventure Center, 5540 College Ave., Oakland, CA 94618 (phone toll free 800/227-8747, 800/228-8747 in California).** ≈

Shopping for victuals

Overlanding

Trekking as a Cheap and Fulfilling Mode of Travel

Organized Walks Along the Lower Slopes of the Himalayas, Andes, and Alps

With Journeys International, in the Himalayas

Like the character from Molière who suddenly discovered that he'd been speaking "prose" all his life, a growing number of Americans have learned that "trekking" is the unfamiliar word for their favorite vacation activity. Though only the barest handful of travel agents understand the term—and some misuse it horribly—international trekking has become a substantial travel activity for at least 20,000 Americans each year, and currently marketed by upward of five major nationwide organizations.

In oversimplified terms, trekking is walking—the healthiest sport on earth—but walking of a special nature, elevated to a high art and mental adventure.

Unlike the hiking and backpacking pursued by individuals, trekking is an intricate, organized, group activity in which porters or pack animals carry your camping gear, cooking utensils, and food from one overnight campsite to another. Relieved of that weight, you're able to go where roads and paths aren't, through the most exotic of nations, over breathtaking terrain, but without performing feats of endurance or possessing mountaineering skills. Persons in their middle age are a familiar sight on treks, as are families and even seniors into their 70s.

That's not to say that minimal vigor isn't required—it is. Yet hundreds of perfectly ordinary, normally sedentary (even chubby) Americans are today found in such unlikely locations as the historic, 18,000-foot-high base camp in Nepal used by intrepid climbers for the assault on Mount Everest. They get there by trekking—organized walking—without setting a single metal wedge into stone or tugging a single rope.

And they achieve that forever-memorable trip for total land costs of less than $70 a day (plus air fare to and from Nepal, in this instance); trekking is one of the cheapest of travel modes, considering the distance you've covered and the highly personal nature of your travel arrangements (groups are never more than 15 people in number). No money goes toward hotels or restaurants, because no such places exist in the areas for trekking. Apart from the one-time purchase of tents and gear by the trekking company, labor alone—the chief guide, the cook, the Nepali or Peruvian porters, let's say—are the only major expense of the venture.

Trekking Destinations

I used the example of Nepal and Peru advisedly. For reasons not entirely clear to me, almost all international treks are operated to mountain areas of the world: the Himalayas, the Andes, the Swiss Alps in particular. (While you don't go atop them, you walk along their easy lower slopes, usually at elevations of 8,000 to 10,000 feet.) Though it is theoretically possible to trek through lowland valleys supplied with roads, it is apparently felt inappropriate and uninspiring to do so.

The mountain kingdom of Nepal, at the northern border of India, is the chief trekking destination, accounting for nearly 40% of all treks. The associated Indian states of Kashmir, Sikkim, and Ladakh, and portions of Bhutan, Pakistan, and Tibet, draw another 10% of all trekkers. Together these areas flank the full length of the most remarkable geographical feature on earth—the 1,500-mile-long chain of the Himalayas, the world's tallest mountains.

It was Nepal, almost entirely covered by mountains, that set off the trend to trekking. A country with scarcely any roads at all, isolated from the outside world until the 1950s, its widely scattered mountainside villages harbor 35 different ethnic groups whose ways of life have been scarcely touched by outside influences.

The people of Nepal have a particular tradition of hospitality to strangers. As you trek the trails from village to village along the south slope of the Himalayas, you are invited to tea in small council chambers, sometimes to stay the night in the homes of villagers or in monasteries.

With unlimited access to the world's greatest mountains, in this peaceful Shangri-La whose half-Hindu, half-Buddhist population coexists without conflict, your own near-spiritual reactions are almost too intimate to describe. You awake at 6:30 a.m., when a cup of steaming tea or coffee is thrust through the flaps of your tent by a member of the cooking staff. Accompanied by experienced Sherpa guides, you take to the

Trekking is walking of a special nature, elevated to a high art and mental adventure.

Sherpa porters

In the Andes

Relieved of your backpacks, you're able to go where roads and paths aren't, but without performing feats of endurance or possessing mountaineering skills.

In the Himalayas

trails, trekking seven to ten miles a day at your own pace. The trip starts and ends in the other-worldly capital of Katmandu, reached by air via New Delhi or Bangkok.

The Peruvian Andes, and that section of it known as the Cordillera Blanca, is next in popularity, accounting for perhaps 30% of all treks. From Lima you fly to Cuzco and there, your gear stowed atop a mountain burro, you embark on a 5-day, 35-mile walk along the ancient Inca Trail to the lost city of Machú Picchú, passing awesome Incan ruins unseen by conventional tourists. Again from Lima, you go by car to Huaraz to embark on an 8-day trek through the heart of Peru's highest mountain area. For an enhanced 11-day (Inca Trail) or 21-day (Inca Trail and Cordillera Blanca) trip of this nature, as packaged by some of the trekking companies, you pay $745 and $1,600, respectively (plus air fare to Peru)—an average of $72 a day for your all-inclusive needs in Peru.

In the Swiss Alps (a 10% share of the trekking industry), hut-to-hut trekking replaces the traditional variety, with vans bringing your food, clothing, and bedding to austere and unattended mountain lodges scattered among the mountain trails, a day's march from each other. The classic trip is of the Mount Blanc massif, on a trail dominated by the tallest of Europe's mountain peaks. Trips cost as little as $895 for 15 days (plus air fare to Switzerland), including lodging, meals, and the services of a support vehicle that moves camp each day.

The Major Trekking Specialists

Himalayan Travel, Inc., of Greenwich, Connecticut, proudly occupies the low end of the trekking industry in price: its consistently low rates for land arrangements ($60 and $70 a day, all inclusive) are matched by similar marvels in air fares, bringing you round trip between New York and Katmandu for $1,285 to $1,425, plus $13 tax (compared with the $1,600 from East Coast cities and $1,400 to $1,500 from West Coast cities charged by most other companies). How that fare is achieved is shrouded in secrecy and the subject of controversy. Its specialty, naturally, is Nepal

(40 different treks there, 200 yearly departures), but all other mountain areas are also offered; and through its representation of a leading British trekking company, Sherpa, an extensive program of low-cost treks in the Swiss Alps, the Pyrénées, the Tyrol and Turkey, is also available. Ask for the Sherpa catalog when requesting other literature from: **Himalayan Travel, Inc., P.O. Box 481, Greenwich, CT 06836 (phone 203/622-6777, or toll free 800/225-2380 outside Connecticut).**

Wilderness Travel, of Berkeley, California, is the price competitor to Himalayan Travel, offering similar treks (including those to Nepal and the Alps), but with a much greater emphasis on the mountain areas of South America, to which more than a quarter of its passengers go. Both founders of Wilderness Travel have spent considerable time in Peru and the Patagonian region of Argentina and Chile; fittingly, the company's 24-day Patagonia Expedition is a highlight of all trekking programs. Impressive, too, is the expertise and experience of Wilderness's tour leaders, many with Peace Corps backgrounds or graduate degrees in the destinations of the treks. For interesting literature, contact **Wilderness Travel, 801 Allston Way, Berkeley, CA 94710 (phone 415/548-0420, or toll free 800/247-6700 outside California).**

Mountain Travel, of Albany, California, is the largest and oldest of the companies, operating an extraordinary variety of treks on at least five continents. Called "deluxe" by its competitors, its rates—in my reading of them—are only slightly above the industry level: an average of $80 a day in Nepal, from $80 to $150 a day in other mountain regions (plus air fare, of course). Those other areas include India, Peru, Bolivia, Patagonia, Turkey, and Tibet. Like all trekking companies, Mountain Travel provides the tents, foam sleeping pads, and cooking gear; you provide the sleeping bag. For free, four-color literature, contact **Mountain Travel, 6420 Fairmount Ave., El Cerrito, CA 94530 (phone toll free 800/227-2384),** but for the fully unabridged, 105-page Mountain Travel catalog, add $5 (which includes postage and handling).

Journeys, of Ann Arbor, Michigan, stresses the cross-cultural aspects of a trek to a far greater extent than the adventure-oriented others. It makes an intense effort to bring about meetings between trekkers and the hill people of each area. Even prior to departure, it involves its trekkers in cultural training for the trip, then delivers daily briefings en route and along the trail by speakers ranging from Buddhist monks and naturalists to ordinary villagers (through interpreters). Specialists to Asia, especially Tibet, Nepal, and Ladakh, since 1978, and highly regarded, even by its competitors, Journeys also offers some departures to Latin America, and charges the "going rate." Contact **Journeys, 4011 Jackson Rd., Ann Arbor, MI 48106 (phone 313/665-4407, or toll free 800/255-8735 outside Michigan).**

Above the Clouds Trekking, of Worcester, Massachusetts, is still another small company whose strong suit is Nepal (and the Andes), with Europe (Transylvanian Alps, Yugoslavia) a strong second. "Everest from the East," using the less-traveled route there, is among its innovative, $70-a-day offerings in Nepal; the "Mountains, Monasteries, and Markets" trek its most popular tour. Like Journeys, the company stresses cross-cultural lessons, and designs its treks to maximize contacts with local residents. For brochures, contact **Above the Clouds Trekking, P.O. Box 398, Worcester, MA 01602 (phone 508/799-4499, or toll free 800/233-4499 outside Massachusetts).**

Trekking! Is this not the ultimate trip, the answer to the vapid vacation, the plastic "package," the madding throng? "When you have to walk six days to a village," a trekker once told me, "you can be pretty sure it is unspoiled by tourism." ≈

A Search for Reliable Sources of Bicycle Tours

A Dozen Companies That Take You Biking to All Parts of the World

Franklin Roosevelt did it in his youth, gliding for weeks along the country roads of Switzerland and Germany in the course of an enchanted summer.

John F. Kennedy, Jr., did it several years ago, on vacation from prep school. And so have many more from other wealthy, or at least moderately well-off, families.

On the lanes and roads of rural France, on the always-level pavements of cycle-loving Holland, over the softly rolling hills of Vermont, in Oregon, and even in Hawaii, increasing numbers of Americans—of ever-increasing age—are flocking to the group bicycle tour.

But why is the activity so expensive—often $100 and $110 a day? Why are bicycle tours more costly, on occasion, than tours by escorted motorcoach? After all, it is you and your two legs that provide the transportation, eliminating a costly vehicle.

Or is that the case?

What most of us fail to consider, in scanning the bicycle brochures, is that a vehicle almost always does accompany the group, to carry luggage. Unless you've opted for the most rugged form of tour, carrying nothing but your cycling costume, a van or truck and a paid driver follow the bicycling tour at a discreet distance.

Because that group is usually limited to 20 or so people, the cost of the vehicle and driver is also divided among fewer people than on a 45-seat motorcoach trip. And because this mode of travel appeals to a more limited audience, all other costs—marketing of the tour, scouting the itinerary, escorting the group—are also proportionately higher per person.

Thus bicycle tours, except in rare instances (see below), will continue to cost a hefty sum—but one that's justified by advantages aplenty: the best sort of exercise in the open air, the closeness to nature and contact with rural people, the scenery, and the relief from urban pressures.

But there are pitfalls; they mainly stem from the ease with which underfinanced or inexperienced people can schedule a bicycle tour. Because so many shaky operators flood the mails each year with ill-conceived programs destined to cause trouble, I've sought to ferret out the firms that have made a substantial, long-term commitment to this travel sport. The list is by no means complete; if you know of others, please write to me at the address given in the preface.

Unless otherwise stated, all tours accept members of any age, provide a supply van, and will rent you a bike (for an extra charge) if you haven't brought your own.

Sixteen Bicycle Tour Specialists

Vermont Bicycle Touring, of Bristol, Vermont: The pioneer in country inn cycling, 18 years old, it operates almost wholly in the unspoiled state of Vermont, with its well-maintained and relatively traffic-free roads. The tours of interest to most are five days long, cost an average of $105 a day, and include two high-quality meals daily and lodging in charming country inns, some of luxury standard. A mouthwatering, four-color, 40-page catalog can be had by contacting **Vermont Bicycle Touring, P.O. Box 711, Bristol, VT 05443 (phone 802/453-4811).** There you'll also learn about an experimental new summer trip to England ($1,599 plus air fare for 14 days) and two winter programs to Hawaii and New Zealand. Vermont, however, remains the chief emphasis.

Vermont Country Cyclers, of Waterbury Center, Vermont: The chief competitor to Vermont Bicycle Touring, with similar tour features, prices, and policies, and an excellent catalog. Its five-day tour of the coast of Maine ($100 a day) is a popular addition to its Vermont repertoire, as are several cycling trips to Western Europe and the Caribbean. Contact **Vermont Country Cyclers, P.O. Box 145, Waterbury Center, VT 05677 (phone 802/244-8751).**

Country Cycling Tours, of New York City: A well-established (12 years) operator of bicycle tours through the eastern United States and to Europe. Domestic itineraries are particularly novel, and go "island-hopping" in New England (Martha's Vineyard, Nantucket, Newport), to the horse-and-wine country of northern Virginia, along the eastern shores of Maryland; they also include the unique feature of

transportation from Manhattan to the place where tours start. To Europe, tours go (for two weeks) to the Cotswolds of England, County Donegal in Ireland, the Loire and elsewhere in France. Lodgings are comfortable country inns in the U.S., two-star or three-star hotels in Europe; two meals a day are always included; and tours average $120 a day in both the U.S. and Europe ($105 a day in Ireland), plus air fare. Contact **Country Cycling Tours, 140 W. 83rd St., New York, NY 10024 (phone 212/874-5151).**

Euro-Bike Tours, of DeKalb, Illinois: Well-priced tours of Europe (by the pricey standards of bike touring; about $115 a day, plus air fare), almost all of two weeks' duration. Interesting itineraries (the Dordogne of France, the islands of Scandinavia, Hungary and Austria, the "Romantic Road" of Germany) operated June through early October, on which you receive room, breakfast, and 30% of your dinners, in lodgings ranging from first-class hotels down to intimate inns without private bath. Contact **Euro-Bike Tours, P.O. Box 40, DeKalb, IL 60115 (phone 815/758-8851).**

International Bicycle Tours of Chappaqua, New York: Primarily Holland (though elsewhere in Europe too), for one or two weeks, as organized by a native Amsterdammer, now a longtime resident of the U.S. Tours to Holland include high-quality hotels with breakfast, and three dinners, and cost $850 for one-week tours and $1,200 for two-week tours (not including air fare)—the latter tour works out to about $80 a day, a value. Because the flat terrain of Holland makes cycling easy for even older Americans, some departures are designated for people over the age of 50 only. Contact **International Bicycle Tours, 12 Mid Pl., Chappaqua, NY 10514 (phone 914/238-4576),** and ask, too, about their bike tour to Russia, first time ever (you fly into Warsaw, take a bus to the border, then cycle to Moscow; $1,850 plus air fare for two weeks).

Butterfield & Robinson, of Toronto: A highly elegant (and expensive) company active as well in the United States. Its major bike program is to Europe (France, Italy, England, especially); uses high-quality villas, castles, country homes, and châteaux; includes two meals a day (with minor exceptions) at top restaurants; throws in "wine tastings"; and averages $200 (some tours more, some less) per person per day, not including air fare to Europe. Special student departures cost considerably less. For a 100-page catalog, like a costly picture book, contact **Butterfield & Robinson, 70 Bond St., Suite 300, Toronto, Ontario, Canada M5B 1X3 (phone 416/864-1354, or toll free 800/387-1147 outside Canada).**

Far West Tours International, of Los Angeles: Offers an unusually broad array of European itineraries, on which it uses good, middle-class hotels; supplies two meals a day; and (unlike the practice of most companies) includes the use of a seven-speed Swiss bike for free. Prices average $125 a day, plus air fare. Contact **Far West Tours International, 4551 Glencoe Ave., Suite 205, Marina del Rey, CA 90292 (phone 213/827-8181, or toll free 800/533-1016, 800/648-8827 in California),** and inquire as well about their trips to Southeast Asia (Bangkok and Singapore).

Gerhard's Bicycle Odysseys, of Portland, Oregon: From May through September, two-week tours to Germany and Austria, France, and Norway, at $120 a day, plus air fare. All are personally led by German-born Gerhard Meng, now in his 16th year of bicycle-tour operation. Fine country hotels are used; cyclists receive daily breakfast and almost all dinners. Contact **Gerhard's Bicycle Odysseys, 4949 S.W. Macadam, Portland, OR 97201 (phone 503/223-2402).**

Backroads Bicycle Touring, of San Leandro, California: All-year-round tours of the western states, Baja, California, Hawaii, New Zealand, Tasmania, Bali, and, new in 1989, France and Ireland—all well described in a slick, 50-page free catalog. Groups are of all ages; if seniors find some itineraries too taxing, they can ride in the support van (the aptly named "sag wagon") for part of each day. Tours include three meals daily, plus accommodations in fine inns, and average $120 a day, though some are cheaper. Contact **Backroads Bicycle Touring, P.O. Box 1626-Q406, San Leandro, CA 94577 (phone 415/895-1783).**

Paradise Pedallers, of Charlotte, North Carolina: Two-week and three-week tours of New Zealand, December through March, at the remarkable price of $70 a day (plus round-trip air fare) for inns or motels and two meals a day; and yet a support van accompanies the group, in addition to two experienced guides pedaling alongside. Contact **Paradise Pedallers, P.O. Box 32352, Charlotte, NC 28232 (phone 704/335-8687),** and ask about their new-for-1989 one-week tours of North and South Carolina at the same $70-a-day price.

Arrow to the Sun, of Taylorsville, California: Energetic, exotic tours of Baja California, the central Pacific coast of Mexico, the Yucatán, and the Costa del Sol (in addition to weekend trips through the West), camping out most nights in tents carried in a support van and supplied by the tour operator, and including three meals a day. Prices average $60 a day, plus air fare. Write to **Arrow to the Sun, P.O. Box 115, Taylorsville, CA 95983.**

China Passage / Asia Passage, of Teaneck, New Jersey: Bicycle tours of China, Thailand, and Mongolia, 16 to 24 nights in duration, all inclusive except for lunch and dinner in Hong Kong. Because of the high air fares, included in tour prices, total charges range from $2,200 to $3,900, but actual land costs average about $115 a day. Contact **China Passage / Asia Passage, 168 State St., Teaneck, NJ 07666 (phone 201/837-1400, or toll free 800/247-6475 outside New Jersey).**

Forum Travel International, of Pleasant Hill, California: In Business for 22 years, it claims to be the oldest and largest of America's bicycle operators, but achieves that status in part by representing a number of foreign operators, for which it accepts bookings. Aside from going to all the standard places (it has particularly cheap tours to France), it operates where the others don't: Peru, Kenya, Turkey, Czechoslovakia, New Zealand, Hungary, Sweden, Norway, North Africa, China, Australia, the Caribbean. Almost all tours use quality hotels and provide two meals a day and a support van, and average $80 to $120 a day, plus air fare. Contact **Forum Travel International, 91**

Gregory Lane, Suite 21, Pleasant Hill, CA 94523 (phone 415/671-2900).

Bicycle Africa, of Bellevue, Washington: For a very special type of traveler, full of adventure and insight, this is a program of one-month bicycle tours to either Kenya, Cameroon, or several countries of West Africa, operated throughout the year. Because no traveling van is used, and accommodations are spartan, costs average only $35 to $50 day, including everything except air fare to Africa (around $1,100, round trip, to West Africa; from $1,365 to $1,650 to Kenya and Cameroon respectively). "We journey through cultures, history, landscapes, cuisines, and lifestyles, close enough to touch them," says a spokesperson; "we enjoy this fascinating and diverse continent on a personal level not usually attainable by tourists." And, says a recent participant, "the trip, a month long, is worth four years of college anthropology courses; it was the greatest experience of my life." For detailed information and brochures, contact **Bicycle Africa, International Bicycle Fund, 4247 135th Pl. SE, Bellevue, WA 98006 (phone 206/746-1028).**

The Sierra Club, of San Francisco: Operated by the fierce and powerful environmentalist organization, 400,000 members strong, this is my own personal favorite of all the programs, a nationwide array of one-week to ten-day tours within the United States, on which no "sag wagon" is provided and leaders are unpaid volunteers. Because of that, costs average only $45 to $50 a day, including all lodgings and meals. You provide your own bike and are responsible for its upkeep. Programs run from late spring to early autumn; sample tours are of the "North Carolina Outer Banks" (six days for $285), "Arcadia (Maine) Hike and Bike" (six days for $250), "Cape Cod and Islands" (six days for $310), "Wisconsin Hills and Valleys" (seven days for $345), "Lake Michigan Shorelines" (Michigan and Wisconsin; seven days for $325), "Colonial Virginia" (seven days for $275)— you get the picture. Tours are always planned to allow maximum independence to participants; you are required to reach the destination each evening, but are otherwise free to wander and detour as you like. Pace is vigorous but not agonizing; changes of clothes are carried in panniers attached to hub caps or in handlebar bags; groups are limited to 15 people. For detailed listings, contact the **Sierra Club, 730 Polk St., San Francisco, CA 94109 (phone 415/776-2211),** and send $2 for the yearly, January/February edition of *Sierra,* the club's magazine, which contains a directory listing of all bike tours scheduled for the year.

American Youth Hostels, of Washington, D.C.: The price champion of all the bicycle operators, for people of all ages, its trips average $25 to $35 a day in the U.S., $65 to $75 a day in Europe, including all three meals (cooperatively prepared by the group) daily, but plus air fare to the jumping-off point in the U.S. (air fare to Europe is included in the cost). That's because spartan hostels are used for lodgings, and no van accompanies the group; rather, you balance a knapsack over the rear wheel. Contact **American Youth Hostels, P.O. Box 37613, Washington, DC 20013 (phone 202/783-6161).** ≈

Good News for Devotees of the Meandering Cruise by Freighter

After Declining to a Dangerous Level of Capacity, the Passenger-Carrying Freighter Is on the Rise Again

Typical freighter cabin

Passenger-carrying freighter
Opposite page: *Freighter dining area*

What's up with passenger-carrying freighters? Are they still around? Still a viable vacation possibility for retired Americans with lots of time?

Had those questions been put a year ago, the answer to them might have been a shaky "No." Capping a ten-year decline, the number of such ships sailing from U.S. ports fell to a paltry 45 or so in 1986. The departure from the field of two major cargo lines, Moore McCormack and Delta; the replacement of several older passenger-freighters with newer, all-freight vessels; a spasmodic reluctance by younger cargo executives to bother with passengers—all threatened to end the activity.

Since freighters are limited to a passenger complement of only 12 persons (otherwise they'd be required by law to carry an expensive doctor), the 1986 decline reduced the U.S. openings to fewer than 400 berths a month.

Gradually, you heard less—saw fewer ads and newsletter mentions—about those long, leisurely sails to Durban and Dar es Salaam, to Mombasa and Yokohama. Die-hards fretted and festered on waiting lists for a year and more; others, more desperate, flew to Hamburg, or Gdynia, Poland, to board the few Europe-originating passenger freighters.

Yet suddenly—in 1987—the picture changed. As with a pendulum, a Hegelian counter-reaction, 1987 saw a sharp, upward swing to more than 60 passenger freighters. And 1988 and early '89 still more. A recent, radical mechanization of ship functions has reduced the need for crew, freeing additional cabin space for passengers. A cyclical glut in cargo capacity has forced lines to search for new revenue sources, which can only come from passengers.

Thus the German-owned Columbus Line (phone 212/432-1700) has reentered the field with eight new passenger freighters sailing from both coasts to Australia and New Zealand; the British-owned Pace Line plies the same route with several passenger-adapted ships in 1989.

The Cast Line now carries passengers on a number of vessels from Montreal to Antwerp. Mineral Shipping

You visit exotic, untouristed ports. Time stretches before you, unlimited, unpressured. You have the run of the ship, dine with the ship's officers. You delight in the intimacy of a lengthy, shared experience.

In port

In the lounge

has assigned additional ships to the classic task of "tramp steaming"—wandering the seas like a driven Ahab, dashing here and there as radio messages direct, changing course in mid-Atlantic to pick up containers from South America, diverting them to the west coast of Africa, and providing 12 lucky passengers with the cruise of their lives.

(By freighter tradition, passengers pay for a fixed number of days; if the trip comes in early, they receive a refund; if it takes longer—as it often does—they receive the extra days free.)

Come 1989, we also see the return of the "cargo liner"—freighters deliberately built to carry 90-and-more passengers. The Norwegian-owned Navaran Line will provide us with one such vessel, sailing from the East Coast to South America on a near-regular schedule.

Waiting lists are thus back to a normal six weeks to four and five months. Last-minute berths are increasingly available. Freighter fans are once again full of expectations and plans.

Why such eagerness? Because the activity is incomparable.

You visit exotic, untouristed ports. Time stretches before you, unlimited, unpressured. You dine with ships' officers, have the run of the ship, attend periodic barbecues on deck and biweekly parties, dart into the galley to fix your own sandwich or pour a beer, as the mood hits. You delight in the intimacy of a lengthy, shared, unstructured experience, gathering at night around the VCR and its extensive library of tapes that all the ships now carry.

You incur half the daily cost of the average passenger liner. While benchmark rates are an average of $90 a day, some budget-style ships charge as little as $70 or $80 a day, some overseas-originating freighters as little as $60 a day.

What is asked of you is flexibility (you rarely know exact sailing dates until a week or so ahead) and time: voyages last for 30 days, 45 days, even 70 and 90 days.

Because of that, passengers are invariably in their 60s and early 70s and retired (unless they're professors on sabbatical or writers seeking seclusion—author Alex

Haley sails on three or four freighter cruises each year). Interestingly, most freighter lines have recently raised their maximum age limits from 69 to 79 (and occasionally higher)—a tribute to the increasing vigor of today's senior citizens.

The largest of the passenger/freight companies is the Lykes Line (phone toll free 800/535-1861), with upward of 28 ships in service; Columbus Lines is the next most numerous, with 10 ships. Polish Ocean Lines is among the cheapest ($60 to $85 a day), occasionally sailing from Port Newark.

Sources of Freighter Information

Freighter World Cruises, Inc., of Pasadena, California, is the base of 60-year-old George Henck, an industry pioneer who has personally propelled a number of freighter companies into the passenger business.

He derides the widely held notion that freighter capacity is incapable of meeting the demand. "There is always space around if you don't care where you go," he says. "We can move a person in two weeks. Only when you insist on, say, New Zealand, or hot-weather ports in winter, must you wait three or four months for a ship."

To prove the point, Henck's 26-times-a-year "Freighter Space Advisory," a smartly edited six-page newsletter, devotes itself to photos and descriptions of ships leaving in the next month or two from both U.S. and foreign ports.

The recent show-stopper: a periodic departure from Charleston, sailing to New Orleans, then to Houston, then through the Panama Canal to Sydney, Melbourne, and Brisbane (Australia), from there to three ports in New Zealand, back to the Panama Canal, and finishing in Philadelphia—a full 70 days at sea. Off-season cost (June through September): $5,900 per person, whether single or double, amounting to $84 a day; in high season (October through May), $8,100 single, $7,300 per person in a double.

Contact **Freighter World Cruises, Inc., 180 S. Lake Ave., Suite 335, Pasadena, CA 91101, (phone 818/449-3106),** and send $27 for a one-year subscription to the "Freighter Space Advisory"; the same firm then makes the reservations and handles all details.

Trav L Tips, of Flushing, New York, is the other combination freighter-travel agency/newsletter company, except that its publication, a bimonthly, is a slick and elaborate 32-page magazine (*TravLtips*), devoted not only to "freightering" (through first-person accounts by subscribers of their own recent trips), but to exotic or long-term sailings by ordinary passenger ships—the kind that would appeal to the heavily traveled, sophisticated devotees of freighters.

Currently edited and administered by the 34-year-old son of its founder, the late Ed Kirk, the publication/organization is staffed by several experienced reservationists and other cruise experts.

Send $15 for a one-year subscription (and membership) to **Trav L Tips, 163-07 Depot Rd. (P.O. Box 188), Flushing, NY 11358 (phone 718/939-2400).**

Unlike the first two organizations, the 31-year-old Freighter Travel Club, of Salem, Oregon, makes no reservations, sells no trips or tickets, and simply confines itself to publication of a monthly eight-page (and rather crudely typewritten) newsletter. Send $16 (for a one-year subscription) or $28 (for two years) to **Freighter Travel Club of America, P.O. Box 12693, Salem, OR 97309.**

The larger companies are supplemented by a handful of smaller travel-agency specialists on freighters—usually a single individual—of which **Pearl's Travel Tips, 175 Great Neck Rd., Great Neck, NY 11201 (phone 516/487-8351),** is perhaps best known for long expertise. ≈

The Trend to the Tiny Ship

Increasing Numbers of Vacationers Are Opting for Intimate Vessels Able to Take Them to Secluded Places

Windstar Sail Cruises

On the quays leading to a store-lined main street, a scraggly group of hawkers fidgets nervously as they await the imminent onslaught of 1,400 visitors. At curbside stands bearing English-language signs, they will have short minutes to dispose of their cheap straw hats, their gaudy T-shirts.

As the tenders deposit a regiment of humanity from the giant vessel anchored offshore, noise and confusion erupt. A military band blares away. The first arrivals go dashing to a celebrated perfume shop, while others rush to ranks of foul-smelling tour buses or to stand in line for casino admission.

And that is the scene encountered as many as seven times in a single week by Americans sailing through the Caribbean on certain massive cruise ships. Others, repelled by the urban qualities they traveled so many miles to avoid, are opting for a wholly different sea-going experience, on a "tiny" ship—one that accommodates from 60 to 150 passengers and goes to quiet ports or secluded beaches.

In a backlash from current cruise-ship trends (one line is contemplating construction of a 5,000-passenger behemoth), a market is growing for yacht-like vessels with shallow drafts enabling them to go directly onto palm-lined shores or to small marinas in cozy bays.

Their customers often are an affluent but unpretentious lot who relax on board in shorts and sandals, follow no schedules at all and attend no ship "events" —there aren't any.

Ashore, they dine quietly in the fresh-fish restaurant of a backwater town, or lie reading a paperback novel in a rope hammock, hearing nothing but sea gulls and waves.

Among the "tiny" ships that bring you that form of paradise are:

Windjammer Cruises

Like that cabin boy in *Two Years Before the Mast,* you'll stumble in dazed excitement onto the teakwood decks of an actual ocean schooner with sails—as sleek as a greyhound, but with the tiny, cot-equipped cabins you'd expect on so narrow a vessel.

You have the run of the entire ship: bowsprit, rigging, even crow's nest and at the wheel—and are actually encouraged to help the professional crew with steering the ship. Each day you anchor off a quiet beach or tiny port, to which your lunch is brought by kitchen crew wading through the surf. You live throughout in shorts and sandals, in sheer relaxation or happy camaraderie with like-minded, unpretentious, adventure-seeking people from all over the world who have heard of these renowned ships. They range in size from the "giant" S/V *Fantome* (126 passengers) and S/V *Polynesia* (126 passengers) down to the S/V *Flying Cloud* (80 passengers) and M/S *Yankee Clipper* (66 passengers, a former scientific survey ship equipped with two large sails). You sail through the Grenadines, the exotic Leeward Islands of the Caribbean, the British Virgin Islands, and to other highlights of the West Indies. And you pay only $725 to $850 for a six-day cruise in most cabins, plus air fare from the U.S. ($299 from the East Coast, $399 from the West Coast). For literature, contact **Windjammer Barefoot Cruises, P.O. Box 120, Miami Beach, FL 33119 (phone toll free 800/327-2600, 800/432-3364 in Florida).**

American-Canadian Caribbean Line

Budget-priced cruises of the Caribbean in winter, the inland waterways of Rhode Island, Montréal, and Québec in summer, on yacht-like ships carrying as few as 60 and 70 passengers apiece. Rates range from a low $85 to $165 per person per day, not including air fare to embarkation cities. On each ship, "bow ramps" allow passengers to walk, not climb, from the ship to the most isolated and inviting beaches. For literature, contact **American-Canadian Caribbean Line, Inc., P.O. Box 368, Warren, RI 02885 (phone 401/247-0955, or toll free 800/556-7450 outside Rhode Island).**

Yugoslavian Sailing Yacht

On the 48-passenger *Marco Polo*—a "motor/sail yacht" operated by a crew of 11—you sail in summer along the enchanting Dalmatian coast of Yugoslavia,

A market is growing for yacht-like vessels with shallow drafts enabling them to go directly onto palm-lined shores or to small marinas in cozy bays.

Bow landing in Glacier Bay

Walking ashore at Lamplugh Glacier, Alaska

135

You have the run of the entire ship: bowsprit, rigging, even crow's nest and at the wheel.

Arriving at San Blas Islands

on seven-day cruises costing $95 per person per day, plus air fare to Dubrovnik. For literature or reservations, contact the ship's U.S. representative, **Love Holidays, 15315 Magnolia Blvd., Sherman Oaks, CA 91403 (phone 818/501-6868, or toll free 800/456-5683 outside California).**

Ocean Cruise Lines

On the borderline of bigness, this company's 250-passenger *Ocean Islander* has all the facilities of a much larger ship, but the intimacy of a private yacht. In the summer of 1989 (early May to late September), it will cruise between Venice and Nice, and between Nice and Athens, yet at the surprisingly low rates of as little as $170, an average high of $300, per person per day (plus air fare from the U.S. to Italy). For literature, contact **Ocean Cruise Lines, 1510 S.E. 17th St., Fort Lauderdale, FL 33316 (phone 305/764-5566 in Fort Lauderdale, or toll free 800/556-8850, 800/528-8500 in Florida).**

Exploration Cruises

Largest of the mini-ship fleets, these consist of half a dozen vessels with drafts so shallow that they can take you where the big ships can't. You cruise to such odd and lightly touristed places as Glacier Bay and the magnificent Prince William Sound of Alaska; to Jost Van Dyke, Norman Island, and Virgin Gorda in the Virgin Islands; the Columbia, Snake, and Willamette Rivers of the Pacific Northwest; to Tahaa and Raiatea in the Tahitian Islands.

The line's largest ship, the *Explorer Starship*, carries 220 passengers; but its average-sized vessel—the *Colonial Explorer, Majestic Explorer, Pacific Northwest Explorer, Glacier Bay Explorer*—is limited to 96, 80, or even 64 passengers. Though some of the smaller ships resemble large ferry boats or multideck catamarans, they are wonderfully endowed with modern comforts and generally cost a hefty $285 to $350 per passenger per day, but usually including air fare from the U.S. to their embarkation points. For literature, contact **Exploration Cruise Lines, 1500 Metropolitan Park Building, Olive and Boren Streets, Seattle, WA**

98101 (phone 206/624-8551, or toll free 800/426-0600 outside Washington).

Clipper Cruise Line

Elegant luxury yachts carrying only 100 passengers apiece, the *Newport Clipper* and the *Nantucket Clipper* limit themselves to "American" waters, even in the Caribbean. Winter, they ply the Virgin Islands, visiting such peaceful ports as Cruz Bay in St. John and Christiansted in St. Croix. Spring, they explore the "Colonial South"—the ports and historic coastal cities and islands of Florida and Georgia. Summer, they head farther north, to Yorktown, Annapolis, Chesapeake City, Newport, and Nantucket. For all their exquisite attentions and amenities, prices are not extreme: $200 to $250 per person per day for most cabins, but plus air fare of $150 to $370 for Caribbean departures, $80 to $180 for domestic embarkation points. For literature, contact **Clipper Cruise Line, Windsor Building, 7711 Bonhomme Ave., St. Louis, MO 63105 (phone 314/727-2929, or toll free 800/325-0010 outside Missouri).**

Windstar Sail Cruises

Newest (1987), longest (440 feet), tallest (masts 20 stories tall), and maybe the largest of the world's sailing ships is the *Wind Star,* berthed at the island of Martinique, from which it makes weekly one-week cruises to such magical spots as Mustique, Bequia, Tobago Cay, Palm Island, St. Lucia, and other unlikely ports of call (for the standard ships). It places its passengers in cabins 185 square feet in size, and plies them with every luxury (like impulsively buying 300 pounds of lobster at a native market for consumption at a beach barbecue that day). The total passenger complement is 148, on ships whose sails are directed by computer; the mood is casual elegance, the charge about $300 per person per day—which is not as high as you'd expect for an experience as exclusive as this. A sister ship, the *Wind Song,* sails year round from Tahiti, while still a third vessel of identical size and design, the *Wind Spirit,* sails along the French and Italian Rivieras in summer, the islands of St. Thomas, St. Barts, St.

Maarten, and Virgin Gorda in winter, all for approximately the same rates (which do not, however, include air fare to and from embarkation points). For literature, contact **Windstar Sail Cruises, Ltd., 7205 N.W. 19th St., Suite 1410, Miami, FL 33126 (phone 305/592-8008, toll free 800/341-SAIL outside Florida).**

I have not mentioned the *Sea Goddess* ships of the Cunard Lines because their rates are truly high, and out of reach for the great majority of our readers; nor have I included several vessels whose 500-passenger size disqualifies them from inclusion in this discussion. Here we're interested in proving that "Small Is Beautiful." Viva the smaller ship! ≈

American-Canadian Lines in the Caribbean

VII ≈ ENLARGING YOUR MIND THROUGH STUDY VACATIONS

A Yank at Oxford— or Cambridge (Summer Style)

Short Summer Study Courses at the Great British Universities Offer an Unusual Supplement to the Standard English Holiday

View of Oxford
Opposite page: *Cloister of New College, Oxford*

They are known as "Quads" because they spread between the enclosing wings of a quadrangular building, and they are magical beyond compare—otherworldly and still, their silence challenged only by the chirpings of a thrush, yet the very air within seems to pulse with the joy of human achievement, 800 years of learning. They are the "quads" of the colleges at Oxford and Cambridge, some so old that one built in the 1300s is still known as New College.

Who among us hasn't dreamed of studying there? How many of the most eminent Americans still harbor a secret disappointment over having failed to win a Rhodes Scholarship or some other form of admission to the ancient universities of Britain?

Well, life in this instance affords a second chance (for a week to a month, at least). From late June through early September, most of the major British universities —Oxford and Cambridge among them—offer study courses of one, two, three, four, and six weeks' duration, to overseas visitors of any age, with adults quite definitely preferred. While a summer week or more in the quiet, near-deserted quads isn't quite the opportunity you may have craved in younger days, it provides a memorable communion with these awesome institutions, and a learning experience that has edified and enchanted many discerning visitors before you.

By the end of spring, the undergrads of Oxford and Cambridge, in their abbreviated black cloaks flung over tweedy suits and dresses (you won't be wearing one), have all departed for the beaches and hills; but instruction in summer is by the unvarnished "real thing": eminent dons (teaching masters) who pursue a clipped and no-nonsense approach to learning that contrasts quite refreshingly with some American pedagogy. The mind responds—stretching to accommodate difficult concepts and queries, directly and sometimes brutally put. At night you join your instructors in the always-active pubs of the university towns, enjoying conversation as heady as a glass of good brandy. Though individual tutorials aren't provided to summer students, opportunities abound to continue classroom discussion in less formal settings.

While a summer week or more in the quiet, near-deserted quads isn't quite the opportunity you craved in younger days, it provides a memorable communion with these awesome institutions.

Kings College Chapel, Cambridge

In all other respects the experience is reasonably akin to that of British university life. You live in the temporarily vacated quarters of an Oxford or Cambridge student. You dine at the long, wooden, refectory tables of an Oxford or Cambridge dining hall—though "high table," the elevated realm from which faculty members take their wine-accompanied meals, is normally vacant at these times. You roam the stacks of the historic Bodleian Library of Oxford, browse among ancient tomes in the hush of Cambridge's Pepysian Library, lie on the sunlight-flecked grass as you cope with the heavy reading load that most courses entail.

Curricula

What courses do you pursue? While Shakespeare and other giants of English literature dominate the lists—and attract the greater number of international students—most remaining studies deal with contemporary aspects of British life and institutions: "Political Thought in England," "The English Educational System," "The United Kingdom Economy," "History of English Painting," among a wide selection of others.

The top summer programs are those offered by departments of the two great universities that concern themselves with extension or continuing education. Cambridge's "official" program, the International Summer School, offers the broadest choice of courses and, unlike Oxford, makes no great point of imposing deadlines for application. It operates a first "term" of four weeks in July, a second "term" of two weeks in early August, permits you to take either or both, and charges upward of £725 ($1,232) for the first term and £425 ($722) for the second. Charges include all tuition, a single room in a university residence, the services of a "scout" to clean your room (but not otherwise to wait upon you), and two meals a day (breakfast and dinner) in a soaring Gothic hall of ancient stone. For catalog and application forms, contact **The Director, Board of Extra-Mural Studies, Madingley Hall, Madingley, Cambridge CB3 8AQ (phone 0954-210636)**, and specify your preference among the International Summer School,

Literature Summer School, and Art History Summer School, attended in total by more than 1,500 people each year.

Oxford's "official" summer course is a six-week session from July to mid-August, for which three-week enrollments are also permitted (and heavily chosen by most people attending). Here, all students pursue the single theme of "Britain: Literature, History, and Society from 1870 to the Present Day," vividly presented in an integrated series of more than 50 lectures by noted Oxford academics (including such major "names" as Professors Richard Ellman, A. H. Halsey, Terry Eagleton, and Christopher Ricks). Tuition for the entire six-week term is £1,290 ($2,195) and about half that for three-week sessions, which includes your room (in Exeter College, founded in 1314) and all three meals daily—as well as the occasional invitation to dine at "High Table" with tutors and lecturers. For further information, contact the **Summer School Secretary, Department for External Studies, Rewley House, 1 Wellington Square, Oxford OX1 2JA (phone 0865-270360).** For applications, contact **U.S. Student Programs Division, Institute of International Education, 809 United Nations Plaza, New York, NY 10017 (phone 212/883-8200).**

If the "official" programs are full, or you have only two weeks available for study, you can opt for a number of "unofficial" courses organized by various Oxford and Cambridge dons on a purely private, entrepreneurial basis; the latter simply rent the use of classrooms and lodgings, and announce their own programs, some for durations of as little as two weeks. Typical are the courses offered at Oxford in "Modern British History and Politics" by the so-called Institute for British and Irish Studies; these are given in July and early August, for either two, three, four, or five weeks, intensively from 9 a.m. to 6 p.m., for a cost to you of about $575 a week, including tuition, lodging, all three meals daily, and occasional theater tickets and excursions. Contact the Institute c/o its U.S. representative, **Dr. E. C. Johnson, IBIS, Camford House, Almont, CO 81210 (phone 303/248-0477, or toll free 800/327-4247 outside Colorado),** or call the institute directly in England (phone 011-44-865-270-980 or 011-44-865-248-451, extension 225). Dr. Johnson and the institute (both highly regarded by me) also offer summer courses to adults in history, literature, and international law at Trinity College, Dublin, and University College, London.

No one suggests that courses such as these should be the sole activity of a British vacation; they can be combined, instead, with the most standard sightseeing and recreation. But what an opportunity awaits! The smart traveler seizes the chance, if the chance exists, to experience these hallowed institutions of learning in the manner they deserve: not as casual tourists, but as students, in the endless quest for light. ≈

Punting on the River Cam, Cambridge

Meet the Danish "Folk High School," and Never Be the Same Again

A Winter Week or Two at a Residential College for Adults

New Experimental College, Thisted

We began the day singing. From our places at a table of polished light pine, drenched in the sunlight reflected from a silver fjord, we sang a secular hymn to life and brotherhood, to goodness and sharing. "Would you care to attend my seminar this morning?" asked a young Danish beauty as she passed me a breakfast bowl of peaches and yogurt. "I shall be inviting people from other disciplines to help me over a rough spot in my paper on producer cooperatives."

I was at a Danish folk high school (folkehøjskole), more properly translated as a "peoples college," one of 102 such residential centers of adult education in Denmark, of which two are conducted in English. They represent a massive contribution by Denmark to educational policies emulated all over the world, and they can be visited this coming fall and winter, for stays of as little as one and two weeks, by "intelligent travelers" from the United States and Canada.

Without Tests or Admissions

A "folk high school." The basic characteristics are easy to describe, but infinitely more complex in their application. There are no entrance requirements or admission exams; hence "folk" (meaning open to all). Students are adults, of post-school age (hence "high school," the term used sensibly, without the unfortunate meanings we Americans ascribe to the words). The schools are residential, and thus radically different from those attended on adult education programs in other lands. Folk high school theorists believe that adults, throughout their lives, should periodically wrench themselves from familiar routines and accustomed settings to go live in a rural residential college with their fellow citizens of all income classes, in a spirit of equality. In Denmark a full 20% of the current population has passed through a folk high school at least once.

Within the schools there are no tests, no final examinations, no certificates or degrees awarded. Learning is for the sheer love of learning. Students and teachers are equals. They are collaborators in the quest for learning. Though teachers initiate some discussions, they quickly cede to their students, and allow inquiries to develop as they naturally do. "It is not the teachers who ask their students questions," explains one folk high school principal, "but the students who interrogate their teachers."

The focus is always on discussions, oral presentations, lively seminars in which students confront their preconceptions and prejudices, their inner and often unexamined beliefs. A goal is to achieve democratic communication between persons of widely divergent backgrounds. Another goal is to tap creative talents lying hidden or subordinated to the harsh realities of earning a living. A Danish farmer with gnarled hands checks into a folk high school near Aalborg, for one month; there he applies himself to easel and canvas, determined to give vent to a hitherto-submerged artistic urge. An operating-room nurse positions herself at a desk near a window looking out onto vistas such as Ibsen might have seen and patiently begins writing a play. While pursuing a thousand different educative tasks, students rediscover their better selves, delight in their nationhood, experience maturation. They study not a single practical subject, but return instead to the liberal arts: poetry, philosophy, history, music. "What did you get out of it?" was the challenge posed to an American businessman completing a two-week stint at one of the two English-language folk high schools. "I got absolutely nothing out of it," he replied, "but I left with my spiritual batteries recharged."

Some observers credit the high Scandinavian regard for law and various forms of community cooperation—including the vaunted Scandinavian cooperative movement itself—to the 140-year-old tradition of the folk high school.

One Is More Traditional

Of the two English-language folk high schools in Denmark, one is very much in that tradition, while the other has passed light-years beyond even the radical formlessness of most schools. The "traditional" establishment is the International Peoples College (Den Internationale Højskole) at Elsinore, an hour by train from Copenhagen, in a Scandinavian-modern complex

They are a massive contribution by Denmark to educational policies emulated all over the world, and can be visited for periods of as little as one or two weeks by travelers of all ages.

Library of the New Experimental College

International Peoples College, Elsinore

Folk high school theorists believe that adults, throughout their lives, should periodically wrench themselves from familiar routines to go live in a rural residential college.

Lodgings at the New Experimental College

of low, glass-sided buildings on expansive grounds. Recognized (and subsidized) by the Danish government, it earns that support by officially offering 26 one-hour classes a week and by publishing a printed, purported curriculum of subjects ("alternative societies," "comparative religion," "life in the Third World"), but there all resemblance to the usual college ends. New subjects spring spontaneously to life, wholly unplanned subject matter grips the imagination of a particular term, while students rush to complete projects and papers that they themselves have conceived. Drawing its student body half from English-speaking Danes, half from other widely scattered nations; employing as "faculty" (read: fellow students) a Greek sociologist, a Ugandan lawyer in exile from successive regimes, an Australian poet, an Indian playwright—some without actual academic credentials—the school shimmers with international vitality, excites even the casual visitor. Tuition, reduced by government grants, runs to all of $158 per week, including all three meals each day and lodging in single rooms.

While most students attend the International Peoples College for periods of four months and more in the fall/winter season, reserving short courses for the summer, the school will occasionally accept three-week and four-week students in winter, if space exists, and particularly if they start near the January 27 opening of a winter term. Address your applications to the white-bearded, cigar-smoking, prominent Danish educator, Eric Hojsbro-Holm, who heads the school. He's a notorious "softie" about making a place available for American adults anxious to attend, if only for a fortnight or so. Contact **Den Internationale Højskole, Montebello Alle 1, Elsinore 3000, Denmark (phone 45-02-213-361).**

The competing, English-language folk high school has no problem at all in accepting short-term students. The New Experimental College (NEC) will eagerly clasp you to its side at any time of the winter, for as little as one, two, or three weeks, and regardless of whether it has on-premises sleeping space still available for you; if it doesn't, it will board you at nearby, comfortable farmhouses or at modern hotels less than ten kilometers away.

The Other Far More Radical

So radical in approach as to lack recognition and subsidy from even the permissive Danish government, NEC is still a highly regarded institution lauded by such celebrated educators as Harold Taylor and Paul Goodman. Yoko Ono and the late John Lennon are among its "graduates." Located at the crest of a gentle hill overlooking a Danish fjord at the northern tip of the Jutland peninsula, it enjoys an enthralling setting supplemented by the comforts of a sprawling Danish farmhouse capable of housing about 38 students. Because of its lack of subsidy, it charges $171 a week for those able to pay, for tuition, room, board, evening sauna, and assignment to a sleep-inducing, overstuffed leather chair in an extensive, quiet library sprinkled with U.N. publications, among its other resources.

At NEC there are no regular or recurring classes at all, not even an initial published curriculum. There are, in fact, no paid faculty members, no "teachers" at all. Every individual pursues his or her study interests, without interference or outside influence, the only element of discipline being the requirement to report, at a Saturday morning meeting, on what they have done the preceding week. If students should feel an earlier need for reporting their results to others, or obtaining comments from them, they "announce" a class or seminar, which they then present, and which others are free to attend or not, as they see fit. They select their own educational goals, define their own education, conduct a raging inner battle, award their own "certificate of completion" to themselves. In effect, they commence a lifelong process of continually discovering what it is they wish to learn and how to go about doing so. They learn best, according to NEC, when that discovery is their own.

Throughout this process of self-realization, akin almost to a self-analysis, NEC remains almost coldly neutral. When outsiders "ask the question 'but what do you do there—what do people learn?'" writes founder Aage Rosendal-Nielsen, 65, "we take our

stand and . . . simply refuse to answer the question."

There is still social interaction. You, as a scholar/student, attend the seminars so continually announced by others. You participate in the *ting*—a Scandinavian-style town hall frequently invoked to pose a general question to the assemblage; anyone can call a ting. At a Friday-evening "celebration meal," you dress for a special candlelight meal at which volunteers deliver speeches on their work or thoughts. You converse on walks into the heather-covered hills. And occasionally at night you relax within a sometimes-coed sauna so hot as if almost symbolically to burn away the inhibitions, unthinking patterns, communications barriers, or narrow provincial attitudes with which you entered NEC.

To attend the NEC at any time of the year, but especially in winter, and for as little as a week or two, write to **New Experimental College, Skyum Bjerge, Thy, 7752 Snedsted, Denmark (phone 45-7-936234).** The school is reached from the airports of either Thisted or Ålborg, 50 or so minutes by S.A.S. jet from Copenhagen, or 6½ hours by train from Copenhagen's central station. You will never be the same again—and isn't that the hallmark of intelligent travel? ≈

Class at the New Experimental College

147

Low-Cost Language Schools Abroad

The Careful Use of Travel to Acquire Fluency in a Foreign Tongue

Language class in Salamanca, Spain

"**O**f course you don't get our business! Of course we don't send you our orders! You don't speak our language!"

Such words of reproach from a normally courteous European surprised even the speaker, stirred some long-smouldering resentment, led to further indictment.

"It isn't that we're asking you to engage in technical discussions with us. But at a simple dinner party you can't carry on the most routine conversation with the lady on your left. You Americans take the cake!"

Why, among all the achievers of the world, do the overwhelming number of Americans fail to possess a second language? Or a third?

Sheer indolence is a first explanation. Torpor. Thoughtless indifference, largely stemming from unpleasant, subconscious memories of uninspiring language courses at ol' State U. Mistaken smugness ("they all speak English"). And failure to make the proper use of travel opportunities. Since languages can be acquired with surprising ease in situations where you are "immersed" in them, the mere decision to travel *solo,* unaccompanied by English-speaking spouse or companion, can yield the most remarkable results. When that vacation trip is further pursued at a European language school, in an off-season period when the tourists have fled and all you hear is one foreign language, at breakfast and in classes, on television and at the movies, in restaurants and bars, one language unendingly—the results are astonishing indeed. You speak!

This fall and winter a great many bright Americans will enhance their cultural perspectives, careers, and lives by pursuing short language courses overseas, partially funded by European governments. They will achieve fluency, or near-fluency, in one of the four major European tongues—French, Spanish, German, or Italian—at schools whose glorious traditions, European settings, and remarkably low costs provide the greatest of travel pleasures in addition to instruction.

Most of the schools share common features, of which the most important is the timing of one-month classes to begin near the first of each month; schedule your applications and arrivals accordingly. Most will provide you with lodgings in the homes of private families, where you'll again be immersed in the local language. State-operated schools are usually considerably cheaper than private ones, without a loss of quality or intensity. Schools in secondary cities will send you to cheaper accommodations than those in famous ones: thus the families with whom you'll stay in Perugia will charge a third of what you'll pay in Florence.

You choose from the following:

For French

Ancestor to all the great European language schools, founded in 1883 to advance French culture and the French language to all the world, is the powerful Alliance Française. Directly funded (in part) by the French Foreign Ministry, it operates low-cost French-language schools in more than 100 nations, but its soul remains in a great gray building on Paris's Left Bank, at 101 Boulevard Raspail, steps away from the trendy cafés, art galleries, and way-out boutiques of the busier Boulevard St. Germain.

In the large stone courtyard of the giant school, teeming with Egyptian caftans, African turbans, Canadian blue jeans, the atmosphere may be international but only one language is spoken: French. And French is spoken at every moment and exclusively throughout the day, in the very first class you attend, in the on-premises cafeteria where you take your meals, at theatrical performances and lectures in the school's auditorium. You are in class at least 3½ hours a day, then in earphone-equipped language laboratories for supplemental practice, then at near-mandatory social events—yet you pay only 480 francs ($75) a week, quite obviously subsidized, for all tuition—and house yourself in any of dozens of inexpensive Left Bank hotels clustered in this section of the Latin Quarter; there, too, you hear and speak French exclusively.

Alliance Française classes must be taken for a minimum of four weeks, starting at the beginning of each month, and application should be made at least a month in advance. For further information and forms,

write: **Alliance Française de Paris, 101 Boulevard Raspail, 75270 Paris CEDEX 06, France.**

For Italian

Choosing from a score of major, Italy-based, Italian-language schools, the clear consensus of the experts (I've spoken with three) favors the state-operated University for Foreigners of Perugia (Università Italiana per Stranieri) and the Cultural Center for Foreigners of Florence (Centro Culturale per Stranieri). Both are in that broad region of Italy (Tuscany and Umbria) where the purest form of Italian is said to be spoken.

At Perugia, an Intensive Preparatory Course (5½ hours of classroom instruction a day, of which 2 hours are devoted to conversation and language laboratories) is priced at only 400,000 lire ($320) for a month—$80 a week. A normal beginner's course (4 hours a day), for either one, two, or three months, costs only 150,000 lire ($107) per month. Compare those rates to what you'd pay to a private language school at home!

Non-intensive courses start every two weeks, and may be taken for as little as a month. Students attend classes in a vast, baroque-style palazzo, stay with Italian families in private homes ($110 a month), and take their meals ($1.25 apiece) in one of two University of Perugia canteens. Weekends, they journey for culture and conversation to nearby Assisi, Orvieto, Spoleto.

At the more leisurely Florence school, where classroom time occupies only 2½ hours a day, but is supplemented with homework and language labs, courses run for ten weeks, start at regular quarterly intervals, and cost 350,000 lire ($250) for the entire term, independent of room-and-board costs. If you're fixed on Florence but can't stay ten weeks, or can't get into the official school, try the one-month, four-hour-a-day sessions of the prestigious-but-private (and costlier) Dante Alighieri Society ($250 a month, not including room and board).

Write for information and/or application forms to: **Università Italiana per Stranieri, Palazzo Gallenga, 4 Piazza Fortebraccio, 06100 Perugia, Italy; Centro Culturale per Stranieri, Università**

The brightest of travelers achieve fluency, or near-fluency, in one of the four major European languages at schools whose glorious traditions, settings, and remarkably low costs provide the greatest of travel pleasures in addition to instruction.

Salminter School, Salamanca

degli Studi, 64 Via Vittorio Emanuele, 50134 Florence, Italy; or **Società Dante Alighieri, 4 Via Gino Capponi, 50121 Florence, Italy.**

And for a list of additional language schools in other Italian cities, contact the **Italian Cultural Institute, 686 Park Ave., New York, NY 10021 (phone 212/879-4242),** or one of their branch offices: in Chicago at **500 N. Michigan Ave., Suite 530, Chicago, IL 60611 (phone 312/822-9545);** in Los Angeles at **12400 Wilshire Blvd., Suite 310, Los Angeles, CA 90025 (phone 213/207-4737).**

For German

The influential world role of German commerce and culture (one out of every ten books on earth is published in German) lends continuing importance to German language study. West Germany's own government provides heavily subsidized instruction via its Goethe Institutes, of which more than 100 are found in 60 countries, and 13 are maintained in Germany itself. The latter are marvelously diverse, in both large cities (Munich, Berlin), university towns (Göttingen, Mannheim), and idyllic countryside locations (Prien and Murnau in rural Bavaria).

If you've the time for an eight-week course, you can make your own selection of a Goethe Institute (and city) from the 13 available. Busier people able to devote only four weeks to it are confined to three locations: Rothenburg-ob-der-Tauber (that perfectly preserved medieval village on the "Romantic Road" near Nuremberg, from June through January), Prien (an hour from Munich, December through March only), and Boppard (in the Valley of the Lorelei, along the Rhine, from February through May).

In each you are given 24 hours a week of classroom instruction, supplemented by at least 10 hours a week of private study, and additional sessions of conversation with German residents dragooned in for the purpose. Each institute makes all the arrangements for your room and board with a private family, and charges a total for the entire month—tuition, materials, room, and board—of 2,060 marks (approximately $1,100).

For further information and application forms,

contact **Goethe House, 1014 Fifth Ave., New York, NY 10028 (phone 212/744-8310).** The U.S.-based branch will then forward your completed form to the Goethe Institute you've selected.

For Spanish

Salamanca is the place. Emphatically. Without a second thought. It is the heart of Old Castile, where Spanish is noble and pure, untainted by the Gallego accents of the northwest, the Catalán of the east, the assorted dialects of the south.

Its monumental University of Salamanca (dating from 1226) is one of the world's oldest. Together with similar medieval academies in Padua and Bologna, it developed an early tradition for attracting international students, and that reputation—even stronger today— has a wholesome impact on language studies there. Because students are from dozens of countries scattered from Japan to Yemen, the only common language among them is Spanish. You either speak it or suffer muteness.

Though Salamanca is only 2½ hours from Madrid, it is no Madrid in cost: $14 a day is more than enough for room and all three meals at scores of guest-accepting private homes. And tuition at the private language schools is as low as the University of Salamanca's, enabling you to study one-on-one with your teacher, or in small groups of seven or eight, for as little as you'd pay elsewhere in a class of 20. I like, for that reason, an intensely personal school called Salminter (Escuela Salmantina de Estudios Internacionales), which charges only $250 per month for four hours of instruction, five days a week.

Dominant among the other, all-year-round, private schools is the Colegio de España, whose intensive four-week course starting at the beginning of every month (four hours daily, in classes limited to 15 students) costs a remarkable 22,500 pesetas ($195) a month, to which you add about $80 a week for room and board. Weekends, its students travel by short bus rides to Ávila, Segovia, and Valladolid, though the older adults among them (like me on previous trips) scarcely budge from a sidewalk café seat on the historic

Plaza Mayor—barred to traffic, and like a baroque drawing room, except out-of-doors. Churches and museums with the next-equivalent of Goyas, Velázquezes, and El Grecos are short steps away.

When people ask why I don't prefer the more accessible Spanish-language schools of Mexico to those of Spain, I answer diplomatically that Mexico is Mexico, but Spain is . . . well, Spain.

For applications or further information on the Salminter school, write to its U.S. representative, **Elisabeth Nebehay, 251 E. 32nd St., New York, NY 10016 (phone 212/689-2636),** or directly to **Salminter, Apartado de Correo 575, Salamanca, Spain (phone 011-34-23-211-808).** For the larger Colegio, write to: **Colegio de España, 65 Calle Compañía, 37008 Salamanca, Spain (phone 011-34-23-214-788).** ≈

Conversation class, Salamanca

151

The Love Boat and the Learn Boat

Expedition Cruising Brings Education to the High Seas

Ashore in Bulgaria

Opposite page: *Ashore at Jeronymos Monastery, Lisbon*

You step aboard to the strains of Vivaldi and search in vain for a single casino. At night you amuse yourself not in a seagoing cabaret, but in that long-forgotten art of serious conversation with fellow passengers, over a brandy in a relaxing lounge. If a film is shown, it's of exotic tribespeople in an actual setting or of humpbacked whales off the Patagonian fjords.

And when you retire to cabin or bunk, you're first handed a half-hour's reading for the day ahead.

You've heard of the "Love Boat." Now meet the "Learn Boat." Though it may seem like a contradiction in terms, the combination of cruising and education is creating a potent new vacation lure for thousands of intellectually curious Americans.

Every week nearly a dozen small ships—and their number seems to be growing—depart from Mediterranean, Central and South American, and South Pacific ports on so-called expedition cruises staffed by naturalists, anthropologists, and cultural historians.

The major programs are three in number:

Swan Hellenic Cruises

Cheapest of the lot—a remarkable value—are two-week cruises of the eastern Mediterranean aboard the 300-passenger M.T.S. *Orpheus,* operated continuously from mid-March to late November each year by the distinguished Swan Hellenic organization of the venerable P & O Lines of Britain.

Here you look in depth at the origins of the Greco-Christian-Judaic civilization, accompanied at all times by a minimum of four—often as many as five—British university lecturers, museum people, clergy, and authors. The dean of Merton College, Oxford, frequently lectures on board and ashore. So do several professors of ancient history at Cambridge, the archeology editor of *The Illustrated London News,* a former dean of Salisbury Cathedral, a director of the Imperial War Museum.

"I so treasured our afternoon at Ephesus," wrote one passenger, "because as we sat in the theater, the guest lecturer read to us from Acts 19 and instantly brought alive the story of the silversmiths who demonstrated

They depart from Mediterranean, South American, and South Pacific ports, staffed by naturalists, anthropologists, and cultural historians.

Tower of the Winds, Athens

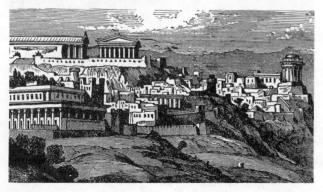

against St. Paul in defense of their livelihood—the making of idols to the goddess Diana."

For such a profound combination of cultural discovery and water-borne pleasures, 16 days in length, you pay a total of $3,900 (in the bulk of cabins), which includes round-trip air fare between several U.S. East Coast cities and London ($190 more from the West Coast), and round-trip air between London and either Athens, Thessaloniki, Venice, or Dubrovnik, from which the ship departs. You're put up for two nights at a first-class hotel in London (one night before the cruise, one night after), and then cruise for a full 14 nights to the "isles of Greece," the coasts of Turkey, Yugoslavia, Bulgaria. The trip is so very all-inclusive—such a splended example of the refreshing British insistence on moderate travel costs—that even the daily shore excursions (with their eminent lecturers) are thrown in at no extra charge.

Swan Hellenic Cruises are represented in the U.S. by **Esplanade Tours, 581 Boylston St., Boston, MA 02116 (phone 617/266-7465), or toll free 800/426-5492 outside Massachusetts).** Contact them for a fascinating catalogue.

Society Expeditions

Now you're on voyages of daring (but deluxe) exploration and discovery, into the most mysterious and remote regions of the earth: the islands of Micronesia, Borneo, Indonesia, and the Northwest Passage, the Antarctic, the Amazon and the Aleutians.

On a Society Expedition, the bent is distinctly naturalistic or anthropological, far less historical or archeological than the themes of Swan Hellenic. You visit untouristed shores, not ports, making landfall on motorized rubber landing boats called "Zodiacs."

Thus conveyed, you go to otherwise inaccessible villages or riverbanks, where at night the beat of a shaman's drum raises appeals to ancestral spirits. You walk among upright penguins gathered by the hundreds on a shore of the Falklands. You meet and interact with Amazonian natives. To avoid "polluting" their natural or cultural life, your visits are scheduled for widely scattered dates.

The trips are realized aboard two luxuriously fitted ships: the 140-passenger *World Discoverer* and the 100-passenger *Society Explorer,* both large vessels, but with the shallow drafts, specially ice-hardened hulls, and bow-thrusters required for expedition cruising.

Each voyage is accompanied by a team of naturalists, marine biologists, and (sometimes) anthropologists. You sail with the likes of Dr. Johan Reinhard, noted anthropologist; Peter Harrison, who has won international acclaim with his books on sea birds; or Frank Todd, senior research fellow at Hubbs Sea World Research Institute.

Both ships go circumnavigating the globe, on different itineraries, throughout the year. Passengers, essentially, book segments of the voyage—usually from two to several weeks—and are flown to and from ports at both ends of the segment. Costs average $300 a day for the bulk of cabins and trips.

For a set of mouthwatering, award-winning, large, glossy brochures, contact **Society Expeditions, 3131 Elliott Ave., Suite 700, Seattle, WA 98121 (phone 206/285-9400, or toll free 800/426-7794 outside Washington).**

Salen-Lindblad Cruising, Inc.

This final firm operates the smallest of expedition ships, some carrying as few as 36 passengers. An example, and its major pride, is the twin-hulled *Kimberley Explorer,* with an astonishing draft of only five feet, enabling it to cruise inlets of the world's last frontier: the virtually unsettled Kimberley Coast of Australia. A trip lasts 17 or 21 days, of which 13 are spent on ship and the remainder in various major Australian cities; departs once a month from January through December; and is led by naturalist Tom Richie, aided by an expert on Australia's aborigine population, who precedes your party ashore, equipped with walkie-talkie, to arrange meetings with these proud and capable people. Cost, including round-trip air from Los Angeles, meals, shore excursions, and all else, averages $4,800 for 17-day trips, $5,400 for 21 days.

Other year-round programs of Salen-Lindblad: To West Africa and New Guinea; to Indonesian waters, embarking from Djakarta on a 36-passenger luxury catamaran yacht (world-renowned divers and naturalists accompany you); and to the Galápagos Islands (a specialty). Seasonal programs: along the Volga River of the USSR, and to the North Cape of Norway. For brochures, contact **Salen-Lindblad Cruising, Inc., 133 E. 55th St., New York, NY 10022 (phone 212/751-2300 or toll free 800/223-5688).**

So what will it be, the "Love Boat" or the "Learn Boat," the libido or learning? Some say that expedition cruising allows the best of both. ≈

M.S. Society Explorer

VIII
VACATIONING FOR HEALTH, AT A MEDICALLY SUPERVISED RESORT

It's Smart to Vacation at a Reducing Center

Our Own Durham, North Carolina—"Fat City"—Has Become Dieting Capital of the World

Low-impact aerobics at DFC

Student meals at the DFC
Opposite page: "Portion control" at Duke Diet and Fitness Center

We felt a bit sheepish as we entered the steak-house, carrying our tiny scales and concealed measuring cups.

But we needn't have worried. Here in Durham, North Carolina, dieting capital of the world, people are used to the sight of overweight visitors on a "dining out experience." Every week of the year, hundreds of reducers from across the country are in attendance at five different nutrition/exercise schools in this key southern hub, with its equable climate and accessible location.

Some come because they are seriously obese, and with associated illnesses; others simply to devote their vacation time to the loss of 10 or 15 pounds of excess weight. And why not? What better use of leisure than to improve one's health?

At the Mecca of Fat

I arrived in winter, flying from the February storms and sub-zero chills of the Northeast, into the brisk but spring-like weather of the Raleigh/Durham Airport, which is fast becoming a major destination for more and more airlines (American, Piedmont, others).

By the time I left six days later, I had lost seven pounds. But more important, I had gained lessons of nutrition that dozens of earlier diet books and articles had always failed to drive home. Durham's success, in my view, results from the unique quality of a residential dieting experience, in which one is wrenched from normal routines, isolated from family pressures, and forced to reflect, without distraction, upon a lifetime of thoughtless and destructive eating habits.

While most short-term "fat farms" and fad diets have an overwhelming record of recidivism—people quickly regain the weight they've lost—some of Durham's establishments claim a 70% record of "wins": patients, upon returning home, either maintain their weight loss or continue to drop additional pounds.

That's probably because most of the Durham centers preach the use of a balanced assortment of popular foods, close in taste and appearance to the

average American diet, but prepared without harmful fats and saturated oils, and served in moderate—but filling—portions. Though most Durham programs restrict their patients to a daily intake of only 750 calories over the two-week to four-week duration of their stays (a quantity of food that, to my surprise, proved entirely adequate and caused no great discomfort), their aim is to prepare the student for resumption of a far more normal, but properly chosen, 1200- to 1500-calorie diet upon returning home.

The lesson is taught in a hard, daily round of classroom lectures, seminars, laboratory workshops, and one-on-one counsultations.

My own "rehabilitation" occurred at what may well be the largest of the Durham schools, Duke University's Diet and Fitness Center ("DFC"), where my fellow students, among others, ranged from a seriously overweight minister of the Gospel, to a portly legal aid lawyer, to an only slightly pudgy drama teacher from a midwestern high school. Despite the wide diversity of weights and backgrounds, there emerged a touching camaraderie among us, sensitive and supportive. Though we joked about food, we knew the depth of commitment on each one's part to break harmful eating habits.

At night we drove with one another to various Durham movies so that we could fill the hours between dinner and bed, but unaided there by a single kernel of popcorn, let alone the buttered kind. One afternoon and evening we ourselves planned and prepared a festive, calorie-conscious banquet. Accompanied by a nutritionist, we shopped at a supermarket, bought only the healthiest of ingredients, cooked the meal in one of Duke's well-equipped kitchens, and then consumed it—blackened redfish, baked potato, a Caesar salad without a single yolk, an exquisite Key lime parfait of skim milk, egg whites, and sugarless pudding—at candlelit tables.

Daytimes, we flocked to the gym for low-impact aerobics, later in the day to a heated pool for water aerobics. We walked and cycled, played hilarious games of volleyball, memorized calorie-counts in our moments of rest. One memorable night we had our restaurant experience and learned how to cope with the realities outside our diet center. But mostly we went to class after class, consultation after consultation, with nutritionists, behavioral psychologists, and fitness experts.

Five Centers

All this costs considerably less than a trendy spa (the cheaper ones are usually $1,300 a week) or a Pritikin Longevity Center (the two most prominent charge $8,000 single, $6,000 per person double, for a month). At Duke's DFC, the fee even for single patients is $2,500 for two weeks, only $3,000 for four weeks, and covers everything except lodging: meals, exercise, complex medical and psychological evaluations, swimming and gym work, classroom lectures, seminars, and workshops. Most participants then stay in a $40-a-night, one-bedroom apartment in Duke Towers (a comfortable, modern, but low-rise hotel) across the road, or in a number of cheaper (as little as $400 a month) nearby motels (and one large B&B house) recommended by the DFC. For brochures and application forms, contact **Duke University Diet and Fitness Center, 804 W. Trinity Ave., Durham, NC 27701 (phone 919/684-6331).**

Space doesn't permit a lengthy discussion of Durham's several other diet centers. Structure House follows much the same approach as at the DFC, but with a far greater emphasis on behavioral and psychological counseling, and is nearly the same size. It maintains its own lodgings on its own impressive grounds and rarely permits its patients to live "off campus." Guests may stay from one to eight weeks, and total charges, including lodging, run $1,500 for one week, $2,500 for two weeks, $3,600 for four weeks, to cite but a few examples. Contact **Structure House, 3017 Pickett Rd., Durham, NC 27705 (phone 919/688-7379).**

The Stuelke Institute, still another major center, regards overeating as an addiction, and treats it in much the same manner as Alcoholics Anonymous deals with drinking. It advises a four-week stay, but occasionally accepts you for two or three weeks. Guests stay on a 700-calorie daily diet, served in a private dining room at the large Imperial Motel, where they also live; total charges, including lodging, run to approximately $2,300 for three weeks, $2,600 for four weeks. Contact **The Stuelke Institute, P.O. Box 2894, Durham, NC 27705 (phone 919/683-5547).**

DUPAC (Duke University's Preventive Approach to Cardiology) emphasizes cardiovascular fitness, gained through diet and exercise, with weight loss simply an added dividend. It is visited, in roughly equal portions, either for preventive purposes or following an actual heart attack. And it requires a four-week stay. Four-week charges for meals, exercises, medical tests, and supervision amount to approximately $2,000; but participants provide their own lodging, which most do by staying either at the Duke Motor Lodge, the Durham Sheraton, the Brownstone Inn, the Campus Oaks Apartments, still others. Contact **DUPAC, Finch-Yeager Bldg., Box 3022, Duke University Medical Center, Durham, NC 27710 (phone 919/681-6974).**

Rice House (the Kempner Clinic), in a modest white frame residence, prescribes a far more radical regimen than the other four (initially, simply rice and fruit), provides little behavioral counseling or fitness exercises, and is primarily for seriously ill or seriously obese persons who need to lose weight fast and massively. Although administrators of several other diet centers disagree with its approach, they always speak of it with great respect; but a stay there, in my opinion, is to be prescribed only by your physician.

Rice House is administered from the more elaborate offices of the **Kempner Clinic, Box 3099, Duke University Medical Center, Durham, NC 27710 (phone 919/684-3418),** where patients undergo an exhaustive, initial checkup ($1,000 to $1,500). After that, they pay about $1,100 per month for continual medical evaluations, lab tests, and those three—spartan—daily meals at the modest Rice House. The program is apparently based on the belief that modifications to the normal American diet—the goal of the other centers—are not sufficient, but rather a wholly new and healthier diet (low salt, low protein) must be

substituted; and people need also to be taught to eat far less.

As for me, I'll stick with the more moderate adjustments to the typical American diet prescribed by DFC; they seem capable of being sustained after you have returned home from Durham—and isn't that the point?

Bear in mind that some dieters simply check into a low-cost motel in Durham for a week or two, without entering a center, and take their meals at the several Durham restaurants that now cater to them and cook in fat-free, low-calorie style. One such is that of the **Triangle 400 Motor Inn, 605 W. Chapel Hill St. (phone 919/687-4666).** ≈

Water aerobics at DFC

On the Trail of Eternal Youth, at a European Spa

Can 200 Million Europeans Be Wrong? Or Is There Validity to the Treatments at European Health Resorts?

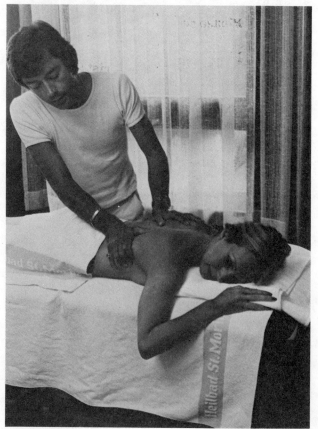

At Heilbad, St. Moritz

As I lowered my limbs into that unheated tub of carbonated water, piped in from peat bogs of the Belgian Ardennes, I felt slightly chilly, faintly embarrassed, and more than a bit dubious about the whole thing.

Yet in 20 minutes my arms and legs were as heavy as lead, my head drooped to my chest, and I could barely stagger to a nearby cot before falling asleep. Hours later I awoke vigorous and refreshed.

I was at a "baths establishment" in the Belgian city of Spa, taking a cure of the sort pursued each year by hundreds of thousands of Europeans.

American doctors think "water cures" are unscientific garbage. European doctors think American doctors, on this point, are boobs.

For centuries, physicians overseas have been sending their patients to spas chosen as carefully as specific medicines for particular ailments—this spa for arthritis, that spa for asthma, still another for neuritis or gallstones or worse. And today so many thousands of Americans are following their lead that a small but thriving segment of the travel industry—close to a dozen U.S. tour operators—has emerged to package the transatlantic health vacation as its sole activity.

Beauty vs. Health

Why the trend to foreign spas? Let me suggest a reason or two.

Compared to a European spa, the average American spa is like an elementary school next to Harvard, like a pickup softball team next to the New York Mets. Such dazzling resorts as The Golden Door, La Costa, The Palms, and Rancho La Puerta are almost wholly concerned with diet, exercise, and massage. Their aim is cosmetic; their methods are hardly the stuff of medical journals.

European spas pursue therapy, the prevention of illness. They operate under strict medical supervision and are recognized by national health plans, which reimburse their costs (if a doctor has prescribed the treatment) to residents of all E.E.C. countries. They screen patients and turn away those for whom their particular treatments are inappropriate. In short, they practice a form of "alternative medicine," stressing natural, health-giving substances in the earth, waters, and minerals around us, or biological substances taken from our fellow animals.

Though none of this has impressed the American medical profession, neither did acupuncture years ago, or the Lamaze method for natural childbirth, or numerous other overseas-originating practices until they were forced upon our M.D.s by popular insistence. That thousands of distinguished European doctors opt for spa therapy is unsettling at the very least, and indicates the wisdom of keeping an open mind.

Certainly no such doubts are harbored by the tour operator specialists in the health-and-fitness field. "Have you ever noticed," says Gerrie Tully of Santé International, "that many Europeans are far less prone to winter colds and other common ailments than we are here? They visit a spa once a year, for two weeks or so, and renew themselves for the next 12 months." "While the statistics are difficult to verify," says Willy Maurer of HBF Resorts, "there is simply no denying the effectiveness of spa therapy. Too many centuries have proven it, too many case studies, too many strong reactions. And remember: this is the chosen course of highly intelligent people, in mature, sophisticated nations."

Though overseas spas are frequently identified with mineral waters and hot mud—"thermal cures," "balneotherapy," "taking the waters"—their concerns extend to three other significant treatments: live-cell injections (heavily done in Switzerland), Procaine-based cures (Romania), and anti-psoriasis regimens (Israel, in resorts along the Dead Sea). For each there's a tour operator (or several), and each has a "package" for every purse.

Live-Cell Therapy

Not the dream of Faust, or eternal youth, but at least a slowing of the aging process is the aim of this radical treatment created by the legendary Paul Niehans in the early 1930s, at his Clinic La Prairie near Montreux. Niehans, who remained active until the age of 89,

administered the therapy to thousands of rather affluent persons (including Pope Pius XII, Winston Churchill, and Joan Crawford), and his clinic has since given it to a total of 50,000 seekers from around the world. Fetal cells from an unborn lamb are injected into the muscles; because the embryo has not yet developed the properties that would normally cause it to be rejected by other human tissues, it remains in the body, causing other cells to stay active and dynamic (so goes the theory).

As you'd expect, the treatment is fiendishly expensive in the main Swiss clinics: as much as $6,500 plus air fare at the ultra-deluxe Biotonus Bon Port Clinic (classic Niehans injections) overlooking Lake Geneva; $7,500 to $8,500 for six nights at Clinic Lemana ("cell-vital" injections) near Montreux; but only $5,000 to $6,000 at the Transvital Center (injections of antibodies and RNA) near Lausanne; and a "low" $4,300 at the still highly reputed Baxamed Institute for Revitalization (classic Niehans) in Basel—including full board at all such centers.

Cheaper versions are had outside of Switzerland. In London, the much-publicized "youth doctor," Peter Stephans, injects a serum of cells and placenta, at fees including examination and post-injection care of about $1,950 (but without room and board, for which patients make independent arrangements). In Montecatini, Italy, Dr. Antonio Caporale charges $3,000 (including room and board) for injections of a carefully prepared "biological cocktail" (and also provides a nine-week supply of suppositories containing such cells for continuing treatment). And in Paris, the president of the International Association of Physicians for Age Retardation, the English-speaking Dr. André Rouveix, charges approximately $1,350 (without room and board) for his own approaches to cell therapy (which include placenta "implants") at his heavily visited Clinique Nicolo.

For one-week packages using the services of the above three physicians, or for a stay at the Transvital Center in Switzerland, contact **Santé International, 850 Seventh Ave., New York, NY 10019 (phone 212/247-3830)**; its president, Gerrie Tully, a former

American doctors think "water cures" are unscientific garbage. European doctors think American doctors, on this point, are boobs.

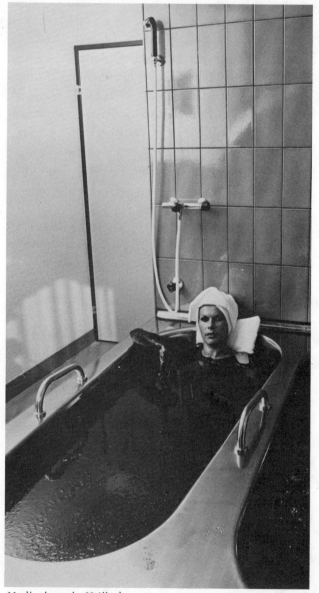

Mudbath at the Heilbad

patient of Dr. Stephans and recipient of such therapy, is a stunning blonde looking 15 years younger than her true age. For one-week packages to La Prairie, Lemana, or the Baxamed Institute in Switzerland, contact **HBF Resorts** (formerly Health and Fitness Vacations), **2911 Grand Ave., Coconut Grove/Miami, FL 33133 (phone 305/445-3876, or toll free 800/ FITNESS outside Florida).** And for the costly Biotonus Clinic, contact **Biotonus, 135 W. 50th St., Suite 1105, New York, NY 10020 (phone 212/ 541-8291 or toll free 800/437-7200 outside New York).**

Procaine-Based Therapies

One of the rare chemicals used at European spas, Procaine is a derivative of Novocaine, widely reputed to dilate the blood vessels and thereby bring greater oxygen to tissues and cells from increased blood circulation. Mixed with other substances into a serum known as Gerovital H3 and Aslavital (both denied admission into the U.S. by the F.D.A.), it is administered to many thousands of elderly Europeans each year as a treatment for diseases and declines of the aged. But though the substance is found in every spa (and in unauthorized forms, highly controversial and of disputed effectiveness, in European pharmacies), the cognoscenti get their Procaine in Bucharest at the clinics and resorts founded by the late Prof. Dr. Ana Aslan, who created Gerovital and Aslavital in the mid-1950s, and remained active until her own mid-80s.

The key Procaine clinics are at the modern Flora Hotel in the parks district of Bucharest, and the more traditional Otopeni Sanatorium on the outskirts of the city, about eight miles away; both provide the classic Gerovital H3 and Aslavital treatments. The key tour operator is **Litoral Travel, 124 E. 40th St., New York, NY 10016 (phone 212/986-4210, or toll free 800/445-1514 outside New York),** charging a winter-season (November through March) price, at either establishment, of $1,360 for two weeks, $1,610 for three weeks, including round-trip air from New York on Pan Am or Tarom Romanian Airlines. Since full board, laboratory tests, and daily treatments are also included, the value is considerable. For comparisons, you might also request the Romanian brochures of **Health & Pleasure Tours, 165 W. 46th St., New York, NY 10036 (phone 212/586-1775, or toll free 800/443-0365 outside New York).**

Anti-psoriasis Treatments

Called "climatotherapy"—climate therapy—it consists of only sea and sun. But it's pursued in the briny sea and ultraviolet sun found only at the lowest point on earth, along the shores of the Dead Sea in Israel, 1,300 feet below sea level. There, in waters with the world's highest concentration of salts, whose constant evaporation produces a mist that prevents sunburning rays from reaching the earth, victims of skin-blemishing psoriasis lie safely under the burning sun and bathe for half an hour daily in the jelly-like sea.

What results is like a biblical miracle: remission of psoriasis for substantial periods in a remarkable percentage of cases. The subject of weighty medical studies for more than 20 years, the benefits of these Israeli spas are today confirmed by exact clinical data of which other therapies can only dream; many physicians are no longer skeptical—and one weeps for psoriasis sufferers who are unaware of the healing Dead Sea.

Along the Dead Sea, the specialist spas for psoriasis are the Moriah Gardens (not to be confused with the Moriah Dead Sea Spa), Galei Zohar, the Hotel Lot, and Ein Bokek. The major U.S. tour operator for them is **Jericho Spa Tours Co., 555 Fifth Ave., New York, NY 10017 (phone 212/286-9291, or toll free 800/538-8383).** And the rates are unusually cheap: in a seven-month, split off-season (June through August and November through February) prices average $650 to $775 for two weeks (the suggested bare minimum), $1,250 to $1,530 for four weeks (the recommended stay), including two meals a day and all treatment, but with air fare extra. Summer is the best time for treatment.

Water Cures

And finally you have the classic treatments—"carbogaseous baths," "fango mud," "vapor inhalations," underwater massage, saunas, "Kneipp foot baths," "thalassotherapy," "algae baths" and repeated draughts of mineral water—as practiced with exquisite deliberation (different treatments, different spas, for different ailments) at quite literally hundreds of spas in Italy, Austria, Yugoslavia, France, Belgium, Germany, and Switzerland. While your average, celebrated U.S. spa charges $1,800 a week and up (to as much as $3,000 a week at The Golden Door) for its "beauty care" and "weight loss," a European spa can be had for as little as $600 a week in the Yugoslavian locations, for an average of $1,200 a week (depending on spa) in Italy (where Abano, Montecatini, and Ischia are the key names), and for $1,250 and up per winter week in Switzerland. The properties and programs are all lavishly described in glossy catalogs mailed free by Santé International and HBF Resorts from the addresses set forth for them, above.

The Ultimate Question

Is there anything to it? I tend to think there is; but whether or not, it is surely the worst smugness, a form of jingoism, to dismiss the claims of European spas out-of-hand and without investigation, as so many do.

Shakespeare warned that "there are more things in heaven and earth, Horatio, than are dreamt of in your philosophy." Perhaps there is more to medicine than the chemical-based prescriptions of U.S. doctors. ≈

Time off at the Dead Sea

Vacationing at a Holistic Health Resort

A New Variety of Spa, Not for Weight Reduction, Not for Stress Reduction, But for "Wellness"

Walking at Bluegrass Spa

Main lodge at Heartwood Institute
Opposite page: *Hot tub at Heartwood*

"**M**achines receive preventive maintenance; why not people? Why should we wait until illness strikes us down, before we attend to our health?"

With those words, a wise, old doctor once explained to me why he had turned at the end of his career to the practice of "holistic" medicine. An eminently sensible approach to life, with which almost no one can disagree, holistic methods of strengthening the body to fend off future illness have attracted the attention of millions of Americans, and created a thriving vacation industry of "holistic health farms" and "holistic health resorts."

None of these institutions, to my knowledge, disavows traditional approaches to medicine. "Holistic physicians" will readily prescribe an antibiotic for infection, or even perform surgery if it is needed.

But the same physicians believe in supplementing the standard therapies with alternative ones: better nutrition, exercise, stress reduction, and relaxation. People, they claim, should actively pursue "wellness" before they become sick, a process—essentially—of self-education and modifying lifestyles. The decision to vacation at a "wellness spa"—holistic centers where guests receive "preventive health workups" and seek to adapt to a healthier mode—is an obvious first step.

Heartwood Institute

On 200 acres in the mountains of northern California, five hours by car north of San Francisco, this is the classic "holistic retreat," and astonishingly cheap: it charges $280 a week in single rooms, $150 per person in doubles, $110 on a campsite, including three vegetarian meals a day and use of sauna, hot tub, and pool. Accommodations are mainly bunkhouses with small, simple rooms, not far from a "community center" and restaurant in a picturesque log lodge with outside dining deck. When guests arrive to pursue a one-week or two-week "wellness retreat," trained counselors aid them to choose from a variety of therapies in massage and bodywork, nutrition and exercise, at nominal extra costs. The institute's credo? That illness results from imbalances in the body's

normal state; that balance can be restored, as it often is in Asian medicine, by alternative therapies such as acupuncture or Ayurveda, lifestyle changes, modified nutrition, herbal preparations, homeopathy, still other treatments. Throughout the year, more intensive workshops are then scheduled at Heartwood in the full range of therapies under study by holistic practitioners: massage and yoga, "bodywork" and hypnotherapy, "energy balancing" and hydrotherapy—all, of course, for tuition charges (though fairly reasonable ones) not imposed upon people participating in a simple retreat. For information, contact **Heartwood Institute, Ltd., 220 Harmony Lane, Garberville, CA 95440 (phone 707/923-2021 or 707/923-3182).**

Rates at other "holistic resorts" vary widely from those of Heartwood, and from each other:

Northern Pines Health Resort

For instance, in the lake district of southern Maine near Portland, about 2½ hours by car from Boston, Northern Pines Health Resort charges $425 to $595 per person for a full week, for which it places you in lakefront log cabins or rustic country cottages on 80 acres of pine forests and rolling hills. Although some guests here simply lie in a hammock and read for that week, most pursue an active daily schedule of exercises, hikes, canoeing, swimming, and classes in aerobics, yoga, nutrition, stress management, weight control, shoulder massage, and "morning stretch." Meals, served in a large, lakeside lodge, are vegetarian, but supplemented twice a week with fish and eggs; and rates throughout the year, including all three such meals, classes, hot tub, sauna, and use of boating equipment, are $425 per person per week in a lakeside cabin, $485 in a better hillside or "yurt" lodging, $595 in a cedar or pine cottage. Add $105 for stays in July and August. For information, contact **Northern Pines Health Resort, Rte. 85, R.R. Box 279, Raymond, ME 04071 (phone 207/655-7624).**

Foxhollow

On stately grounds in the heart of the Berkshire mountains of western Massachusetts, Foxhollow is an imposing stone manor house of long vintage and varying uses, that reopened in late 1988 as a wellness spa under the supervision of noted holistic physician Dr. Stephan Rechtshafen, aided by other doctors; it hopes to become one of the nation's foremost preventive health centers. Rates in 1989 are expected to average $870 a week (double occupancy), and include vegetarian meals (with some fish, some chicken), massage and loofa rubs, yoga and aerobics classes, Japanese baths, sauna and whirlpool, flotation tanks, swimming, hiking and boating, and considerable instruction in diet and nutrition. "We aim to help guests return to a healthy lifestyle that seems to get lost in the day-to-day concerns of living," says a staff member. For information, contact **Foxhollow, Rte. 7, Lenox, MA 01240 (phone 413/637-2000).**

Murrieta Hot Springs Resort

Ninety minutes south of Los Angeles on 47 acres of rolling hills dotted with palm trees, this is a rather upscale version of the more typical health farm, with Spanish-style buildings, tiled walks, and elaborately manicured grounds. Yet rates are rather reasonable by health-spa standards: $795 per person per week in a double room ($945 single), including all three vegetarian meals daily, spa mineral baths with "energizing bodywrap," exercise program, mud bath, energy-balancing massage, and full use of all hot springs pools and saunas. Accommodations are in cozy cottages or terraced lodgings, where smoking is forbidden and alcohol is forbidden. Throughout the day, courses in stress management, exercise, diet, bodywork, "awareness," and health information are presented to guests free of charge. For information, contact **Murrieta Hot Springs Resort, 28779 Via Las Flores, Murrieta, CA 92362 (phone 714/677-9661, or toll free 800/322-4542 outside California).**

Harbin Hot Springs

On 1,100 wooded acres in a valley of northern California, 2½ hours by car from San Francisco, Harbin Hot Springs is a simpler (rooms without private bath), and far less expensive West Coast alternative to Murrieta; guests enjoy the very same species of natural, warm mineral-water pools (one of 112° Fahrenheit, open all night and all year), but stay in dormitories, unpretentious private lodgings, or even on campsites. In addition to soaking (without speaking, a requirement) in the celebrated hot springs, hiking, sunbathing, and enjoying—according to one staff member—a "meditative atmosphere," guests sign up for one of numerous courses in exotic massage—Swedish, shiatsu, acupressure, watsu (water shiatsu)—at rates as low as $25 for a "walk-in" course of a weekend's duration. Room rates per person are $60 a week on campsites, $75 a week in dorms, $125 a week in rooms ($80 for the second person), to which you add $12 a day for two vegetarian meals. For information, contact **Harbin Hot Springs, P.O. Box 82, Middletown, CA 95461 (phone 707/987-2477 or 707/987-0379).**

Bluegrass Spa

In the rolling horse country of central Kentucky a few miles north of Lexington, Bluegrass Spa is an antebellum mansion with large white columns, set on expansive lawns amid clusters of guesthouses and spacious exercise facilities. Rooms are quite comfortable, almost elegant. Your day begins with yoga; goes on to include fitness and nutrition lectures, tai-chi exercises, walks and jogging, swimming and saunas, country-road biking and spa aerobics; and ends with optional massage and Jacuzzi bathing. Meals are mainly vegetarian, but often with chicken or fish, and always low in fat, salt, and sugar. Rates are $1,042 per person for a seven-night week, in shared accommodations, including meals, classes, and use of all fitness facilities, as well as complimentary transportation to and from Lexington Airport. For information, contact **Bluegrass Spa, 901 Galloway Rd., Stamping Ground, KY 40379 (phone 502/535-6261).**

For reasons of space, I have obviously compressed the theories of "holistic health" into almost absurdly simple form. For a more complete exposition, request a program guide of the Heartwood Institute described above, enclosing $2 to cover costs. ≈

It seems a sensible approach to life, with which almost no one can disagree.

At Northern Pines

Guests at Heartwood

Warm mineral-water pool at Harbin Hot Springs

Vacations at Pritikin Centers Are High Priced But Healthy

Bland Meals and Mild Exercise at Miami Beach, Santa Monica, and Downingtown, Pennsylvania

Lounge at Pritikin Center, Santa Monica
Opposite page: *Pritikin treadmills*

The good news is that the approach seems to work, restoring your health, lengthening your longevity.

The bad news is that it's rather expensive: an average of $3,750 for two weeks, $6,500 for a month, even when two people are taking the "cure" together.

Yet Americans continue to throng the three Pritikin diet centers, devoting their two- to four-week vacations to a disciplined regimen of bland meals and mild exercise. And a major expansion of the Pritikin facilities—as planned by the 36-year-old son of the company's founder, the late Nathan Pritikin—will soon bring Pritikin-style vacations or treatments into the geographical reach of more and more people.

Residential Pritikin centers are currently in operation in Santa Monica, California; Miami Beach, Florida; and Downingtown, Pennsylvania. Each advances the message first proclaimed by Pritikin in 1974: that most of the major degenerative diseases of our time—heart disease, diabetes, atherosclerosis—are largely caused by excessively high blood-fat levels, and that their prevention and cure could be brought about by reducing those levels through diet and exercise.

Sounds commonplace now, doesn't it? But it was revolutionary then. Heart-disease patients were being routinely treated by drugs and surgery, told to avoid exercise, and then sent back to eating the standard American diet of meat, eggs, and dairy products.

Instead, Pritikin advocated a diet that consisted only 10% of fat, only 15% of protein, but a full 75% of complex carbohydrates, the latter mainly from fruits, vegetables, and whole grains. He counseled an avoidance of all extra fats and oils (other than those naturally in grains and lean meats), all simple sugars (honey and molasses as well as sugar), all salt, coffee, and tea, and all foods rich in cholesterol (eggs, shellfish, animal organs and skin).

And each Pritikin patient or vacationer, regardless of age, was to engage in daily exercise, mainly walking.

On such a program, he maintained, the middle age of life could be stretched to cover the years between 40 and 80, rather than those from 40 to 60. Old age would begin at 80, not at 55 or 60.

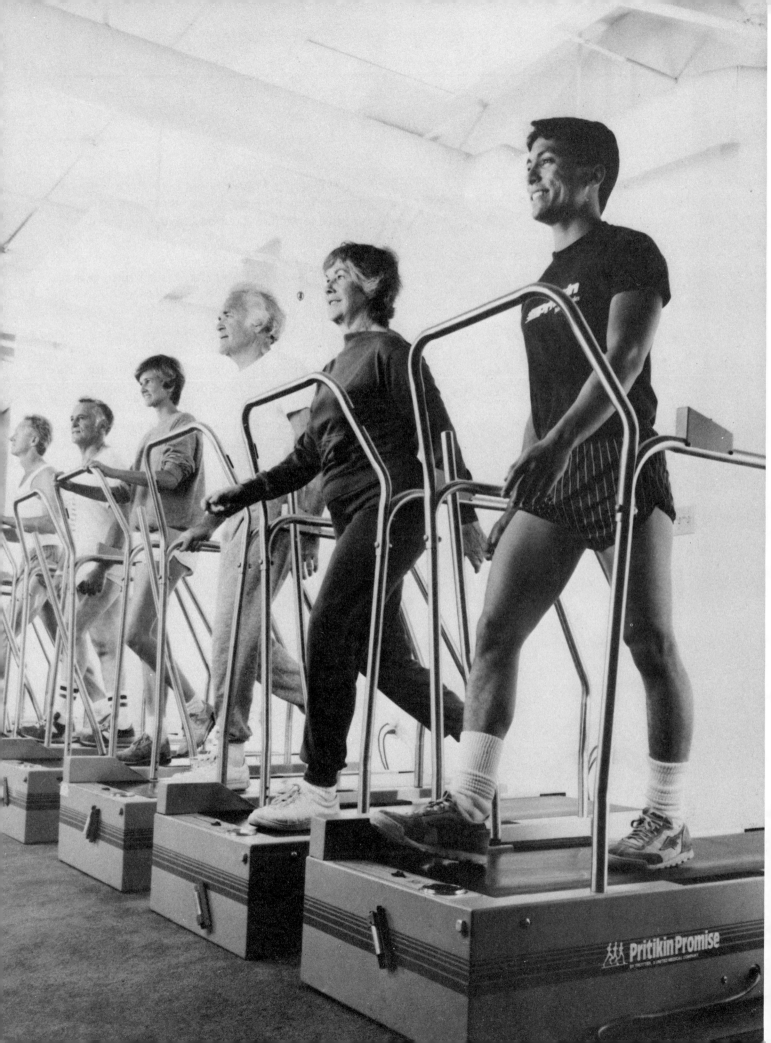

Each of the centers advances the claim that most degenerative diseases are caused by excessively high blood-fat levels.

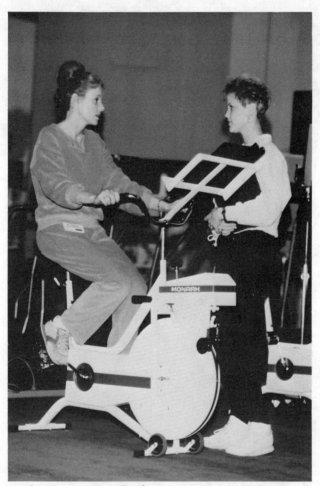

Pritikin Center, Miami Beach

Pritikin staff will cite all sorts of statistics—I won't repeat them here—to bolster their claims that the treatment has had remarkable results for the 40,000-odd people who have thus far passed through the three residential centers. What is unarguable is that strong word-of-mouth comment has kept all three facilities busy and well occupied, despite the founder's death from leukemia in 1985.

Programs, Costs, and Meals

Each center offers programs for 13 and 26 days. The shorter course is for those overweight or interested in preventing future illness or reducing stress, or who have hypertension or mild diabetes (currently treated by oral medication). The second program, while available to anyone, is primarily designed for those suffering from the more serious health problems of heart disease, insulin-demanding diabetes, obesity, gout, or claudication.

No matter which program you select, you're busy from early morning till early evening, taking pre-breakfast walks along the beach or on country lanes, exercising three times a day, attending cooking classes, lectures, or supermarket expeditions.

Personalized medical supervision is a major feature of the program. Depending on their health needs, guests are assigned to a specialist in either cardiology or internal medicine (Pritikin physicians are all Pritikin enthusiasts and live the programs themselves).

As for the meals, they are—reportedly—much better than in the early years of Pritikin. Although no extra fat is added to foods, and no salt, sugar, or caffeine is permitted, chefs still manage to turn out tasty fare. Meals are largely vegetarian, but with some fish served several times a week. You eat six times a day, so you never get hungry. Snacks might consist of vegetables and soup, Pritikin "chips" and salsa, fresh fruits. Dishes include "enchilada pie," potato pancakes, Moroccan orange-and-carrot salad, sweet-and-sour cabbage, ratatouille, paella, vegetable pot pie, and yogurt-marinated chicken. Desserts might be carrot cake or strawberries Romanoff.

For all this, you pay a substantial price if you are

traveling alone, but considerably less on a per-person basis if you are accompanied by a spouse or companion. For a 13-day session, including medical costs, the fees total $5,000 or so for one person, but only $7,500, at most, for two. For a 26-day session, fees are as much as $8,900 for one person, but only $13,000 for two. Major-medical plans may cover that portion of the cost that is attributed to medical attention. And some guests have been known to treat the entire expense as tax deductible, provided they have been directed to take the program by their doctor (consult your tax adviser).

Is it necessary for the Pritikin experience to be so very expensive? Physicians with whom I've spoken think it well worth the price and not out of line with costs in the more exclusive spas (not to mention alternative costs of surgery, hospitalization, time lost from work).

The other, lower-cost alternative is a planned new chain of health-and-fitness clubs for people over 40, embodying the Pritikin principles. Three are currently in operation in Los Angeles and Houston, with several more due to open soon. These, in essence, are "outpatient" facilities, with Pritikin-style restaurants on the premises and a 30-hour program of instruction presented three nights a week for four weeks, all at the moderate charge of $300 to $400.

Vacationing at the Residential Facilities

Meanwhile the better course—if you can afford it—is to spend a two-week or four-week vacation at an actual Pritikin residential facility. The **Pritikin Longevity Center, 1910 Ocean Front Walk, Santa Monica, CA 90405 (phone toll free 800/421-9911, 800/421-0981 in California),** is the largest (150 guests) and the mother center (some would call it the "mother church"). It enjoys a superb beachfront location facing ten miles of boardwalk on which, conceivably, you might walk from Malibu to Palos Verdes.

The **Pritikin Longevity Center, 975 E. Lincoln Hwy., Downingtown, PA 19335 (phone 215/873-0123, or toll free 800/344-8243, 800/342-**

2080 in Pennsylvania), in rolling hills an hour and ten minutes from downtown Philadelphia, at the gateway to the quaint Amish country, provides both indoor and outdoor swimming, tennis, a golf course across the street, two driving ranges within walking distance, and bowling available less than 100 yards from the main building. There's also a climate-controlled indoor gym for the 45 to 60 guests enrolled per session.

And finally, the **Pritikin Longevity Center, 5875 Collins Ave., Miami Beach, FL 33140 (phone 305/866-2237, or toll free 800/327-4914 outside Florida),** is housed in a small resort hotel on an ocean beach that is swimmable year round. A recent expansion of facilities permits the center to accommodate up to 132 guests at a time. There's a large beachfront pool, and an oceanfront gym.

At all the centers, visitors are welcome to take a free tour. At Miami Beach, says the general director, you may even be invited to take a meal with guests. ≈

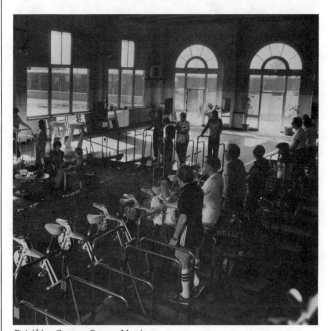

Pritikin Center, Santa Monica

Vacationing with the Seventh Day Adventists

A Less Costly Form of Pritikin-like Treatments for Mature Americans

At Living Springs, Putnam Valley, New York

Yⁿou are 55 and you feel yourself—faintly but perceptibly—slowing down. You are overweight and high in cholesterol. You are anxious and stressed. You have heard of the Pritikin Centers, where health can supposedly be restored, but you can't afford the tab (as much as $6,000 to $7,000 for a month).

So what do you do?

You call the Seventh Day Adventists (and I am perfectly serious). For prices averaging $2,600 a month they offer residential health retreats all across the U.S.A., where diet, exercise, and atmosphere are akin to those maintained in the costly health resorts, but at less than half the price.

The Adventists have long been known for their interest in health and nutrition, and for the consequent longevity of their lives. Studies in California have revealed a much smaller incidence of heart attacks and strokes among them, as compared with other population groups in the state. Early in the century an Adventist named Kellogg began producing strange but effective breakfast foods called "wheat flakes" and "corn flakes," while his brother in the same town founded the famous Battle Creek (Michigan) Sanitorium. Today Adventists operate large and prestigious hospitals—notably, Loma Linda in California and Castle Medical Center in Hawaii—from which smaller, no-frills, nonprofit, inexpensive health retreats have been spun off.

Diet and Exercise, Not Religion

At each such center the policy is determinedly vegetarian. Adventists are normally advised (but not required) to consume a purely "Vegan" diet of fruits, vegetables, legumes, and for those able to handle them, modest amounts of such high-fat foods as nuts, avocados, and olives. Scarcely any "free fats"—i.e., those not found in whole foods—are used.

Which means no butter or marmalade on rolls, no oils in salad dressings, and foods sautéed in water rather than oil (the Adventists and the Pritikin people are in agreement on the virtual elimination of "free fats"). Complex carbohydrates are the basis of their diet (again in agreement with Pritikin; Pritikin, however, does allow small amounts of poultry, fish, and dairy products).

For all its spartan features, Adventist food can be surprisingly tasty. At my own recent lunch in the Adventist-run Living Springs of Putnam Valley, New York, I took repeated helpings from a buffet of salad, steamed vegetables, and cashew chow mein.

Careful attention to diet is combined, at the centers, with exercise in the open air, sunbathing, a mammoth intake of water (six to eight glasses a day), hydrotherapy treatments (saunas, alternate hot and cold showers), and temperance: the total avoidance of coffee, alcohol, tobacco, and irritating spices.

Those strictures are translated into programs that begin early in the morning with brisk outdoor walking, followed by a hearty breakfast, daily lectures by physicians, hydrotherapy, classes on remedies utilizing water, vegetarian cooking classes, more walking, a large meal at lunch, educational seminars, more walking or exercising, a light evening meal, then perhaps a slide show on some aspect of health.

What does not take place is religious proselytizing. "People of all persuasions and no persuasion come here," says Leatha Mellow of the center known as the Weimar Institute, in California. "We've had Catholic priests, Jews, Christians, and atheists. We do maintain a spiritual emphasis, but it is nondenominational and nonsectarian."

In health matters, by contrast, the centers are fierce advocates. Like Pritikin, they believe a proper diet can avoid the major degenerative diseases of our time—heart disease, diabetes, atherosclerosis—and pursue their cures intensively in two- to four-week programs at the various locations.

The Eight Major Centers

Living Springs Retreat, Rte. 3, Bryant Pond Road, Putnam Valley, NY 10579 (phone 914/ 526-2800): In the foothills of the Berkshire Mountains, about an hour's drive from New York City, it is a large but homey building overlooking an 18-acre pond with swans. Guests occupy attractive private and

Says one Adventist nurse: "We believe our services should be made available to all, and not simply to those with money."

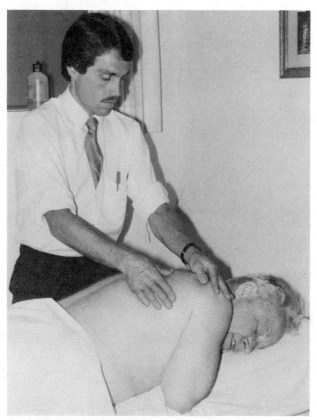

At the Weimar Institute, Weimar, California

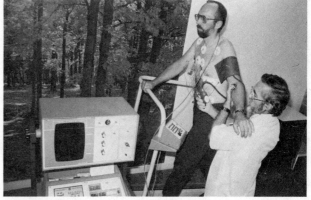

Stress test, Weimar Institute

What does not take place is religious proselytizing.

Preparing the meals at Weimar

semiprivate rooms, all with private bath, for which they pay weekly high-season rates (Memorial Day through Labor Day) of $595 in a semiprivate room, $695 in a private room, $875 for two persons staying together. Off-season weekly rates are $495, $635, and $805 respectively, including all three meals daily and all treatments.

Hartland Institute of Health and Education, P.O. Box 1, Rapidan, VA 22733 (phone 703/672-3100): On over 700 acres of gently rolling hills, an hour from the Blue Ridge Mountains and two hours from Washington, D.C. When its current expansion program is completed by the spring of 1989 it will house up to 30 guests in two lodges. Programs are 25 days long, and cost $3,750 for one "patient," $2,750 for a companion patient. Says head nurse Linda Ball: "We believe services like these should be made available to everyone, and not just those with a lot of money. Some people call and say, 'I'll pay any price.' Others still say, 'I can't afford it.' "

Wildwood Lifestyle Center and Hospital, Wildwood, GA 30757 (phone toll free 800/634-9355): A modern facility on 500 acres of trails and hills, at an elevation of 700 feet, between Mount Raccoon and Mount Lookout. Rooms are attractive, and each has its own sunny patio. On a 24-day program, rates are $2,950 in a semiprivate room, $3,525 for a private room with bath, $3,364 for a private room with shared bath. On the 17-day program, rates in a semiprivate room are only $2,395, a private room with bath is $2,796, $2,683 without bath.

Uchee Pines, Rte. 1, Box 440, Seale, AL 36875 (phone 205/855-4764): In a climate that is generally warm the year round (though rainy in winter), this is a country house set in 250 wooded acres, with lovely gardens and trails. A 21-day program is offered, at charges of $2,520 for the first "patient," $2,320 for a patient/companion. Occasionally guests will be accepted for shorter programs, and fees will then be prorated.

Poland Spring Health Institute, RFD 1, Box 4300, Summit Spring Road, Poland Spring, ME

04274 (phone 207/998-2894): Smallest of the retreats (seven guests only), but with a broad variety of activities, including cross-country skiing in winter. It is an old New England farmhouse with attached barn housing the guests and various hydrotherapy facilities. Down the road is a clinic with medical offices. Rates are $595 a week for semiprivate rooms, $795 a week for private rooms; but most rooms share a bath. The average stay is two weeks. And, oh yes, this is the same Poland Spring of the world-famous mineral waters; the institute has its own well, and guests therefore drink the same water as in the bottled product.

Weimar Institute, P.O. Box 486, Weimar, CA 95736 (phone 916/637-4111, or toll free 800/ 525-9191): It enjoys the most idyllic of Adventist retreat locations—on some 450 acres in the foothills of the Sierras, about 50 miles northeast of Sacramento, off Interstate 80—but is atypically expensive: $3,670 for the first "patient" on a 19-day program, $3,125 for that patient's companion. Guests do a great deal of walking through hundreds of acres of hiking trails, and occupy rooms that are all supplied with private bath.

Black Hills Health and Education Center, P.O. Box 19, Hermosa, SD 57744 (phone 605/ 255-4101 or 605/255-4687): In the Black Hills of South Dakota in a scenic valley surrounded by rimrock cliffs, this is a "change-your-lifestyle" retreat whose diet is free from refined products and cholesterol, low in fat and salt. Daily exercise is stressed, including visits to a large, natural indoor pool fed by hot springs; physical examinations and numerous blood-chemistry tests are administered by a medical doctor. The emphasis is on a 25-day program costing $1,980 for a single room (including meals and all else), $1,495 per person double, only $1,315 per person if you park your own motorhome on one of the center's camping sites.

Total Health Foundation, P.O. Box 5, Yakima, WA 98907 (phone 509/965-2555): An 18-room country mansion in fruit orchards of the Yakima Valley, ten miles from Yakima; it's operated by a number of physicians who first subject patients to a complete medical evaluation and then supervise a program of meals made up solely of natural foods, and

considerable physical therapy. Some (but not all) insurance programs cover a part of the treatment at T.H.F.

Write for literature, then call. Staff members at all eight centers are, in my experience, gentle, caring people. ≈

The New World of Travel 1989

The lifeblood of the Arthur Frommer travel guides is the correspondence received from readers, commenting on the establishments recommended in the texts, and recommending new establishments. Each such letter is carefully studied, and when a particular lead seems promising, it is followed up and personally checked.

It is hoped that *The New World of Travel* will receive similar assistance from its readers. A yearly publication, issued near the start of each year, the *New World* will constantly grow. And since much of its content relates to organizations that lack the means to properly market themselves, or come to the attention of a travel journalist, your help is invaluable in alerting me to the organizations—hospitality exchanges, alternative resorts, new travel clubs, and the like—that you have discovered.

If you become aware of a new travel organization, program, or development that deserves to be described in our next edition, *The New World of Travel 1990,* won't you please let me know about it? Send your letters to Arthur Frommer, *The New World of Travel,* c/o Prentice Hall Press, One Gulf + Western Plaza, New York, NY 10023. All letters will be acknowledged, and all are warmly appreciated, in advance, by the author.

Vacationing, for a Change, at a Whole-Grain Resort

At Macrobiotic Centers Clustered on Both Coasts, the Cuisine Is As Soothing As the Setting

Vega Study Center, California

Cornellia Aihara leading exercises

Just as you occasionally need a vacation (which is presumably why you are reading this book), so does your stomach occasionally need a vacation. Both can achieve that restful interlude at a macrobiotic center, of which our nation has a dozen. Without necessarily subscribing to the tenets of macrobiotics—a diet of cooked whole grains and vegetables—you can turn for a time to a gentler form of life, lacking in stress, free of fats, and full of companionship among the most amiable people.

Many thousands of Americans make an exclusive use of the macrobiotic cuisine, which they often first encounter and learn to prepare at residential centers clustered on the two coasts.

Contrary to a popular misconception, macrobiotics has no necessary connection to Zen, Zen Buddhism, or even Buddhism, although a great many of the latter persuasion adhere to the theory. It is a purely secular approach to nutrition based on the teachings of the late George Ohsawa, born in Japan, who believed in essence that people should live in harmony with what he perceived as natural cycles and elements of the physical universe. Thus they should eat only those foods that had grown for centuries in the places where those people lived. They should, in the United States, emphasize grains, the staff of life, supplemented by vegetables, beans, vegetarian soups—on occasion a bit of fish.

Translating those ingredients into tasty meals takes skill. Accordingly, all macrobiotic centers include cooking courses in their schedules, taught to all guests. Yet even in the hands of a gourmet cook, the subtly flavored macrobiotic dishes are bland compared with the steak and potatoes of the average American diet, and thus offer a radical change of pace—a soothing one—to the average American.

You pursue that relaxing course in centers operated by disciples of Ohsawa, of whom Japanese-born Michio Kushi on the East Coast and Herman Aihara on the West Coast are certainly the most prominent. Out of a dozen possible choices, you may want to request schedules and literature from:

The Four Main Centers

Vega Study Center, of Oroville, California: Ninety minutes north of Sacramento, in an old and sleepy town of Victorian homes and later shops and stores of the 1920s, is this large, residential, teaching base of Herman and Cornellia Aihara. Their courses (including "hands-on" cooking classes) run for one to three weeks throughout the year, and cost $450 for one week, $850 for two weeks, with full board. Guests live in shared rooms with pine beds and wonderfully firm futon mattresses; wake at 7 a.m. for meditation, Eastern-style exercises, and tea; attend lectures delivered by the charming Aihara himself; and eat classic macrobiotic meals often prepared by Cornellia. Contact **Vega Study Center, 1511 Robinson St., Oroville, CA 95965 (phone 916/533-7702)**, for an interesting catalog.

The Kushi Foundation, in the Berkshires of western Massachusetts: Placid and still, on 600 mountain acres, its main building is an old mansion with spiraling wooden staircases and stone fireplaces for cool evenings. It is an appropriate setting for the calm and gentle lectures of Michio Kushi and his wife, Aveline. Seven-day residential seminars on emotional harmony and healthy food preparation cost $800 for a shared room and all meals. A unique opportunity to study with the "master." Write or phone **Kushi Foundation, Berkshire Center Program, P.O. Box 7, Becket, MA 01223 (phone 413/623-5742)**.

Lady Diane's, on the island of Jamaica: A lavishly decorated macrobiotic hotel near the airport of Montego Bay, with superb views of the bay. There's no classroom instruction, but an imaginative macrobiotic cuisine enhanced with Jamaican touches for holiday purposes: breakfast might consist of hot grits, turnips, miso soup, and whole-wheat biscuits. Rates for room and full board at the charming seafront resort, for a full seven-night week, are $595 per person (double occupancy), and include shiatsu massage. Contact **Lady Diane's, 5 Kent Ave., Montego Bay, Jamaica (phone 809/952-4415)**.

And then there are the macrobiotic summer camps, for a cheap, refreshing, and restorative holiday in the open air. Try the 800-guest Kushi Institute Summer Camp, always in July, in a comfortable Swiss army base in the Swiss Alps, near Lenk ($416 to $480 per person for the week)—contact **Margaret Goodwin, 173 Lyman St., Pawtucket, RI 02860 (phone 401/726-2973)**; the Macrobiotic Summer Conference, in August at Simon's Rock of Bard College in the Berkshires of Massachusetts near Great Barrington ($575 to $895 per person for the week, depending on the accommodations)—contact the **Kushi Foundation, P.O. Box 1100, Brookline, MA 02147 (phone 617/738-0045)**; the Mid-Atlantic Summer Camp, usually held for a week in mid-June, in the Pocono Mountains of Pennsylvania ($495 for all meals and dorm accommodations in rustic cabins)—contact **Macrobiotic Center of Baltimore, 604 E. Joppa Rd., Towson, MD 21204 (phone 301/321-4474)**.

I have, in my description of macrobiotics at the beginning of this essay, compressed a complex subject into a simplistic and inadequate paragraph. I have failed, in particular, to explore the emphasis of the theory on the need to properly balance the expansive (*yin*) and contractive (*yang*) varieties of food, and their counterparts in other areas, or the claims that a macrobiotic way of life can prevent or cure serious illness.

All this you'll hear—and more—in one of the most restful interludes of your life, as you grant time off to your overworked and suffering stomach. ≈

Aveline Kushi teaching at Becket, Massachusetts

IX ⚹ NEW DESTINATIONS FOR BETTER AND CHEAPER TRIPS

If You Haven't Looked at Venezuela Lately, Look Again

What Was Once Among the Most Expensive Nations on Earth Has Now Become One of the Cheapest

Filet mignon dinners for under $5, including wine. Self-drive cars for $12 a day. Gucci shoes for $30. Men's linen suits for $50.

The location of these rub-your-eye rates—Venezuela—is an attractive, tropical nation easily accessible to Americans, but usually shunned because of its former reputation as a fiendishly expensive place. Prior to 1983, when oil was king, oil-rich Venezuelans were a free-spending lot, with a strong currency, stratospheric prices, and lavish habits. "Even our toothpicks were imported," says one government official, caustically, today.

Then, in 1983, came the crash in oil income, and down with it went the Venezuelan currency, the proudly named bolívar (Bs, for short). From an exchange value of 4.3 Bs to the U.S. dollar in 1983, the bolívar has fallen to a level of 33 to the dollar today. Some observers predict it will continue falling to as low a rate as 40 to the dollar by mid-1989. Even at its present level, the bolívar is so cheap as to drive the cost of rooms, meals, shopping, and entertainment down to the levels of Morocco or to below those of Portugal.

Yet surprisingly, although learned economists have written of Venezuela's plight, almost no one in the U.S. travel industry has alerted the public to the travel opportunities resulting from the same condition.

Super-Bargain Tours

No one, that is, except a scattered handful of small tour operators shouting the news to a largely unhearing audience. Their brochures tell the story. Seven nights at a deluxe—indeed, a five-star—resort hotel, with full American breakfast daily, including round-trip scheduled air transportation from New York, Miami, or Houston, for $499 per person in off-season (until December 15), for $599 thereafter, in any of the major Venezuelan centers: Caracas, Puerto la Cruz, or the offshore resort island of Margarita. That's considerably less than similar luxury properties would cost in other Caribbean locations, even on tour packages using charter flights. And of course, properties in the lower first-class or tourist-class range are priced even less.

182

In 1983 came the crash in oil income, and down with it went the Venezuelan currency, the proudly named bolívar.

Cablecar over Caracas

One tour-operator specialist to Venezuela, the long-experienced Bob Thorne of Inter Island Tours, told me he recently arranged an independent, ten-night tour for a young, single woman, that sent her to spend two nights at the Caracas Hilton, then on a two-night air safari to the jungle camp of Canaima and nearby Angel Falls, from which she flew to spend three nights at the posh Melia Hotel in Puerto la Cruz, then onward by air to the five-star Hotel Concorde in Margarita for a final three nights, and home. The bill came to $828, including all air transportation from New York, full American breakfast daily, and the supplement for a single room throughout. Surely that price couldn't be achieved outside of Nepal or Ethiopia!

The airlines flying to Venezuela are VIASA, Avensa, Pan Am, Eastern, and American, daily from such cities as New York, Miami, and Houston to Caracas, and onward from there (or on connecting carriers) to Puerto la Cruz and Margarita. VIASA also operates a weekly nonstop Saturday flight between New York and Margarita. The attractive, round-trip air fare is $320 from New York to Caracas ($300 from Miami, $330 from Houston), while Avensa charges the same fare to Margarita and Puerto la Cruz as well. VIASA and the others ask a bit more ($350) for New York passengers going beyond Caracas, but only $320 for the weekly nonstop to Margarita. Once there, budget-minded independent tourists can pick up modest lodgings for $15 a night.

They'll find plenty of Canadian tourists, and some European tourists, ahead of them. The canny, cost-conscious Canadians discovered Margarita as early as 1984, and 60,000 went there in 1988. Still, the foreign tourist is only a bare fraction of the size of the native Venezuelan market for Margarita and Puerto la Cruz, which leaves both locations refreshingly foreign, exotic, and Spanish-speaking: a window onto the life of Latin America.

Hot Spots

My own favorite is Puerto la Cruz, a sleepy "Spanish" town (which wakes up at night) on the beach-lined coast 250 miles to the east of Caracas. Its main seaside promenade consists of nearly 50 $5-a-meal restaurants lined side by side (each one better than the next), interspersed with occasional bars and discos; it's the perfect setting for those, like me, who like late dining, strolling, and staying in the very center of town, here in the old-world elegance of the five-star beachfront Melia Hotel. A bit outside the center, around the cove, is the Doral Beach Resort, only four stars in category, but with 1,300 rooms (largest in South America), especially cheap and suitable for families. You buy budget breakfasts there for $1.25, dinner for under $2.

Caracas is for two or three nights only, a dynamic South American capital of skyscrapers and boulevards, with two vital sights (the home of Bolívar and the cable-car view of the city), several excellent museums, and evenings in nightclubs, discos, and a spectacular National Theater hosting such traveling troupes as the Bolshoi Ballet or Comédie Française at ticket prices of $6 and $8. Its top two in-city hotels are the Hilton and Tamanaco, but 1½ hours outside of town are two major resorts: the Sheraton Macuto and the Bolívar, both on so-so beaches, but with superb seaside views.

And then there's the mountainous island of Margarita, 40 miles off the coast; it is the chief vacation destination for all Venezuelans. Discovered by Christopher Columbus in 1498, it is historic and Hispanic in its culture and many colonial towns, dotted with good restaurants and discos, filled with churches, small castle-like estates, and friendly people. Its two major hotel properties, on the beach in or near the capital city of Porlamar, are the Margarita Concorde (five stars) and Bella Vista (four stars). Inland by a few blocks are the new four-star Margarita Towers and Aquila Inn, as well as a great many smaller hotels, perhaps unsuitable for the demands of traditional U.S. tourists (mediocre décor, poor service, ceiling fans) but entirely appropriate and wonderfully priced for budgeteers. The best beaches are scattered around the coast and reached by self-drive rental car.

A particular draw of Margarita, and its big town of Porlamar (100,000 population), is shopping: the entire area was made a tax-free port by Venezuela, and products from around the world are on sale at rock-bottom rates.

A fourth grand attraction of Venezuela is the world's highest (3,200 feet) cascade, the breathtaking Angel Falls, whose impact is enhanced by savage rapids, lush jungle, and picturesque but peaceful Kamarta Indians. From both Caracas and Puerto la Cruz, day-long or overnight air tours go there for an all-inclusive price of under $100. On the shorter trips, your plane simply flies alongside the falls (for an unforgettable view), then lands for the day or overnight at the nearby jungle camp of Canaima, at the approach to the Amazon territory of Venezuela. There, tribes of the aforementioned Kamarta emerge from the bush to entertain or trade with you.

Looking for a touristic "hot spot"? All of Venezuela (especially Margarita and Puerto la Cruz) is largely untouristed by Americans, unpolluted by outside influences, cheap. The leading tour operators (from which free literature is available) are the aforementioned **Inter Island Tours, of New York City (phone 212/686-4868, or toll free 800/245-3434 outside New York State)**, where Bob Thorne is your contact; **Turven Tour Express, Inc., of New York City (phone 212/254-0881, or toll free 800/338-0696 outside New York State)**, where you should ask for the exceptionally well-informed Paolo Bastianello; and **Sabrosa Adventures, Inc., of New York City (phone 212/983-0855, or toll free 800/642-2324 outside New York State)**, where your contact should be Berta Zurumay (who worked with the Tourist Board of Venezuela for 14 years, and was its tourist commissioner for 3 years). ≈

Along the beach-lined coast

Costa Rica, for a Different Sort of Tropical Vacation

On the T-Shirts of the Teenagers Here the Words "Costa Rica Air Force" Are Emblazoned Near the Neck; Filling the Space Below Is a Huge Dove

A Costa Rican beach

They abolished the army here more than 40 years ago, and have lived in perfect peace and tranquility ever since. They enjoy the highest per-capita income in Central America, a fully functioning democracy, the presence of North American retirees totaling 35,000 people, and a president who won the Nobel Peace Prize for his plan to end the fighting in nearby Nicaragua and El Salvador.

But the beaches are 80 miles from the capital city, and the seaside hotels are small lodgings that haven't yet attracted masses of foreign visitors. While that's a disturbing fact for traditional tourists, it's a positive plus for special ones. Costa Rica is the destination par excellence for people seeking the pleasures of the tropics without the pressures of crowds and casinos. It affords you a chance to experience Central America without danger, to explore and discuss the politics of the region with open-minded, uncoerced residents, to combine rest for the body with stimulation for the mind, pleasure with learning.

But what exactly do you, as a tourist, do there? Because the capital city of San José is in a central valley, 80 miles from the sea on either side, your initial activities are different from those you scheduled for more standard tropical destinations located on a coast, near beaches. Here, before attending to countryside pleasures, you first experience the distinctly urban life of a great Central American center, conversing with its highly opinionated, politically alert people, visiting attractions of cultural interest, taking Spanish lessons, attending highly charged lectures (in English) on social and regional concerns.

The Life of San José

The opening step is a remarkably cheap and effective, three-day "crash course" in the Spanish language at the Instituto Universal de Idiomas in the heart of downtown San José, Costa Rica's capital. For six hours a day on each of three days (Tuesday, Wednesday, and Thursday) each week, their university-level instructors will provide you with a basic underpinning in that useful subject for a total charge of only $75. Reserve your place by contacting the **Instituto Universal de Idiomas, P.O. Box 219-2120, San José, Costa Rica (phone 506/23-9662).**

More serious travelers will opt for a one-month course in Spanish (three hours a day for five days a week, for four weeks) at the same Instituto, costing an equally remarkable total of only $215, including materials and registration. To ensure your immersion in the subject, the Instituto will then arrange your room and board with one of 20 Costa Rican families in the area, for $70 a week, including all meals and laundry service. Classroom instruction is with a usual total of three or four other students, a maximum of six. Private lessons, either supplementing the group instruction or substituting for it, are $8 an hour, which contrasts radically with what you'd pay for Spanish instruction here at home.

A shorter, but perhaps more elaborate, introduction to the language and culture of Central America, in a country club–like setting within the elegant residential neighborhood of Los Yoses (20 minutes by bus from downtown San José), is provided by the Forester Institute; its classrooms enjoy an awesome view of the surrounding mountains, and the chirping of birds.

At Forester, you choose from either two-week, three-week, or four-week classes (maximum of six students per class) in either "Language" or "Language and Culture." The former involves from three to six hours a day of instruction; the latter supplements classroom instruction with daily excursions, cultural activities, and conferences (on both political and cultural themes), often conducted on the weekends as well. On both programs, students are placed with carefully selected but non-English-speaking Costa Rican families where they receive a private room, breakfasts, dinners, and laundry service.

Charge for Forester's language program, including the homestay, is $425 to $555 (depending on the number of class hours) for two weeks, $545 to $720 for three weeks, $660 to $860 for four weeks. The more extensive language-and-culture program (including hotel stays on weekend excursions, as well as the normal homestay) runs $655 to $715 for two weeks,

The country is peaceful and stable, its cities calm and well ordered.

San José

La Mariposa, San José, Costa Rica

$835 to $910 for three weeks, $985 to $1070 for four weeks. Contact Forester's U.S. representative: **Charlene Biddulph, 249 S. U.S. 101, Suite 226, Solana Beach, CA 92075 (phone 619/792-5693).**

Realities of Central America

With or without a knowledge of Spanish, you can attend courses presented in English on the present-day realities of Central American societies at the Central American Institute for International Affairs ("ICAI") in San José, founded in part by the Organization of American States. ICAI offers numerous short-term (three weeks to one month) programs co-sponsored by about a dozen U.S. universities, to which outsiders are admitted, but only if they have some college training or other background in the social sciences. Lecturers are leading scholars or political figures of Central America; classes are supplemented by field trips, such as to a Nicaraguan refugee camp in Costa Rica's Limón Province; and students are housed (room and two meals a day) with Costa Rican families. Though prices vary, figure about $900 for a three-week course of instruction. For information, contact **Roberto de la Ossa, Director, ICAI, Apartado Postal 3316, San José, Costa Rica (phone 506/33-85-71 or 506/ 55-08-59 in San José.**

More casual learning, and again usually in English: at the Wednesday-evening lectures of the Quaker-run **Friends Peace Center** in San José, or at their periodic, frequent workshops, many of which are conducted in English (phone first—506/33-61-68— to determine if they are). And you can browse through numerous hard-to-find newspapers and magazines dealing with Central American issues at the center's extensive library. Its address, in the strange directional terms of San José, but comprehensible to any taxi driver, is: "C 15, a Central/2." Taxis to most points in San José are rarely more than $1 in cost.

If you would simply like the experience of living with a Costa Rican family on your visit to San José, contact **Señora Soledad Zamora (phone 506/24-79-37),** who serves as a one-woman booking agency for nearly 80 such families in and around the city. For a $15 fee, Señora Soledad will place you with a family that charges $7 to $12 a day, full board. Since she does not speak English, ask to speak with her daughter, Silvia, or with one of the American students usually living at Señora Soledad's home, if you yourself do not speak Spanish. Staying with a host family, you soon will.

Costs and Cultural Opportunities

For the standard tourist to Costa Rica desiring standard accommodations, the choices are broad and at wonderfully low rates. They range from such stand-outs as the deluxe Corobici Hotel (as little as $66 for a double room) to the tourist/first-class Gran Hotel Costa Rica ($52 per double) and Ambassador Hotel ($40 for a double), to the charming Pension Don Carlos ($30 per double) to the more basic Costa Rica Inn ($14.50 per double) to the Toruma Youth Hostel ($2.45 per person per night). Restaurants offer meals with music at such outstanding values as El Balcon de Europa (Costa Rican dishes from $2 to $4.85) and Miró's Bistro (a giant platter of rice with shrimp for $3.30). Nightlife is centered at El Pueblo, a sparkling-white village of Spanish colonial architecture whose varied components—discos, bars, restaurants with guitar players and accordions—could not be exhausted in a week of going out each night. At the complex's La Cocina de Leña restaurant, where musicians wander in to play, a mammoth plate called Gallo Pinto (mixed rice and beans, meat, eggs, and sour cream) sells for the Costa Rican equivalent of $2.70.

Suitably housed and fed in the year-round, spring-like climate of San José, you then attend symphonic or dance performances (tickets for under $5) at the famed National Theater; visit the art exhibits and presentations at the Costa Rica–North American Cultural Center; wander among the modern art, primarily by Central American artists, at the Galería J. Garcia Monge or in the galleries of the Central Bank on the Cultural Plaza; view pre-Columbian art at the National Museum of Costa Rica.

But mainly you meet the politically alert, fiercely independent people of Costa Rica, and hear their varied reactions to conditions in Central America and policies of other nations toward Central America. And then, if you wish, you can head to the beaches, surrounded by jungle-like national parks.

Into the Country

When you then strike out into the hinterland, your vacation is again utterly different from what you've experienced in more standard resorts, in high-rise hotels. It is not only different, it is more human, more removed from urban atmospheres, better.

Because the Costa Ricans are fiercely determined to protect their beach areas from the excesses of a Miami or Acapulco, they have limited seaside hotels to the height of a palm tree, and placed many of them back from the sea, on hillsides or enveloped by trees. About the closest equivalent to a standard resort area is that sector (actually a province) of Costa Rica's Pacific coast called Guanacaste, where the several, small, one- and two-story hotels on four particular beaches—Tamarindo, Ocotal, Condovac, and Flamingo—are the chief draws, but charge no more than $37 to $50 for a single room, $47 to $70 for a double, even in high season. Those rates contrast sharply with the levels of other tropical countries available to North Americans.

Amazingly, you can fly from San José to Guanacaste for only $10 each way, or go by bus for infinitely less, or drive there from San José in four hours on the Pan American Highway.

Rather than stay at the resorts of Guanacaste, however, I'd pursue the more exotic pleasures of the nation's national parks and nature reserves, teeming with wildlife and wonders. They are the true, stand-out attractions of Costa Rica.

Manuel Antonio National Park

Reached by air from San José for only $7.50 each way, this 1,700-acre preserve on the Pacific Ocean is a series of crescent-shaped, white-sand beaches surrounded by lush tropical jungle and verdant volcanic cliffs; mention its name to a "Tico" (a Costa Rican) and you'll provoke exclamatory superlatives, sighs, and dreamy smiles. It is one of the few places on earth

Here are the pleasures of the tropics without the pressures of crowds and casinos.

Costa Rica's Pacific coast

Street artisan

It affords you a chance to experience Central America without danger, to explore and discuss the politics of the region with open-minded residents.

The Jungle Train

La Mariposa dining

where you can luxuriate on a beach and experience jungle (including white-faced monkeys) at the same time. You walk to the beaches along well-marked jungle paths, enjoy breathtaking views of azure seas and sharp cliffs from atop lookout areas on Cathedral Point (a bit more difficult to reach), view wildlife in a hundred forms, then frolic in the warm surf with Tico families, who later tap and sway to salsa music—and prepare enormous lunches for their beachside stays.

Although campers can remain overnight in the park, at designated sites (receiving fresh water, bathroom facilities, and picnic tables, for 50¢), the hotels are outside its grounds, but immediately alongside or less than two miles away. The top lodgings are the Spanish-colonial duplex villas of La Mariposa, built into the otherwise-untouched, lush countryside, with one of the world's most spectacular ocean views and Costa Rica's highest rates: $85 per person per night, including breakfast and dinner served in an elegant pavilion amid jungle flowers and palms. You dine to the strains of classical music, enjoying such treats as stuffed quail baked in red wine or heart of palm brioche. For reservations (which you will need here), phone toll free 800/223-6510 (212/832-2277 in New York), or directly to La Mariposa in Costa Rica at 506/77-0355.

Lesser-priced, but perfectly adequate and just as exotic: the small Hotel Divisamar, directly across the road from La Mariposa ($34 double, without meals), and the nearby Hotel Karahe ($34 double), the latter with a moderately priced restaurant. Rock-bottom in cost, but proper: the Costa Linda Youth Hostel, accepting people of all ages, for $4 per bed per night.

Monteverde Cloud Forest Reserve

By express bus from San José ($3.40), or by rental car, a great many visitors schedule time for still another major attraction: the mystical, cloud-enshrouded, 25,000-acre reserve of Monteverde in the Tilaran Mountains, 6,000 feet above the sea. Protected and maintained by a world-renowned, Quaker-founded science institute, it harbors hundreds of varieties of mammals and birds (including the mythical Quetzal and the elusive golden toad; you'll almost certainly spot the former), lush jungle with 80 miles of wood- or rock-carpeted trails, waterfalls, orchids, and a dense shroud of white cloud—you feel somewhere between land and sky. For $47 per person, including all three meals, you can stay in the lodge/farm known as the Hotel Montana (call 506/61-1846 in San José for reservations) or for $25 including meals in the Belmar Hotel or Pension Quetzal, or for $18 including all three meals in the Flora Mar, or for $3 a night, without meals, in the dorm-like "field station" of the Tropical Science Center ("T.S.C.", headquartered at Apartado 8-3870, 100-San José, Costa Rica, phone 506/22-6241; phone them in advance for a bunk). And at the club known as the Golden Toad in the nearby town of Santa Elena, Latin and rock music is played most nights.

The Jungle Train

Still other visitors take the six- to eight-hour trip on the slow "Jungle Train" from San José to Limón, where they proceed by bus for another hour to the 1,500 acres of coral reef that make up Cahuita National Park of Costa Rica. After that day-long ride through tropical vegetation and coffee plantations along mountains and in green valleys, so close to village life as to enable eye contact with Ticos going about their daily business, they repair for rest to the pleasant Hotel Cahuita ($15 per very basic double room), with garden, pool, and patio restaurant. In the park, snorkeling equipment is rented for $5.40 to explore the exquisite coral reef.

Some of these sights, and still others, can be managed on shorter day-trips from San José (where a dozen travel agencies will make the arrangements), but staying overnight or for several nights at small lodgings affords you a different and better contact with the primeval life of tropical jungles, mountains, and sea—the kind of experience that used to be the accustomed lot of travelers before high-rise hotels standardized the world.

For assistance in visiting these and other attractions of Costa Rica, I like the services of OTEC, a well-staffed, nonprofit organization of student travel which specializes in trips and discounts for the young, but actually handles the needs of all ages and of nonstudents. They're found on the second floor of the Victoria Building in San José ("a 3, c 3/5"; phone 22-08-66), where they answer questions and offer to make you one of their traveling groups, which brings you a radical saving from the price levels of other commercial tour operators. Contact them ahead of time if you're planning a special interest or group tour of Costa Rica, by writing: **OTEC, P.O. Box 323, San José 1002, Costa Rica.**

For additional information on this inexpensive and inspiring nation, contact the Los Angeles office of the **Costa Rica Tourist Board** (phone 213/382-8080, or toll free 800/762-5909) (800/762-5900 in California), or phone their Miami office at 305/358-2150, or toll free 800/327-7033 outside Florida. The national carrier, LACSA, and Eastern Airlines, service San José directly from several U.S. cities, and numerous other airlines go there via their own national gateways. ≈

River-rafting in the national parks

The North Shore of the Dominican Republic, Newest Bargain Spot of the World

It Is the Cheapest Acceptable Vacation Coast in the Caribbean

Luperon Beach

Opposite page: *Playa Grande, on the northeast coast*

If I had less than $400 to spend on a two-week vacation in the tropics, and needed to stretch that sum to cover every expense other than air fare, I'd go to the north coast of the Dominican Republic. Apart from Venezuela much farther to the south, it is the cheapest acceptable vacation spot in the Caribbean.

As late as the mid-1970s the area had no tourist industry to speak of. It had no airport, no hotels of international standard, no modern port facilities, and no transportation from the provincial, seaside capital of Puerto Plata other than *carros publicos,* group taxis, carrying up to 12 people and their live chickens, hooded fighting cocks, an occasional frisky pig, and assorted bundles of merchandise.

Today, all that has changed. At Playa Dorada, and at other beaches along the coast near Puerto Plata, a dozen major hotels and numerous more modest ones have sprouted like mushrooms. And Puerto Plata itself now has a modern airport and docks for receiving the largest of cruise ships. On vastly improved roads, you find air-conditioned motorcoaches.

And yet the scene is still refreshingly traditional, somewhat sleepy and Hispanic in character, without high-rise towers, and not at all overdeveloped as in other Caribbean locations or at Mexican resorts. The line has not yet been crossed that distinguishes an indigenous foreign culture from a stateless stew of modern, cookie-cutter–created hotels and plastic retail shops. When you stroll the village streets along the coast, and chat with the people, and even when you delve into the more distinctly urban Puerto Plata, you are very definitely in the proud, foreign precincts of the Dominican Republic.

And because tourism here hasn't yet reached a total of 300,000 tourists a year (compare that with the one million going annually to Jamaica), the tourist remains submerged in a sea of locals, enjoying prices geared to the needs of the local population. Rates are relatively cheap in even the larger hotels, and dirt cheap in the minor ones.

Why else go to the north shore of the Dominican Republic? Let us count the reasons.

Here, the tourist remains submerged in a sea of locals, enjoying prices geared to the needs of the local population.

Another view of Luperon

Along the "Riviera of the Atlantic"

1. Climate and Geography: The beaches of the northern coast—an 80-mile-long "Riviera of the Atlantic," stretching from Luperon to Samana—enjoy endlessly sunny days, with average air temperatures of 75° to 85°, and average water temperatures in the 70s, year round. The terrain immediately off the beaches is as varied as in the U.S.: high coffee plantations, dry desert lands, rolling sugarcane fields, flat, rich farmland, and large cattle ranches.

2. A Warm-Spirited People: The Dominicans lead a gentle, simple life still dominated by family ties and various neighborly interactions. In the small villages and the country (*campo*), it is not uncommon to be invited into a palmwood shack and served coffee or a cool coconut milk. Since tourism is relatively new to most of the common folk, they still relish the chance to make visitors feel at home.

3. History: Here, as you know, is where Christopher Columbus first landed on December 5, 1492, near a bay called La Isabella, to the west of Puerto Plata. It's well worth a day-long excursion to Santo Domingo, the center of Spanish colonial power, to visit the well-preserved structures associated with that era and the 16th-century cathedral said to contain the remains of Admiral Columbus (Colón). After a turbulent series of invasions, occupations, and dictatorships, the island-nation is today relatively stable, democratically governed, and moving ahead economically.

4. Vacation Options: As the northern perimeter of a populous country, the area offers a far more varied array of activities than is usually found in the Caribbean. You can, in addition to swimming and snorkeling, attend baseball games or local cockfights, ascend cable cars to mountain peaks, visit rum factories, amber mines, and numerous markets, dance the merengue at a dozen locations, and join the *paseo* of strolling couples and singles around the central square of Puerto Plata on Sunday evenings (when there are outdoor band concerts), obtaining a sense of the rich Dominican culture and people.

5. Crafts for Sale: The north coast is also known as the "Amber Coast," from the large deposits of this semiprecious gem formed from the sap of trees which dripped and hardened about two million years ago. For purchasing low-cost jewelry of amber, you have the shops of the Amber Museum in Puerto Plata, an amber "factory" on a corner of the central square (Parque Central) in Puerto Plata, or the Centro Artesanal de Puerto Plata, where Dominican youth are given a year's schooling in making that and other crafts.

6. Vacation Prices: But equally important, you have the values that result from an exchange rate of nearly seven Dominican pesos to $1 U.S., which makes a vacation here one of the best buys in the Caribbean, regardless of the price category you choose.

The bargains are especially breathtaking at the modest hotels, where you meet local people in their own domain, and "touch" their lives. At the Hostal Jimesson, in one of the several, newly renovated, turn-of-the-century Victorian homes of Puerto Plata, rooms for one or two people start at $18 and $20 a night in low season (April 15 to December 15), about 30% more in winter. Owner-manager Maria Jimenez is from one of the town's oldest leading families. You pay even less, as little as $16, at the air-conditioned Hotel Caracol down by the Malecon (the oceanfront drive) or at numerous guesthouses nearby with *cuartos* (look for the room signs) for rent, although you can go to as high as $40 a night for a double room of fully American standard at the Hotel Montemar in town, a training school for aspiring young hotel personnel. I vastly prefer these lodgings to the more costly, self-contained tourist complexes farther down the beach.

For authentic cuisine in Puerto Plata, take a bus or *publico* to Maria's El Portal, just outside the gates of a ritzy condo known as Costambar, a few miles west of town. Maria serves only Dominican dishes on the ten tables of her inexpensive, open-air restaurant under a thatched roof. She makes a memorable *sancocho* (mixed stew), and *carne mechada* (spicy beef, rice, and beans), among many other *comidas típicos,* and is greatly beloved for personality as well as culinary skill.

Sosua

The second major beach of the north coast—small but exquisite—is near the resort-like town of Sosua,

settled by Jewish refugees from Europe in the early years of World War II; it is on the other side of (and equidistant from) the airport servicing Puerto Plata. A good place to meet the locals here is at "El Oasis"— oldest restaurant and hotel in town—where mid-April to mid-December room rates are about $18 a night, including private bath, about a third higher in winter. At the nearby Hostal de Lora, or at the Sun Island Inn, rooms range from $16 to $24 a night, depending on size of room and day of week, while a weighty $40 a night will rent a one-room cottage for two at Charlie's Cabañas, complete with pool and beach overlook. Heading east from Sosua along a spectacular coastline, you reach the tiny town of Cabarete, known for its crayfish, grouper fishing, excellent beach, scuba-diving, windsurfing competitions, and $30-a-day apartments at Tom and Lois Yoder's place. The approach to take, at this and other tiny beachfront towns, is to stroll the central square (there always is one) and ask the local people for their recommendation of a good, family-run hotel. Get clear on the price and write it down, so that you and the owner will later agree on whether you are talking about U.S.$ (dollars) or RD$ (pesos), especially if your Spanish is poor.

For every site along the northern coast, the gateway is Puerto Plata, to which direct flights are scheduled from Miami and New York. From the airport, you can make your way cheaply into town (or to Sosua) by eschewing the taxis in favor of a *concho* or *guagua* (local minibuses) that stops along the main road and costs a couple of dollars at most. Living modestly, treading lightly, remaining open to different ways, you will have traveled in a socially responsible manner, and perhaps brought the world a little closer together. ≈

An Introduction to Belize

Shunned By Many Because of Its Location in Central America, It Is Peaceful, Stable, Filled with Activities—and Cheap

Belizean interior

Weather-beaten wooden homes and streets made of white sand. "Hotels" with ten rooms and "restaurants" with five tables. Barefoot informality and yarn-spinning residents with all the time in the world. Electricity that doesn't always work, schedules that aren't always met.

If you're yearning for the Caribbean as it once was, you'll find it in the Caribbean's newest nation, Belize, only seven years removed from its former status as British Honduras. Two hours by air from Miami, and yet touristically underdeveloped, it awaits you on the edge of Central America—some would say "on the edge of the world"—just below the Yucatán peninsula of Mexico, between Guatemala and Honduras.

It is remarkably peaceful, stable, democratic. Though its tiny population (160,000 people in an area the size of Massachusetts) is split among a dozen ethnic groups—Mayan Indians, Chinese, "Anglos," Créoles, Hindus, mestizos, Hispanics, even a recent community of horse-and-buggy Mennonites—they live in perfect harmony, enjoy a British-style parliamentary government, intermarry, and serve as a lesson for all of us. What's more, their official language is English!

As for its touristic attractions, Belize possesses the second-longest (after Australia) barrier reef on earth, a teeming coral formation of sea life, shapes, and colors that draws scuba-divers and sailors from around the world. Along the reef are then dozens of "cayes" (pronounced "keys")—narrow, beach-lined islands of remarkable beauty, dotted with small hotels (often ten rooms apiece) of modest, friendly pretensions.

On the mainland, only one major city is found, of no great visitor interest. This is Belize City, with only 40,000 people, but site of an international airport well serviced by a number of carriers (I'll list them later). From here, you take smaller planes to the cayes.

Inland of Belize City is of greater appeal: 65% of the country's land area is uninhabited jungle—supporting jaguars, no less—and scattered about are relics, temples, even cities, of the once-mammoth Mayan civilization that flourished from the 3rd to the 10th century in what is now Belize.

You have two vacation choices, therefore, on a trip to Belize, and many tourists combine them both. You can sun, swim, sail, or scuba-dive on and off the cayes. Or you can explore the inner mainland, pursuing bents of archeology, wildlife and other natural history, Mayan ruins and culture, all forms of jungle adventure travel.

The Mainland

The region on the mainland best suited to accommodate tourists is the Cayo District (two hours by car from Belize City), which has several exotic but comfortable lodges, and is accessible to the formidable Mayan ceremonial site of Xunantunich and the impressive natural wonders of Mountain Pine Ridge. Alternatively, you go south down the coast to Dangriga, viewing the world's only jaguar preserve and the life of Garifuna Indians, who allow visitors (if they're so inclined) to participate in their rituals. Because life hereabouts is rustic, with treacherous roads and nonexistent (usually) signposts, you accomplish all this not by self-drive car, but on organized small-group tours operated weekly and well by several Belizean tour operators. In my opinion, it's best to pursue the mainland portion of your trip first (say, for four days) and follow up with R&R on those sunny, pleasant cayes for two or three concluding days of your trip.

Upon the mainland, so rich is the Mayan heritage of Belize, so diverse its wildlife and flora, that the resulting travel choices are fairly dizzying.

If you can somehow manage the time, sign on for Beth La Croix's 12-day/11-night "In Search of the Ancient Maya" (as little as $1,325 per person, and virtually all-inclusive; write **Personalized Services, P.O. Box 1158, Belize City, Belize (phone 011-501/77593)**, which takes you to a dozen ancient ceremonial centers, Mayan trading sites, excavated village ruins dating as far back as 2,500 B.C. Your stops include Altun Ha (the country's most extensively excavated Mayan pyramids, mounds, ball courts, burial chambers, reservoirs) and Xunantunich (tallest man-made structure in Belize, with elaborate stucco friezes); and then your tour darts over the Guatemalan border to view the grandeur of famous Tikal (a Mayan royal city flourishing from 600 B.C. to A.D. 950, when it was mysteriously abandoned). On the way, while still in Belize, you visit the current "digs" at Caracol, which university archeologists believe will ultimately unearth a pre–Classic Age Mayan city three times as large as Tikal and every bit as grand.

Or if you're inclined to less vigorous touring, but in the same prime location (the well-located Cayo District), you can contact the English couple who own the palm-thatched safari lodge called **Chaa Creek Cottages, P.O. Box 53, Cayo, Belize (phone 011-501/092-2037)**, from which every standard tour is offered. Charges here are $45 per person per night, double occupancy, including all three meals. Or you can stay at the newer, basic, but charming, Windy Hill Cottages where double rooms rent for a total of $30 a night. Finally, if you're not up to a jungle camp at all, you can simply base yourself (for $30 double) in the hillside **San Ignacio Hotel, P.O. Box 33, San Ignacio, Cayo District, Belize (phone 011-501/092-2034)**, booking one-day tours, or hiking on your own, from there.

Whatever your hotel choice, you must be sure to include a visit to the mile-long Panti Trail, in the same area and of considerable historic and perhaps scientific interest. It's lined with the remarkably diverse plants, bushes, and trees supplying herbal substances used as medicines by the ancient Mayans, all according to formulas handed down from generation to generation and today known to a 90-year-old Mayan/Belizean priest/doctor (read: medicine man) named Eligio Panti. For four years now, scientists headed by Dr. Rosita Arvigo have been "debriefing" Don Eligio of his secrets, attracting attention from learned groups ranging from the New York Botanical Garden to the National Cancer Society. They also conduct guided tours of the trail (daily except Monday, $12), commenting on the strongly apparent medicinal properties of the growths (a tree bark that cures dysentery, a leaf that stops bleeding).

And don't laugh: fully 25% of the world's commercial medicines are derived from plant-based chemicals found in tropical regions (according to Dr. Arvigo).

The Panti Trail begins at Dr. Arvigo's home, "IX Chel" (named for the Mayan goddess of medicine), just beyond San Ignacio off the Western Hwy. The great Mayan ceremonial site of Xunantunich is not far away. To contact Dr. Arvigo for a guided group tour of the Panti Trail ($30 per group), call the **Environmental Center, Eve Street, San Ignacio (phone 45545).**

The Cayes

After an active and sometimes tiring exploration into the interior, a great many visitors turn to those restful strips of water-surrounded land along the barrier reef.

Ambergris Caye is the most highly developed of these narrow lines in the sea, and that mark of distinction will come as a surprise when you first arrive by small plane at the sleepy frontier town of San Pedro, "capital" of Ambergris Caye. It consists of exactly three white-sand-covered "avenues," the unpretentiously named Front, Middle, and Back Streets. On Front (also known as Beach) Street, within the five intersecting blocks of the city center, are small hotels and cabañas interspersed with the basketball court, police station, town hall, school, and local discothèque (Big Daddy's).

On Front Street, the Holiday Hotel features the colorful tales and excellent cuisine of the charismatic Celi McCorkle, whom many call the "mother of tourism" in Belize. Farther along, the Coral Beach is a favorite of divers and operated by the "father of diving," Allan Forman, who offers inexpensive rates ($36 for the average double room) and generous, family-style meals. You can stay at the Sun Breeze Beach Resort ($80 for a double room, and home of the island's windsurfing school), at Ramon's Reef (in charming, waterside cabañas priced at $75 a day, double), or on the edge of town in the costlier ($80, double) Paradise Hotel much favored by Francis Ford Coppola.

It is also possible, either by simply applying door-to-door, or by using the advance services of Beth La Croix of Personalized Services in Belize City (address and phone number above) to obtain $25-a-night rooms at such family-run lodgings as the San Pedrano and its several affiliates run by four brothers and sisters.

From all these havens, the barrier reef is less than a mile out into the sea, supplying not simply the site for snorkeling and dives, but a wonderfully protected area for invigorating sailing and windsurfing; "there's always a breeze in Belize," goes a local saying.

For on-the-spot information and assistance in San Pedro, contact Pany Arceo (011-501/026-2136); he's a dynamic fisherman-turned-guide who offers insight, instruction, and excursions in bonefishing, snorkeling, diving, and birdwatching at considerably lower cost, and with far greater knowledge, than others I've met. Or seek out his sister, Shelley Prevett, who operates the moderately priced and popular restaurant, The Hut ($8 for turtle curry). She provides hard-to-get information (babysitters, air charters, local black-coral-jewelry makers), and will also prepare your own fish catch at half the normal menu price.

The lower-priced, budget alternative to Ambergris Caye—if you can imagine such a thing—is Caye Caulker, a few miles farther south in the sea. With only two streets along the beach, it's like a stage setting for a W. Somerset Maugham play, and hotel rooms are widely available for $10 to $20 a night, while several inexpensive "restaurants" are in people's homes. At the popular Tropical Paradise hotel, $20 will get you your own cabaña by the sea. Caye Caulker, though, can be reached only by boat from Belize City (on several services operated daily except Sunday), while Ambergris Caye is more easily serviced by air.

Other cayes (often with only a single hotel apiece) are more difficult of access, and thereby more exclusive: Caye Chapel (the 32-room Pyramid Island Resort), St. George's Caye (St. George's Lodge), South Water Caye (Blue Marlin Lodge), and Caye Bokel (the fishing-oriented Turneffe Island Lodge, $150 a day per person for room and all three meals, unlimited use of fishing boats, gas for the boats, and guides, all for the purpose of seeking six-pound bonefish, the chief activity), among them. An exception to the pricey tone of the less accessible cayes is Bluefield Range Cayes (a group of three), where beach huts on working lobster and fishing camps rent for under $25 a night. Ricardo's Beach Huts, also offering tent sites for $2.50 per person per night, is one such place.

Resources for Touring

Always bear in mind that the relative newness of tourism in Belize adds to its appeal, but also has its drawbacks. Tourists are often surprised to find no air conditioning in many hotels (unnecessary, say the Belizeans, because of their cooling trade winds). And visitors should also be prepared for occasional electricity shortages and lack of hot water, particularly inland. Bring a spirit of adventure—and an open mind.

Your best contact for preparing a trip to Belize is **Tropical Travel Representatives, of Houston, Texas (phone 713/688-1985 or toll free 800/451-8017 outside Texas).** A combined travel agency and tour operator, its founders, Tommy and Jerisue Thomson, are so enchanted with the country that they exchanged wedding vows on its white sands four years ago. They also publish a quarterly newsletter, *Belize Currents,* which is widely distributed by the Embassy of Belize and the Caribbean Tourist Association and available to their clients. Other Belize-specializing U.S. travel agents include the high-volume **Ocean Connections (phone 713/486-6993, or toll free 800/331-2458 outside Houston),** and **Triton Tours (phone 504/522-3382, or toll free 800/426-0226 outside Louisiana).**

Another excellent Belize information resource and travel coordinator is **Beth La Croix, of Personalized Services** in Belize City (see above for address and telephone number). She has a wealth of information and welcomes inquiries that state budget limitations and personal interests. For ultra-cost-conscious travelers whom the U.S. agents cannot accommodate, Beth's services will be well worth the time of a letter or the cost of an overseas telephone call.

Good background reading for Belize is the book *Jaguar* by Alan Rabinowitz (published by Arbor House).

Four airlines service Belize from the States, usually for a round-trip "add-on" fare from Miami of $238, a bit more from New Orleans and Houston. **Tan Sahsa Airlines (phone 305/526-4300, or toll free 800/327-1225, 800/432-9818 in Florida)** operates daily service at that rate from Miami, four times a week from New Orleans, thrice weekly from Houston; it also provides advantageous "through" fares from other cities, such as from New York for $424 round trip.

Continental Airlines (phone toll free 800/231-0856), Eastern Airlines (phone 201/621-9450, or toll free 800/EASTERN outside New Jersey), and **TACA International Airlines (phone 305/526-6795, or toll free 800/535-8780 outside Florida)** offer similar services. Eastern charges a dramatically low $191 round trip from Miami, and Continental, $241 round trip from Houston. TACA goes there from Los Angeles ($499), San Francisco ($599), New Orleans ($285), and Houston ($295).

This winter in the Caribbean, you have a choice.

You can crowd into a high-rise hotel and fight for a place at a noisy pool.

Or you can go to Belize.

Guess which I'd choose. ≈

Belizean plaza

A Trip to Eastern Europe

Budapest, Prague, and East Berlin, in a Time of Ferment

Parliament buildings, Budapest

Center of East Berlin

Though some, at times, resemble a Western city, with modern skyscrapers and trendy shops, their street names leave no doubt that you have passed into a different world. They read: "Karl Marx Strasse" and "Lenin Allee," "Engels Utca" and "John Reed Korút."

Yet after several days of touring the capitals of Eastern Europe, you take it all in your stride. Anxiety, the initial sensation, converts to calm curiosity, and eventually you move beyond political preconceptions into an appreciation of the complexity of all human societies, both theirs and ours. A trip to Eastern Europe is one of the great learning experiences for Americans, and one that increasing numbers of our fellow citizens are attempting.

It is also one of the cheapest of current-day trips. To travel here in 1989 is like returning to the Western Europe of the 1950s. Provided only that you strictly avoid the large, grand establishments—as you prudently did in London and Paris, too, 30 years ago—you discover that everything else is priced at a half to a third of American levels. Staying in a private home of Budapest or Prague, eating at cafeterias, taking the local trams and subways, you can live for as little as $15 or $20 a day.

For maximum learning, the best course is to stray from the central areas of cities—those showcases built to impress—and venture instead into the neighborhoods. There you will more quickly discern the radical differences between Eastern European states, some the product more of age-old national characteristics than of modern ideology.

Hungary: Almost frantically consumerist—to some tastes, overly so—intent on amassing material goods, focused heavily on commerce and social competition. East Germany: Austere and disciplined—to some observers, gloomily so. Though the country is one of the "wealthiest" of the Soviet bloc, it is obvious that most resources are being channeled to sectors other than consumer needs. People here live modest, quiet lives, mainly in their homes; they seem still too scarred by turbulent events of their recent history, including the Wall, to speak out as forcefully as some do in other Eastern European states. Czechoslovakia: Poor and repressed, but with an active dissident movement that periodically demands reform; it will obviously come about, perhaps earlier than most suspect.

Though much about Eastern Europe may dismay you, the total effect of the trip is rather uplifting, mainly because the journey is taking place at all. Between the two great ideological blocs, travel is reaching major proportions, tourists and residents are meeting and conversing, dialogue occurring, people on both sides pondering. And though these winds of change were born from causes other than travel, yet travel plays its part, as you begin to see on a visit to:

East Berlin

It is still called Checkpoint Charlie, and soldiers guard the gate. But as you cross the Wall into East Berlin, you get a "Guten Tag" and the hint of a smile from police on the other side. Though perestroika and glasnost aren't exactly welcomed over here, there's been a definite lessening of tensions, and more and more Americans travel from West to East Berlin not simply for the day, but to stay overnight, or for several days, in the capital of the German Democratic Republic.

I crossed the Wall into East Berlin last summer at the start of a whirlwind visit to three nations of the Soviet bloc: East Germany, Czechoslovakia, and Hungary. The experience, in its earliest stages, couldn't have been more unexpected. In this, one of the more prosperous of the Communist states, my lodgings were a brand-new luxury hotel—the Grand—with an eight-story atrium lobby. My post-breakfast stroll was along the elegant Unter den Linden—looking like a boulevard from Switzerland—and then into the vast expanse of the skyscraper-lined Alexanderplatz and along the one-mile length of the Karl-Marx-Allee. I passed multicolored office buildings with mosaic murals, a half dozen new hotels, a newly refurbished opera house, and other impressive structures.

Here was none of the shabbiness or the signs of a disabled economy that one instantly sees, for instance, in Czechoslovakia or in Poland.

But then, as I always do in a large city, I walked into a subway and rode for several stops outside the center, to where the people are. In a famous, low-income district of prewar Berlin called Prinzelauer Berg, I quickly discovered the far more modest life of the average East Berliner, in plain apartment blocks that are sometimes seedy, never grand, and where people shop in often-gloomy stores of limited variety, unlike the big emporiums of the downtown. It is always good to "come back to earth" after viewing the stagy, showy centerpiece of a world capital. But it is equally wrong to assume—as I so quickly learned in East Berlin, as elsewhere—that people there are seething with discontent or that they think our way.

One of the rewards of venturing into the neighborhoods of an Eastern European city is that you talk with people and learn from them. Away from the monuments and museums, the government ministries, flags, and slogan-covered banners, people almost visibly relax. No sooner had I stopped to peer at a street map of that East Berlin neighborhood than a young father with two children in tow asked, in English, whether he could be of aid. Then, after a block or two of talk, and to my sheer amazement, he asked whether I would care to visit for a few minutes with his wife and himself.

Now you would think that in the private apartment of an English-speaking couple who had just invited a Westerner to tea, you would hear blanket condemnations of the regime, the Wall, and the Warsaw Pact. It was more complex than that. I heard wry references to the refusal of East Germany's leaders, to date, to follow the reforming lead of Mikhail Gorbachev. I heard sarcastic asides about the stubborn conservatism of party functionaries. But mostly I heard references to life: how the younger daughter, five years old, was unhappy to enter grade school because she so liked her kindergarten teacher; how the couple would be willing to pay more in rent if the building's superintendent were to repaint the corridors. I heard love of country, and pride in Olympic athletes.

When you again leave the touristic center of an East European city, and dine in the small café of a neighborhood, you are seated quite democratically in any empty chair (I like that), even at a partially occupied table. Next to me, that very same day, was an East Berlin teacher in special education (for the mentally retarded) and his woman friend. In broken German and broken English, we discussed the plight of autistic children, the comparative street life of New York and East Berlin, the backgrounds of our parents.

In short, we rediscovered—across a vast political gulf—the essential oneness of all mankind.

Later in my East Berlin stay, I did the standard things. I toured the great Pergamon Museum with its remarkable Greek temple and actual processional street of ancient Babylon. I dined at the Moscow Restaurant, peered at highly political exhibits of German history, shopped the Centrum department store, saw cabaret and theater.

But nothing matched the impact of that earlier human encounter with people in the East Berlin neighborhoods—the kind of visit made by so few tourists, yet only a 10¢ subway ride from the central tourist attractions. Though the East German regime is among the least open, most authoritarian, of all the Eastern European governments—a one-party state that brooks no organized dissent—it is obviously in ferment, and it is possible to meet with people and ascertain their views. And while you will hear cautiously expressed criticisms of their society, you will find them unconvinced that all political rectitude belongs to one side or another of the world's contending forces. If you will open your own mind to unprejudiced thought as you converse with them, you will be forced to confront grave questions about the inequalities and insecurities of American life, and about our problems of poverty and homelessness.

You will also meet, in my humble view, a somewhat different sort of person than you encountered in West Germany: less bluff and assertive; people who have passed through the crucible and emerged more gentle and kind. The sweetness of the East Berliners—invariably courteous and helpful to the visitor—is the most indelible recollection of my just-completed stay.

Getting there for a single day from West Berlin is easy: you simply go with passport to a border-crossing point, like Checkpoint Charlie, and pass through the Wall in 15 minutes or so.

Going there for a stay of several days is more cumbersome. You must fix your entire itinerary in advance, and make firm hotel reservations for every night of the stay, in order to obtain an East German visa.

Once there, the rewards are many—and inexpensive. But only if you shun the normal tourist paths. Look for a subway station and take any train to a neighborhood, where life is, where people are. And rediscover that all of us on earth have similar human concerns.

Prague

When you drive from East Berlin to Prague, as I recently did, you remain at all times within the Soviet bloc; but when you cross the border from East Germany to Czechoslovakia, you are in a different realm.

From Teutonic to Slavic. In the streets of the East German cities you just left, strollers were sparse, and the few there were had really promenaded, not walked, a bit pompously, as if on display. Suddenly, in Prague, you are surrounded by swift-flowing crowds, people darting here and there, jabbering in excitable Czech, jamming the wine bars and the separate beer bars, rushing into line at small sausage stands and ice cream shops.

Once again you have felt the key attraction of Europe: the total change of cultures and cuisines, languages and attitudes, that can take place in a few miles, almost within minutes, daily. Even in the supposedly homogeneous states of the Warsaw Pact, nations are radically different from each other.

Not to have seen Prague is not to have known Europe. Like Bruges, like Siena, like Rothenburg-ob-der-Tauber, it is one of those few, almost perfectly preserved cities that overwhelms with architecture of the past. Throughout its vast central area it looks today exactly as it did 100 years ago; in parts of that area, it looks today as it looked 500 years ago. When Milos Forman chose to film the exterior scenes of *Amadeus* in the streets of Prague, he found it unnecessary to construct a single set.

And so you stroll in Prague, on streets where often traffic has been banned, through curving, medieval lanes, beneath archways and on arcaded sidewalks, into ravishing squares flanked by structures of every century other than the 20th. You cross the Moldau River on the medieval Charles Bridge with its baroque statuary—a gathering place for students from perhaps 50 lands—and then ascend cobblestone streets to the giant castle (Hradcany) that dominates the city. Behind it is the 14th-century St. Vitus Cathedral, and the Golden Lane of bohemian huts, in one of which Franz Kafka lived. From here he gazed upon the massive, turreted building alongside, and then wrote—in the novel *The Castle*—of the bureaucracy that kept him, even then, from that edifice of power.

The city is richly endowed with ornate opera houses, theaters, and concert halls, but July (my visit) is the wrong time to see them. Since most were closed for vacation, I made do for evening entertainment with the world-renowned Laterna Magika (Magic Lantern), which almost never shuts its enchanting stage. For 30 years it has been causing live actors to walk into and out of a curving, slitted, canvas backdrop of motion picture images to create theater that has the stunning impact of a fairy tale or a basic myth.

They will invariably tell you at the box office that all the seats are sold, but half an hour before curtain time, scalpers crowd the lobby to sell black-market tickets for "hard currency" (West German marks or U.S. dollars). I got mine for $5, U.S.

Not far from the Lantern, a key sight among many is the former Jewish area with its ancient synagogues and centuries-old gravestones crowding upon each other like a surrealistic stack of building blocks—the very image of old Europe. In the adjoining Jewish State Museum are drawings made by 12-year-old Jewish children in 1943 and 1944 as they awaited shipment to the gas chambers of Auschwitz and Buchenwald from Czechoslovakia's infamous Terezin concentration camp. In the Jewish Cemetery is the small mausoleum of the 17th-century religious philosopher, Rabbi Löw,

Anxiety turns to calm curiosity as you embark on a vital learning experience.

Zsambek Church, Hungary

The Castle Hill of Prague

Away from the grand hotels, everything is priced at a half to a third of American levels.

Hotel Gellert baths, Budapest

Wallenstein Palace, Prague

reputed by legend to have built an artificial man, the "Golem." Admirers from around the world have placed small pebbles of remembrance atop his tomb.

The city's contemporary life presents a mixed picture. Czechoslovakia is relatively poor, ranking well below Hungary and East Germany—the two economic leaders—in the eastern bloc. Much of Prague is therefore shabby and without comfort; prices are incredibly low. Subway fares are the equivalent of 10¢; main courses in one of the better restaurants run $2 and $3; meals in an "automat" or cafeteria can be had for $1.50.

While in the food shops and grocery stores there is plenty to buy, food is of limited quality and variety. Last summer, in the meat and fish stalls of a major department store I visited, only one product was available: pork, or rather pork fat laced with thin strands of meat. There was no beef, no chicken, no fish. Clothing is relatively drab, though serviceable, and people have limited funds for exercising their admitted right to travel.

If you have read the recent works of Czech novelists—like Milan Kundera's *The Incredible Lightness of Being*—you have learned there is considerable anger here. For this is the country whose "springtime of democracy" in 1968—the effort led by Alexander Dubček to build "socialism with a human face"—was brutally crushed by Soviet tanks. Yet Dubček was advocating little more than what is now espoused by Mikhail Gorbachev—policies still largely inadmissible to the clique that holds on hard to power in Czechoslovakia. In all of Prague, you will not find a single Western newspaper or magazine of the sort so frequently available today in East Berlin or Budapest.

And yet not everyone is discontent. And people react badly to the Westerner who tries too hard to elicit criticism of the regime or the society. No one wants to be patronized or constantly told that their life is inferior to ours.

To learn that lesson of travel, use the Frommer method of meeting people in an Eastern European state. Stand on a busy street corner with an unfurled city map and gaze anxiously at it. In just a few minutes an English-speaking bystander will approach to ask if he or she can be of aid. (If this doesn't happen, walk to a different street corner and try again.)

Start conversing; tell them you are new in the city, and would they care to have a drink, and answer questions about Prague, in a nearby café?

On three occasions in Prague, I spoke in this fashion to residents, and was thus able to remove myself, for half an hour or so each time, from the tourist's artificial world of monuments and museums. While, obviously, none of the people I met felt free enough to advocate a wholly different system, and while one man even asked me to lower my voice somewhat when we spoke of politics, all were nevertheless eager to speak about the current ferment in the Communist world, and about specific grievances, but with balance, and with unmistakable affection for their city, and some—some, I say—of their achievements.

Any special problem of life in Prague, I asked? The time spent in shopping, all three replied. Sometimes it was necessary, they said, to sneak time from work to stand in line at successive shops to purchase the ingredients of that night's dinner. Another complaint: the under-allocation of resources to the service industries, they said, making service poor; all the while, the factories are awash with excess personnel marking time. On Czech television, remarked one of my informants, hours are now spent discussing these problems of the Czech economy. "But they never talk," he continued, "about political democracy, which you have to have to make economic reforms."

What's good about your economy, I asked? Our rents are only a tenth of our incomes, answered one. The basic needs—the subways and buses, bread, our marvelous Czech beer—are all dirt cheap. We have no unemployment, free medical care, decent vacation time, and can retire at an early age.

Are you happy then, I asked?

"When I travel to the West and then come home," said one, "I get angry over our conditions. But when I then travel to the East and come home, I'm happy to be home."

"Our last real president, Edouard Bênes, said it best," he continued. "Even before the war, Bênes said that peace would come about when the East grew to appreciate the political freedoms of the West, and when the West secured some of the economic securities and equalities of the East. When we begin to be a bit like each other."

Now you, dear reader, may think these comments of an average Czech citizen to be wrong, or at best simplistic.

But think what is happening: we are at last speaking to each other, people-to-people, open-minded. After decades of Cold War, enmities we are conversing, debating, dealing with one another like human beings, over a beer at a Czech café, through travel.

And you, as a traveler to Eastern Europe, can help the process along—by simply standing on a corner and consulting a map.

Budapest

Hungary is the success story of the Communist bloc. When you drive from East Berlin and Prague to Budapest, as I just did, you are suddenly in a scene of consumerism hardly different from that of any major Western capital.

Here are stores and shops by the thousands, many of them privately owned. Goods of every variety filling their windows and decorating their aisles. Well-dressed shoppers stuffing plastic tote bags with purchases. Gleaming, new hotels with names like Hilton, Ramada, Intercontinental, Forum, and Novotel. Residents gorging on gooey strudels and chicken paprikash at restaurants staffed by attentive waiters.

And equally surprising, Western publications— *Newsweek, Time,* the *International Herald-Tribune*— for open sale on the racks of major newsstands.

It isn't communism, and yet it isn't quite capitalism either, but rather a system of mixed elements, unmistakably superior—in economic terms—to the societies of other Eastern European countries. While the Hungarians you meet will repeatedly stress that their nation is now in a serious recession, that isn't apparent at all to the first-time visitor, and those visitors include a great many from the Soviet Union and other Eastern countries, who stare bug-eyed at the products piled up in every store. When Mikhail Gorbachev visited Budapest last spring, he told his hosts that theirs were the results he hoped to achieve in the USSR.

In October of last year the American Society of Travel Agents held its annual convention in Budapest, the first time ever that this giant, yearly event has taken place in a Communist state. Some 12,000 travel professionals—nearly half of them retail travel agents—themselves sampled the charms of Budapest, and their recommendations to clients (most travel agents recommend what they themselves have seen) will undoubtedly set off an increased tourist boom to Hungary in 1989. Already, and long before the A.S.T.A. convention, rooms here were hard to obtain in the peak summer months.

Other straws in the wind: On January 1, 1989, Hungary joined the Eurailpass system of Western Europe, and bearers of that card will henceforth travel here at no added transportation cost.

In what way, then, is Hungary different in a touristic sense from any Western European country? Mainly in terms of cost—it's dramatically cheaper. Although the big-name hotels charge standard rates, everything else—the medium-priced hotels, restaurants, nightspots, and sights—are a third to a quarter the price of similar items in the Western European cities, as remarkable as that may seem. Though Hungary is far more prosperous than Czechoslovakia, East Germany, Poland, or Romania, its prices provide the very same startling bargains that theirs do, except—to stress the point again—at the large chain hotels (and their on-premises restaurants).

Thus, in-city transportation by subway or bus costs the equivalent of 10¢. The average taxi ride within Budapest is under $1; the taxi ride to the airport, about $5. Admission to museums is 10¢ to 20¢. Main courses at good restaurants can run as low as $2 and $3. Often, a three-course meal with Tokay wine, cherry strudel for dessert, and coffee, will run considerably under $10 a person.

Throughout my own stay, I hopped in and out of multiple taxis with abandon, ordered meals with scarcely a glance at menu prices, purchased a new set of eyeglasses for $17, kept busy from morning till night, and still had funds left over from the $50 traveler's check I had cashed that morning.

As in any Eastern European city, the serious-minded visitor wanders from the standard paths, and ventures into the nontouristed areas. In my own case, I rented a car and drove for two fascinating hours into the suburban-like Buda Hills, just behind the Buda half (divided by the Danube River) of Budapest—Pest is on the other side. Through miles and miles of recently built and quite stunning homes and villas, with many more in construction along sloping lawns that afford a perfect vista of the city below, I gazed about in open-mouthed wonder: the scene had more in common with Beverly Hills than Buda, and it was obvious that a sizable part of the city's population had found affluence.

Other nontouristy visits should include the mammoth indoor food market of Budapest—three football fields in size—at the corner of Tolbuhin Kurit and Sohaz Utca, just at the foot of the Szabadsag bridge, on the Pest side of Budapest. There, among other delights, a big bottle of Polish vodka (better than the Russian, say all the stallkeepers) runs $2.50, but the visit is made not to buy—but simply to take in the overwhelming variety of foodstuffs that the Hungarian economy has made available to its citizens. The contrast with the agricultural scarcity of Czechoslovakia—where food markets sometimes display only a single variety of meat—is startling.

Another, more affecting sight: The vast Dohany Street Synagogue (second largest in the world) in central Budapest, where a wedding was in progress when I last looked in. Because the Nazis were late in occupying Hungary, and commenced their horrifying deportation of Jews and others to the gas chambers at a late point of the war, too late to deport them all, a sizable number of Hungarian Jews survived, and a thriving Jewish community of about 50,000 is today found in Budapest—somewhat of an oddity in Eastern European cities. Diagonally across the street was a large "film museum" showing *Dr. Zhivago,* last summer, in

English. Hungary is the freest of the Soviet bloc in matters of expression, and the newspapers were filled with the prediction of the new premier, Karoly Grosz, made while touring the United States, that Hungary might soon enjoy a multiparty political system.

The top touristic activities begin with a visit to the city's resplendent Fine Arts Museum, with its half dozen Goyas and El Grecos, alongside priceless works of every age, especially Flemish and old Dutch masters. The equally grand National Museum, not far away, displays a strangely affecting collection of ornate armor, uniforms, and housewares of those dashing Hungarian hussars of old; the crown and crown jewels of the former Hungarian monarchy; and then—the highlight—Beethoven's piano, presented on his death to Franz Liszt.

After climbing various hillside vantage points, especially to the enchanting Castle Hill of multiple, restored highlights, you then take yourself to any of the scores of baths establishments of Budapest, to sweat in steam or soak in mineral-laden liquids at the lowest costs in travel today. At the gilded and rococo baths of the grand and traditional Hotel Gellert along the Danube, admission is all of 50 forint ($1) to the public baths (which includes both an indoor pool, outdoor pool, and several saunas), and a 20-minute massage by an elderly but strong masseuse comes to another 40 forint—80¢ U.S.

And then, if you haven't the time for a two-hour trip in each direction to the vacation areas of famous Lake Balaton, you take instead a quicker suburban train (fare: 10¢) to the Hungarian "Taos, New Mexico," the picture-postcard-pretty village of Szentendre, whose every structure houses an arts-and-crafts shop, art gallery, boutique, restaurant, or coffee bar. Here again, Hungary's current appeal as an international shopping mart is strongly apparent, and the town is packed in summer with tourists from around the world, snatching up quantities of those distinctive embroidered blouses with string-tied necks and other classically Hungarian styles.

As an alternate to the train, you can also go to Szentendre by Danube river steamer from a dock in the center of Budapest for a round-trip fare of 60 forint ($1.20).

Throughout your day you dine on elaborate stuffed meats with mounds of shredded dumplings overlaid with a paprika-scented sauce, alongside salads of juicy tomatoes and marinated cucumbers. You end with assorted strudels covered with whipped cream, or with heavenly Palacsinta Gundel—thin pancakes covered with a subtle, almost watery but unforgettable chocolate sauce.

Around you are scattered American tourists—the advance guard of what will inevitably be a flood of Americans—some talking about the possibility of purchasing a retirement home in Hungary (attractive houses in countryside settings cost as little as $30,000). I can't go quite that far—the language, as one factor, is incomprehensible—but I am convinced that Budapest, at least, will henceforth become an almost-indispensable stop on the classic circuit of European capitals, especially now that those thousands of U.S. travel agents have seen it for themselves. ≈

Church concert in Budapest

Hot Turkey

Tourism There Is Booming As the World Awakens to Its Attractions and Low Rates

Topkapi Palace, Istanbul

Opposite page: *The Blue Mosque, Istanbul*

No destination on earth has created more tourist excitement this year than Turkey. As if Aladdin had suddenly rubbed his lamp to give the Islamic world its first big travel hit, Turkey is today awash with visitors throughout the year, bestrewn with new hotels in construction, covered with touring motorcoaches.

Why did it happen so late? What delayed the advent of Turkey into massive tourist popularity? Though many will cite the remarkable cheapness of a Turkish vacation—decent hotels for $20 a night; colorful meals of lamb shish kebab, eggplant, and juicy tomatoes for $3; in-city transportation via group taxi ("dolmus") for 30¢—Turkey has always been that cheap, even cheaper a decade ago.

The explanation seems to stem from political changes that bode well for the long-term health of tourism in Turkey. Stable, democratic, civilian government seems to have been achieved after a period of intermittent military rule. No longer do fanatical religious parties control the Ministry of Tourism, from which they frequently sought to block incoming tourism and the liberalizing influences it brought. Most important, Turkey is currently attempting to enter the Common Market (the European Economic Community) and is supporting the application with widespread advertising and exhibitions that stress its openness to commerce and visitors.

Turkey is a pleasant way-station to the Muslim world, a partially Westernized country that nevertheless grounds its culture and religion on the Koran, a safe and familiar base for commencing your study of Middle Eastern institutions. Though there are mosques everywhere, and veiled women, there's none of the tension felt in similar countries, and people are friendly to foreigners. Signs are in Roman letters, not Arabic script; hotels serve cocktails and wine; the female tourist is tolerated at restaurants and cafés, even alone; and women of the West are able to move about without harassment or scorn, at least in the larger cities and at beachfront resorts.

For tourists, as I've already noted, the country is remarkably cheap, the cheapest of any European

No longer do fanatical religious parties control the Ministry of Tourism.

Harem Hall, Topkapi Palace

Farmer of Antalya

nation. With Spain increasingly costly, and Greece getting there, the budget-conscious traveler is especially attracted today to Turkey.

Exploring Istanbul

You start, of course, in Istanbul, the former Constantinople. Once the capital of Christianity, then of the great Ottoman Empire, its downtown is a startling forest of needle-like spires sticking into the sky from the minarets of more mosques than you are ever again likely to see in one location.

The key attractions are rather conveniently grouped on a peninsula of sea-surrounded land known generally as Sultanahmet. Here is the rich Topkapi Palace, where a series of often-decadent, occasionally impressive, sultans, pashas, and caliphs once disported themselves in sensual style, both at water pipes (still seen at cafés in Istanbul) and with harem dancers; the exhibits inside are disappointing, but the harem exquisite. More impressive, just outside the palace walls, are the Museum of Oriental Art (with Hittite ruins), the Archeological Museum, and the Museum of Tiles.

From there you easily stroll to the massive Blue Mosque, removing your shoes to enter inside; and then, across the way, to Aghia Sophia, once the largest domed church in all of Christendom, now a mosque but still bearing Byzantine mosaics of biblical scenes.

From the grand mosques, a street called Divan Yolu leads to the Grand Bazaar (Kapali Carsi), perhaps the largest covered bazaar in the world. As you near the vast emporium, numerous "kebab" restaurants tempt you with savory scents and displays of grilled lamb or chicken kebab or sausage kebab, accompanied by that supreme achievement of Turkish farmers: succulent fresh tomatoes, the highlight of a meal that rarely exceeds $3 in cost. As you then pass into the four-block-wide labyrinth of shops that make up the bazaar, you catch your breath at the bargains that smart shopping can secure: excellent leather wallets for under $6, pantaloon-like "harem pants" for the same, full-length leather coats that can be negotiated down to $200, pages from medieval illuminated Islamic manuscripts—a superb gift—for $10.

The bulk of visitors, after touring Istanbul, head to inexpensive beach resorts on the Antalyan portion of Turkey's Mediterranean coast, but I'd suggest the coast just outside the port city of Izmir ($40 by air from Istanbul); there you can combine sea-bathing with a one-hour trip by dolmus or taxi to the unforgettable Roman ruins at Ephesus, where Paul preached. After all, you didn't fly 4,500 miles from the U.S. just to lie on a beach.

Cappadocia

An even better course is to follow up Istanbul with eery Cappadocia, the highlight of all Turkish visits, in my view, and a great wonder of the world. It is the province of volcanic rock in central Turkey to which tens of thousands of Christians fled in the 7th century from Muslim persecution. And there they proceeded to build and inhabit underground cities—whole cities—carved from the volcanic stone.

Although a military airport at Kayseri, in Cappadocia, receives civilian flights from Istanbul twice a week ($40 for the trip), the timing of that facility permits its use only in one direction—one way, in other words. The other leg is best accomplished by flying from Istanbul to Ankara ($45) and boarding a bus from there for a five-hour ride to Nevsehir, largest city in the region. Motorcoaches leave Nevsehir every two hours and charge only $3.50 for the five-hour journey.

Does all this seem overly fatiguing? Not once you've seen Cappadocia. The trip begins in ordinary style, but gradually, in the triangle of land formed by the towns of Nevsehir, Avanos, and Urgup, you encounter a weird alternation of terrain in shapes you have never before seen: cream-colored hills of solid rock undulating like folds of satin, alongside high, conical mounds formed from the eroded volcanic ash of eruptions occurring a millennium ago. Suddenly, within these strange, cone-shaped forms, you take in hundreds upon hundreds of large, oblong, man-made holes cut into the face of each monolith.

It was through these openings that fleeing Christians built whole cities in the rock: churches adorned with fresco paintings, refectories, dormitories, work rooms—all ingeniously carved, and then hidden from view by giant boulders over each entrance. Gazing at them, wrote a young American tourist, Tracie Holder, in a recent letter to me, "I had feelings of wonderment—wonder that these early inhabitants could have thought to hew entire cities from solid rock. To me, Cappadocia attests not simply to the determination of a particular people at a particular time, but to the timeless human spirit which creates civilizations in the face of adversity."

Most visitors to Cappadocia stay in the pleasant town of Urgup, in one of a cluster of small hotels ranging from the comfortable, swimming-pool-supplied Kaya Otel ($58 per double room, including breakfast for two), Boybas Motel ($53 double), and Turban Motel ($43 double, yet also with swimming pool), to the simple but adequate Pinar Otel ($12 per double room) and other more basic lodgings renting for as little as $10 and $8 per double room. Others prefer to stay closer to the Open Air Museum at the village of Goreme (really, a wide spot in the road), at the three-story, red-stucco Pala Otel, paying $17 for a double and two breakfasts.

For meals, I like the Restaurant Allah Allah in the Cappadocian city of Avanos, on the Red River, where my party of four once paid a total of $20 for appetizers, melon, dolmades (stuffed grape leaves), shish kebab of lamb and chicken, Russian salad, wine, and strong Turkish coffee (sweet, in thimble-like cups).

Turkey is an important country of 50,000,000 people, almost the size of France or Germany. And as you may have guessed, it's also a sybaritic experience at the lowest of costs. Get there before it's too late. ≈

Town of Goreme, Cappadocia

X ≈ NEW WAYS TO VISIT OLD DESTINATIONS

Sweden: A Return to the World of Tomorrow

There's New Ferment in the Greatest Social Laboratory on Earth—and Special "Institutes" Can Reveal It All to You

Stockholm

Opposite page: Stockholm's floating youth hostel

To a teenager in the late 1940s (myself), magazine articles on Sweden supplied the same improbable combination of erotic urges and high-tech fantasies that *Playboy* provides today. Imagine! Swedish men and women, it was seriously claimed, were living together *before* they got married. Wow! Day-care centers, like apparitions from Mars, were sprouting up for the children of working mothers. Neat! As wintry as its weather was said to be, Sweden seemed a dream of the rational future, and I longed to view it.

So did thousands of other foreign admirers, who flocked to Stockholm for special tours of contemporary life that the Swedes, with uncharacteristic immodesty, called "the World of Tomorrow." Then, as the rest of the world began cohabiting before marriage, and women flocked to offices and assembly lines, as progressive schools and cradle-to-grave security became a commonplace in dozens of nations, that special interest in Sweden began to wane, and all but disappeared by the mid-1970s.

Well, it's time to return, but fast. Because those sly ol' Swedes are at it again, testing the limits of the possible, once more enacting the visions of social planners, revamping the rules of commerce, industry, and even family life. And since the rest of the world tends to emulate the Swedish model on a time lag of about 30 years, no thinking person can pass up this foretaste of what, arguably, the world of the future may be.

The Swedish Penchant for Innovation

As early as the ride on the airport bus into Stockholm, you begin to glimpse the Swedish penchant for innovation, if only in a trivial sense. It is a sunshiny, summer day. Yet all the cars have their headlights on. "Why is this?" you ask the stately Swedish woman in the seat ahead. "Statistics show," she answers rather archly, "that even daytime accidents are sharply cut if pedestrians and motorists are made more aware of traffic by oncoming headlights. Our parliament now requires them on, throughout the day."

Then, as now, Sweden seemed a dream of the rational future, and I longed to view it.

Boat tour of Stockholm

Royal Palace, Stockholm

Once in town, engaged in conversation with the largely English-speaking Swedes, you quickly meet up with matters more monumental: all talk is of the awesomely ingenious new "wage-earners' funds" designed to overturn the very basis of industrial ownership in Sweden. Created in 1984 by Sweden's then-governing Social Democrats, the funds are entitled to 20% of the pretax profits of all corporations above a certain size. These monies are then reinvested in exchange for new stock whose voting rights are held by labor unions and other public representatives of the employees in those firms. The aim is nothing less than to transfer control of all such corporations from shareholders to the employees in them, by 20 to 30 years down the road (although the initial legislation expires in 1990), in addition to ensuring the reinvestment of profits instead of their distribution to shareholders. While Sweden's opposition parties have pledged to dismantle the funds if they should win the next election, the razor-thin margins by which most Swedish governments gain and remain in power, and thus the probable Social Democratic reaccession in any event, makes the funds a lively topic for investigation and debate, both within Sweden and abroad.

A lighter topic for study (unless you're 12 or younger): spanking is now illegal in Sweden. Corporal punishment of the young in any form, even "humiliation" visited upon a child (like being made to stand in a corner), can now subject Swedish parents to a fine or term in jail. Though no one has yet been imprisoned, Sweden's child experts expect the altered home environment resulting from this legislation to produce no less than a better human race, at least in Sweden.

Watching Innovation Work

How do you, as a curious student of world trends, gain access to these experiments? How do you progress beyond the purely touristic realms into the actual test-tube settings of Swedish innovation?

You write to an "institute"—in this case, the Swedish Institute. Unknown to 99% of all American visitors, most European governments supplement the work of their tourist offices with "institutes" offering assistance far more profound to visitors pursuing special interests. Unlike the tourist offices, whose function is simply to attract more and more tourists, the institutes are broadly charged with promoting the culture and image of the nation. And although many of the institutes are primarily concerned with language courses or library services—the Institut Français/ Alliance Française, the Goethe Institute, the British Council, the Austrian Institute do that—another batch (including, most prominently, the Swedish Institute and Danish Institute) are heavily involved in arranging interviews and meetings with distinguished local figures or authorities for visitors from abroad.

You are, we'll presume, the vice-president for labor relations of your company, or a teacher of political science, or vice-chairman of your local political club, heavily involved in matters of social welfare. Or you're a medical administrator anxious to visit the Scandinavian hospitals, especially in a country whose life-expectancy rates are two years higher than ours. You advise the Swedish Institute that you'll be in Stockholm, say, from February 3 through February 12 (having first made all hotel and transportation arrangements yourself), and then: you describe your background, enumerate the topics you're desirous of pursuing, and ask whether a "program" might be prepared for your stay. Within a few weeks (faster in winter), and free of charge, you receive a carefully formulated schedule of appointments. At 11 a.m. on February 3 you're to meet for an hour or two with Professor Rasmussen of Uppsala University, an authority in the field you've cited. At 9 a.m. on the 4th, the appropriate English-speaking committee of the Center Party will wait to brief you at their party headquarters in downtown Stockholm. That afternoon, their opposite numbers at the Social Democratic Party will do the same. And so on and on. While none of this will be arranged for persons who simply describe themselves as members of the public (no matter how studious, sympathetic, or concerned they may be), it should not be hard to dredge up the titles or qualifications that will entitle you to receive these introductions to your "professional" counterparts in Sweden.

Next time you visit Europe, try an institute! No more fascinating travel activity exists. Contact the **Swedish Institute (Svenska Institutet), Sweden House (Sverigehuset), Kunstradgarden, Box 7434, S-103 91 Stockholm, Sweden (phone 08-789-2000).** Or the **Danish Institute (Det Danske Selskab), #2 Kultorvet, DK-1175 Copenhagen K, Denmark (phone 01-135-448).** And thus replace those rather mindless vacation weeks of sand and sea with intelligent travel, to destinations that may indeed presage the World of Tomorrow. ≈

Gamla Stan (Old Town), Stockholm

Home Stays in the British Isles

A Number of Impressive Organizations Now Permit Americans to Visit with Britons of Distinctive Social Viewpoints and Achievements

In tweed jacket and suede tie, his bushy white moustache twitching with glee, the ruddy old squire stood beaming at the gates to an imposing English estate, as an American tourist couple came driving up the gravel path. "I'm Underhill!" he boomed. "The bed-and-breakfast man! And if you can stow your gear post-haste, we still have time to view the horse auction in the village!"

In actual fact, this gentleman-farmer was not a bed-and-breakfast host. Britain's B&B proprietors are often fully as warm and spirited, but they tend to be a far more ordinary lot, not given to living in stately country homes. And their offer of bed-and-breakfast means just that: bed, a breakfast the next morning, then a cordial but conclusive good-bye.

Rather, the people of whom Squire Underhill is typical are a wholly different lot whose conversation and companionship are themselves a prime reason for your visit to Britain. They are the source of unique home stays designed to produce a very special travel benefit: the experience of gracious country living, yet in a lively atmosphere of intellect and discourse, among individuals of distinctive social views and lifestyles. The sojourns they offer take place in country homes of the British Isles. The proprietors in question are a form of landed gentry, an aristocracy of sorts, but nontitled, democratic, close to their middle-class origins, and not at all like their often other-worldly counterparts on the continent, the latter frequently removed from life, acting as cultural ornaments or loosely overseeing hereditary estates. English gentry are more often active types, merchant bankers (investment counselors) and retired magistrates, functioning business executives and art dealers, much-traveled former army officers from "good regiments," professors, writers, and dons of awesome reputation.

Why should such persons accept paying guests into their homes? It is because their wealth is often in land and structures, in paintings and heirlooms, and not in cash—which is always welcome. About a decade ago, when various British organizations began discreetly soliciting their willingness to receive overseas visitors, many of them cautiously agreed, some with initial hesitation, some insisting that visitors first be screened for compatability. Thus it was that various firms emerged to match up hosts with guests. It is these screening organizations—some identified by the words "at home" in their titles—that provide the most curious of tourists with the profound delights and insights of a proper British "home visit."

At Home in England and Scotland

Among the oldest of the "at home" firms is Esther Eder's At Home in England and Scotland, Inc. The Argentine-born wife of the former theater critic of the *New York Times,* she agonized in the mid-1970s that friends going to England weren't seeing "her England" because of their limited access to Britons of distinction. She began approaching prospects, explaining, cajoling, and assuring, ultimately tapping into an extraordinary wealth of human resources that proceeded to host hundreds of fortunate Americans in the ensuing years:
• The one-time private secretary to Winston Churchill, now a merchant banker living in Dorset, from which he commutes to important meetings in London, accompanying his guests on the ride into town;
• A retired general, later a professor of political science at the University of Exeter, now a consultant from his home in Wales on responses to international terrorism;
• An active, though middle-aged, administrator of the Bodleian Library of Oxford, his wife a writer in her late 20s, both living near a picture-postcard village near Oxford;
• A woman "don" at the University of Cambridge, an imposing raconteur whose field is the history of architecture, her own Tudor home an impressive example;
• A former governor of the Bank of Scotland, his wife a magistrate, their household completed by the elderly nanny of their now-grown children (for which reason they especially enjoy receiving families);
• And scores more, of every calling: an international stockbroker, once with the Tenth Hussars Regiment, living in the horsey country outside Bristol; an intensely contemporary theatrical agent, also the business man-

ager for a renowned duchess; a retired judge now serving as the arbitrator for industrial disputes. Plus an executive with British Petroleum, and another with Cadbury Chocolates. And leavening the political leanings of these gentlemen farmers, art dealers and auctioneers, chartered surveyors and retired officers: a prominent member of the British Labor Party, now retired to a charming cottage both thatched and covered with vines; a leading left-wing journalist still passionately contributing columns to a literary weekly. Their homes range from 16th-century manors to 18th-century rectories, from rambling Queen Anne country estates to narrow, four-story Georgian town houses (of "Upstairs, Downstairs" memory), from 17th-century farmhouses outside tiny Cotswold villages to modern, but classically elegant, mansions surrounded by miles of open ground. They are in England, Scotland, and Wales, in Lancashire and Gloucestershire, in London and near Brighton. And their charge for hospitality, guest rooms, full English breakfast daily, and use of the entire estate, in Mrs. Eder's program, averages $70 to $80 per person per night, including Mrs. Eder's rather extensive services in matching you up with a suitable host. Minimum required stay is three nights.

At Home Country Holidays

The larger country homes, each with two or three guest rooms to rent, are the specialty of a competing organization known as At Home Country Holidays. But though the latter's appeal is primarily to small groups—say, a family, or two or three couples traveling together—the goal remains the same distinctive and intensely private, noncommercial, and leisurely home stay offered by the others: no paying guests other than your own party of travelers are ever accepted in the same house at the same time. Hosts of At Home Country Holidays tend also, in the view of some observers, to fewer political or business interests than Mrs. Eder's. Practitioners of the good life, they stress the art of country living, and warm to the visitor who shares their admiration for 19th-century prints, hunting and sailing, antiques and gardens. When one possesses a country estate, not simply a country home; when one lives in a near-stately structure of turrets and towers, with croquet lawns and walled kitchen gardens, in dozens of surrounding acres—as so many At Home Country Holidays hosts do—one apparently cares less about Dow-Jones statistics or North Sea oil. "Your host," says one typical At Home Country Holidays entry in their illustrated catalog, "is a former Master of Foxhounds and a member of the Coaching Club. Guests may have the opportunity of hunting in wintertime and driving round the forest in a four-in-hand in the summer. They may also join the family on their 36-foot mahogany yawl, built in Denmark in 1966 and meticulously cared-for." Another points out that he "is a writer and art historian, and his wife lectures and writes on the history of food and garden design." Others stress that "being collectors ourselves, we are happy to act as guides to nearby antiques markets." Most take pains to assure that "there is a swimming pool in the garden and tennis courts in the village." "Our guests dine with candles and flowers in the dining room either with us, or on their own, as they prefer." For such elegance and grace, which always includes a private "suite" (bedroom, bath, sitting room, and garden) and full English breakfast, the charge is £85 ($144) per couple per night, £60 ($102) for a single. They now offer the same service in smaller homes for £60 ($102) for a double, £45 ($76) for a single. Dinner, at an extra £12.50 ($21) per person, can also be arranged.

The most expensive of the home-stay firms is Country Homes and Castles, headed by Susan Uda, who uses a carefully defined ratings system to set apart her renowned member establishments. "Grade A" consists of "Stately Homes and Castles in Extensive Parklands," charging £230 ($391) per couple per night, including cocktails, a three-course dinner with wine, coffee, and liqueurs, overnight accommodations, full English breakfast, and the many facilities individual to each home—a very considerable value. "Grade B" comprises "Country Mansions and Castles," and costs £170 ($289) per couple per night, again including dinner for two and full English breakfast the next

morning. On arrival at each home, usually in late afternoon, one joins the family for cocktails in the drawing room, then enjoys that full-scale dinner with wine, and retires to an elegant bed, steeped in the history and heritage of each house and family.

Typical of the firms offering budget-priced home stays are Wolsey Lodges, a loose marketing association of independently owned country houses clustered in the southern half of England, heavily in the Cotswolds and East Anglia, but throughout Scotland and Wales as well. Though some resemble the more commercial variety of bed-and-breakfast, they are all a cut above, and by studying the Wolsey literature carefully, one can find homes owned by Oxford graduates, retired lieutenant-colonels of the Royal Air Force, people actively engaged in demanding professions and business activities. Their charges range from as little as £15 ($25) per person to rarely more than £25 ($42) per person, a cooked breakfast included, and although they engage in none of the elaborate screening and matching of guests with hosts, of the sort promised by the costlier firms, they offer the opportunity (through careful selection of homes, this time by yourself) to socialize with English people of above-average intelligence and tastes.

Minding Your Ps and Qs

Having made the choice of firms, how then do you comport yourself as a house guest in Britain? You act exactly as if you were staying with friends or relatives. You make your own beds. Except at Wolsey Lodges, where it obviously isn't expected, you bring a small house gift. Again except at Wolsey Lodges, you make no on-the-spot payments of any sort to your hosts—you have already prepaid through your "at home" booking organization. Primarily, you talk—about wide-ranging topics, enjoying the lively, articulate views of the obviously gregarious people who engage in hosting. In the morning, you wander through home and grounds. You take long walks. Sometimes you are escorted by your host to worthwhile sights of the vicinity. One host in London invariably takes her guests to an unforgettable luncheon in Parliament!

In the predominantly countryside settings of home stays, you also gain a rare opportunity to observe British attitudes toward leisure, which they take as seriously as work, pursuing the life of sport, which they practically invented, and to which they devote ever-constant attention. In this, and in still other areas, you witness the life of England from an utterly unique vantage point.

In short, you act as a traveler, not as a mere tourist, enjoying intellectual growth as well as profound pleasure.

Names and Addresses

For the descriptive literature and booking forms of the firms I've cited, contact **Esther Eder, c/o Barbara Gurwitch, At Home in England and Scotland, Inc., 101 Hickory Grove Dr. West, Larchmont, NY 10538 (phone 914/834-4625)**—Mrs. Eder requests completion of an elaborate questionnaire, including an optional short essay on your background and interests; **Angela Rhodes-James, At Home Country Holidays, The Stone House, Great Gransden Sandy, Bedfordshire SG19 3AF, England (phone 076/77-300); Susan Uda, Country Homes and Castles, 118 Cromwell Rd., Kensington, London SW7 4ET, England (phone 01/370-4445 or 370-0322, or 404/231-5837 in the U.S.);** or **Wolsey Lodges, 17 Chapel St., Bildeston, Suffolk IP7 7ED, England (phone 0449/741-297).**

For still another organization somewhat similar to Mrs. Eder's, contact the Countess of Denbigh's **Welcome Stranger Ltd., Stable Cottage, Newnham Paddox, Monks Kirby, Rugby, Warwickshire CV23 ORX, England (phone 0788/832-173),** which is also represented in London by **Mrs. Worbory, 11 Lower Common South, London SW15 1BP England (phone 01/788-7047).**

And for a less expensive form of homestay, all over the world, see the homestay discussion in the Appendix to this book.≈

The sojourns they offer take place in country homes of Great Britain.

A Trip to the Other Hawaii

If Our Vacation Budget Confines Us to the Tourist-Jammed Island of Oahu, How Can We Nevertheless Escape the Tawdry?

Volcanic eruption on the Big Island

Mission Houses Museum, Honolulu

Wall-to-wall hotels. Awestruck, first-time visitors in matching muumuus or gaudy shirts. Fast-food restaurants with lines stretching far outside. Hokey Hawaiian performers leading organized songfests and drawn-out chants of "ah-loh-hah."

And if you present a tour voucher upon arrival at Honolulu airport, you get kissed on the cheek. No voucher, no kiss.

Hawaii's Tourist Ghetto

Let's face it: some sections of modern-day Hawaii, especially overbuilt Waikiki, leave much to be desired. Some visitors to the 50th state are less than enchanted with the development of mass-volume tourism there, and seek an option—a pathway to the "other Hawaii," the "real Hawaii."

So do many longtime residents of Hawaii's heavily populated Oahu, who feel resentful of tourism, even enslaved by it. That, in part, is why Waikiki remains "ghettoized," in the words of a University of Hawaii anthropologist. And as he further notes, that's just fine for many locals. It gives them the rest of the island to enjoy for themselves, a space in which they needn't be endlessly reminded of Hawaii's dependence on tourism.

The thoughtful visitor follows the same path, to areas of Oahu outside of Waikiki, and to the people who work in or inhabit those areas. But it isn't easy—it requires sensitivity and work.

The key word is "respect." That's the quality voiced to me by a dozen residents as lacking in tourists to Hawaii, and the essence of what would otherwise give them access to the "real Hawaii." People here have an overweening appreciation for courtesy—perhaps a by-product of the Japanese culture of the islands' largest ethnic grouping. They like questions to be prefaced with "Excuse me, could you please tell me? . . ." And if the resulting conversations should lead to an invitation to someone's home, where shoes are left outside the door, leave yours outside also. "Don't ask if you should take your shoes off. Just do it, said a long-suffering Hawaiian of my acquaintance."

People Places

Certainly the finest place to meet or mingle with the locals is the Ala Moana Shopping Center, largest outdoor shopping mall in the world, with close to 200 shops. Its Makai Market features dozens of food stalls offering international cuisine at low prices (less than $5 for large portions), and there you join locals in that ultimate, conversational "bond" between tourists and residents: food.

After walking around the mall, go across the street to the pleasant Ala Moana Park, which has grass, picnic tables, and a lovely beach favored by locals. You can bring lunch from the Makai Market, or stop off at the Ala Moana Farmer's Market behind the nearby Ward Warehouse shopping complex; the latter features specialty foods of Hawaii: for example, a Hawaiian plate, from Haili's Hawaii, of lau-lau (dumplings made of ti leaves and stuffed with meat or fish), poki (raw fish), lomi salmon (smoked with tomatoes and onions), poi (sticky, pudding-like starch made from taro root), and haupia (coconut pudding), for a total of $3.50. And you won't see a single other tourist.

Traveling Elsewhere

For getting about and meeting friendly folk at the same time, the essential device is Honolulu's wonderfully efficient and inexpensive public transportation system, "The Bus" (60¢ to any point in Oahu; call 531-1611 for the routes, or buy *The Bus Guide* for $2 at any drugstore). According to many locals, use of The Bus distinguishes locals from tourists. If you are friendly, you will soon find yourself in conversations about the food and weather, which often lead to weightier things. Cultivate the habit of listening to the residents; one local's explanation to me of what makes tourists so offensive is that they are "abrupt" and cut people off.

The Nonprofits

In preference to the commercial attractions and events assaulting you from every poster and glossy, ad-filled brochure, patronize the attractions that aren't operated for money. Go to the Campus Center of the

A thoughtful visitor runs from the tourist ghetto of Waikiki.

Mission frame house, Honolulu

Volcanic lake near Kalani Honua

Oriental Court at Honolulu Academy of Arts

University of Hawaii at Manoa and look at any of the numerous bulletin boards publicizing time and location of such cultural events as a Western Samoan music concert. Pick up a copy of the weekly *University Bulletin* (at Brachman Annex no. 6), which lists several activities each day, including art exhibitions, theatrical productions, films, and lectures (a recent example: a breakfast meeting to discuss "The Pacific Attitude Toward Work"). Visit the University Bookstore for its "Hawaiiana section" of works on whatever aspect of Hawaii most interests you: from poetry and healing practices to mythology, ethnic difficulties, marine biology, whatever.

You can plan your activities, read your books, or perhaps participate in lively discussions at the Coffeeline, 1820 University Ave., open Tuesday through Saturday for both breakfast and lunch. A comfortable, open-air, but roofed meeting place for the university community, the Coffeeline serves healthy, old-fashioned cooking at low prices (seafood gumbo, biscuits, lime pie, and coffee for $3; meals are prepared by food science/nutrition teacher Brigitte Campbell and the students she trains). You can also go to the sometimes boisterous university hangout, Manoa Garden in Hemenway Hall, open weekdays only: from 10:30 a.m. to 8 p.m. when school is in session, from 11 a.m. to 6 p.m. during vacations.

And then there's the East-West Center, established by Congress in 1960 to "bring together people from the United States, Asia, and the Pacific in studying and seeking solutions to problems of social, economic, and cultural change." By dropping in at Burns Hall on the East-West Center Campus (adjacent to the university), you can pick up a copy of the event-listing *Centerweek*. From it, I was quite recently able to attend a free storytelling event by Hawaiian, Samoan, and Maori performers, "Na Mo'olelo O Ka Pakipiki—Legends of the Pacific" (followed by an engrossing, lively discussion). You can also scan the more detailed bulletin called "Today at the East-West Center" posted in Burns Hall, or phone 944-7283 for schedule information. Be sure to ask how early you should arrive to obtain a seat.

More Options

The thoughtful visitor can also obtain information on Hawaiian ethnic festivities by reading the local newspapers (*Star-Bulletin* and *Honolulu Advertiser*), or by calling the Hawaiian Visitors Information Office at 923-1811. There you'll learn about such celebrations as the Japanese Bon Dance, which takes place at temples for the purpose of sending ancestral spirits to the "other world." Or you'll be given word of cultural activities in which you also can participate, such as Japanese tea ceremonies. If you'd prefer to arrange for this particular item on your own, contact the Urasenke Foundation of Hawaii at 923-3059, which offers tea ceremonies to the public on Wednesday and Friday from 10 a.m. to noon.

An excellent way to have a taste of Oahu's Asian communities is to walk around Chinatown. Wander down the main street, Mauna Kea, and look in the glass windows to see people making leis. Sample local foods—yellow bean cake and lotus root candy. Ask to be directed to a Chinese herbalist, Dr. Fook Sau Tong, who charges $25 for acupuncture treatment and herbal prescriptions, and by whom several of my Hawaiian friends swear. Stroll through the open-air market on King Street (most active on Saturday mornings), which displays produce, poultry, and exotic fish. Eat dim sum (assorted dumplings) for lunch, or at the famous Wo Fats, at the corner of Hotel and Mauna Kea Streets, for which dinner reservations are required. Take in the Kuan Yin Temple on Vineyard Street, whose impressive statues, altars, offerings, joss sticks, and incense reflect a mix of Confucian, Taoist, and Buddhist influences.

And if you must take a tour, at least opt for the smaller companies using ten-person vans. E Noa Tours (phone 941-6608) will take you on a full-scale exploration of Chinatown and the Old Oahu Market District, dropping in at a Chinese noodle factory, cake shop, acupuncture clinic, herb shop, open-air fish market, and Asian food processor—a total of four hours and $23 (including a Peking duck buffet at Oahu's oldest restaurant, Wo Fats, a separate sampling of authentic local food, and a visit to the Kuan Yin Temple).

Around the Island

Now let's escape the city altogether, and taste the pleasures of the "other Oahu." Following which, I'll talk about specific institutions that introduce you in general to the "other Hawaii."

The Road Less Traveled

Kamehameha Highway is your "yellow brick" path to the dream of Hawaii; it almost circumscribes the island, along the ocean on one side, with farmland and sloping volcanic hills on the other (where you'll see families hanging octopus to dry in the sun). In a rental car (as little as $19 for the day), you'll find numerous points from which to enjoy beaches unspoiled by tourists or development, cane fields, quaint towns, fruit stands, and lunch wagons. One visitor at a roadside pay phone was recently overheard calling home to complain about learning of this "paradise" so late in her stay.

For surfing and such, you use Sandy Beach on the far side of Hanauma Bay, or Sunset Beach on the north shore (but beware the dangerous waves). For simply enjoying the ocean and clear air, Waimanalo Beach Park and Kailua Beach Park are favorites of the residents whose town sits on their shores. Haleiwa, also on the north coast, is the quaint village site of still another charming beach.

Closer to Honolulu is the suburb of Kailua, with its soft, white sand beach of Lanikai flanked by aquamarine waters; from here you can take a 3½-hour excursion by inflatable boat (and for $36) to five uninhabited islands and a legendary sea cave—the kind of approach to unspoiled, breathtaking nature that many visitors mistakenly assume can only be had on the more expensive outer islands of Hawaii. Contact Windward Expeditions (phone 808/263-3899) for reservations. In Kailua, too, is the moderately priced L'Auberge Swiss, 117 Hekili St. (phone 263-4663 after 2 p.m. for dinner reservations), which many regard as among the islands' best.

In the course of your self-drive journey prior to reaching the Kamehameha Highway, you can stop to visit Manoa Falls, an easy, one-mile hike through lush tropical rain forest entered by scarcely a single other

The quality voiced as lacking in tourists to Hawaii is "respect."

Hawaiians at play

Oahu, away from Waikiki

225

Use of "The Bus" distinguishes locals from tourists.

Japanese pine and bamboo decorations

Hawaii's premier art museum

tourist; if they did, they'd enjoy a major reward: a freshwater pool created by the gentle but high-up cascade. Drive to Paradise Park at 3737 Manoa Rd. (a popular tourist attraction for bird enthusiasts), but head behind the parking lot to the well-marked but scarcely used road leading to the falls.

And for other "roads less traveled," inquire of the Sierra Club of Hawaii (phone 946-8494) about their $1 hikes through still other unspoiled terrain of Oahu. These are generally scheduled for every Sunday (but occasionally on Saturday) and are often available on the other islands too.

The Institutions That Assist You

Kawaiahao Church at 957 Punchbowl St. in Honolulu, which many call the Westminster Abbey of Hawaii, dates back to 1842 and figured prominently in the early Christian period as the church of the Ali'i (chiefs and chieftesses). Viewing the 21 graceful and lifelike portraits of the Ali'i here gives one a sense of the former Hawaiian kingdom and its rulers. Services, though open to everyone, are still conducted largely in the Hawaiian language, and there's no more awesome experience than the Sunday 10:30 a.m. program, suffused with the true aloha spirit, and frequently attended by parishioners dressed in the pageantry of Hawaii's past—not, mind you, to entertain the tourist, but in celebration of their heritage.

The Bishop Museum, at 1525 Bernice St., displays relics of the art, transportation, war practices, and worship of ancient Hawaii. It's important, too, and charges an entrance fee of $4.95 for adults, $2.50 for children 6 to 17.

The Mission Houses Museum, also in downtown Honolulu at 553 S. King St., where it displays home and workplace furnishings of 19th-century Protestant missionaries, is less interesting for its contents, in my view, than for its twice-weekly (Monday and Friday at 9:30 a.m.) guided walking tours of the historic downtown center of Honolulu. Tours depart from the museum, cost $7 for adults and $2 for children, require reservations (phone 531-0481), and are another introduction to the "other Hawaii."

Honolulu Academy of Arts, 900 S. Beretania St., is home to one of the world's finest collections of Asian arts, and is unusually pleasant to visit in its airy setting of courtyards with sculpture gardens. Open free of charge six days a week (closed Monday), it also offers classes, lectures, and films on the culture and art of Asia, the Pacific, and Hawaii, and serves lunch in its café for $4.95.

Temari Center for Asian and Pacific Arts, 1329-A Tenth Ave., provides semester-long courses to residents in Asian crafts, but also serves the tourist by scheduling single-evening lectures and demonstrations in such subjects as lei-making ($15 for three hours) or Japanese paper-making ($50 for a Friday-night lecture followed by Saturday and Sunday workshops). Phone 808/735-1860 for detailed information.

Discovering Authentic Culture

Tune your Walkman or your transistor radio to AM 1420—KCCN—the island's only Hawaiian-music radio station. Watch the newspapers for appearances by the Brothers Cazimero (best known of all the contemporary Hawaiian music groups), the Makaha Sons of Niihau, the Sons of Hawaii, or the Kahuano Lake Trio. Or go for dinner and/or dancing to the Metco and Rockchild's, both at 5156 Kalanianaole Hwy. in Ainahaina (phone 373-2177 for the Metro, 373-5310 for Rockchild's), where the most authentic melodies accompany every meal.

Waimea Falls Park, at 59-864 Kamehameha Hwy. in Haleiwa, on the north shore (phone 638-8511), offers exact performances of the original hula—considerably different from the contrived variety performed at Waikiki's Royal Hawaiian Shopping Center—daily at 11:30 a.m. and 1, 2:30, and 4 p.m. Additionally, a covey of shrines, burial caves, ancient game sites, waterfalls, and arboretums make the park well worth visiting, even for its steep admission charge of $8.50 for adults.

"Luaus" are another means for entering into the life of Hawaii, but only if they are of the kind designed for local residents. If the newspapers or bulletin boards fail to announce one of the periodic community-sponsored luaus ($10), then phone Larry Lim of Vacations Unlimited at 949-5559, and book onto one of his half-day (1 to 5 p.m.) "participatory" luaus, on the 75-acre farm of a Hawaiian family in Punalau. You'll help to catch (via weighted nets cast into the sea), scale, and clean the fish, place the pork into the imu, and make lau-laus. All for $37.95, including transportation there, and all you can eat. Alternatively, and if you'd rather be entertained than participate, try the commercial evening luaus at Paradise Cove (phone 945-3539), about $40 for the giant repast, and highly regarded by residents.

Nonstandard Resorts

Finally, with their other-worldly airs, their remoteness from industrial concerns, their mid-ocean location, it was inevitable that the islands of Hawaii would become capitals of the "New Age."

And that's exactly what is happening. Though Honolulu and its crowded Waikiki Beach have remained determinedly mainstream—with fast-food restaurants and souvenir stands at every turning—the remainder of the lush Pacific state is sprouting everywhere with "holistic spas," "Buddhist retreats," "channeling centers," and "meditation lodges." Even the brand-new, $300-a-night Hyatt Regency Waikoloa on the Big Island of Hawaii has announced that its central health facility will be devoted to "A New Age Restorative Approach" ("A.N.A.R.A.") consisting not simply of spa-like treatments, but of therapies with "depth and meaning . . . promoting a state of inner peace," according to a Hyatt official.

Should you, who may have no sympathy at all for New Age concepts, nevertheless consider the use of such facilities for your next Hawaiian vacation? Yes, in my view, for the following reasons:

• The New Age resorts of Hawaii are all far from the overly developed areas, in remote settings of untouched, awesomely lovely nature. They assure you a noncommercial vacation.

• Their cuisine avoids the gluttony and overindulgence of the tourist restaurants; you'll feast on bran muffins for breakfast, on tofu and sprouts for lunch.

- They tend to be cheaper than the standard resorts in all but a few instances. And finally,
- They put your own, standard views to the test, provoking thought, perhaps awakening your mind to new values, at least reducing stress and anxiety.

All this is found on three particular islands:

Maui: Here's the most visible evidence of the burgeoning new philosophy in the form of countless herbal and health-food stores, holistic medical centers, offices of "transformational counseling," and alternative bookstores, along the length of Central Avenue in the town of Wailuku, a short drive from the airport. The impressive commerce attracts large numbers of sympathizers from the mainland, who congregate particularly among the New Age books and crystals on sale at **Miracles Unlimited, 81 Central Ave., Wailuku,** where they gaze at a notice-filled bulletin board and peruse Suzi Osborne's monthly "Island Calendar of Events" listing massage classes, fire dance celebrations, acupuncture demonstrations, nutritional lectures, and other such esoterica across the island.

Maui's key New Age resort, though tiny in size, is Old Maui Zendo, a former Buddhist monastery taken over two years ago by a 28-year veteran of the Los Angeles police force, Rick Smith, who himself had experienced a life-change in the awesome natural setting of the tropics. He thereupon resolved to create a center for other establishment people—standard, conservative types who had not yet been exposed to the liberating ideas of the newer generation. "My ideal guests," he recently told me, "are Mr. or Mrs. Middle America, usually 40 to 60, who've been stuck in certain phases, but are ready to open up to a beautiful place."

A single big house with enormous porch, Old Maui Zendo lodges fewer than 20 guests at a time, but looks out onto vast grounds filled with surprises: natural pools, waterfalls, hot tubs. Instruction is informal and eclectic, often unplanned, and by Tai Chi masters or lecturers on mythology, who make periodic, unscheduled appearances. Total charge for a full week, including airport pickup, room, three meals daily, and all surprises, is exactly $1,000, plus air fare there. Contact **Rick Smith, Old Maui Zendo, 915 Kaupakalua Rd., Haiku, Maui, HI 96708 (phone 808/572-8795).**

Larger, and altogether different in mood, is the several-structure retreat complex known as Hale Akua, which consciously caters to persons already well versed in New Age approaches; neophytes, or nonbelievers, would not, in my view, be comfortable in this million-dollar estate whose ideal guest, according to manager Donny Regalmuto, is "arty, together, clear-minded, and happy." On the awesome tropical estate with seaside views are hot tubs, a large swimming pool, waterfalls, fountains, and considerable classroom space for periodic workshops on topics dealing with frontiers of the mind. Expect to pay about $55 to $65 a night for most double rooms, and to prepare your own meals in the kitchen facilities of each building. Write for a schedule of retreats to: **Hale Akua, P.O. Box 1425, Paia, Maui, HI 96753.**

A place called Pualani is Maui's "fitness retreat," a luxurious, spa-like center with only occasional New Age overtones (yoga, meditation, biofeedback), but rather a fairly normal stress on exercise, massage, saunas, Jacuzzis, and gourmet vegetarian meals limited to 1,200 calories a day. Price for a Saturday-to-Saturday package, all inclusive except for air fare, runs $1,500 to $1,600 per person. Contact **Pualani, P.O. Box 1135, Makawao, Maui, HI 96768 (phone toll free 800/PUALANI).**

Hawaii: Less evident to the eye, the New Age facilities of the Big Island are still vital and popular. The leading New Age location is a laid-back retreat called Kalani Honua, consisting of 32 rooms grouped into four wooden lodges, rustic but elegant, on 20 acres of scenic lawns and forests across the road from a black sand beach (and 30 miles down the coast from Hilo). Though outside groups schedule one-week workshops there during much of the year, individuals are always welcomed to occupy the small but charming rooms, and to imbibe meals prepared with a careful attention to good nutrition—for example, homemade granola, sprouted grain bread with fresh berry topping, and fresh fruit, for breakfast. Hiking is particularly popular, to hidden lagoons, lava tubes, natural steambaths, and volcanic lakes. Room and board: a remarkable $40 per person per day, on average, exclusive of optional workshop costs. Contact **Kalani Honua, Kalapana, HI 96778 (phone 808/965-7828).**

On the same island, Wood Valley Retreat is a Tibetan Buddhist center (actual Buddhist temple and adjoining two-story residence) nestled in the woods near Pahala. Contemplation and calm prevail here, as contrasted with the sharing and sociability of other centers. Prices for retreats vary greatly, but often range about $40 a day for room and full board. Contact **Wood Valley Retreat, P.O. Box 250, Pahala, HI 96777 (phone 808/928-8539)** or send $5 to receive its mailings.

Finally, the Big Island seems to have the world's only New Age tour operator, a company called Lokahi (meaning "dynamic balance"). It conducts visitors on several-day journeys of "inner discovery" and "personal growth" as they explore active volcanoes, ancient temples, remote areas, and fields of petroglyphs, on that largely undeveloped terrain. A five-day, four-night tour costs $395 per person, including the services of two host-guides. Contact **Lokahi, Inc., P.O. Box 2154, Kailua-Kona, HI 96745 (phone 808/329-7569),** and enclose a stamped, self-addressed envelope for a reply.

Oahu: The pickings here are slimmer, but accessible even to visitors staying at the standard hotels. By scanning the large bulletin board at the **Sirius Bookstore, 2320 Young St., Honolulu,** open until 7 p.m. on weekdays, until 6 p.m. on Saturday, you'll learn of a wide range of New Age seminars and meditations in the area away from Waikiki, and especially about the popular yoga classes taught for 17 consecutive years (and for $6 per hour) by the much-respected Rick Bernstein at the Kilauea Recreational Center, two miles from Waikiki, at 9 a.m. on Tuesday and Thursday, and at other times (Tuesday and Thursday at 5:30 p.m., Saturday at 9 a.m.) in the airy structure behind the Japanese temple in Oahu's Nu'uanu Valley.

A better base than a standard hotel would be Oahu's small Plantation Spa, occupying elegantly manicured grounds on the north shore, near Ka'a'wa. It qualifies for the New Age with its emphasis on preventive health, warding off illness with yoga, aerobics, and a lacto-vegetarian cuisine, but its hefty rates are very much of the "Old Age": $1,250 per person for a six-night, Sunday-to-Saturday stay, all inclusive. Contact: **The Plantation Spa, 51-550 Kamehameha Hwy., Ka'a'awa, Oahu, HI 96730 (phone 808/237-8685).**

Even if you stay on Oahu, you can visit the more exotic New Age facilities on Maui and the Big Island by flying there for a day visit; Aloha Airlines charges only $44.95 for any point-to-point trip within the islands.≈

At the Mission Houses Museum, Honolulu

Spanish Court, Honolulu Academy of Arts

On the Trail of van Gogh

Basking in the Glow of Genius, in Arles, St.-Rémy, and Auvers-sur-Oise

Pont Langlois, Arles

Pont Langlois, by van Gogh

Opposite page: Self-portrait with a Straw Hat

He went there in February of 1888, in search of light, obsessed with a vision of colors such as the world had never known. And in that sun-drenched village of southern France, today's city of Arles, he experienced a burst of creativity without parallel in the history of art—at times, almost a canvas a day.

From February of 1888 through April of 1889 his abode was a tiny hotel room in Arles, where he painted *The Night Café, Portrait of My Room, Harvest Landscape, The Drawbridge,* and many more.

From May of 1889 to mid-May of 1890: the nearby village of Saint-Rémy, and its mental asylum in the Monastery of St. Paul, to which he voluntarily committed himself. From there he ventured forth on lucid days to perfect the "swirly" style of *Starry Night, The Olive Orchard, The Huts,* and others still.

In mid-May of 1890 he returned north for a last two months to the Paris suburb of Auvers-sur-Oise, where a strange combination of torment and creative joy drove him to do *The Church, Banks of the Oise, Town Hall on Bastille Day,* and nearly 30 other towering masterworks, before ending his life with a pistol on July 29, 1890.

Astonishing, isn't it, that in so fevered a two-year period—of which the world celebrates the centenary in 1989—Vincent van Gogh could have produced the great body of his work, become an immortal? And that the setting should have been such unremarkable sites as Arles, Saint-Rémy, and Auvers-sur-Oise?

However minor they are, all three will be visited in the next two years, the centennial period, by large numbers of art lovers anxious to see the structures and fields, the trees and flowers, the people of suburban Paris and Provence, whose essence was so dramatically captured by van Gogh. If you're to be among them, you must start planning now, because Arles and Saint-Rémy, in particular, will be jammed to the eaves with seekers wishing to bask in the glow of genius.

Arles

The dates are from January 18 through April 30 of 1989, in the new cultural center of Arles to be known

They will be jammed to the eaves with curators and museum trustees, art students, connoisseurs, and ordinary folk.

His abode in Auvers-sur-Oise

Docks at Saintes-Maries-de-la-Mer

The Cloister at Arles

as L'Espace van Gogh. There, art historian Ronald Pickvance, who organized the 1984 showing of "van Gogh in Arles" at New York's Metropolitan Museum, will apparently out-do himself with an even larger exhibition drawn from collections all over the world, of paintings done by the great impressionist in that eventful, 14-month period. For information on it (and on continuing exhibitions of van Gogh in Arles), contact the **Association des Amis de Vincent van Gogh, 35 Place de la République, 13200 Arles (phone 90/93-49-11).**

The exhibit will provide the main—for some, the exclusive—reason for visiting Arles in the winter/spring of 1989. Because the city was heavily bombed in World War II, little remains of the actual structures here that were portrayed by van Gogh. The *Little Yellow House* is gone, as are the two dingy hotels at which he stayed. But you will see the still-surviving clock tower which appears in several paintings, and more important, the courtyard of the Arles cloister—now adjoining the town museum—which once served as the hospital to which van Gogh was brought after severing his ear (*Courtyard of the Hospital in Arles* now hangs in the Rijksmuseum of Amsterdam, but hopefully will be brought to Arles for the centennial showing). Then, by walking to the Place du Forum, you can catch a glimpse of the overhanging balcony appearing in *Café Terrace by Night*. And by proceeding up rue Diderot to Place Balechou, you'll see, at no. 32, the house of Madame Ginoux, the famous *L'Arlesienne* in the masterpiece hanging in the Musée d'Orsay of Paris.

Most memorable of the Arles sights is *The Drawbridge*—the Pont Langlois—bringing goose pimples to your arms in its location about 1½ miles from the city. Facing the tourist office at Place de la République, walk to the right for three blocks to Avenue Sadi-Carnot, and turn left on Carnot for two to three kilometers until you reach a sign reading "Pont Van Gogh." You'll pass, on that short stroll, through countryside closely resembling that which van Gogh painted: sprawling, yellow wheatfields dotted with red-roofed farms. The bridge, with its distinctive, vertical spars, stands as it did in the painting, next to a charming barn with chickens running freely about.

Although van Gogh made a five-day visit to the nearby port of Ste-Marie-de-la-Mer, and painted docks and boats there, as well as a memorable landscape of the town fronted by vibrant lilac fields, you ought not to waste a day in Ste-Marie-de-la-Mer (as I did), because the surviving traces of van Gogh there are virtually nil.

Saint-Rémy

The same cannot be said of Saint-Rémy, an hour by bus or car from Arles. For there you find the asylum of his illness, in the Monastery of St. Paul (where van Gogh painted the gardens; they are still as they were), and the surrounding hills of Alpilles, where he did *The Olive Orchard, Pietà,* and *Starry Night.* All about are woods with the same twisting pine that van Gogh immortalized.

Saint-Rémy will be mounting its own centennial exhibition of van Gogh works in 1989–1990, starting in the month of May with the opening of the permanent Centre van Gogh (exhibit area, information center, and research library) in the 18th-century Hôtel Estrine in the heart of old St-Rémy. For details, contact **Catherine de Logères, Fondation van Gogh, 1163 Fifth Ave., New York, NY 10029 (phone 212/996-9287).**

Auvers-sur-Oise

But the real treasure trove of van Gogh structures and locations is Auvers-sur-Oise, less than an hour by rail from Paris. At the Gare St-Lazare, take one of the hourly trains to Pontoise and change trains there for Auvers-sur-Oise. Arriving at the little town—as serene and unindustrialized as during van Gogh's short stay—walk to the left for 100 yards to the tourist office, which could be lifted from a van Gogh–lover's dreams. It is a mini-museum in itself, displaying reproductions of his work and supplying literature and van Gogh–oriented maps with specific walking routes.

Quickly you'll find the large, majestic white building that is the Town Hall portrayed in van Gogh's masterwork of it, and across the street, the inn at which he stayed. In a ten-minute walk from that inn, and along a hill, is the Notre-Dame Church with its small flying buttresses and round stained-glass window—all portrayed in an equally famous work. Discover, as you gaze upon it, how van Gogh made that structure live—it trembles upon the canvas. Elsewhere you'll see *La Maison du Père Pilon,* on rue François-Villon. The well-kept house looks today exactly as it does in the painting. Or walk to the outskirts of town, across the bridge, and onto the banks of the river; you'll see the same luxuriant vegetation and peaceful stream depicted in *Bord d'Oise à Chaponval.*

Then, from the Notre-Dame Church, walk farther up the hill to the cemetery, on a path between wheatfields on either side that seem to go on and on, even beyond the horizon (remember the painting?). You reach the graves, side by side, of Vincent van Gogh and his art dealer brother, Theo, who encouraged, loved, and supported the unsuccessful Vincent throughout his life. Atop them is a single "blanket" of thick green ivy, placed there by Theo's wife, who felt the two brothers should be entwined in death as they were in life.

To share the drama and ultimate triumph of Vincent van Gogh, plan now for a 1989 or 1990 trip to Paris and the south of France. For information on hotels in Arles, consult your travel agent, or call the nearest French Government Tourist Office, or contact the Arles Tourist Office, the **Syndicat d'Initiative, 35 Place de la République, 13200 Arles, France (phone 90/96-29-35).**

Then make a reservation, fast. ≈

Sunflowers today, Arles

Reflections on a Chilly Cruise

The Waters of Alaska Are a Valid Alternative to the Difficult-to-Tour Interior

Juneau

Humpback whale breaking water

Mt. Edgecumbe, Sitka

On an ocean bay as smooth as glass, the giant ship glides silently toward the face of a mile-wide glacier. As the blue-white ice looms overhead, dwarfing the ship, the captain stills each engine aboard so that passengers can hear the remorseless advance of the eerie structure, grinding its way forward, as it has for 10,000 years.

A mammoth shard of ice the size of a 20-story building suddenly collapses from the front wall of the glacier into the iceberg-strewn waters; the resulting boom is like a rumble of dynamite. Throughout the morning, as you stand entranced at the rail of a promenade deck, smaller pieces break off with a sound like rifle shots.

Around you is a forest primeval, a coastline untouched, an unexplored mountain range against the full horizon. No one has ever lived here, or even trodden on the shore, and probably no one ever will. It is like returning to prehistory, as you view the world in the state it was in upon emergence from the Ice Age.

What I have just described is but a single moment out of the many awesome, breath-stopping episodes of an Alaskan cruise. For years I've been reacting with skepticism to friends who returned from similar cruises with stars in their eyes, groping for words to describe their reactions to the awesome coast of Alaska. How could a mere coastline provide such an experience? Why would people, in the midst of summer, send themselves up north to the chilly winds and frigid nights of Alaskan waters?

Now I've returned from my own first Alaskan cruise, and now I know. It's several weeks later, and still at night, as I lie abed, I remember:

• Humpbacked whales within 200 yards of our ship, a dozen of them, breaking water, and requiring several seconds for their entire length to arc above the waves and disappear beneath the surface.

• The sight of majestic mountains all around the ship, still green in the half-dark evening haze of an Alaskan summer at 10 p.m., still snow-covered and clearly visible at their topmost peaks.

• A bald eagle several feet tall, sitting erect and still on a tree branch over a spawning place for salmon, patiently awaiting their inevitable return; a school of seals swimming near the shore; a young deer unafraid of my human form, picking its way along a forest stream, no more than 50 feet from where I stood.

• The graceful takeoffs and landings offshore of small, pontoon-equipped seaplanes as they came and went on medical or supply flights to isolated posts in the interior.

• Lying snugly in a blanket on a reclining canvas deck chair, sipping a hot Irish coffee, watching the receding, moonlight-reflected image of the Russian Orthodox church of Sitka, with its onion-shaped dome, as our ship sailed away at midnight, southward through the Inland Passage to Vancouver.

Alaska, Not the Cruise Ship, Is the Destination

From mid-May to mid-September 24 of the world's largest passenger ships—a considerable portion of the world's cruise-ship fleet—sail the waters off Alaska. That figure is scarcely down from the peak of 28 ships assigned to Alaska in the summer of 1986, when fears of terrorism in Europe and the Mediterranean caused a number of lines to position their vessels in what was then, for them, a wholly unfamiliar area. Heartened by the public's response, they repeated that pattern in 1987 and again in 1988, making it clear that summer cruises of the Alaskan coast have become a large, standard, permanent part of the vacation scene.

Among the lines most prominent in Alaskan cruising: Holland-America Cruises (all three of its large ships in summer 1988; all four of its expanded fleet in 1989), Princess Cruises (again, four ships in 1989), Sitmar, Cunard (the elegant S.S. *Sagafjord*), Exploration Cruises (smaller ships, enabling passengers to debark at raw, unsettled coastal points), Regency Cruises, Costa Cruises (the *Daphne*), Admiral Cruises, and still others. The price per person per day, exclusive of air fare to Vancouver or Juneau, the two major embarkation points: a general, uniform average of about $190, except in the more luxurious *Sagafjord*, and except for top-of-the-line cabins in other ships.

In Caribbean cruising, the ship is generally regarded as the "destination," more important by far than the islands visited, a place of endless fun and games. In Alaskan cruising, although the ship is endowed with the very same casino and nightclub activities, the same deck buffets, sports, and hi-jinx, it is Alaska that is quite clearly the destination and the prime preoccupation: passengers spend a large part of their time lining the deck and gazing out with binoculars (be sure to bring them), or going on elaborate shore excursions into the wilds, often by seaplane.

Because of this emphasis on relatively sedate, nature-oriented pursuits, the average age of passengers on Alaskan cruises—about 55—is 10 years higher than on tropical sails. But though many of the passengers are elderly, they are among the liveliest of all Americans: educated and intellectually curious, experienced travelers taking the ultimate trip.

Viewing the Interior

Many of the cruise lines own large and active Alaskan touring companies, and therefore supplement their seagoing voyages with extensive excursions into the interior, by train or plane. From various, small, seaside ports, you fly north to visit the Eskimos of Nome or to the oil installations at Prudhoe Bay or to hike "taiga" forests (stunted trees growing in permafrost), or else you venture inland to wildlife preserves alive with elk and moose, or to see the remains of gold-rush days. By mixing and matching land tours with ocean cruising, you "bump up" the standard 7-day cruise to a varied adventure of 9, 11, 12, 14, 19, or even 21 days in Alaska. The average cost of a multi-modal 15-day Alaskan vacation, including a 7-day cruise: $2,500 to $2,600, plus air fare to Vancouver or Anchorage and back.

Alaska, with only half a million residents, will welcome nearly one million visitors in 1989. Yet so vast is the area that the tourist presence is hardly felt; it remains a land of prehistory, of nature unsullied by development, untouched by mankind, forever wild, the living earth, evoking emotions rarely felt.

You still have time to book an Alaskan cruise this summer. ≈

XI ⚍ OTHER
CHEAP AND/OR
UNDISCOVERED
DESTINATIONS

Frommer's Favorites

The Largely Unvisited Destinations That Haven't Yet Been Spoiled By Mass Tourism

Malta, the Mosta Church

Island of Gozo, Malta

Saltworks at Bonaire

Think back on it. Your fondest travel memories are always of the islands and cities you visited before they were discovered by hordes of others. Beaches on which you alone dozed beneath a sheltering palm. Cafés in which you chatted for hours on end with residents eager and open to a newcomer's questions. Places unique in their distinctive characteristics, excitingly foreign or fresh, as unfamiliar in appearance and attitudes as a South Seas island.

Do they still exist? They're obviously harder and harder to find! Yet in a world crammed with sightseeing buses, amid the wailing jet engines and the cacophony of tourist voices, five refreshingly unspoiled destinations come immediately to mind. Some are small and only slightly known, others are giant urban centers, but all are places not yet thronged with visitors from remote cities—the key to a magical sojourn of the sort you once knew.

1. The Island of Bonaire

Here is the Caribbean as it used to be, without high-rise hotels or daily charter-loads of "packaged" tourists. A member of the politically stable Netherlands Antilles, located less than 30 miles from the coast of Venezuela, Bonaire is a good-sized island but one with only 8,000 permanent inhabitants; a destination serviced on direct flights by major airlines, but with only two major hotels (neither more than three stories tall) and a handful of smaller ones; the proud possessor of two tiny casinos, a disco, and nightly entertainment by native dance troupes, but a haven of calm and repose for all of that. In the village square off the stone counters of a tiny fish market, residents still smile at the tourist—as if they were the first to visit the site—and lead you by the hand to view that morning's catch of rainbow-colored fish.

The chief attraction is scuba-diving, practiced here with an intensity found elsewhere only in the Red Sea; scuba-diving experts rank Bonaire with Elath as enjoying the two top underwater sites of the world. Off the white sand beaches fronting the island's two large hotels are coral reefs and sea life famed throughout the world. Numerous certified divers provide you with "resort courses" enabling you to don a tank and mask after only two days' instruction and attempt a dive of, say, 40-foot depth. Nothing you ever viewed from the surface of the sea while snorkeling can possibly prepare you for the awesome beauty far below; though you may never have considered this rather difficult sport before, you'll quickly yearn to be a diver of ever-greater depths—in Bonaire.

For less venturesome sorts, the island offers almost constant sun throughout the year, magnificent beaches, a high level of continental cuisine in several restaurants (more than enough for your needs), birdwatching of great variety and appeal (the island's second major attraction), pink flamingoes roaming in flocks over expansive salt flats—and relatively moderate prices by Caribbean standards. For detailed information, contact the **Bonaire Government Information Office, 275 Seventh Ave., New York, NY 10001 (phone 212/242-7707),** and for tours to Bonaire, contact either a travel agent or the airlines flying directly to Bonaire (ALM Antillean Airlines) or to nearby Curaçao (Eastern and American Airlines), from which small planes then shuttle you to Bonaire, 20 minutes away.

2. The Resorts of Silicon Valley

With more BMWs per capita than anywhere else on earth (Germany included), Santa Clara County south of San Francisco is home to the golden youth of high tech, the scientific yuppies whose microchip factories and computer think tanks have caused the entire area to be known as Silicon Valley. Their very presence here has, in turn, spawned a secondary resort industry well known to most residents of San Francisco, but to scarcely anyone else at all. It is centered about four remarkable towns: Los Gatos, Santa Cruz, Aptos Beach, and Capitola.

The inland gem of Silicon Valley is little Los Gatos, sandwiched between a double range of low-lying mountains about 30 miles from the sea. A relatively compact city by California standards, its trendy downtown area can be covered on foot, passing boutiques by the dozen, chic ethnic restaurants, crafts stores and art galleries, a movie house showing foreign films, and—most delightful—a block-long garden/courtyard fronting a theater in a restored old mercantile building, all of this alongside still other restaurants patronized by many of the most accomplished young and middle-aged people of America.

The chief seaside location is sprawling Santa Cruz, almost wholly suburban in appearance, but with that most appealing of urban attractions: a pleasant boardwalk lined with ferris wheel, roller coaster, and other smaller entertainments for families with kids. Behind the boardwalk are suburban-like areas of charming modern residences, as well as wooden Victorian homes made into low-cost apartments. These, and the city's mild, year-round climate (better than San Francisco's), have attracted flocks of writers, artists, and musicians to a community that grows ever more vital with their arrival. Immediately adjoining Santa Cruz: the more sophisticated Capitola (again, art galleries, colorful restaurants and boutiques, hotels in Spanish style directly facing the sea) and Aptos Beach, where waters are warm enough for swimming in almost every month. If hotels in these stylish sections are too pricey for your budget, you'll find numerous lower-cost bed-and-breakfast establishments nearby.

If you were now to proceed southward along coastal Highway 1 for another 30 miles, you would reach that stretch of Pacific Ocean beachfront of which everyone in America knows: the famed Monterey Peninsula, with its awesome "17-Mile Drive." But don't neglect the resorts of Silicon Valley in your search for the better-known sight. While these havens of high tech can be contrived—a bit pretentious—in their architecture and décor, sometimes "tea shoppe" in character, screamingly quaint, they house a special breed of American, alive to every human possibility, ambitious and educated in the best sense, open and eager to new ideas and people—like you.

3. Malta, in the Mediterranean

The British tourist goes there. And so does the German. But to date, very few Americans have experienced the unique charms of this odd Mediterranean island, a former member of the British Commonwealth, located 60 miles south of Sicily. It is accessible via cheap flights (as little as $224 round trip from London) on its own flag carrier, Air Malta, operating from major European capitals to a coral-covered surface of about 100 square miles. And once there, the tourist discovers top hotel resorts (the Malta Hilton, the Phoenicia) charging but $82 to $110 a night for a double room, lesser hotels for much less, restaurants with an Italianate flavor charging $6 and under for meals, an outgoing, sociable population of about 300,000 people, well-disposed to visitors—and sun, sun, and more sun.

After a checkered history of successive domination by many different foreign lands, Malta burst into world prominence in the 1500s when it came under the control of the historically important Knights of the Order of St. John, a quasi-military organization of the Roman Catholic Church. In later centuries—particularly the 17th and 19th—the "Knights of Malta" brought artistic riches to the island's many churches, and covered its cities, particularly the capital of Valletta, with white stone structures of great architectural merit; most of these ancient buildings still stand and impart a distinctive cast to the island's appearance. In World War II, as a key outpost of the British Empire, Malta withstood the most constant but unavailing attacks by the German air force.

For today's tourist to Malta, there are more intact historical remnants per square mile than perhaps anywhere else in the world: both Megalithic and later Roman temples, catacombs and palaces, formerly inhabited grottoes and caves. There are medieval fortifications and structures built by the Knights, more recent façades from the era of the baroque, the homes of ancient nobles, art treasures of extraordinary value and variety—it requires a full week to take in the most minimal list of sights.

For less exalted recreation: low-priced resort hotels with pools, casinos, and tennis courts; intermittent beaches scattered about (particularly on the small neighboring islands of Gozo and Comino); sightseeing boat cruises through the Grand Harbor and along the coast; those Italianate restaurants to which I referred; and those friendly Maltese people, themselves an attraction. Among the undiscovered gems to which you haven't yet been, Malta ranks high; don't omit it when planning your next European itinerary. Contact **Air Malta, 345 California St., Suite 2560, San Francisco, CA 94104 (phone 415/362-2929).**

4. The Colorful Nation of Belgium

Neglected by the tourist throngs, lightly visited and often casually dismissed—"If it's Tuesday, it must be Belgium"—Belgium is a nation with museums to rival the Louvre, a cuisine rated tops in the world, a friendly, sympathetic population, and low to moderate prices. Why, then, is it so widely bypassed by the major travel movements?

The fault, I suggest, lies in the tourist and not in Belgium. We tourists were incorrectly taught that the Middle Ages—the period of Belgium's greatest glory—was a time of "darkness," when nothing much happened, and mankind passed into sloth and illiteracy. Because the greatest Belgian sights are medieval cities preserved from that period—Bruges, Ghent, Antwerp, Tournai—we assume them to be unimportant, and either eliminate a stay from our itinerary or schedule only a scant two days for Belgium.

In actual fact, the latter half of the so-called Middle Ages—the High Gothic era—was a time of extraordinary human achievement, in which Belgium was a world leader. It was then that people embarked upon construction of the great Gothic cathedrals, began painting the never-again-equalled masterworks of the Flemish primitives, erected the gilded city squares and soaring belfry towers that so enchant us today, and formulated most of the legal, commercial, and theological concepts that continue to govern our lives. As you pass beyond Brussels to the magnificently preserved medieval cities of Belgium, you literally stagger under the impact of great art and architecture, revising all your previously mistaken notions about those "terrible Dark Ages."

In addition to drinking in these remarkable visual sights, you eat—oh, how you eat! You dine from the wares of chefs as celebrated as movie stars. You choose from 300 varieties of Belgian beer. Suitably aglow, you watch ballet companies and colorful religious processions, outdoor markets and masked revelers, festivals peopled by papier-mâché giants, massed ranks of dedicated diamond cutters, equally intent croupiers at elegant seaside casinos on the 60-mile Belgian coast.

Don't pass up Belgium—it is the example par excellence of another undiscovered geographical delight! An enthralling nation well represented by the capable **Belgian National Tourist Office, 745 Fifth Ave., New York, NY 10151 (phone 212/ 758-8130),** from which further information is readily available, it more than repays the tourist who approaches its resplendent city sights with the proper, advance historical preparation—and attitudes.

5. Wales and Its People

For most of us, our awareness of Wales—that separate "country" in the western part of the British Isles—is based on poems by Dylan Thomas, as read by Richard Burton, or from *How Green Was My Valley* and its picture of the harsh life of coal miners occupying the section's southern industrial belt. Mainly it is a grim image we remember, and grimmer still now that the coal mines are mainly abandoned and Britain's "sunset" industries (steel, in particular) winding down. In actual fact, the greater part of Wales is a green and verdant landscape, given over to large national parks and impressive mountain ranges, to white sheep with black feet grazing on heather-covered slopes, to picturesque villages and terraced farms, with scarcely a single soot-darkened miner trudging wearily home at dusk. Though the Welsh economy is sharply depressed, its tourist appeal is undiminished and increasingly looked to as a source of Welsh employment. Yet only a bare handful of Americans travel on to this unusual "nation" found only three or so hours by train from London.

You reach the underpopulated center of Wales, or the alpine-like north, in less than four comfortable hours from London's Euston Station, usually changing at Shrewsbury (pronounced "shroze-berry") and pro-

ceeding from there through the "harp-shaped" hills of Wales (Dylan Thomas's phrase) either through the center or to the northwest. If you choose the central route heading toward the quaint and dreamy town of Machynlleth (pronounced "mah-hun-lith"), with its several hotels and guesthouses, you can pause for a day or two to view an oddity (described in a separate essay)—the Centre for Alternative Technology—located atop an abandoned slate quarry just outside the town. A utopian community of 30-or-so extreme ecologists, fully self-sufficient from the use of renewable energy sources only (solar power, wind, water), the centre actively encourages visits and conducts all guests on extensive tours of the grounds, seven days a week. One continues from Machynlleth to the delightful Welsh university town of Aberystwyth on the sea, or northward to Snowdonia Park containing the highest mountain peaks in Britain.

With its distinctive national culture and history, its use of the Welsh language by nearly 25% of the population, Wales is an exotic travel experience too complex to summarize here, but one that shouldn't be passed up. It is the classic example of an untouristed (by Americans) "find," possessing all the attributes and attractions of more heavily visited destinations, but reserved, for the time being, just for you! ≈

Grand' Place of Brussels

241

My Own "Little Black Book" of Cheap Destinations

Six Holiday Areas with Prices in Pennies and Values Galore

Lisbon

A rather cynical Boston tour company once operated charter flights to Copenhagen in the frigid month of February, when snowdrifts pile up five feet deep. Because the trip cost only $299, including everything, passengers returned with stars in their eyes. "Whatta city!" they cried.

Now, cheapness alone is scarcely a reason for travel; North Yemen is cheap, but not exactly thronged with visitors.

But cheapness combined with other attractive features is a valid basis for choosing a travel destination. When everything is cheaper than you are normally accustomed to paying, you tend to love the city or country in which those prices prevail.

Based on that powerful truth—that travel enjoyment generally runs in inverse proportion to cost, that places are unusually pleasant if unusually cheap—I've searched for the world's cheapest (but at least minimally attractive) destinations. Discarding the many "cheapies" that lack any appeal at all (Albania, Bangladesh), eliminating others that aren't cheap enough, I remain with six that combine dramatic cheapness with dramatic travel excitement:

Orlando, Florida

Cheapest of all the world's resort cities, cheaper even (on a relative basis) than Barcelona and the Costa Brava in the 1950s, Orlando got that way (in my view) because of unjustified expectations as to its future growth following the opening of Walt Disney's EPCOT in late 1982. Not content to predict a simple doubling or even tripling of tourism, it now appears that the citizens of Orlando were convinced it would rise tenfold. Because each of its most solid citizens— every taxi driver and dentist, every housewife with a nest egg stashed away—proceeded to build a motel (I am only exaggerating slightly).

With 75,000 rooms now available, Orlando suffers from an unprecedented hotel glut, and units at good-quality, medium-level establishments (not simply budget motels) are often available for $25 per night and less during at least seven scattered months of the year (mid-August to mid-December, January, May, and June). Add the prevalence of all-you-can-eat buffet breakfasts (with grits!) for $2.99, add the endless offers of western-style chuckwagon lunches or dinners for $3.99, add the Duff's Cafeterias serving multicourse, Rabelaisian repasts for $5.46 (which include make-it-yourself ice-cream sundaes and banana splits that alone would cost $5.46 in most other cities)—and you have price levels lower than Las Vegas once offered to its frantic clientele.

The result is that Orlando has now become a resort area of broad appeal, and not simply a place to bring children. I suggest that smart adults without a single child in tow—utter misanthropes without the remotest intention of visiting the Magic Kingdom—can now enjoy a proper, adult-style vacation of tennis, sunning, nightlife, and swimming in the Orlando area for less than they'd spend anywhere else on earth.

Cities of Central Mexico

As unlikely as this may seem, the Mexican peso presently sells at a rate of 2,260 to the dollar (it was 23 to the dollar short years ago). But don't expect dramatic savings in the popular, typical coastal resorts of Mexico (the Acapulcos, Puerto Vallartas, and Ixtapas on the Pacific; the Cancúns and Cozuméls on the Caribbean). There, with tourists numbered in the millions each year, people charge what the traffic will bear.

Rather, it is within the deep interior of Mexico—and especially in that diadem of colonial locations surrounding Mexico City—that the normal, remarkably low price structure of Mexico asserts itself. In the fabled urban centers of the 17th-century conquistadors—in such cities as San Miguel de Allende, Patzcuaro, Guanajuato—quite decent hotel rooms rent for $30 and under, quite adequate meals are available for $4, long intercity bus rides cost less than $2 an hour, and every other expenditure is a happy surprise.

Most important, one encounters a culture in these storied cities of Mexico's past that is fully as colorful, fully as profound and important, as any other on earth—but available here at a fraction of normal costs.

Cheapness alone is scarcely a reason for travel; North Yemen is cheap, but not exactly thronged with visitors.

Central plaza, San Miguel de Allende

But when everything is cheaper than you are normally accustomed to paying, you tend to love the city or country in which those prices prevail.

Downtown Orlando

Patzcuaro, Mexico

One may fly to Mexico City (using reduced, midweek fares of several airlines) and rent a car from there to descend in three hours into a deeply enjoyable and reliably safe area of colonial sights so cheap as to warrant inclusion on any list of the "cheapest six."

The Nation of Portugal

Cheapest country in all of Western Europe, cheaper even than Greece, Portugal is also the least developed of the Old World nations, a time machine transporting you to the past, poor but proud. Even in Lisbon, modern structures are few; but in the countryside outside the capital, life is simpler still, intensely human. And thus on the beaches of Portuguese fishing villages, anxious wives still peer out to the sea at dusk, awaiting the return of their fishermen husbands; in time-worn roadside cafés, grizzled farmers sit nursing a glass of raw red wine as they discuss the harvest or the prospect for jobs abroad, never too preoccupied to offer a seat or a kindly glance at the tourist who wanders into their midst.

The Portuguese escudo, which sold at 38 to the dollar a few years ago, is now exchanged at a rate of 150 to the dollar, and the always-inexpensive Portugal has clearly become the bargain paradise of Europe. Only the most elegant of Lisbon hotels charge more than $70 for a double room with two breakfasts; other quality establishments lower the price to $50, while budget lodgings in pensions and small hotels sell for under $30—often for $25—for two people. Pay particular heed to the *pousadas* (government-owned inns, in period buildings, the equivalent of Spain's better-known *paradors*) in the north of Portugal; although priced (on average) as high as $68 for a double room, with dinner at $12, their castle-like settings and amenities will remain in your memory for years to come.

Rio de Janeiro and Buenos Aires

Here, local currencies haven't simply fallen against the U.S. dollar, but virtually "collapsed" against it. At current rates of exchange, a pair of men's shoes can be bought for as little as $12 in both cities, a high-fashion women's suit for $40, and other exquisite articles of apparel for a fraction of what you'd spend at home. Because the world's most celebrated designer fashions are manufactured under license in both Brazil and Argentina, you obtain the most stylish of dresses, blouses, coats, and boots at ridiculously cheap rates.

At restaurants, steak dinners are served in Buenos Aires for $3.50 and less, high-quality meals in Rio for $6 or so. Long taxi rides cost $2. Hotel rates are appropriately low, movies cost a third the rate in North America, and there is scarcely anything (except scotch whisky) that doesn't sell for well below the levels you are normally accustomed to paying. As chic and glittering as they may initially seem, these are among the world's most remarkable bargain spots for possessors of the U.S. dollar.

The Soviet Union

Though it may be depressing at times, it is never uninteresting. And the USSR is also among the cheapest of European nations for high-quality hotels and meals at the lowest of costs. In Moscow and Leningrad, skilled French and Scandinavian construction firms, brought in for the job, have now erected deluxe hotels (swimming pools and all else) for use on package-tour programs priced at wonderfully low levels; the tourists requesting these properties receive one of the greatest of all tour values. At mealtime, in the hotel restaurants of most Russian cities, caviar is often available at no extra charge to your tour package, as are such appetizers as smoked salmon, delightful hors d'oeuvres (*zakuski*), succulent borscht (beet soup), and other gourmet-level dishes. So eagerly sought is the hard currency spent by European and American tourists that the Russians respond with extraordinary tour features: tickets to the Bolshoi Ballet, continual sightseeing, long flights within the country to destinations thousands of miles away, yet all for a price that would barely purchase a scaled-down trip by escorted motorcoach in the Europe to the west. For satisfying the most demanding of tastes at the lowest of costs, Russia vies with Portugal and Greece.

Nova Scotia

Finally there is Canada, and that most quaint and underdeveloped of its provinces, Nova Scotia. In a country where the U.S. dollar sells at a full 25% advantage against its own currency, almost all Canadian areas have become refreshingly priced, but Nova Scotia is cheaper than most. You'll find lobster dinners for $8.95 (U.S.), motel rooms for $40 and less, local crafts at bargain rates, and inexpensive recreational and sporting activities conducted in the clearest, briskest air in all of North America.

And Nova Scotia is accessible, almost ridiculously so. The U.S. tourist in the eastern United States need only drive north along the Atlantic coast to Portland or Bar Harbor, Maine, from which car-ferries make the six-hour crossing (from Bar Harbor) to Nova Scotia. Once there, one roams the villages and towns, or urban Halifax, seeking that perfect lobster, that ocean trout, that exquisite seafood dinner that the "Scotians" prepare and price so well.

The site as well of a fascinating history (which includes the exile here, for a time, of Victor Hugo, banished from France), Nova Scotia is excitingly foreign, pleasantly friendly, a bit backward (in modern structures and amenities), always close to nature—in short, the type of vacation destination of which most of us dream.≈

Fishermen of Portugal

XII ≈ 20 TRAVEL ORGANIZATIONS THAT WORK FOR YOU

Twenty Varied Travel Organizations That Bring You Better, Cheaper Travel

Clubs and Exchanges, Schools and Retreats, Passes and Programs, Fitting into No Established Categories—An Assortment of Travel Firms That Can Change Your Travel Life

Participating in a cattle drive

If Adam Smith returned to life (and I'm referring to the 18th-century economist, not the current-day journalist), he'd be rather pleased with the travel industry: it's largely a free-market dream. Except for the transportation element of it—increasingly dominated by a few large carriers—the activity consists of thousands upon thousands of relatively small and little-known entrepreneurs scrambling to improve upon their competitors' products.

Among those mini-units are a thousand particular firms whose approach to travel, in my view, is meaningful, innovative, and exciting, and it is that charmed number of organizations—1,200 or so, to be exact (see the index at the back of this book)—that account for the bulk of our discussion.

A remaining 20 firms fail to fit, however, into any of our preceding categories. Hence, the following chapter dealing with a few last, miscellaneous, and sometimes-rather-odd organizations that can nevertheless have a major, beneficial impact on your next trip:

1. The Ultimate Travel Club

Its only membership requirement is that you have "an aenemic wallet," and a zest—despite that condition—to rove the farthest reaches of the world. Its members of all ages make the readers of my $30-a-day books seem like plutocrats. They walk across all of Nepal; take local buses, regional jitneys, occasional mule trains, to cross the wastes of sub-Saharan Africa; sleep in the huts of Indonesian villages, cadge meals at the communal fires of New Guinean fishermen, trade bars of soap for trinkets crafted in the yak tents of Ladakh.

And then they return home to tell about it, at monthly public meetings in St. Martin's Lane, London; in southern California or New York; or in the pages of their six-times-a-year newsletter, *The Globe*.

Surely the most distinguished travel group on earth—despite their "aenemic wallets"—is the 40-year-old **Globetrotters Club, c/o BCM Roving, London WC1N 3XX, England** (an oddly truncated, but perfectly adequate, mail-drop address). Since officers are all volunteers lacking a full-time office and frequently changing, they use that simple pickup point to receive membership applications and communications. The fee is $14 per year, $24 for two years, for receiving *The Globe* every other month, as well as *The Globetrotters Directory,* listing names, addresses, ages, and travel experience of members (be sure to provide that information while applying), as well as purely optional offers by them of free accommodations or advice to other members. Because a great many members do, in fact, make such offers of lodging (in spare beds or cots of their living rooms or dens), the *Directory* is a rich source of free travel opportunities, though not primarily designed as such.

London Globetrotters (and visitors from abroad) meet at 3:30 p.m. the second Saturday of each month in the Friends Meeting House, 52 St. Martin's Lane, (entrance at 8 Hop Gardens), London WC1; monthly sites and dates for the same in New York, Toronto, and southern California are listed in *The Globe*—as are those accounts of members' adventures in touring the Third World.

2. Networking the "A.T.'s"

"Appropriate Technology" or "Alternative Technology" ("A.T.") is a massive worldwide movement of people who believe in a simpler, gentler, human-scale life, non-industrial, cooperative, participatory—the dramatic opposite of the factory-polluted, harshly competitive, and hierarchical world of autos and metallic wastes in which most of us live. Its advocates are found in every nation, on organic farms and in vegetarian restaurants, at "New Era" bookshops and solar-energy centers, in consumer co-ops and small utopian communities. And because they believe in pressing their views on others, they are the easiest people on earth to get to know. Regardless of your own beliefs, you add a new dimension and intellectual growth to your travels when you meet and interact with these mild-mannered but highly motivated, free-thinking people.

But how do you meet them? Though it wasn't intended for that purpose, the quarterly newspaper/

newsletter called *TRANET,* for *Transnational Network for Appropriate Technologies,* is a highly useful "guidebook" to alternative technology people in every nation. Its primary goal is to apprise alternative technology advocates of developments in their specialties in other lands. But recent editions have contained extensive directories of addresses for the specific purpose of encouraging well-focused, carefully planned, international travel by persons exploring "A.T." Thus, issue 48 for the spring of 1988 listed 200 sources of "alternative travel," while issue 42 for the summer of 1986 listed organizations engaged in "cross-cultural, people-to-people linkages" across national boundaries; by contacting them, one arranges to meet "people who are changing the world by changing their own lives . . . adopting alternative technologies." Issue 43 for winter 1986 was called "Alternatives Down Under" and provided the addresses of scores of contacts in Australia and New Zealand for experiencing those approaches. The spring 1987 issue has a similar directory to alternative movements and peoples in the otherwise highly conformist nation of Japan, and issue 53—out in early '89—does the same for Southeast Asia.

Such contacts are the supreme essence of meaningful travel, says *TRANET.* Journeys should produce not simply a "tolerance" of foreign people, but "a love of our differences. . . . We need to invite them to our homes, to visit them in theirs. We need to participate in their alternative celebrations, to eat their foods, to honor their ceremonies, to explore their wild places, to understand their human-rights issues, to see how they confront their governments."

Though a year's subscription to *TRANET* is a hefty $30, back issues will be sent to you for $5 apiece. You'll want to start with the remarkable directory to Australia and New Zealand (no. 43), then perhaps go to the earlier one on "People-to-People Networking" worldwide (no. 42). Contact **TRANET, P.O. Box 567, Rangeley, ME 04970 (phone 207/864-2252).**

3. The Other Elderhostel

You've just been placed on your third waiting list for a popular Elderhostel course; your first two choices are hopelessly sold out. Soaring in popularity, the 13-year-old system of foreign and domestic study tours for seniors over 60 is expected to draw 180,000 participants in 1989, causing a moderate, but still irritating, number of "close-outs."

So try Interhostel. It's administered by the same University of New Hampshire officials who created Elderhostel, but then "spun it off" when the baby grew too big for the campus. The university continues to operate Interhostel, which at this time sends people over the age of 50 to pursue intensive two-week tours and bouts of classroom instruction at foreign universities around the world. While topics are a bit more general and geographical than Elderhostel's, they're taught by leading academic figures. Price: $1,095 to $1,295 for two weeks, including everything (housing in university residences, all meals, all tuition) except air fare, usually from Boston or New York.

For information, contact **Interhostel, University of New Hampshire, Division of Continuing Education, 6 Garrison Ave., Durham, NH 03824 (phone 603/862-1147 Monday through Friday from 1:30 to 4 p.m. EST).**

4. The "Reader's Digest" of Travel

Once a week throughout the year, Miriam Tobolowsky of West Los Angeles—a part-time English teacher—travels to a public library to scan the Sunday travel sections of two dozen major newspapers. Pausing for breath, she then proceeds to read every major U.S. magazine, searching for their occasional words on travel. That done, she composes highly abridged "précis" of the latest travel news and publishes them in her bimonthly newsletter, *Partners-in-Travel*.

No matter how extensive your own reading of the travel press, you will always encounter surprising new tidbits of travel lore in her chatty but incisive condensations. Though her focus is on the mature traveler, and her newsletter was initially intended as a match-up service for retirees seeking travel companions (and still performs that function), *Partners-in-Travel* is fast emerging as a valuable compendium of travel discover-

ies that would otherwise appear in only isolated form, lost to the great majority of us.

Where else would you learn about a club for single persons owning recreational vehicles ("Loners on Wheels")? Or about swim-up blackjack tables in Las Vegas, a golf school for senior citizens, a pet hotel in Arizona? One issue even preserves the advice of a certain Arthur Frommer (on how to override the airline computers when they show an absence of discount fares) for those deprived communities, dark holes of ignorance, where this book isn't sold.

A subscription to *Partners-in-Travel* (still devoted in part to "Travel Personals") is $30 for six months, $45 for a year. Address: **P.O. Box 491145, Los Angeles, CA 90049 (phone 213/476-4869).**

5. Hospitality Exchanges

In theory, it's simplicity incarnate: you offer to accommodate people free of charge as they pass through your home city (using a spare room or cot in your home); they offer to accommodate you as you pass through their home cities. Both of you live for free on all your travels, whenever they occur.

In practice, this intermittent exchange of hospitality requires a great deal of administration, and a number of well-meaning "hospitality exchanges" have collapsed under the weight of address changes, heavy correspondence, and other pesky paperwork.

One with considerable staying-power—possibly because it is not entirely free—is **INNter Lodging Co-Op, P.O. Box 7044, Tacoma, WA 98407 (phone 206/756-0343).** With several hundred members well scattered across the country, it provides you with instant friends (and accommodations) in all the states other than Utah and Nevada for an initial fee of $47, plus $4 or $5 per person per night paid to your actual hosts (for the cost of fresh linen, towels, and other usables). Children with their own sleeping bags pay only 50¢. On an INNter Lodging Co-Op trip, says founder Bob Ehrenheim, you learn that "strangers are friends you haven't met yet."

Slightly smaller, but growing fast, is **Visiting Friends, Inc., P.O. Box 231, Lake Jackson, TX**

77566 (phone 409/297-7367), the "guestroom exchange network." It charges $25 for a "lifetime membership," then a total of $25 for your stay of up to six nights at a member's home. It also centralizes the reservations process, keeps all addresses to itself (and not in a published directory), and thus preserves both your privacy and occasional desire to receive no inquiries at all for a number of months.

Note that a "hospitality exchange" is different from a "home exchange" or "vacation exchange"; it does not require a simultaneous swapping of accommodations. You use the service, or provide accommodations, only when you choose, and without having to coordinate your travel plans with those of another.

Surely there are other, struggling "hospitality exchanges"; if you'll send me their names, to the address listed in the Preface, I'll spread the good word.

6. Cheapest Caribbean Cruises

It's not a sailing offered by the lower-quality ships, or even a cruise heavily discounted in price by the cruise "bucket shops." Rather, it's a cruise on which four people squeeze into a single cabin. Though travel agents told them they were crazy to try, a small-but-distinguished tour company called Singleworld (formerly known as Bachelor Party Tours) recently offered to guarantee quad accommodations for individuals traveling alone. By stuffing four unrelated persons (of the same sex, of course) into a quad "room," Singleworld reduces the price of some one-week Caribbean cruises to less than $800 a person, including round-trip air transportation to the embarkation point.

Do people then chafe at their cramped condition? Are they at each others' throats after only a few hours? Not so, says Singleworld—they're rarely *in* the cabin assigned to them!

For a free catalog of Singleworld's offerings, contact **Singleworld, 401 Theodore Fremd Ave., Rye, NY 10580 (phone toll free 800/223-6490).**

7. Cattle-Herding Holidays

Consider, now, the latest initiative of the tireless Patricia Dickerman of New York City.

In theory, it's simplicity incarnate: you offer to accommodate people free of charge as they pass through your home city; they offer to accommodate you as you pass through their home city.

An Elderhostel visit to Scotland

Elderhostel cross-country skiing class

TRANET caters to that massive, worldwide movement of people who believe in a simpler, gentler, human-scale life, non-industrial, cooperative, participatory.

NICA volunteers cutting cane

Coffee-harvesting brigade in Nicaragua

In 1948, alone in a battered coupe, she bumped along the rural dirt roads of American, persuading skeptical farmers to accept her guests and thus create a new holiday industry and a new source of income for themselves: farm vacations. She later did the same at working ranches. Her classic book of 1949, *Farm, Ranch, & Country Vacations* ($11 postpaid from Pat Dickerman, 36 E. 57th St., New York, NY 10022), updated approximately every three years, is the oldest continually published travel guide in America.

Now, fulfilling everyone's secret desire to lead the life of a cowboy, she arranges for actual participation by us city types in real-life cattle drives in Wyoming, Nevada, Colorado, New Mexico, and Montana, moving herds to pastures with better grass. Costs range from $50 to $100 per person per day, including everything: chuckwagon meals, tents or sleeping bags under the stars, your own horse to ride. If nothing else, says Pat, "you'll have a new respect for a hamburger and the hard work that goes into producing it."

For a free newsletter on cattle drives, send a self-addressed, stamped no. 10 envelope to **Adventure Guides, Inc., 36 E. 57th St., New York, NY 10022 (phone 212/355-6334).**

8. Mexico Study Groups

Gayle Savelsberg, of Phoenix, Arizona, is a retired teacher who felt that school-based Spanish-language courses were lacking in one key element: immersion in the home life of a Spanish-speaking family.

So she darted from Cuernavaca to the Yucatán, from San Miguel de Allende to Guadalajara, laboriously persuading Mexican families to put up students (aged 15 to 85) in their homes, on a three-meals-a-day basis. That exposure to everyday Spanish, coupled with four hours a day of instruction in distinguished Mexican schools, catapulted her courses over those of the competition—while keeping prices at rock-bottom levels.

The study tours last for 30 days, are each accompanied by Gayle (who stays near you, but at a discreet distance, and without intruding into your Spanish-speaking life); and they are operated at renowned "institutos" or "academias" in San Miguel and Cuernavaca in summer, in Merida and Cuernavaca in winter. Rates are a remarkable $1,045 for 30 days (thus, $35 a day), including everything (housing, meals, instruction) but round-trip air fare to Mexico.

Contact **Mexico Study Groups, P.O. Box 56982, Phoenix, AZ 85079 (phone 602/242-9231).**

9. A Reputable Student Exchange

The very finest form of travel, bar none, is a several-month stay in a foreign home, enjoyed in the teenage years of one's life. I weep for those students who miss out on these life-enhancing, maturing experiences simply because their schools haven't publicized the offerings (which happens more than you'd expect).

The solution: Acquire the information yourself and then deal directly with the sponsoring organization.

A 131-page publication from the Council on Standards for International Educational Travel describes the student programs offered by 49 reputable U.S. organizations and provides the facts for selecting the group from which to request further information. Listed are not simply the "giants"—Experiment in International Living, Youth for Understanding, American Field Service—but also the smaller, specialized ones as well—like the Educational Foundation for Foreign Study ($3,590 all inclusive, for ten months in Europe with volunteer host families, while attending European public schools; note its full scholarship for students creatively talented in the arts); or the Iberoamerican Cultural Exchange Program ($500 for a six-week stay with a Mexican family, $1,500 for a full school year, excluding air fare). Scholarship aid is heavily stressed.

Request the *Advisory List of International Educational Travel and Exchange Programs 1988—1989* from **CSIET, 1906 Association Dr., Reston, VA 22091 (phone 703/860-5317),** and elclose $6.50 for the cost of the booklet, postage, and handling.

10. World's Finest Cruise Value

Forget the source and focus on the price. You pay as little as $125 a day (plus air fare), perhaps an average of $140 a day (more familiar cruise ships average $200 to $225). You cruise with largely English-speaking passengers on unusual routes through the Baltic Sea, or to the North Cape (of Norway) or the South Pacific, or you sail around the world in 100 days for as little as $10,000.

Only thing is: you do it on a Soviet ship. Proud possessors of the world's largest passenger-carrying fleet, the Russians have launched a determined effort to enter the international cruising market. And thousands of British vacationers, Germans, and more recently Americans, have responded favorably, booking themselves onto the world's cheapest ocean-going cruises.

From Tilbury, England, on the River Thames, the 17,000-ton *Leonid Brezhnev* and *Azerbaidzhan* sail in summer on 14-day itineraries along the fjords of Norway's North Cape, and on alternate departures through the Baltic to Helsinki, Stockholm, Copenhagen, Gdynia (Poland), and Leningrad—the latter visited on group excursions requiring no visas. In spring and fall the same large ships depart from Genoa or Venice to wander the eastern Mediterranean, and then go to the Greek Islands and Turkey, occasionally darting through the Black Sea to Yalta or Odessa (again no visa needed). In January, and again from Tilbury, the *Leonid Brezhnev* sets off to sail around the world (at even lower daily rates than its normal $125 minimum).

From Bremen, Genoa, or Venice, the M/V *Odessa* makes similar 14-day cruises, but is best known for its yearly round-the-world sailings, on which 50% of all passengers are now Americans. From Australia, the M/V *Belorussiya* cruises through the South Pacific.

Meals on board are "continental," with Russian touches: borscht among the soups, chicken à la Kiev and beef Stroganoff among the entrees. Entertainment is so-called international cabaret adapted to Russian talents: balalaika groups perform, and sailors dance the *kasatski*. But movies, thankfully, are U.S. or British, all cabin and deck staff are reasonably multilingual, and politics is never discussed. "You are in America when you use the ships catering to the U.S. market," says a Soviet shipping official, "but on our ships, you are in Europe more than America."

For brochures and sailing schedules, contact the U.S. general agent for the Soviet shipping lines: **International Cruise Center, Inc., 250 Old Country Rd., Mineola, NY 11501 (phone 516/747-8880, or toll free 800/221-3254).**

11. King of the Discount Books

Though more than 2,000,000 are sold each year, scarcely a copy appears in bookstores, and use of the so-called Entertainment Books is thus confined to those relatively few savvy Americans who purchase them from nonprofit clubs, service groups, and other civic organizations. Yet each book entitles the bearer to near-50% discounts at restaurants, sporting events, movies, live theaters, and other recreational facilities, even at scattered hotels in that person's home city—or in the 73 other major U.S. cities for which Entertainment Books are published.

Bulky as dictionaries, the books consist of perforated cardboard discount coupons offering "two-for-one" dining or admissions, or straight 50% reductions, at scores of establishments. Some 74 books are published each year, one for each of the 74 largest American cities.

Of course, the discount doesn't always work out to 50%. When two of you order a $15 and $11 entree, respectively, at a listed restaurant, it is the cheaper entrée (the $11 one) that comes free; and drinks and dessert aren't included in the "two-for-one" offer. As for the hotel discounts, a major portion of them are valid for lightly booked weekend stays only. Yet though the dining discount works out to 30% on average, and some of the weekend hotel discounts are of dubious value, the savings overall are substantial indeed. Two million families wouldn't budge from their homes without their Entertainment Books.

Individual-city books cost $25 to $45 apiece, depending on the city, and often pay for themselves in one or two days of travel or use. Almost all are sold in bulk to nonprofit organizations that then quietly resell them to members in fundraising programs. But since Entertainment Publications, Inc. (a 28-year-old publicly owned company), has offices in most of the 74 largest cities, they can usually be contacted directly by the public (and books purchased) by simply looking up the words "Entertainment Publications" or "Entertainment Passbooks" in your local phone directory. Or you can go directly to the headquarters of **Entertainment Publications, Inc., 1400 N. Woodward Ave., Birmingham, MI 48011 (phone 313/642-8300).** If you do contact them directly, consider buying the condensed, one-volume, nationwide Entertainment Book called *Travel America at Half Price* ($26.95).

12. The Second Night Free

With nearly two million members currently enrolled, the Encore Travel Club of Lanham, Maryland, has become the largest discount organization in travel history. Reason: It has signed 2,300 hotels to provide "the second night free" to Encore members (usually without weekend limitations). Thus, stay for two nights and you pay for only one; stay for seven nights and you get two free nights; and so on. If you are constantly traveling and staying in hotels, you can scarcely afford not to join (membership is $48 a year).

But will success spoil (or even ruin) Encore? As an ever-greater percentage of the American public joins, won't these 2,300 hotels find that they are giving discounts to almost everyone, thus eliminating the potential for purely incremental business that led them to give "the second night free"? That's a problem that puzzles me. Still, until the day when hotels dig in their heels and say no to Encore's entreaties, it remains an attractive organization for frequent travelers. And it supplies its members with a growing list of other services: the lowest air fare available on domestic flights, a six-times-a-year magazine listing discounts on tour programs and packages, still more.

For further information, or to join, contact **Encore Travel Club, 4501 Forbes Blvd., Lanham, MD 20706 (phone toll free 800/638-8976).**

13. Finding the "Poor Man's Spa"

A glossy, four-color publication called *Spa Finders* ($4 through the mails) is currently enabling a narrow segment of the public (those who know about it) to enjoy wholesome spa vacations here in the United States at a fraction of the cost that others incur. It achieves that feat simply by revealing the existence of a broad range of spas heretofore known only to spa-lovers residing in the immediate vicinity.

A cottage industry by normal commercial standards, the average U.S. spa is a small, family-owned resort hotel, chronically strapped for cash and barely able to advertise outside its own small region.

There is no trade association of spas, no publication devoted to the activity.

The industry has for years been dominated by the glitzy names—La Costa, the Golden Door, Maine Chance—charging a king's ransom for a week of their health-bestowing attentions. Most Americans have consequently assumed these slimming spa vacations to be outside their financial reach.

Unless they had a copy of *Spa Finders,* that is. A remarkable product of nationwide research, presented with glamorous flair but punctilious attention to detail (prices to the penny, seasons, facilities), it claims to contain listings and descriptions of all major U.S. spas, bar none, alerting us to underutilized facilities that have long catered to a purely local clientele. Included are places with all the features and facilities of the big-name resorts—Jacuzzis and rubdown tables, saunas, aerobics, and scientifically measured meals—but at rates as low as $200 a week for room, all meals, and all traditional spa treatments and programs. Some of the establishments in it are making their first appearance before a nationwide audience.

(*Spa Finders* also lists and describes the higher-priced varieties, of course, but proudly claims to be the first such publication to gather particulars on every one in every price range, in a widely dispersed activity).

For a copy of the 100-page, magazine-size catalog, send $4 to **Spa-Finders, 784 Broadway, New York, NY 10003 (phone 212/475-1000, or toll free 800/ALL-SPAS).**

14. Britain with Elsie

"Elsie from England" is a Cockney from south London named Elsie Dillard, who immigrated to the state of Washington in 1957, tried her hand at real estate and insurance, but preferred offering advice to friends about travel to the British Isles. "You don't want a dull hotel," was her most frequent litany. "I've got this darling bed-and-breakfast house for only 32 shillings 6 pence."

Soon she was a retail travel agent, and then a wholesaler, the single leading source to other travel agents of low-cost bed-and-breakfast accommodations in scores of locations throughout England, Scotland, Ireland, and Wales. Her product currently ranges in price from $25 per person per night (breakfast included) for the standard English guesthouse, to $35 for an upgraded version that can sometimes be a comfortable country estate. (She charges $10 additional for every reservation made.) And although her clientele originally was mainly travel agents from the western states, she is perfectly willing (indeed, eager) to deal directly with the public from every state.

If you've a craving for the "real England," call Elsie for even a single reservation in a single location. Or else put yourself entirely in her hands for a full three-week tour. She'll start you in a B&B in London, then place you in a self-drive car, and provide you with other prepaid B&Bs for all remaining nights, as you follow a classic, planned-by-Elsie itinerary into Wiltshire (Somerset) and the West Country (Devon and Cornwall), up to Bath and through "the Potteries" into North Wales, thence to Chester, on up to the Lake District, and all the way up to the Hebrides and northern Scotland, then south to Edinburgh, and into York, the Cotswolds, and Heathrow or Gatwick Airport for the homeward-bound flight. With pre-reserved, classically British, marvelously cheap guesthouse rooms all the way! Write or phone "Elsie from England," P.O. Box 5107, Redondo, WA 98054 (phone 206/941-6413).

15. Vacations from a Barter Firm

"Barter" is the exchange of product for product, and nowhere is the activity more intensely pursued than in the travel industry. Airlines trade seats for radio commercials, cruise ships trade cabins for stationery and supplies, hotels trade rooms for ads on the sides of buses. Since each of the "traders" has unused capacity or excess merchandise, they are exchanging items that might have gone unsold in any event—thus the trade costs them nothing (so goes the theory).

But who ends up sitting in the airplane seats, or sleeping in the hotel rooms and cruise-ship berths, that have been "bartered"? Since there's an obvious limit to the number of trips that radio station personnel and staffs of advertising agencies can themselves use (or else they'd be on perpetual vacation!), the excess "travel credits" are sold by dozens of so-called barter companies to large corporations or special groups, at prices heavily discounted from normal levels. Among those firms, a small but growing number (a handful, really) are currently selling their credits—sharply reduced air tickets, cruises, car rentals, tour packages, hotel stays—directly to individual members of the public, among others.

In the Southeast, the behemoth of the barterers is **Lino and Associates, 5665 Central Ave., St. Petersburg, FL 33710 (phone 813/384-6700),** and it is willing to deal with the public (I asked). Call, write, or visit, and you'll pick up a broad variety of trips and tickets at substantial discounts. In the East and West, the leading firms are **Travel World Leisure Club, Inc., 225 W. 34th St., Suite 2203, New York, NY 10122 (phone 212/239-4855),** and **Communications Development Corp., 1454 Euclid St., Santa Monica, CA 90404 (phone 213/458-0596),** respectively. Both sell deeply discounted tour packages, cruises, and air tickets, and have no objection to selling them in "ones and twos," to even a single person or couple contemplating a trip. For precisely what were these tours, cruises, and tickets originally exchanged? For a TV spot late at night, or a billboard in the country, or even a paint job in the airline's office!

16. Adventures in Nicaragua

Though no one ever dreamed of going there in the days of Somoza—a tropical paradise it wasn't—today you can't beat them away. So many Americans are

currently traveling to Nicaragua, to "see for themselves," that a sizable segment of the travel industry (at least a dozen specialized tour operators) has emerged to service the trend.

One of the largest is NICA (Nuevo Instituto de Centroamerica), which sends you to study Spanish in the town of Esteli (pop. 70,000, Nicaragua's second largest) in the north of the country, quite near to Contra activity, but thus far unscathed by it. There you live with a Nicaraguan family for either four weeks ($875, including meals but not air fare) or five weeks ($980), sharing their lives in toto, studying Spanish in classrooms for four hours each morning, performing volunteer work on two afternoons weekly, attending seminars and lectures (by Sandinistas and oppositionists alike; you even meet one weekend with U.S. Embassy officials) several times a week. Median age of participants is 31 years, but people of all ages make the trip. For literature, contact **NICA, 1151 Massachusetts Ave. (P.O. Box 1409), Cambridge, MA 02238 (phone 617/497-7142).**

Shorter, one-week ($795 from Miami) or two-week ($1,080 from Miami) study tours on topics ranging from "Health and Education in Nicaragua" to "The Role of Women in Nicaragua" are operated throughout the year by **Marazul Tours, Inc., 250 W. 57th St., Suite 1312, New York, NY 10107 (phone 212/582-9570),** from which brochures are available. Rates include economy-style hotel accommodations, two meals a day, all transportation to and within Nicaragua, and the services of bilingual guides.

For the fully committed, **Nicaragua Network, 2025 I St. NW, Suite 212, Washington, D.C. 20006 (phone 202/223-2328),** works with regional organizers all over the country to coordinate volunteer work brigades to Nicaragua. (There are three types of brigades: coffee harvesting, construction, and reforestation). Stays are for four weeks, and cost a total of about $700 from Mexico City. Monthly, the **Casa Nicaragüense de Español, 2330 W. 3rd St., Suite 4, Los Angeles, CA 90057 (phone 213/386-8077),** provides four-week stints of Spanish-language study in the capital city of Managua, plus meetings with political leaders, family living, and community work. At other times the organization known as **TECNICA, 3254 Adeline St., Berkeley, CA 94703 (phone 415/ 655-3838),** sends skilled Americans to consult with or assist their counterparts in several business or technical areas for periods of two weeks to one year. If you're worried about such things, ask to be assigned to southern locations, as Contra attacks are mainly directed at civilian activities and civilian communities in the north.

17. Visits to a "Homestead"

Finally, a short trip to bask in the glow of the late Scott Nearing, who remained handsome, vigorous, and creative until his recent death at the age of 100. He, as you may recall, was the 1920s radical ousted from teaching positions because of his far-advanced views. Whereupon he and his wife, Helen, determined to end their dependency on society by moving first to Vermont and then to an abandoned farm in Maine, where they developed the practice of homesteading to a fine art: producing goods and services for their own consumption, self-sufficiently, without the intervention of a market or the use of cash.

A stream of books from their fertile pens—*Living the Good Life, Continuing the Good Life,* and *Simple Food for the Good Life,* among others—brought thousands of visitors each year to their Forest Farm and stone house built with their own hands, where Helen and Scott demonstrated the virtues of a fresh-food diet, gardening, composting, pond and dam building, and lectured on other, broader social themes. Despite Scott's death, 84-year-old Helen is still willing to receive visitors, provided they make advance contact with the nearby **Social Science Institute, Harborside, ME 04642 (phone 207/326-8211),** to which royalties from the Nearings' books are assigned, and which also sells their books through the mails (request a catalog). According to Helen Nearing, it is possible to visit Forest Farm during the summer and fall. She devotes the other seasons to travel and writing. Accommodations and meals are available in the town of Blue Hill, approximately 20 miles away.

She persuaded Mexican families to put up language students in their homes, on a three-meals-a-day basis.

Visiting a Nicaraguan school

"Bullfight" in Central America

Dancefest south of the border

Though the dining discount works out to only 30% on average, the savings are substantial indeed.

Care to change your life? The farm and books of Scott and Helen Nearing have done that for multitudes before you.

18. Foam-Rubber Bus Travel

From the innards of a large motorcoach, all the seats have been removed and then replaced by a foam-rubber platform. Why? So that 35 adventurous souls can stretch out to sleep, their heads on knapsacks or rolled-up coats, while the bus hurtles through the night. Daytime, the same passengers recline in varying positions, while some strum guitars or play the classics on a reedy flute. In vehicles so oddly outfitted, enabling an obvious lowering of travel costs (and an obvious camaraderie), the most casual (but perhaps the most insightful) of American tourists are today exploring geographic wonders of the U.S.A., Mexico, and Canada.

Some use the foam-rubber method to cross the country. Once every two weeks or so from May through September, from each coast (New York and Boston in the East, Los Angeles and San Francisco in the West), buses of the celebrated Green Tortoise line embark for an eleven-day transcontinental adventure traversing 5,000 miles each way, yet costing only $249 per person. The buses drive mainly at night. In the day, passengers go river-rafting on the Colorado, explore major national parks (Bryce, Zion, Yellowstone, Badlands, Tetons, depending on itinerary), and go wandering about all over the continental states.

Other Green Tortoise trips go to Baja California and mainland Mexico in the winter, to Yosemite throughout the year, up and down the West Coast. Though singles predominate, Green Tortoise urges—and receives—patronage from families and senior citizens. On one four-week tour to Alaska, the average age aboard was 45.

On all trips, passengers contribute about $6 each per day to a food "kitty" used to purchase vittles for a twice-daily cooperative cookout. Breakfast is coffee, eggs, and rolls purchased at various truckers' stops, or else "gourmet vegetarian" if participants are bestirred to purchase and prepare the necessary ingredients.

One of the few survivors of a number of alternative bus companies established in the late 1960s—they included the Briar Rabbit and the American Gypsy—Green Tortoise is no Greyhound, but still a flourishing company that publishes an irresistible, periodic tabloid, *Tortoise Trails,* about its most recent tour successes. For detailed information, write to **Green Tortoise, P.O. Box 24459, San Francisco, CA 94124 (phone 415/821-0803, or toll free 800/227-4766 outside California).**

19. Realities of Asia

Life Tours of Bangkok, Thailand, is surely the ideal example of an "alternative travel" company—the kind we so urgently need in more and more nations. Instead of simply guiding its clients to temples and shrines, to see quaint native dancers and exotic canals, it brings them in touch with the realities of life in Thailand. "Ours is an attempt," says its brochure, "to see and know how people who have less of the goods of this world live and interact among themselves, how creative they are and how they adapt with their indigenous technologies." Orientation lectures precede each tour; visitors spend several days in a Thai village, sharing the daily lives of villagers. They enjoy a learning experience, offered to them by concerned Thais, and made available to both individuals and groups, at costs that range from $20 to $60 a day per person, including accommodations, meals, inland transport, guides and all else. Write, in advance of your arrival, to: **Life Travel Service Co. Ltd., 15 Soi Soonvijai 8, New Petchburi Road, Bangkok 10310, Thailand,** or to its mailing address, c/o **P.O. Box 10-1014 Petchaburitadmai, Post Office Bangkok 10311, or phone 318-1287.**

20. Servas

Finally, and for every trip, you'll want to know of "Servas," to me the most exalted travel organization on earth, which arranges for you to stay for free in the homes of thousands of Servas members around the world—not simply in terms of occupying a bed, but even to the extent of sharing family tables for meals, and without being obligated to provide reciprocal hospitality at some later date in your own home. And why do they do this? Because Servas members believe that such people-to-people contacts serve the cause of world peace. An outgrowth of the peace movement, Servas has built its remarkable roster of thousands of hospitality-givers over forty years, and yet maintains a relatively-low profile in the United States.

Applicants are screened for membership (through interviews designed to weed out frivolous seekers of cheap "crash pads"); membership fees of $45 a year are charged; and free stays in any one city are theoretically limited to three nights—although the latter provision is meant, in my experience, simply to give hosts a graceful out if unusually obnoxious types should appear on their doorsteps ("I'd love to house you for longer, but the rules won't permit me . . ."). A great many Servas travelers, known to me, invariably stay for a week and longer in the homes of their hosts. If you're endowed with the proper attributes—you enjoy meeting people, conversing with them and ascertaining their views, sharing the daily rhythms of their lives—then you'll want to join Servas. Write to: **U.S. Servas Committee, 11 John Street, Suite 706, New York, NY 10038, or phone 212/267-0252.** ≈

Central American children

XIII ⚅ TRAVELING IN THE MATURE YEARS

Our Greatest Retirement Bargains— Extended-Stay Vacations

A Month in Spain for $769, Including Air Fare—and Similar Stays in Yugoslavia and Australia

Equinox Sun Resort, Queensland, Australia
Opposite page: *Inlet of the Dalmatian coast*

If I could bestow an Academy Award for travel, it would be to the operators of extended-stay vacations to Spain, Yugoslavia, and Australia in the winter months. Next to the values offered by these one-month (and longer) sojourns, all other tour programs seem tawdry ripoffs, high-priced scams.

I am standing, in my fantasy, on the great curving stage of the Dorothy Chandler Pavilion in Los Angeles. I rip open the envelope and shout to the world: "The winners are:" (pause) "Sun Holidays of Stamford, Yugotours of New York, and Aero Tours International —for their 'Extended Stays'!"

And as they drag me to a psycho ward (overlooking the blue Pacific), I struggle to explain the concept:

Almost by definition, an extended-stay vacation takes place overseas in the off-season setting of a popular summer resort.

The hotels are desperate. Built to accommodate the great warm-weather crowds, they now stand empty and losing in the chillier months. Along comes a U.S. tour operator with the following pitch: "If you will rent us your rooms for $6 a night, we'll fill them off-season with retirees staying for at least 30 days. You'll still lose money, but you'll lose less. And your staff will be happy to stay active and receiving tips."

To the airlines, a similar appeal: "Our one-month clients don't need the popular dates. Give us seats for $300, and we'll fill your flights on Tuesday nights."

To the public: "Why go in the winter to a mildewed motel and the plastic meals of fast-food chains? We'll fly you for less to glamorous foreign resorts. Sure, it's no longer hot in those places. But it's sunny and mild, and filled with exotica."

Thousands of mature U.S. travelers (and their numbers are growing) now say "Yes" to these attractive offers. They receive one of the great travel bargains, which seem particularly well packaged by the following:

Sun Holidays, to Spain's Mediterranean Coast ($769)

The undoubted price champion of the extended-stay companies, Sun charges a flat $769 in January, $789

in February, slightly more in late March, for a full winter month on the Costa del Sol of Spain, including air fare. It flies you there and back from New York, Boston, or Miami ($137 more from Miami) on Iberia Airlines, meets you at the airport of Malaga, and transfers you by bus to the modern, high-rise Timor Sol Apartments on the beach of bustling Torremolinos (Europe's most heavily visited resort city in summer) with its dozens of hotels and varied tourist facilities. And there you stay for four weeks in a studio apartment with fully equipped kitchen, either making your own meals or taking them at restaurants nearby, enjoying maid service, an entertainment program, and the mild winter climate of Spain's southernmost shores (where it's too chilly at that time for ocean swimming, but otherwise entirely pleasant—and emptied of its often-oppressive summer crowds). For $130 more per person, you get a one-bedroom apartment for the month; for $78 per person per week, you get additional weeks. And thus, for as little as $1,081 per person, including air fare, you can stay for a full eight weeks on the Mediterranean coast of Spain!

Sun Holidays has been operating these tours in close concert with Iberia Airlines for eight years. Though a dozen other companies attempt the same thing—including such well-known senior-citizen specialists as Grand Circle Travel ($875 for a winter month in Nerja on the Costa del Sol) and AARP Travel Service ($868 for a winter month in Torremolinos on the Costa del Sol), no one else comes remotely close in price or value. An Oscar is clearly deserved. For a colorful, free catalog describing several such lengthy stays in various resort areas of Spain, and a similar miracle of pricing for one-month winter vacations on the Algarve Coast of Portugal, contact **Sun Holidays, 26 6th St., Stamford, CT 06905 (phone 203/323-1166, or toll free 800/243-2057 outside Connecticut).**

Yugotours, to the Dalmatian Coast ($1,216)

Some seven years ago, the leading tour company of Yugoslavia—a remarkably elegant organization despite its somewhat brutish name—discovered ahead of everyone else that a large number of Americans could greatly enjoy a long-stay winter vacation in the then largely empty modern hotels of the medieval resort cities of the Dalmatian (Adriatic) Coast of Yugoslavia.

Thirty thousand U.S. travelers, mostly 55 and older, have since leaped at the chance. Somehow they sensed that the colorful atmosphere, setting, cuisine, and deliciously old-fashioned pace of these ancient ports would provide a unique vacation. They had heard, of course, that the Dalmatian Coast was among the most scenically awesome spots on earth. And they were soon to learn that it is also remarkably cheap.

Today, from a busy office in New York's Empire State Building, Yugotours publishes an eagerly awaited, and quite handsome, 16-page catalog of "extended stays" in the fall, winter, and early spring to Dubrovnik, Opatija, Hvar, and Split, among others. Their rates are like from a Slavic fairytale. They include not only air fare and accommodations, but two meals a day—and other remarkable features (like a trip by passenger steamer between one resort town and another, on tours that feature more than one resort).

The best of the tours (but not the cheapest) are those assigning you to three different cities in your three-week stay—with the option to stay an extra week. For a grand total of $1,216 to $1,462 per person (depending on dates), you fly on Yugoslav Airlines from New York or Chicago ($50 to $70 more from Chicago) to Zagreb, go by bus to Opatija for several days, proceed from there by steamer to a week apiece in Hvar and the walled city of Dubrovnik, stay in modern seaside hotels with heated swimming pools, eat two meals a day, and receive all sorts of charming extra features: cocktail parties and candlelight dinners, a Dalmatian band at several meals, orientation tours, films about Dubrovnik and Hvar, much else. This short summary can't begin to do justice to the program as a whole.

From all resorts you have cheap, and almost daily, optional excursions to a variety of enchanting, unspoiled villages and seaside locations—especially to those in historic Montenegro: Sveti Stefan and Budva, the Bay of Kotor. So hand me that golden statuette for Yugotours! And for a free catalog, contact **Yugotours,**

350 Fifth Ave., Suite 2212, New York, NY 10118 (phone 212/563-2400, or toll free 800/223-5298 outside New York).

AeroTours, to Australia's "Gold Coast" ($1,530)

Here is the sole exception to the "off-season" timing of most extended stays: our American winter is Australia's summer, and the ocean is filled at that time with swimmers, who later bask in the 80° sun. The low value of the Australian dollar, which sells for only 80¢ U.S. (you greatly increase the value of your money there), explains why the seven-year-old AeroTours International can sell such a reasonably priced, month-long holiday to a peak-season resort so far away.

For a total of $1,579 in early April, $1,530 from mid-April through September, $1,730 in October and November, and $1,930 from December through the end of March, AeroTours will fly you round trip from the U.S. West Coast direct to Brisbane and then bus you 40 minutes south to the 26-mile-long beach known as the Gold Coast; it is lined with luxury hotels, condominiums, and even a casino or two. Near a town called Surfers Paradise (its actual name), you'll stay for a full month in a 15-story beachfront apartment-hotel (the Equinox Sun Resort) in a balconied studio with wall-to-wall carpeting, fully equipped kitchen, and dining nook. Downstairs are restaurants, shops, squash and tennis courts. Fifteen minutes away are rain forest–covered mountains with horseback and walking trails, and most of the wildlife sanctuaries of Australia.

When you consider that the peak-season air fare from the West Coast to Australia is alone $1,545, you glimpse the value this package represents. And if you can yourself improve on the air fare to Australia—using a local bucket shop, for instance—AeroTours will sell you just the accommodations, at a considerable saving. Once in Australia, you enjoy marvelously low prices for everything else, including the memorable trip to the Barrier Reef.

Persons of any age can book these tours (and so can retirees of any age on the programs of Sun Holidays and Yugotours).

For brochures and further details, contact AeroTours International, 115 W. 29th St., New York, NY 10001 (phone 212/594-7575, or toll free 800/223-4555 outside New York City). And for giving me this chance to tell you about AeroTours, I want to thank the Academy, my travel agent, the Rand McNally Atlas, my typewriter repair shop. . . . ≈

Street of Dubrovnik

"Gold Coast" of Australia

The Battle for the Older American Traveler

Four Major Travel Firms Are Following a Unique Approach in Their Sale of Vacations to Seniors

Orientation get-together, Locarno, Switzerland

Touring Torremolinos

In the world of travel, what do older Americans really want?

That inquiry is the topic of the year among airlines and tour operators. As if, without warning, a new planet had swung into their sight, they've discovered that a startling percentage of all travel expenditures are made by people 55 and older. Not yuppies, not preppies, not even baby boomers, but rather senior citizens are today the "name of the game" in travel.

Young folks, it appears, go to the movies; older ones go on vacation.

"Our senior citizens," says one tour operator, "are feeling better about themselves, and that's why they're traveling more. They're healthier, living longer, more affluent. They have a new conviction that life is to be enjoyed for quite a while more, and this fairly recent attitude makes them the fastest-growing segment of the travel market."

Given that fact, it is surprising, as an initial note, to find so few companies serving the needs of the older American traveler. Apart from local motorcoach operators and purely ad hoc programs by regional firms, only four really major U.S. companies deal exclusively with the marketing and operation of far-ranging tours for seniors, and three of these are headquartered in one city: Boston. They are: Saga Holidays, Grand Circle Travel, Inc., Elderhostel, and AARP (American Association of Retired Persons) Travel Service.

Having journeyed to Boston to view the first three, and phoned the fourth in California, I've been alternately impressed, startled, dismayed, and educated by several uniform ways in which they do business. Traveling seniors may want to consider the following observations on the major "tour operators for older Americans":

They Mainly Sell "Direct"

Not one of the "big four" deals with travel agents or sets aside a single percentage point of income for the latter. Each one heatedly insists that the processing of seniors' tours is a specialty requiring direct contact between them (the tour operators) and their clients (the actual senior travelers), usually via toll-free "800" numbers. Because the four firms adhere fiercely to their position, their brochures and catalogs are unavailable in travel agents' racks and can be obtained only by mail. Nor do they advertise in the general media. If you are not already on their mailing lists, you must specifically request their brochures by writing to the addresses listed above. Once you do, you'll soon receive a heavy packet of attractive, four-color literature and application forms.

They Cater to "Older" Americans

Although people can theoretically use the services of the senior citizen tour operators when they reach the tender ages of 50, 55, or 60 (50 for AARP, 55 for Grand Circle, 60 for Saga and Elderhostel), in practice they don't. The average age of Grand Circle's clients is 67, that of the others only slightly less. The apparent reason is that Americans no longer feel removed from younger age categories until they reach their early or mid-60s. Advances in health care and longevity, better diets, and attention to exercise keep most of us youthful and vigorous into our late 50s, and reluctant to cease socializing—or vacationing—with younger people. (I recall growing apoplectic with rage when, on my 50th birthday, the mail brought an invitation to join AARP.) Who any longer even retires at the age of 65?

Their Clients Insist on the Exclusion of Younger Passengers

But when those mid-60s are in fact reached, the newly elder turn with a vengeance to services of the specialists. After an initial reluctance to confine their travel companions to a single age group, today's 65-year-olds discover that they are of a different "mind set" than their younger co-citizens. Brought up during the Depression, sent to fight or work in World War II, denied the easy travel opportunities enjoyed by our blasé younger set, they better appreciate the joys of international travel, react with gratitude and awe to wonders of the world, enjoy the companionship of people who feel the same way.

Not yuppies, not preppies, not even baby boomers, but rather senior citizens are today the "name of the game" in travel.

Yugoslavian village

267

The bad news is that the tours planned for senior citizens only are generally higher priced than similar trips sold to all ages.

National Palace, Mexico City

Golfing in Orlando

They Possess a Historical Perspective Denied to the Younger Generation

Clearly, they share a wealth of experience and a common outlook; come from an education in the broad liberal arts as contrasted with the crudely materialistic, vocational outlook of so many of today's youth. And when they travel with younger people, they are often upset by the young folks' failure to share the same values or to be familiar with the events that so shaped their own lives. What mature American can enjoy a trip through Europe or the South Pacific with people who are only dimly aware of Franklin Roosevelt or Winston Churchill, of Douglas MacArthur or Field Marshal Rommel, of the Invasion or the Holocaust? Accordingly, they respond with eagerness to tour programs limited to persons of their own age.

Their Clients Receive Distinctly Different, Custom-Tailored Travel Arrangements

In addition to confining their groups to an older age range, the major tour companies earn their allegiance by providing arrangements that are significantly different from those designed for a general clientele. "We avoid the modern hotels, with their small public spaces, their in-room videos and bars," explains a specialist. "We look for traditional buildings with large lobbies for congregating and sitting—our clients prefer camaraderie to in-room movies! We also insist on a location within distance of everything important."

"We pace our tours to avoid overly long hours on a bus," explains another. "But we keep our passengers active, always on the move. Older travelers have had enough of sitting around at home; they want constant experiences and encounters."

Though the tours are of a longer duration than the normal variety, they are rarely for more than three weeks at a time. "People in retirement like to take two and three trips in a year," says the president of one firm. "They tour a particular destination for two or three weeks, then want to try something else."

In planning tours for the older American, the great majority of departures are scheduled for off-season periods—not in July or August to Europe, for instance, but in the "shoulder" and "off-peak" months when retired people are the best possible prospects for travel. "We get better rates for them that way," says a tour official. "And they're better appreciated at that time by the suppliers. They get more and better attention."

But Their Prices Are Higher Than the Norm

So much for the good news. The bad news is that the tours planned for senior citizens only are generally higher priced than similar trips sold to all ages. This is not to say that the former do not use better hotels, provide closer and more personal attention, supply more tour ingredients. They may or may not. But except for Elderhostel—whose prices are truly remarkable—not one of the senior-citizen specialists has opted to service the needs of intensely cost-conscious Americans; their tour products are generally $100 to $300 higher than the motorcoach programs or "stay-put" holidays available from several of the low-cost tour operators serving a general public, sometimes for suspiciously similar features. This, to me, is a serious mistake on their part, limiting their programs to an upper-middle-class clientele and bypassing the budget-limited majority of the older generation. When a tour company—perhaps a wholly new one—begins offering modestly priced tours for exclusive use by older citizens, they will, in my view, be flooded with bookings (as Elderhostel is).

The Programs Themselves

What do the specialists offer, and how do they differ one from the other? Here's a quick rundown:

Saga Holidays, 120 Boylston St., Boston, MA 02116 (phone 617/451-6808, or toll free 800/343-0273 outside Massachusetts), is perhaps the largest of the lot, resulting from the activity of its British parent company, which each year sends over 250,000 senior citizens on vacation. To tap into that major movement (and the bargaining power it represents), the U.S. organization routes all its transatlantic tours through London, there to combine its older American travelers into one group with older British and Australian passengers. Such blending of English-speaking nationalities adds "zip" to any tour, they claim, and I agree. On board the buses, frolicsome passengers quip that Saga means "Send-A-Granny-Away" or "Sex-And-Games-for-the-Aged" (the latter very much tongue-in-cheek).

Headed by an ebullient, walrus-mustached, former educator named Jerry Foster, a one-time official of Elderhostel, the Saga staff also provide technical travel arrangements for Elderhostel's programs (see below) to Britain, Ireland, Spain, Portugal, and Turkey—a potent endorsement. Saga's passengers (who must be 60 or older) are later invited to join the Saga Holidays Club and receive a quarterly magazine supplemented by newsletters. The latter's most appealing feature is a page of travel "personals"—older people seeking other older people to join them on a trip.

Saga's major stock in trade is escorted motorcoach tours: heavily (and throughout the year) within the United States, heavily in Europe, but also in Mexico, in Australia, and in South America. Although it also offers cruises and extended stays, it is the escorted motorcoach, competitively priced, that most of its clients demand.

Grand Circle Travel, Inc., 347 Congress St., Boston, MA 02210 (phone 617/350-7500, or toll free 800/221-2610), is the oldest of the U.S. firms dealing only with senior citizens, but recently rejuvenated through its acquisition by an enterprising travel magnate, Alan E. Lewis, who has injected considerable new resources and vigor (quarterly magazine, *Pen Pal,* and travel-partner service) into it. In business for 31 years, it enjoys a large and loyal following who respond, especially to offers of extended-stay vacations in off-season months, and to low-cost foreign areas with mild climates. The greater number of Grand Circle's passengers are those spending, say, 2 to 20 weeks on the Mediterranean coast of Spain, in a seaside, kitchenette-apartment supplied with utensils, china, and cutlery. Others go for several weeks to Dubrovnik on the awesome Dalmatian coast of Yugoslavia, or to Portugal and Madeira, the Canary Islands, the Balearics. Wher-

Tour companies earn their allegiance by providing arrangements that differ significantly from those designed for a general clientele.

At a Senior Vacation Hotel

ever, the tour company argues (and quite successfully) that older Americans can enjoy a "full season" at these exotic locations for not much more than they'd spend to Florida or other domestic havens. While neither Spain nor Yugoslavia offers swimming weather in winter, their low prices enable seniors (even those living mainly on Social Security) to vacation in dignity, enjoying good-quality meals and modern apartments in place of the fast-food outlets and shabby motels to which they're often relegated here at home. Grand Circle's extended stays are supplemented by nearly a dozen other programs—Alaskan cruises, Canadian holidays, tours to Europe and the Orient—booked by thousands, but not yet as popular as those "stay-put" vacations for several weeks in a balmy, foreign clime.

AARP Travel Service, 5855 Green Valley Circle, Culver City, CA 90230 (phone toll free 800/227-7737), is the "new kid on the block," less than eight years old, but obviously destined for big things. As the official travel arm of the 28-million-member American Association of Retired Persons, it draws upon a massive potential following and contacts them quickly and efficiently via the organization's impressive bimonthly magazine, *Modern Maturity,* sent to all members. They, in turn, can request upward of 30 separate travel catalogs dealing with cruises, escorted motorcoach holidays, "long stays," and jaunts of every description.

But though the audience is on such a mass scale, the programs themselves are operated for AARP by a "carriage trade" tour operator, Olson-Travelworld, known for its quality accommodations, careful attention to travel details, and substantial price structure. Olson, in its early stewardship of the AARP program, has surprised the travel trade by placing a heavy emphasis on cut-rate cruises; it offers (with considerable success) a lengthy series of sailings on celebrated ships already heavily patronized by seniors, but discounted for the AARP membership by as much as $150 to $1,000 per person. While the strong response to these ocean-going values has tended to overshadow the remainder of the program, AARP's buses, planes, and tours are operating to every major destination.

Elderhostel, 80 Boylston St., Boston, MA 02116 (phone 617/426-7788), is, in a nutshell, the much-discussed, increasingly popular, nonprofit group that works with 1,000 U.S. and foreign educational institutions to provide seniors 60 and over with residential study courses at unbeatable costs: $215 to $250 per week for room, board, and tuition (but not including air fare) in the U.S. and Canada; an average of $1,700 for three weeks abroad, this time including air fare. Accommodations and meals are in student residence halls or underused youth hostels.

Those are the "nutshell" facts, which can't do justice to the gripping appeal of Elderhostel's course descriptions. Who can withstand "The Mystery and Miracle of Medieval Cathedrals" (taught at a school overlooking the Pacific)? Or "Everything You Always Wanted to Know About Music But Were Too Afraid to Ask" (at a university in Alabama). Or "Gods, Kings, and Temples" (at a classroom in Cairo)? They make you yearn to be 60!

With more than 180,000 traveling students anticipated for 1989, Elderhostel is the once-and-future travel giant, fervently acclaimed by its elderly devotees. "Thank you, Elderhostel!" wrote one senior in a recent publication. "We've built beaver dams in Colorado, explored temples in Nepal, ridden outrigger canoes in Fiji, sat on the lawn sipping coffee at Cambridge University, eaten with our fingers at private homes in Bombay, where they venerate older people!"

The Prices They Charge

Those are the four specialists. Why aren't they (with the exception of Elderhostel) cheaper? With such huge resources and immense followings, the senior-citizen tour operators are capable of achieving major price breakthroughs for their elderly clientele. The disquieting thing is that they don't.

In the area of extended stays, a well-known nonspecialist, **Sun Holidays, 26 6th St., Stamford, CT 06905 (phone 203/323-1166, or toll free 800/243-2057),** takes people of all ages to modern apartment-hotels on Spain's Costa del Sol, in winter, for a charge per month (the first month) of $769 per person, including round-trip air fare from New York on Iberia Airlines. Two of the major senior-citizen specialists (I am of course excluding Elderhostel) charge $100 to $400 more on most of their winter departures for virtually the same one-month stay (although the costlier tour includes a night, with meals, in London at both the start and end of the trip, and a slightly larger apartment). The senior-citizen companies also include insurance worth about $30.

In the field of escorted motorcoach tours, the well-known **Trafalgar Tours,** selling to young and old alike, charges $1,688 for a 15-day tour of Britain, air fare included, and $1,888 for a classic 16-day tour of Europe, air fare included. One of the major senior-citizen specialists (I am again excluding Elderhostel) charges $1,899 for a 16-day tour of Britain, air fare included, and charges $2,159 for a quite similar 17-day tour of Europe, air fare included. Another so-called specialist charges over $2,000 for nearly everything. While hotels on the highest priced of these tours are marginally better than Trafalgar's, they do not support (in my opinion) a differential of that magnitude; and most other features of the tours are similar.

Should companies be surcharging the senior citizen by $100 to $400 per person for the right to travel only with other senior citizens? Shouldn't older Americans, of all people, enjoy the lowest of travel costs? Especially when they are dealing directly with the tour operator, saving that company a travel agent's commission?

In private conversations, travel industry people will speculate as to whether the senior-citizen companies are relieved of normal competitive pricing pressures by the semi-captive nature of their clientele—who have no independent travel counselor to steer them to a cheaper course. Whether or not this is so—whether, as the companies claim, their tours are worthier because of their attention to needs of the elderly—those prices quite obviously need some analysis, and perhaps revision. ≈

Traveling Alone in the Mature Years— Plight or Opportunity?

The Problem Is Not Confined to Women; the Question Should Be Rephrased to Ask: "Can a Single Woman, or Single Man, Travel Enjoyably Alone? And Can This Be Done at a Mature Age?"

On an archeological dig, Spain

Out-of-breath and weary, I end my eager speech— that overlong lecture on travel that I deliver, some- where, each month—and throw open discussion to the floor. Within four minutes, never more, it comes, that inevitable, inescapable, and utterly harrowing question: "Can a single woman travel safely, and enjoyably, alone?"

Amazing how persistent the inquiry, how it reveals a major, near-universal concern among a large portion of all potential travelers.

The questioner is usually a widow in her late middle age, her forehead furrowed with worry. She explains that she and her husband had enjoyed memorable trips abroad, that travel for her is a cherished activity, but that now she is anxious, even frightened, about undertaking further journeys on her own.

As she talks, a nervous movement occurs in the auditorium among men of a similar age. Though they—the men—never initiate the question, they now lean forward in rapt attention, concentrating on every word. And suddenly it is obvious: the problem is not confined to women; the question should be rephrased to ask: "Can a single woman, or a single man, travel enjoyably alone? And can this be done at a mature age?"

The Glib Response

Though my answer, generally, is "Yes," I wish I could state it with greater conviction than I do. But the issue is complex, surrounded by ifs, perhapses, and maybes.

In this respect I differ from a great many more impulsive travel lecturers who teach one-evening courses at urban night schools, under the title "Traveling Solo: The Joys of Going It Alone." These people claim that we should always travel unaccompanied, even if we don't have to. Why? Because such is the road to romance and adventure, to chance encounters with foreign citizens, invitations to foreign homes. And the practice, as they tell it, is deliciously selfish: you do only what you desire, without compromise. You do not alter your itinerary or schedule to suit the tastes of another human being. For the first time in your life, you are Free.

The message of these trendy singles (almost all in their mid-20s) is of course based on the assumption that a compatible travel companion doesn't exist; that, almost as if by some law of nature, two people traveling together must necessarily have widely divergent views, inclinations, and tastes. Having themselves never experienced true friendship, love, or compatibility, they proclaim the resounding advantage of traveling alone.

I can't go quite that far. For surely, only the most naïve pollyanna can believe that the pleasure of traveling with a cherished companion—the joy of sharing reactions to renowned sights and experiences—can now be duplicated or replaced in the absence of that person. At best they can be experienced differently, with adequate enjoyment, but not usually with the profound satisfactions of discovering them in the company of a like-minded friend.

The Alternatives to Solitude

Therefore, before I discuss the ways to enjoy a solitary holiday trip, to "make a go" of traveling alone, it's important to note that you don't have to. By simply mailing $5 for a three-year membership in the Saga Holidays Club operated by **Saga Holidays Ltd., 120 Boylston St., Boston, MA 02116 (phone 617/ 451-6808, or toll free 800/343-0273 outside Massachusetts)**, or $5 for a similar membership in the Grand Circle Travel Club, operated by **Grand Circle Travel, Inc., 347 Congress St., Boston, MA 12210 (phone 617/350-7500, or toll free 800/ 221-2610)**—both of them companies dealing exclusively in travel for mature persons—you can obtain the names of potential companions for your next trip. Both clubs distribute quarterly magazines with "Pen Pal" or "Penfriend" features listing dozens of applications by mature singles for travel partners. These, in effect, are "travel personals," but proper to a fault, and fascinating to read as they detail the varied goals of the mature, experienced travelers submitting them.

For more extensive listings (over 200 "travel personals" per bimonthly publication), send $45 for a one-year subscription (but only $30 for six months) to **Partners-in-Travel, P.O. Box 491145, Los Angeles, CA 90049 (phone 213/476-4869)**. Its newsletter, issued every 60 days, is by the irrepressible Miriam Tobolowsky, who attracts a zestful following and ads peppered with jaunty exhortations: "Let's go—life is for living!" One recent listing assures that the applicant is "caring and considerate, but won't hover. Want ardent traveler who travels light, dependable driver, honest and open communication, brisk walker." Though Partners-in-Travel does not limit its services to mature persons, a full 70% of its subscribers appear to be over 50, most in their 60s.

And for a near-guarantee that you will find a suitable travel "match-up," but at rates varying from $3 to $11 per month (with a six-month minimum), contact **Travel Companion Exchange, P.O. Box 833, Amityville, NY 11701 (phone 516/454-0880)**, founded by the well-known travel figure, Jens Jurgen. His is the most elaborate of all travel match-up services, supplying you with literally thousands of available listings, all carefully grouped by computer into helpful categories ("special interests," "special travel plans," and the like) to enable a wise choice.

Traveling Only with Singles

As a substitute for seeking a travel companion, one can travel with groups consisting only of singles. Although the prestigious **Singleworld Cruises & Tours, Inc., 444 Madison Ave., New York, NY 10022 (phone 212/758-2433, or toll free 800/ 223-6490, 800/522-5682 in New York State)**, does not limit participation to mature persons only, its programs are heavily booked by the mature, and its tours are only for single people. Join them and your problems of "singlehood" vanish.

Loners on Wheels, Inc., c/o Marcelle Phillips, 1206 Sunset Dr., Ennis, TX 75119, or c/o Dick March, 5824 Cowden, Fort Worth, TX 76114, is still another travel organization confined to singles. An RV club, it forms caravans of singles only, and takes them to rallies and campouts all over the country and occasionally to Mexico, too.

Before discussing the ways to travel alone, it's important to note that you don't have to.

Earthwatch volunteers in Panama

Activities Where It Doesn't Matter

Your other option is to travel abroad with groups pursuing an intense social, political, scientific, or educational purpose. In that context, the fact that some are singles, some couples, becomes of minor significance: people are engaged in a communal activity, living helter-skelter in group lodgings, so intent on their work that they mix and mingle easily.

The study tours operated by the famous **Elderhostel, 80 Boylston St., Boston, MA 02116 (phone 617/426-7788),** are that kind of program. Elderhostel sends people over the age of 60 to attend one- to three-week classroom courses of instruction in the U.S. and around the world, using university residence halls—sometimes even dormitories, segregated by sex—for lodgings. It makes no guarantee of single or double rooms, charges one standard fee without single supplement, and thereby attracts a heavy number of singles to its continually fascinating curriculum (singles make up a full 30% of Elderhostel's volume, and two-thirds of those singles are women). But because Elderhostel passengers are focused so intently on ideas outside of themselves, the fact that they are alone or accompanied dwindles in importance, fades from consciousness; and people glory in the camaraderie and joint activities of the entire group.

The trips sponsored by **Earthwatch, P.O. Box 403N, Watertown, MA 02272 (phone 617/926-8200),** are also that sort of program. It sends its volunteers on scientific research projects (tagging fish, measuring acid rain, interviewing rural residents), making use of a catch-as-catch-can array of housing accommodations (local schools and community centers, tents, and private homes) in which people are lodged as conditions permit. Its charges ("contributions") are uniform per person, with no single supplement, and the composition of its "teams" is heavily slanted to singles. "We were an unlikely group," wrote one recent Earthwatch participant, ". . . a history teacher from Ohio, a Long Island college student, a retired real estate investor from Arizona. . . ."

Similar in character, largely erasing the distinction between couples and singles, and attracting a heavy percentage of singles, are the "adventure tours" (camping safaris, treks in Nepal and the Andes, outdoor nature expeditions) sponsored by an increasing number of tour operators. Though they require a certain minimum vigor (but less than you might think), they cater to people of all ages, attract a heavy turnout of mature singles, and house them in tents or improvised accommodations. Scan the catalogs of **Overseas Adventure Travel, 349 Broadway, Cambridge, MA 02139 (phone 617/876-0533, or toll free 800/221-0814)**—which carried an 82-year-old woman on a recent camping safari to Tanzania—or **Sobek Expeditions, Inc., P.O. Box 1089, Angels Camp, CA 95222 (phone 209/736-4524),** for additional examples of purposive trips in which all participants became undifferentiated members of a cohesive group, without regard to marital status. The same applies to volunteer "workcamp" tours engaging in socially conscious projects around the world: contact **VFP International Workcamps, Tiffany Road, Belmont, VT 05730 (phone 802/259-2759),** and specify the trips open to all ages; or to politically oriented trips, some heavily feminist in nature, organized by such as **Schilling Travel Service, 722 Second Ave. South, Minneapolis, MN 55402 (phone 612/332-1100).**

While all such trips appeal to only a segment of the mature audience, they provide the perfect antidote to the "single travel blues."

It is primarily—let me suggest—on the standard, traditional trips, with their single supplements and couples-only atmosphere, that the problems of traveling alone are most sharply felt.

Enjoying the Standard Trips

So how, then, do you travel alone for normal sightseeing or recreational purposes? How, as a mature single person, do you best vacation in new lands, or travel to visit important cultural exhibits or simply to refresh the mind and body?

The problem centers on that edifice known as a hotel—that ultimately boring and impersonal institution, with its inescapable "single surcharges." (One wise observer recently speculated that Hell consists of

As a substitute for seeking a travel companion, one can travel with groups consisting only of singles.

Birdwatching in the tropics

Your other option is to travel abroad with groups pursuing an intense social, political, scientific, or educational purpose. In that context, the fact that some are singles, some couples, becomes of minor significance.

Earthwatch volunteer with black bear

being condemned to stay, unto eternity, in a different modern hotel each night.)

The obvious solution is to avoid the use of standard hotels, and replace them with a people-friendly form of lodgings. Staying with families while abroad serves the triple purpose of avoiding loneliness, gaining new friendships and insights, and lowering costs: you not only escape from that burdensome single supplement, but start from a radically lower base of costs. Indeed, some mature singles even lower their lodgings expense to zero by joining the public-spirited, worldwide membership of **Servas, 11 John St., Suite 706, New York, NY 10038 (phone 212/267-0252),** which believes that free and frequent people-to-people contacts, through home visits, serve the cause of world peace. On the eve of a trip, they obtain from Servas the names and addresses of families in every major city who have expressed their willingness to receive other Servas members into their homes (for short stays) free of charge, because they believe in the profound moral aspect of such hospitality. (Yearly fee for Servas membership: $45.)

Other mature singles opt for a more commercial form of homestay, but inexpensive and without the single supplement, by utilizing the services of homestay organizations in every major country. For a comprehensive list of several dozen national homestay organizations (and of other interesting travel activities), send $4.95 (plus $1 for postage and handling) to **Pilot Books, 103 Cooper St., Babylon, NY 11702,** for a copy of the 72-page *Vacations with a Difference*. This little book lists homestays in Canada, France, Australia, Tahiti, and Scandinavia; homestays with Unitarians, humanists, Mennonites, and Quakers; homestays with farmers and wine growers; homestays for as little as $85 a week, including all meals. What you yourself may have done as a teenager—a month and more abroad with a foreign family—is now available in your mature years, and for reasons obvious and profound, no other travel experience quite compares to it.

The most relaxed and adventurous of mature singles stay in youth hostels both here and abroad, now that the international youth-hostel organization has removed all maximum-age restrictions on the right to use their facilities. Particularly in the fall and winter months, when young people are in school, the predominant clientele of many youth hostels is today middle-aged and elderly! But even when one shares these multibedded rooms or dorms with young people, one pays an inexpensive charge, without a supplement. And one stays in a lively setting of international conversations and encounters. For information, contact **American Youth Hostels, Inc., P.O. Box 37613, Washington, DC 20013 (phone 202/783-6161).**

One rather affluent and mature U.S. lawyer of my acquaintance, who has traveled extensively by herself in the South Pacific, actually favors hostels, though she could afford much better. "They offer a wonderful way to meet people, including local people traveling in their own country," she points out. "The kitchen is a great social center, with perhaps 12 people each attempting to cook dinner for one—a hilarious scene. By the time the various dinners are ready, you're all old friends."

Revising Your Attitudes

If, despite this advice, you're determined to keep going on the standard trips and to use standard hotels, you may need a new mental outlook for coping with the problems of solitary travel—a confident and positive outlook. Though at the outset, I was careful to stress, my own view that traveling in twos is usually superior to traveling alone, there are nonetheless some attractive aspects to the latter experience.

You might regard that first experience as a zesty challenge, a chance to shape yourself for the better. Whatever your usual personality, you must of necessity attempt to be more outgoing and convivial.

Introduce yourself to the people around you. Ask other tourists for advice on restaurants and sights. Suggest the sharing of a meal at some celebrated establishment. Just as the same human necessities breed invention, so traveling by oneself often leads to increased openness, receptivity to new people and ideas, greater self-assurance and pride.

Among some single travelers—certainly not all, but some—the experience soon takes on a mood of surprised exhilaration. They find they're more sensitive to the people and culture of the destination. The absence of a familiar companion removes them from the familiar cocoon of their own language and culture, and teaches them a new language, a new culture. (And, incidentally, traveling alone is the fastest—some say the best—way to learn another language).

These new solitary travelers become less self-conscious. After that first nerve-wracking dinner alone in a large hotel restaurant—when every eye seems focused, accusingly, on them—they suddenly realize that in reality no one is terribly concerned with or interested in the fact that they are dining alone. It is a liberating bit of knowledge. On all subsequent evenings they bring a book or magazine to the dinner table, and revel in the luxury of thus relaxing at a high-quality meal.

Though it may not be all that it once was, traveling while alone is soon recognized to be immeasurably more satisfying than the alternative: moping at home alone. And with every succeeding trip, the experience gains in pleasure, ease, and depth; it keeps us alive. As that canny voyager (Miriam Tobolowsky) who operates Partners-in-Travel puts it: "Travel isn't something you do in old age; it is something you do *instead of* old age."

Travel is thus far too important to be dispensed with when a companion is unavailable; it is part of a civilized life, our birthright. The most vital of our fellow humans travel, whether alone or not—and so should you! ≈

Volunteers, digging up the past

Some Travel Options— Good, Bad, and Indifferent—for the Mature American

As the Travel Industry Scrambles to Win Over the Senior Citizen, a Mixed Bag of Programs Emerges

Retirement Explorations group in Costa Rica

Opposite page: *On a "retirement exploration"*

Maybe it's my widening girth, my whitening hair, my increasing nostalgia for "slow music." But the travels of senior citizens interest me more and more, and provoke these comments on recent developments.

That 10% Lure: Call me a grouch, but I'm not impressed with the discounts for mature travelers offered by most hotel chains and airlines. In the majority of cases these consist of 10% reductions off room rate or air fare. Since that's the exact amount that hotels and airlines pay out to travel agents, and since most senior-citizen travel programs require (in effect) that passengers avoid the use of travel agents in making reservations, the hotels and airlines are frequently saving 10% on their senior-citizen programs—and then simply passing on that 10% saving to the senior citizen.

In other words, they're not spending a red cent to obtain their senior business. Which seems a bit chintzy.

Best Hotel Bets

Does anyone do better by America's elderly? A few do. And they deserve acclaim as a means of nudging the others to do more. Here's a sampling:

Sheraton Hotels: Though they caution that the discount can be withheld during periods of peak business, and is not applicable to minimum-rate rooms, virtually all Sheratons give a 25% discount to persons 60 and older. Phone 800/325-3535.

Ramada Inns: Many (about three-quarters) give the same 25% off to persons 60 and up. Phone toll free 800/2-RAMADA.

Marriott Hotels: At more than 100 Marriotts in the U.S., Europe, and the Caribbean, a 50% discount off regular weekday rates is given to persons 62 years of age and older, and 25% off on lunches and dinners (the latter whether you're a guest or not). Reductions are subject to availability and occasional seasonal close-outs, and require advance reservations at the reduced rate. Phone toll free 800/228-9290.

La Quinta Inns: Offer 15% off to people age 55 and older. Phone toll free 800/531-5900.

Holiday Inns: Give 20% off room rates, 10% off meals, to those over 50 joining their Mature Outlook club for $7.50 a year. Phone toll free 800/336-6330.

Days Inns: From 15% to 50% (usually 15%) off at 536 participating inns, to members (50 years and older) of their September Days Club; send $12 to September Days Club, P.O. Box 4001, Harlan, IA 51593 (phone toll free 800/241-5050).

Howard Johnson's: Take 15% off for seniors 60 years and older at more than 85% of the nation's H.J. hotels. Phone 800/634-3464.

Airline Offerings

As for the airlines, some of them also confine their senior-citizen air-fare discounts to 10% and simply pass on the 10% they've saved by subtly influencing senior citizens to book direct. To add insult to injury, they then charge a $25 "membership" fee to enjoy that 10% off, and a $100 charge for the "companion" who accompanies the senior (American Airlines' "Senior SAAvers Club" and Continental's "Golden Travelers Club" are typical examples; United Airlines' "Silver Wings Plus" charges $50 for life membership, but does give two $25 travel certificates good for the first year, in addition to the standard 10% discount). In fairness, they also provide self-promoting newsletters and diverse other discounts and features (as do the others). Braniff, in handsome, contrasting style, gives 15% off to travelers 65 and older, and asks no fee. TWA sells coupon booklets or yearly $1,399 passes entitling the senior citizen to unlimited domestic travel for one year; international flights are an add-on option.

Such programs have been overtaken by events. The introduction of radically reduced "MaxSaver" fares, and the continuation of "Super-Saver" fares—as little as $59 to fairly distant points—lessens the worth of these programs considerably. Unless one travels with absurd frequency, it is often cheaper simply to pay individual advance-purchase rates than to commit to the use of a yearly pass.

Clearly, unless the airlines now devise new programs keyed to the levels of, and kept below, their own "Saver" fares, they must—in my view—brace for outcries of protest from the seniors who purchased their fixed-price coupons or year-long passes.

Rehearsals for Retirement

Happier news—of a bright, new use of holiday travel to scout potential sites for retirement. Though the idea is obvious, it's easier said than done.

When middle-aged people go off to test the retirement attractions of Florida or Arizona, of Costa Rica or Cuernavaca, they often return as uncertain as when they left. Simply to look at a retirement area is not to ensure that you obtain reliable, relevant information about its suitability for retirement. For the latter, you need to meet with real estate people and lawyers, with municipal officials and other retirees.

So reasoned Jane Parker, a retired schoolteacher of Saratoga, California. And thereupon she formed a tour company called Retirement Explorations that performs all the advance preparations for a meaningful research trip. Arriving at the destination, her groups engage in scheduled interviews, appointments, seminars, and briefings on the pros and cons of that area's retirement possibilities. The information is supplied by on-the-spot specialists, who undergo a withering cross-examination by tour participants; the latter stay at the area's best hotels and enjoy gala dinners while doing so.

Retirement Explorations' most popular trip is to Costa Rica. Three are scheduled each year, in February, July, and November, and at least two of these consist of two groups at one time. The cost for ten days from Miami is $1,200, with a single supplement of $250. Groups are limited to 35 people.

Twice a year, Retirement Explorations takes groups to the Algarve coast of Portugal and Spain's Costa del Sol (on the Mediterranean). The 15-day trip is $2,400 per person, with a $325 single supplement, and can be booked by up to 40 people per departure.

In the offing: tours to South America, and to the Colonial Towns (San Miguel de Allende, Patzcuaro, Guanajuato) of Mexico.

For additional information, or to book, contact **Retirement Explorations, 19414 Vineyard Lane, Saratoga, CA 95070 (phone 408/257-5378), or—**

if Ms. Parker has moved (a possibility)—contact her permanently based representative, **Marty Scutt, 2900 Scenic Bend, Modesto, CA 95355 (phone 209/ 526-1887).**

A "Club Med" for Seniors

At $22 to $27 per person per day (based on double occupancy), including three meals, private facilities, and morning-till-night activities—all limited to people over the age of 60, from November until April 30—that, in a nutshell, is the pricing policy of "Florida's Club Meds" for senior citizens: four large hotels in highly desirable cities on the west coast of the Sunshine State.

These are not, of course, real "Club Meds"—that's only my term for them. The owning company is Senior Vacation Hotels of Florida, in business for 26 years—longer than any Club Med in the Western Hemisphere.

But the offerings—and atmosphere (adapted for an older generation)—are exactly that of a Club Med: you receive not only your room but also three grand repasts daily, parties, live entertainment and free movies, bus excursions, theme nights, beach trips, and more—for one fixed, and remarkably low, price.

What's the catch? Well, first, there's the required minimum age, and I should point out that most guests appear to be over the age of 65 (but they're an unusually lively lot of over-65ers). More important, you must normally stay for a minimum of one month, usually starting at the beginning of the month. Provided you do, you pay only $700 per person per month (based on double occupancy) in November, December, and April, $800 per month in January, $875 per month in February and March.

The hotels in question are the large Sunset Bay and Courtyard in St. Petersburg, the Regency Tower in Lakeland, and the Riverpark in Bradenton. For a lively four-color brochure on these veritable "Club Meds for Senior Citizens," and for application forms, contact **Senior Vacation Hotels of Florida, 7401 Central Ave., St. Petersburg, FL 33710 (phone 813/345-8123, or toll free 800/247-2203, 800/872-3616 in Florida, 800/843-3713 in Canada).** ≈

Call me a grouch, but I'm not impressed with the discounts for mature travelers offered by most hotel chains and airlines.

Party at a Senior Vacation Hotel

Songfest at a Senior Vacation Hotel

XIV ⚬ CAREERS
IN TRAVEL

Working Your Way Around the World

The Strategies and Schemes for Remaining Housed, Fed, and Alive as You Satisfy Your Fondest Travel Dream

Picking grapes near Bordeaux

Harvest in the Languedoc

Opposite page: *On an Israeli kibbutz*

Can you work your way around the world? Yes. Would any reasonably sane person do so? No. Do thousands do so nonetheless? Very definitely yes!

And thousands more seek out the secret of that feat by attending three-hour night-school classes on the weighty theme. Indeed, at my own travel lectures, questions about working abroad are second in frequency only to that perennial champion among inquiries, "Can an unaccompanied woman travel alone?"

Some Guiding Principles

Having spent a large part of my life among indigent Americans who were working at casual jobs to prolong their sojourns overseas, I can let you in on a few leading principles of the art.

Nearly every major country—a prominent exception is Switzerland—turns a blind eye to its own labor regulations during periods of seasonal need. When the grapes want picking in France, when beds want making in British hotels, when the ski resorts of Austria are aching for additional busboys and waiters, they hire foreigners to do the job and ask no questions about work papers and such. It all resembles the former attitudes of our California lettuce growers toward migratory farmhands.

It is important to realize that the vast percentage of available overseas jobs for traveling Americans are wholly menial in nature, and you will be deluding yourself—in most cases—to hope for something better. A great many of our itinerant countrymen take counter positions for a week or two in the local equivalent of Burger King. "The whole point," I was told by one, "is to get it into your head that you are not above anything. At home, you would never have thought of Burger King. Here—go for it!"

Although some resourceful types land jobs teaching English, or even in clerical fields—I'll detail those success stories further on—the great majority follow agricultural pursuits. The standard route, starting in early summer, is picking raspberries in Scotland (May-June), pears in northern France (June-July) or fruit in the Peloponnese of Greece (July-August), harvesting

But keep in mind that the vast majority of overseas jobs for traveling Americans are wholly menial in nature.

Waiting on tables at the Oktoberfest, Munich

Seasonal needs at Oktoberfest time

grapes for wine in southwest France, mainly near Bordeaux (late September, early October), grapes for cognac in the Cognac region of France (mid- to late-October), olives in Crete (November to March), oranges in Israel (February to May). The work is back-breaking and lodgings can be in a barn, but the company good (other international adventurers), the food excellent (hearty, farm-style lunches and dinners with wine), and since there is absolutely nowhere to spend money, you generally save enough to finance several additional weeks on the road.

The travel industry in Europe provides the second-largest source of temporary, unskilled jobs for foreigners. At alpine resorts in winter, and along the French Riviera in summer, short-term work in hotels and restaurants is plentiful, and because much of it is menial in character (busboys and *plongeurs*—dishwashers—mainly) and therefore scorned by the locals, work-paper requirements are quickly forgotten.

Short-term labor shortages occur in other months as well: the autumn in Paris (when hotels bulge with congresses and trade shows), Oktoberfest in Munich (late September to mid-October), Christmas in Rome and Florence (entire month of December), spring recess in Greece (March).

In the Far East (and to a lesser extent in the Middle East), the teaching of English is an activity that sustains a great many American travelers. In Japan, Korea, and Taiwan especially, English-language instructors are continually sought by both companies (for their employees about to be sent abroad), individuals (for their own needs, in one-on-one conversation sessions), and schools. There, formal teaching backgrounds are rarely required, and persons speaking with American accents preferred (unlike Hong Kong, where the British accent is *de rigueur*).

Prime Sources of Information

Apart from simply applying directly to the job opportunity—walking from hotel to hotel or restaurant to restaurant; showing up unannounced at pubs, freighters, farms, cafés, tour companies (for guide jobs), and the like—travelers learn to use four on-the-spot institutions as prime sources for information about "undocumented work":

Youth hostels: At these ubiquitous, international lodgings which—despite the name—are now open to people of all ages, the air crackles with news of job openings for "casual" work. From the bulletin boards, but also from your fellow hostelers, and especially from the staff and hostel "warden," you'll quickly learn what's available in the vicinity. Some employers actually visit the hostels to seek out workers for temporary short-term jobs, and some job-seekers stay on at the hostels (sometimes earning their keep by work performed there) in the hope of receiving such offers.

English-language newspapers: In capital cities all over the world, English-language newspapers published for expatriate communities are often chock-a-block with want ads for short-term employment. On the newsstands in Tokyo, English-language newspapers carry ads placed by people seeking private instruction in English. Other standard, local newspapers occasionally carry English-language ads for such instruction in the midst of their incomprehensible ideographs.

Government employment agencies: Amazingly enough, even official job organizations in many countries often join in the hunt for undocumented aliens to perform seasonal work of the sort that local residents won't consider. In France, you visit local branches of the A.N.P.E. (Agence National pour l'Emploi) in Bordeaux, Reims, Macon, Beaune, Dijon, or Colmar to sign up for grape picking in the season of the *vendange* (harvest). In West Germany, you visit the Arbeitsamters for much the same reason.

Private employment bureaus: Or you go to a private agency that specializes in "temps." Just as we have our "Kelly Girls" and such, so do other nations (under different names); and while you can't expect them to find you a clerical job if you're not fluent in the local language, you'll often discover a variety of other unskilled, short-term jobs to which, as an American, you'll be sent with alacrity (Americans have the reputation of "workaholics" overseas).

You always start in England, where job opportunities are ample in the south, and it's somewhat of a status symbol to hire Americans. One young person of my acquaintance obtained a hotel list from the British Travel Authority, photocopied an application letter to 30 or so hotels that seemed promising, and received three offers of summer employment. He proceeded to spend two successful months behind the front desk of a hotel in Cornwall, where his exotic nationality appealed not simply to British visitors, but to American tourists. "Oh look, Herbert, an American working his way across Europe, let's give him a big tip."

From Cornwall, a succession of similar triumphs: cutting trees in the outskirts of Paris, grape picking in the champagne vineyards near Reims, dishwashing in Florence, working for passage aboard a freighter to Greece, the olive harvest and then olive oil bottling at a factory in Crete, teaching English for a month to "two bratty kids at a big mansion in Turkey," then by bucket-shop air fare to Bangkok (more English teaching) and Djakarta (guiding tourists to commission-granting batik shops), then home.

And so it goes. This is not for your everyday tourist. It's a modern-day adventure for travelers, not tourists. A big adventure, full of experience and learning.

But take credit cards—and a return ticket home. ≈

"Traveling" As a Flight Attendant

Does an Airline Job Enable You to See the World? Yes and No

In the early years of commercial aviation, when planes flew the Atlantic three times a week, working as a flight attendant (then called a "stewardess") was a wonderful way to see the world. You landed in Lisbon, let's say; repaired for a bit of rest to a grand, traditional hotel; and then spent a couple of leisurely days seeing the city before flying back.

How is it now? Are those jobs aboard a plane, pushing carts of prepackaged meals up and down the aisle, still the route to take for travel-loving Americans? Are the rewards of travel sufficient to justify what is, from common observation, an unusually arduous sort of work, consisting largely of repetitive functions?

To answer those questions, I interviewed six flight attendants from as many airlines, plus a supervisor of flight attendants at one mighty line, and the director of an information service for aspiring flight attendants. And their answers were more complex than I had anticipated.

Better Routes and Schedules Come with Seniority

For people seeking an immediate, constant access to the world's great sights—right now, without delay—the prospects are apparently disappointing. Rules of seniority restrict access to the better routes and schedules. For the first five or so years, until they've acquired a bit of status, most fledgling flight attendants are assigned to dull domestic itineraries, flying constantly from one industrial city to another. Only after they've "paid their dues," so to speak, are they able successfully to "bid" for Rome or Hong Kong, for Rio or Kathmandhu.

Even when the destination is an attractive one, the rapid turnaround of jet aircraft and the constant flow of flights restricts the amount of time available for enjoying that city. The average domestic layover is 10 to 24 hours. You fly to Phoenix, let's say, arrive at 10 p.m., are taken for a night's sleep to an airport hotel, and have little more than the next morning in which to sightsee or relax at the pool before returning to the airport for a return flight.

"It starts out as a crummy job," said one flight attendant, "but gets better as the years roll along."

On a long-distance international flight, the average layover is longer, but still no more than one or two days: you leave New York on Monday evening, for instance, arrive Paris on Tuesday morning, and fly back from Paris to New York on Wednesday afternoon. But since your outbound flight has gone throughout the night, you need to sleep for much of Tuesday in order to recover. Therefore you have little more than late Tuesday afternoon and evening, and Wednesday morning, for enjoying Paris.

Off-Duty Flying

How about the chance to travel and sightsee on your own time, and not simply when you're flying for the airline? Isn't it true that flight attendants can themselves fly free, and to almost anywhere, when they're off-duty?

The answer, generally, is yes. After first working for an initial period, flight attendants receive the right to fly free (on a chancy, "space available" basis) on services of their own airline, and often—using reciprocal privileges—on the flights of another airline. That's a considerable fringe benefit, and it extends to the spouse and dependent children of the flight attendant, and (sometimes) to their parents as well.

But again, and in the early years, the rules of seniority often limit the ability of a flight attendant to make an off-duty use of his or her fly-for-free privileges. That's because most flight attendants, in their first one to four years of flying, are placed on a "reserve" status: made to fly as and when the airline determines, and often on as few as four hours' notice. Although most flight attendants are guaranteed at least 12 scheduled days off each month (and some get 15), it can happen that those days (for a junior flight attendant) can be so scattered throughout the month as to leave insufficient blocs of time for anything resembling international travel. Only with the gaining of seniority can one effectively plan to make use of free ticket privileges.

The time needed for such seniority varies drastically from one airline to another, as some are more liberal than others in this regard. On a recent flight aboard

United Airlines, a travel-happy flight attendant told me that she was able within only a year of starting her employment to schedule two periods of five consecutive days each month for leisure time (in addition to other scattered days), and was thus able to plan a series of rather ambitious off-duty trips. A fellow flight attendant told of other patterns that could result, even for a junior employee, in at least one bloc of seven consecutive leisure days for travel each month. While, admittedly, this was under the policy of an unusually generous airline, it is illustrative of the ability of flight attendants to escape the Monday-through-Friday, nine-to-five routines of most deskbound jobs, which is of course the major lure of the flight attendant position.

At all airlines, seniority of about five to seven years confers considerable flexibility of scheduling (and thus constant, free travel possibilities) upon the flight attendant willing to "stick it out." Once endowed with seniority, one bids for the most attractive cities and patterns of flights. "In other words," as I was told by another flight attendant, "it starts out as a crummy job, but gets better as the years roll along."

Why else is it a "crummy job" at first? Because the airline reserves the right to assign the fledgling flight attendant to a "domicile"—a home city—of the airline's choosing. Many flight attendants must relocate upon starting work. Only after several years are they able to "bid for" the more popular "domiciles," which are currently the West Coast cities, Hawaii, and Florida. And there they schedule themselves, as few other Americans can, for widely varying dates of work, which can differ each month.

Flight Attendants Give Their Views

You've probably gathered from the above that the job is suitable only for people who enjoy a carefree lifestyle, full of change and variety, but also replete with scheduling mishaps, and never the same as the patterns chosen by family and friends. If I were to compose a composite of the statements made to me by experienced flight attendants, they would go like this:

"It's a crazy life, and you have to like irregularity. It definitely infringes on social life; you can't date or be married to someone who is a rigid person." "It's for those who don't require a lot of structure in their lives. You work nights, weekends, holidays, and don't know from one month to the next what your time will be like. You work with different people all the time. Things change constantly, a new set of problems pop up at every turn. Currently, schoolteachers and nurses are our largest group of applicants, because they are chafing in their predictable life patterns, and are seeking constant change."

"Yet quite a few flight attendants are married with kids, and find the job gives them more time with their kids. Then, when they're on duty, they have time with themselves. This gives them both more time with family and more private time."

"Rather than fly a set schedule to the same cities, I 'bid vacations'—that is, I opt to substitute for other people who are on vacation. They take two weeks off and I fly their trips. That way, I fly with different crews and to wholly new destinations each day. I also work different positions on the aircraft, which I like."

"The worst part of the job? Being stuck in a strange city and not knowing anyone. You've got a dinner date at seven o'clock, and all of a sudden Boston's snowed in and you're stuck in Boston for four days, and you've missed the wedding of your best friend and your mother's birthday and Christmas—and you're sitting in a hotel room."

Do Americans crave that kind of life? Consider the statistics. On some airlines, applicants for flight attendant positions outnumber openings by 80 to 1; on others, it's 30 to 1.

Yet the openings exist, and many thousands are hired each year. Call the personnel office in the airline's headquarters city, ask for their leaflet of "recruitment information," and you, too, may become one of those "gypsies of the sky." ≈

Can You Really Become a Part-Time Travel Agent?

As Many as 100,000 Americans Earn Income from the Sale of Travel While Holding Down Full-Time Jobs in Other Fields

It's a zinger, a stunner, a title bound to appeal. But to pound the point home, they place dollar signs, in boldface, at the start and the end: "$Become a Part-Time Travel Agent$."

At "urban night schools" all over the land, lecturers charge as much as $25 for three hours, even $47 for six hours, to present a topic that I think can be treated in 1,200 words. Here goes:

Anyone can become a "part-time travel agent" by 10 a.m. tomorrow morning, because part-time travel agents receive no salary, and are paid only when and if they produce clients for their agency. Though some travel-agency owners are weary of the part-timers they already employ, and will refuse to take on more, most will instantly respond "Yes" when you offer to work for them "free."

While you wait for your business card to be printed, you hang around the agency for an hour or so each day, to familiarize yourself with its personnel and with the travel packages most frequently requested of them. You browse among the brochures on the racks. You do not learn the technical end of the travel-agency business, and no one offers to teach you. As a part-timer, you are not really a "travel agent," but rather an "outside sales rep," in the parlance of the trade.

On the day when your cards arrive, you ask to borrow 200 pieces of letterhead stationery and envelopes, which you take home. You then proceed to compose a list of every human being you have ever met: relatives, friends, alumni, business associates, fellow church members—anyone. To them, you compose and duplicate a letter, which might read like this:

Dear Friend:

You will be delighted to learn that I am now associated with XYZ Travel Agency. And in that capacity, I should like to arrange your next vacation trip.

Give me a chance—I won't let you down! I'll send you on journeys of unequalled joy, I'll weave rainbows into your holiday plans.

And it won't cost you an extra cent. My

services are free (to you); my income is from the airlines, cruise ships, and hotels I use.
Hoping to hear from you.
Alice or John Jones

To your amazement, the phone begins to ring. Why? Because most people don't already have a travel agent to whom they owe allegiance. Or else they're accustomed to making their own reservations by calling airlines and hotels direct. When you offer to take those burdens off their hands—at no cost to them—they often rush to agree.

If all you then do is refer the booking to the travel agency you represent—without performing any of the work—you generally receive one or two of the percentage points of commission they earn. After all, you have brought them a client they might not otherwise have had.

If you do more, you earn more. Thus if you consult with the client and "hone" their vague vacation desires into a finite, complete decision—get them to agree on the exact date and flight of their departure, a specific hotel property, all else—and then present that virtually complete transaction to the agency for processing, you are generally able to up your income to three or four percentage points. After all, you have saved the agency one or two hours of nonproductive time. Instead of engaging in repeated discussions over the phone or across a desk, the agency can limit its services to a few minutes of processing: placing the booking, then issuing tickets and documents.

Gradually you—the "outside sales rep"—learn to do even more. As your knowledge of the industry increases, you actually phone the suppliers and make the needed reservations. Though you still can't work the computer, issue tickets, or perform a dozen other tasks, you do much of the other paperwork and all of the contact with the client. And then, because you're saving the agency additional time, you ask them to "split the commission," receiving an average of five percentage points on the income your clients bring.

With growing pleasure, and while retaining your daytime position as a nurse, teacher, or paralegal, you

begin receiving a steady stream of small commission checks. If you are diligent about it, you discover that you are supplementing your income with two or three thousands of dollars a year, maybe more.

And then you generally make that other all-important travel discovery: that it is often just as easy to book 20 people on a trip as to sign up one. You begin actively to "sell" travel, creating holiday motivations where none might exist. On the bulletin board of a large, nearby office, you post a notice: "Hey, gang, if I can sign 20 of you aboard a charter to Rio on September 17, I can get us a full week's trip, including air fare and a good Copacabana hotel, for only $599."

If you are good at it and enjoy a following—which most often happens if you're a "joiner" known to large numbers of people in your community—you find that your part-time "outside sales" position is so promising as to warrant your taking an evening vocational course in the retail travel business. Every city of size offers such instruction—look in the *Yellow Pages* phone directory under "Schools."

How about free or reduced-price travel privileges? Do part-timers enjoy that fringe benefit of the travel agency? Depends on the agency. Under deregulation, no legal obstacle any longer bars airlines or others from offering free trips to anyone. But different agency owners pursue differing policies in allocating their reduced-price trips, free "junkets," or "familiarization trips." Ask before you make your choice of agencies. Certainly, if you're a heavy producer, you should be entitled to your pro-rata share.

And that, so help me, and in my humble opinion, is all there is to it. Obviously, it doesn't work for everyone, as nothing in this life does. But with so many travel bookings being placed directly with airlines, cruise lines, and hotels—and not presently through travel agents—opportunities abound for dynamic, sales-minded individuals to steer much of that business their way, earning a commission.

Thereby they not only enhance their incomes, but share in the emotional rewards of the travel industry.

And they don't have to pay $25 for a course to learn how. ≈

Flying for Free (or for Peanuts) As an Air Courier

By Permitting Your Baggage Allowance to Be Used for Freight, You Fly at the Cheapest Rates in Travel Today

In the novels of an Ian Fleming or a John le Carré, full of spies and foreign intrigue, the "courier" is typically seen sitting uneasily in an airplane seat, a black leather briefcase chained to his sweating wrist. In the somewhat less-pressured world of holiday travel, the "courier" wears no chain at all, carries no briefcase, and simply relaxes en route with a tall iced drink. Occasionally he breaks into a grin, or chuckles aloud over having won the air-fare game.

Doing nothing shady, and without assuming the slightest risk or major responsibility, an increasing number of Americans are acting as occasional "couriers," hired a trip at a time by overnight air-freight companies anxious to avoid the normal long delays in clearing goods through Customs or cargo sheds. Through the use of air "couriers" and the baggage checked by them, freight clears Customs or cargo as fast as baggage does—in a half hour or so. And the "couriers" receive either free or sharply reduced air fares for accomplishing that feat.

Though it's a rather weird way of going on vacation, you may want to consider doing exactly the same.

Anyone can become a courier. Most are ordinary working people who love to travel and act as couriers to take advantage of super-low air fares for vacations.

"It's absolutely wonderful," says Sylvia Roberts, who has flown to Europe 20 times in the last three years. "How else could you fly to London for $250 round trip, which includes flying on the Concorde on the return trip. I recommend it to all my friends."

The main drawback to flying as a courier is that you give up your baggage allowance. Couriers are permitted to take only one piece of carry-on luggage, because the courier company uses their baggage allowance to ship its clients' packages, which are mostly documents.

"People worry that we'll have them transporting drugs or guns, but in fact most of our packages are from stock market firms or advertising agencies—anybody who's willing to pay a premium to ensure that a document gets to Europe the next day or to Japan in two days," says Barry Pearlstein of Airsystems Courier in New York.

One courier firm charges $35 to transport an envelope weighing less than a pound from New York to London for next-day delivery, so it's easy to see how the courier companies use a passenger's 44-pound luggage allowance to make a profit.

Duties of the Courier

People traveling as couriers are asked to carry a sealed envelope which contains a "manifest"—a list of items, usually mail in sacks, which travels with them— but the sacks are handled entirely by employees of the courier company. "You never touch anything at all," says Carl Radebush. "When you get to the airport, they unload the van and put everything through the baggage check-in. Then they give you your ticket and a yellow envelope (the manifest) and off you go.

"At the other end, somebody from the courier company is waiting to meet you. You wait while the stuff clears Customs, which can take anywhere from 15 minutes to an hour, then off you go on holiday. You do the same thing coming back."

In international travel, the courier must declare to Customs the contents of the bags accompanying him as shown in the manifest, but the accuracy of the manifest is solely the responsibility of the courier company.

Drawbacks of the Courier Life

Flying as a courier involves several distinct disadvantages, although most people feel these are outweighed by the savings. The first, mentioned earlier, is that you're limited to traveling with just one in-flight bag. One employee of a courier company who was interviewed for this article said, "Personally, I can't even conceive of going to Europe with one piece of carry-on. I would be a mental case."

Sylvia Roberts, on the other hand, says the baggage limitation taught her to travel light, whereas she used to lug three big suitcases.

A potentially more serious limitation is that, in an emergency, a courier can be bumped from a flight, although the companies make every effort to see that this doesn't happen often. The fee a courier pays for his passage is usually referred to as an "administrative

Though it's a rather weird method of earning your trip, it's easily accomplished.

Couriers take "carry-ons" only, because the courier company uses their baggage allowance for the shipment of small parcels and documents.

charge" or some such, and the company makes it clear that they are not in the business of selling airline tickets. This means that if your flight is cancelled, or if you are bumped by the courier company, you may not have the same rights as a regular passenger.

For two or more people traveling together, special arrangements are necessary. TNT Skypak, the company Sylvia Roberts flies for, will make arrangements for two traveling companions to fly on consecutive days. Sylvia took advantage of this to arrange a ski trip to Europe for herself and three friends. Sylvia flew to Geneva on a Monday and her friends followed on Tuesday, Wednesday, and Thursday. They came back on a similarly staggered schedule. Was it worth the hassle? "It cost us $150 each for the air fare, and the hotel was $100 each for the week. That's skiing in Europe for a week for $250. You bet it was worth it!"

Another TNT Skypak courier is Frank Sansone. "I'm not a wealthy man," he says. "But how many people have been to three continents and the West Coast in two years?" As a present, he gave his mother a trip to Europe. "To be able to do that, it's great," he says. "It's like being a Rockefeller."

Where, When, and How Much?

Courier companies operate from major U.S. cities, like Los Angeles, San Francisco, New York, Chicago, Miami, and San Juan, flying overseas to Rio de Janeiro, Tokyo, Hong Kong, London, Brussels, Amsterdam, Geneva, Milan, Madrid, Sydney, and Auckland.

Fares vary according to season and the popularity of the run. The least expensive flights seem to be those to Europe in the winter months and unpopular runs, like New York to Hong Kong, which is such a long trip that most people prefer not to fly straight through.

The length of your stay abroad is determined before you go. To Europe it's usually a week; to the Far East, two weeks; to Frankfurt, Geneva, Amsterdam, and Brussels, the return date is often open.

To Become a Courier

Though your *Yellow Pages* phone directory may list a local firm using on-board couriers, under the heading

"Air Courier Services," your best bet is to write to the "biggies," of which most will urge you not to use the phone (see below). Rather, at least eight weeks in advance of departure, write a letter describing yourself and your travel desires, include a phone number where you may be reached during the day, enclose a stamped, self-addressed, #10 envelope (for application forms), and send the lot to:

TNT Skypak, 400 Post Ave., Westbury, NY 11590 (phone 516/338-7760 from 10 a.m. to noon and 3 to 4 p.m., and ask for Laura), or 845 Cowan Rd., Burlingame, CA 94010 (phone 415/692-9600, and ask for Pauline) (flights from New York to Rio, London, Frankfurt; from San Francisco to London, Sydney, Tokyo, and Hong Kong).

World Courier, Attention: Barbara Whitting, 137-42 Guy R. Brewer Blvd., Jamaica, NY 11434 (currently has on-board couriers flying to London, Amsterdam, Frankfurt; discourages phone calls and requires a personal interview at the above address).

A-1 International Courier, 6930 N.W. 12th St., Miami, FL 33126 (phone 305/594-1184) (Miami to Caracas, with "open return" dates).

Now Voyager Freelance Courier, 74 Varick St., Suite 307, New York, NY 10013 (represents a number of the smaller courier companies flying to all points, and charges a fee of $45 a year for its own services as a broker; it also encourages calls to a "hot line" recording at 212/431-1616 from 8 a.m. to noon on weekdays, using the same number that afternoon to book).

Halbart Express, 147-05 176th St., Jamaica, NY 11434 (phone 718/656-8189) (flies from New York to Milan, Amsterdam, Madrid, Frankfurt, Paris, and Brussels at fares ranging from $150 to $300; call at least six to eight weeks ahead).

Rush Couriers, Inc., 481 49th St., Brooklyn, NY 11220 (phone 718/439-8181) (flies to San Juan, Puerto Rico; fares range from $100 to $160, depending on the season; there's no time limit on your return and you can occasionally check one bag in addition to the carry-on).

Air Facilities, 3100 N.W. 72nd Ave., Suite 111, Miami, FL 33122 (phone 305/477-8300) (flies from Miami to Quito or Guayaquil for $200 round trip, to Rio for $350 round trip, and to Buenos Aires for $400 round trip; call at least one month in advance).

Graf Airfreight, 5811 Willoughby Ave., Hollywood CA, 90038, Attention: Ernie Kiefer (phone 213/461-1547), has flights to Chicago and New York's JFK Airport and expects to go to Dallas–Fort Worth by the summer of 1989. There's no limit to your stay and costs are $50 one way. Reservations are accepted by mail or phone—beginning on the first working day of a month for flights the following month (i.e., the first working day in December for January flights). ≈

Traveling for Free as a Tour Escort

Pursuing the Dream Job, the Fantasy Career: The Companies That Hire, the People They Hire

Checking the manifest

A "tour escort": the words imply a dream job, the fantasy career. In blue blazer and natty scarf (one typical vision), you stroll through life with well-mannered groups of sensitive adults as they view the storied sites of antiquity.

Just think: you are traveling for free, and getting paid, to boot!

The reality can be jarringly different. As a paid travel professional, on call around the clock, your phone rings at all hours of the night with unreasonable demands: change my room, get me more blankets or towels. You learn that awful truth: that of every 40 persons on earth, 38 are gentle, caring souls and 2 are monsters. In my own past life as a tour operator, I sent an escort to China with 20 auto dealers and their spouses, of whom 2 refused to eat Chinese food after the first day. The poor tour escort, in addition to her other tasks, labored in a hot hotel kitchen at mealtimes to prepare hamburgers or spaghetti for the obstinate duo.

Still another member of the group was a surly drunk who slipped pitchers of Mai Tais onto the bus, creating scandal and problems in a dozen Chinese towns.

Want an additional whiff of reality? Well, people get sick while on tour, and you, the tour escort, rush them to the hospital at 3 a.m. and pace the waiting room. People occasionally die while on tour—that being a tiring activity—and you, the tour escort, trudge to a grisly foreign morgue to ship the body home.

Yet for all the horrors, thousands of Americans—in love with travel, in love with people—are joyfully at work as tour escorts, either part-time or full-time; and many thousands more would kill to land a like position. In this essay I appraise that dream vocation, and provide pointers—based on interviews with the personnel directors of nearly a dozen tour operators—on how to be hired.

The Companies That Hire

As travel becomes increasingly group-oriented (economies of scale bring lower prices to groups), creating an obvious need for one escort per group, more than 450 tour companies are now making use of tour escorts—some hiring fewer than 10 a year, others as many as 200.

The largest users of tour escorts are, beyond any doubt, Tauck Tours of Westport, Connecticut (for domestic trips, mainly by motorcoach), and Maupintour of Lawrence, Kansas (going worldwide). Beyond the two leaders, precise rankings are difficult to make, but the major escort-hiring firms include, quite clearly: American Express of New York City (primarily for incoming groups to the U.S.); Four Winds of New York City; West Tours of Seattle, Washington; Mayflower Tours of Downers Grove, Illinois; Olson-Travelworld of Culver City, California; Pacific Delight of New York City and San Francisco (but this one requires fluency in one or more Asian languages); Collette Tours of North Providence, Rhode Island; Paragon Tours of Bedford, Massachusetts; Globus Gateway/Cosmos of New York City and Los Angeles; Allied Tours of New York City and Los Angeles (foreign incoming tours, mainly); and Rural Route Tours of Overland Park, Kansas (the last-named, of increasing significance).

To obtain a more comprehensive list of every such potential employer, including escort-using companies in your own immediate vicinity, I'd go to a local retail travel agency and ask (politely and shyly) to look at their current copy of one of the "travel trade personnel directories." These yearly publications, some the size of a small telephone book, are issued by the three major trade periodicals: *Travel Weekly, Travel Agent,* and *Travel Trade.* Each lists all the major companies of the travel industry. By scanning the sections called "tour operators," and reading the descriptions of each, you can usually spot the many firms that hire tour escorts.

Two other important names in tour escorting are those of the major schools purporting to train and place "tour managers" (their loftier title for a "tour escort" or "tour courier"): **American Tour Management Institute, 271 Madison Ave., New York, NY 10016 (phone 212/889-5990),** with classes in New York; and **International Tour Management Institute, 625 Market St., Suite 1015, San Francisco, CA 94105 (phone 415/957-9489),** with classes in

San Francisco, Los Angeles, and Boston. Although I've long been skeptical about their ability to teach what seems to me a commonsense function, I was surprised to learn, in interviews, of the high regard in which both companies are held by the professionals. While the vast majority of tour escorts obtain their positions without formal instruction in the subject, an increasing number of tour companies are currently saying they will "give an edge" to school-trained applicants; one or two even look exclusively to the graduates of such schools for openings in their ranks.

The People They Hire

The activity is largely a women's profession—to such an extent that some personnel managers say they now give preference to men to redress the balance! And contrary to the popular conception of tour escorts as vigorous yuppies in their early 30s, the actual average age level is fairly high. A recent private study of tour escorts by George C. Guenther of Talmage Tours in Philadelphia (which he was kind enough to show me) asserts that the typical tour escort is, in addition to being female, between 50 and 59 years of age, married, but retired and working part-time as an escort (she is also "caring, patient, outgoing, and well-organized").

The maximum age limit for service? None, say the personnel managers, provided the applicant is physically strong and able to work the long hours (hopping on and off buses, doing considerable walking) that tour escorting entails.

The Places to Which You Go

By a three-to-one ratio (and probably higher than that) domestic tours outnumber international ones as opportunities for escorting; you are far more likely to crisscross New England than New Zealand. And this numerical imbalance has an important part in determining the duties you'll perform.

On an international tour you'll seldom be asked to deliver the lectured commentary on what the group is seeing. That's done by local art historians or other specialists picked up along the way (who accompany the group, say, to the Uffizzi Galleries in Florence) or by full-time, highly trained British tour guides assigned to the bus for the entire tour. The tour escort from the U.S., if there is one, performs the homelier tasks: dealing with mishaps and travel emergencies, overseeing transfers of luggage, watching the air connections, acting as liaison between the group and their hotels, or between the group and the tour operator's head office. Ironically, the foreign tour is thus the easiest to escort.

In the United States, by contrast, both practice and tradition cast the tour escort, in most cases, as the commentator: you provide a running lecture on all that passes by.

Accordingly, virtually all tour companies cite "a knowledge of place," "experience in the area," as one of the prime requisites for a majority of their escort positions. That's not to say that you must memorize scores of facts about various destinations to get the job; no escort is made to "solo" on a particular tour until he or she has first accompanied a trained escort on at least two departures of the same tour. But to the extent that you are already heavily traveled, or know particular areas well, you become a prime prospect for domestic escorting.

(In this respect, tour escorting is radically different from most other careers in travel. In a retail travel agency, for instance, the fact that you have traveled a great deal in life has almost no bearing on your ability to do the job; rather, it is first and far more important that you master a body of technical details on booking and pricing flights, cruises, tours, and the like.)

Therefore: if you know New England like the palm of your hand, if you grew up on the coast of California, if Alaska was your kindergarten or Florida your life-long home, say so. Lead off your résumé with travel experience and half the job is done.

The Criteria They Use

With ten applications for every opening, tour escorting rivals the theater world in the brutal competitiveness of its job-seeking process. The analogy is apt. "We're looking for stars," says Nancy Jepson of Globus Gateway/Cosmos Tours. "You have to be a bit egotistical to be a tour director, which is why unemployed actresses are often our best prospects."

To find out the criteria leading tour companies use for choosing escorts, I interviewed (by phone) the personnel managers for a dozen large tour companies. Apart from a knowledge of the destinations to which the tours go—a talent heavily stressed by most—what other attributes cause ten résumés to be plucked from a stack of a hundred?

"Let me tell you first what we're not seeking," says John Stachnik of Mayflower Tours, Downers Grove, Illinois. "We're not impressed by people in a mid-life crisis seeking a 'cure' through travel or escaping from reality—and we can read those aims in a great many of the applications we receive."

"We're looking for people who like being leaders, responsible for the welfare of a group," says Bruce Beckham of Beckham Travel, Canton, Massachusetts (50 miles from Boston). "I scan the résumés mainly for organizational background, prior experience as the head of a group or effort, however small: teachers, high school principals, former YMCA directors, people who have been involved in social volunteerism: Elks, Knights of Columbus."

"The underlying quality," says Rohan Wanigatunga, director of tour managers for Olson/Travelworld, "is that they be caring; they must enhance the tour on a personal level, go all out. In the very first interview with them, perhaps by phone, we are looking for that caring quality."

"Too often," says John Stachnik of Mayflower Tours, "we hear applicants stressing how much they love to travel. We would rather hear them say, 'I love to be with people.'"

"They must be a bit like psychiatrists," adds Kathy Ackers of Rural Route Tours, Overland Park, Kansas, "able to cope with varying personalities, eager to mold 40 people into a happy group, a family. If you get tired of 40 people after seven days, and have seven more to go, you're in the wrong business. And if you don't like change, you won't survive."

The subsidiary qualities for success in the field? "The strength of Superman and the patience of God" (says Joan Dunne of Pacific Delight Tours, New York City); "good grooming; we stress appearance very, very strongly" (Bill Strickland, American Express, New York City); "good communications skills" (Bob Sanger, director of New York's American Tour Management Institute); "high energy level, liking to have fun" (Kathy Ackers, Rural Route Tours); "incredible patience, mature judgment, and the vigor to bear up under a physically demanding job: the end of the day is not the end of their day; that's when problems start" (Dick Sundby, tour escort supervisor for Tauck Tours).

"The ideal candidate," concludes John Stachnik of the fast-growing Mayflower Tours, "is a recent widow, completely flexible in her time requirements, still vigorous, who has feelings within herself to give, a great deal to share, and is herself well-traveled."

Possessed of such qualities, how do you bring them to the fore and snare the job? Through persistence, answer all my interviewees. The mailing of a résumé to multiple tour operators is only the first step in a protracted campaign. You follow up by phone, perhaps two or three times in a season. You regard turndowns as mere temporary setbacks—the simple lack of an opening in an industry whose needs are notoriously volatile, fluid. You shrug off rejection, press on in requesting interviews, submit updated résumés. One reason why some companies prefer graduates of the two major schools of "tour management" is because attendance at such a school evidences a profound determination to enter the field.

If some companies demand prior experience of their potential tour escorts (as American Express, for one, does), you obtain that experience by leading a small, local tour for one of your own local tour companies or travel agencies, even for free. And then you headline your résumé with that event. Either way—with or without experience, with or without tour-school training, but through persistence—you obtain an interview and presumably obtain the job.

The Job Itself

Once employed, do you work full-time or part-time? In most instances you work seasonally, say all my informants; at least 70% of all tour escorts do it on a part-time basis, and only 10% to 20% of the 450 companies hiring tour escorts are able to employ people year round (Collette Tours is one of the latter). Even the giant Tauck Tours employs the great bulk of its escorts during the May-through-October season only (but operates every day of the week throughout that season). Actually, according to Tauck supervisor Dick Sundby, that intense seasonality is well suited to the type of escort Tauck seeks to hire. "We like people who have other things in their lives. We look for escorts willing to work their heads off May through October and use the other months to pursue life goals."

How much do tour escorts earn? While arrangements vary broadly from firm to firm, most companies report an average of $80 to $100 a day while on tour (and tours can extend for as many as 14 to 21 days), much of it from the tips that escorts traditionally receive from their passengers. And since escorts are usually housed and fed at the tour company's expense, most of that income can be retained as savings. "You live a rather high life when you're a tour director," says Nancy Jepson of Globus Gateway/Cosmos Tours. "If you're doing it full-time, you often don't pay rent, because the company will put you up when you're between tours. If you're away seven months, you make a lot of money."

But: "It's a 24-hour job," Ms. Jepson continues. "You have to be a little crazy to do it, and you have no social life. At the same time, it's the most rewarding job you'll ever have."

Which is why those résumés keep arriving in an endless stream, seeking the dream job, the fantasy career. ≈

The Quick and Simple Means of Becoming a "Cruise-Only" Travel Agent

Some Conduct the Business from Their Living Room and Control Their Own Hours

Mary Pat Silberman, a "cruise-only" agent

Her office is her living room, amid couches and plants, without a single metal desk, and no computer anywhere in sight.

Nor is she burdened with bulky directories of flights and hotels, or by wire racks bulging with a forest of brochures.

Because she sells cruises, and nothing else, the tools of her trade are a telephone with two buttons, and a small pile of catalogs. Yet she earns a handsome income, controls her own hours, and goes on five to six luxury cruises a year.

To that multitude of Americans wishing to enter the travel industry, but unwilling to make the investment of time and money needed to operate a full-service travel agency, a new opportunity has presented itself: the "cruise-only travel agency." Managed at times by a single person, infinitely less complex than the standard variety, easily spotted by such names as "Ship Ahoy" or "Anchors Aweigh," at least 1,000 such firms are now in existence, and doing well.

Indeed, people have been known to open cruise-only agencies with but a few weeks' preparation and a modest investment, and yet to become successful in a very short time.

The Key Is Specialization

Before the arrival of significant numbers of cruise-only agencies three or four years ago, nearly all retail travel firms held themselves out as offering all things to all people: every type of trip and tour, to every geographical destination, using every form of transportation and lodging, in every price category.

That lack of focus required—and still does—work of an often-staggering complexity: long hours of continuing study, mastery of difficult computer programs, securing endless information sources. And because the traditional travel sale is low in price—a few hundred dollars for the average air ticket or hotel stay, earning commissions of $30 or $40 at best—the traditional travel agent needed to attract thousands of clients or transactions a year, a daunting task. Although many agents craved a more confined sort of business, no one segment of travel enjoyed sufficient volume by itself to support the agency; you had to handle everything.

Then came the explosion in cruises. From being a rather elitist and relatively small-scale activity as recently as 1979, cruise sales are today approaching four million passengers a year, and billions of dollars in revenues, as the world's shipyards labor to turn out one vessel after another. A properly specialized agency can today prosper on cruise sales alone, and can enter the field without meeting any of the requirements needed to sell air tickets.

Because cruise-ship capacity is growing so fast, and needs all the sales help it can get, most cruise-ship companies are happy to accept bookings from any company that styles itself an "agency."

Unlike the airlines, the cruise lines do not permit agents to stock their blank tickets, and extend credit to no one; they mail their tickets to agents only after full payment has been received for them. Therefore they need not concern themselves with whether the agents are creditworthy, and (again unlike the airlines) impose no "licensing," bonding, or appointment procedures on the person who wishes to earn commissions by selling their cabins and berths.

While some cruise lines will pay commissions only to agents affiliated with the Cruise Lines International Association (C.L.I.A., a loose marketing group), membership in C.L.I.A. costs only $35, plus $90 annually in dues, and no screening is done of applicants, who simply submit a statement that they are in business on a full-time basis to sell travel.

With entrance so easy, why aren't there more than a thousand cruise-only agents in the business? Because in the hotly competitive world of retail travel sales, the decision to open a cruise-only agency—as simple as it may be—must be combined with a great deal of imagination, sales ability, and status in the community. The people who succeed best are gregarious "joiners," known to many and respected, able to create enthusiasm about the prospect of taking a cruise. Some do it without heavy advertising expenditures by requesting low-cost videos from the cruise lines and then organizing "cruise nights" for screening the video at a

The tools of her trade are a telephone and a small pile of catalogs.

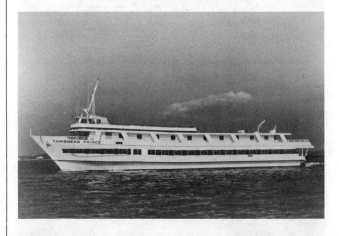

You spot them by their catchy names: "Ship Ahoy," "Anchors Aweigh."

club or organization. Others send out brightly written mailings, or give speeches about cruises at various social gatherings. Because the subject matter is relatively simple, and the technical procedures virtually nil, it is innate marketing ability that makes a successful cruise-only agent. Virtually all the other details are handled by the cruise line, which even prepares and sends out air tickets transporting the passenger to and from the embarkation point.

Obtaining Advice

Where, nevertheless, can you obtain advice on opening a cruise-only agency in your area? Some do it by contacting an already-established firm a hundred or so miles away and retaining the proprietor for a week's consultation.

Others go it the franchise route, by purchasing use of a name (and training) from one of a growing number of cruise-only franchise companies, like Cruise Holidays of San Diego, or Cruiseships Ahoy of New Orleans. But some of the latter charge as much as $25,000, plus a percentage of the take, and the value of such franchises is hotly disputed by several in the industry.

Still others join **C.L.I.A.** (see above), **500 Fifth Ave., New York, NY 10110 (phone 212/921-0066);** the moment they do, their name is placed on the master mailing list for receiving quantities of catalogs and brochures from all the major cruise-ship companies. They also then have access to an extensive, year-round C.L.I.A. program of workshops and seminars in all parts of the country, dealing with every phase and aspect of the sale of cruises.

Or they join **N.A.C.O.A.** (National Association of Cruise-Only Agencies), **P.O. Box 942, East Northport, NY 11731;** N.A.C.O.A., representing some 600 cruise-only agents, is the ardent advocate of the activity, and also schedules periodic workshops and seminars in several parts of the country to hone members' skills. Several prominent members and/or officers of N.A.C.O.A. are also available to answer phoned inquiries about the cruise-only field (or to sell you a cruise); they are Jay Silberman of Cruise

Consultants Company of San Antonio, Texas (phone 512/349-7700); Debbie Adams of The Ship Shop of Independence, Missouri (phone 816/795-0570); and Caroline Mozdean of Anchors Aweigh Cruise Agency of East Northport, New York (phone 516/757-2630).

Income and Fringe Benefits

Most professionals estimate that successful, individual cruise-only agents need to sell at least $500,000 of cruises a year, yielding about $50,000 in commission income. If expenses can then be kept to below $20,000, a yearly income of $30,000 results. By then pursuing group business, and the occasional family-reunion bonanza, some individual agents can push their sales to as much as $1 million a year, yielding $100,000 in commissions, before expenses. Since the average one-week cruise costs about $1,400 per person, annual sales of $500,000 requires that an agent book around 350 persons—or about 175 couples. That, say the experts, is within the reach of a capable person, even one operating out of their homes.

Moreover, agents can increase their commissions beyond the 10% level by concentrating their business among a small number of ships; volume given to a particular line results, usually, in commission "overrides." Or they can place their bookings through a travel agency "consortium" and increase their commissions by three or four percentage points; one such consortium, GEM (Go Earn More), charges only nominal yearly membership fees. Finally, they can use one of a growing number of cruise "consolidators" to obtain their tickets at a commission level higher than 10%.

How about free cruises for the agent's own vacations? That, of course, is the compelling fringe benefit that causes a great many to enter the field. By joining C.L.I.A. (see above), agents are able to apply to the cruise lines for "reduced rate privileges," enabling them to book aboard for as little as $20 to $50 per day, on a "space-available" basis. Even more effective are repeated bookings given to a single cruise line; those will inevitably result in an invitation to take a free cruise.

The Only Barrier

A single barrier to the operation of a modest one-person or two-person "cruise-only" agency is the apparently inadvertent application to them of bonding laws recently enacted in four states; these are aimed at thwarting what are generally non-cruise-related travel scams. Although one such state specifically exempts N.A.C.O.A. agents from the bonding requirement, the three others have failed to do so; but some cruise-only agents believe that the laws permit them to substitute more easily obtained insurance or escrow arrangements for the costly bonds.

Meantime, more people each day become "cruise-only agents," and quickly acquire a reputation for specialized travel knowledge. Wouldn't it be nice to rely on similar expertise in other specialized areas of retail travel? ≈

The World of the One-Man (or One-Woman) Tour Operator

Offering Specialty Travel, Exploring the Most Narrow of Interests or the Oddest of Destinations

Irma Turtle on tour

She had reached the well-paid pinnacle of her profession.

And she felt miserable.

After 12 years with a glamorous New York advertising agency, she had grown bored with business and began asking all the standard questions: "Is this all there is to life?"

One thing she knew: that she loved to travel. So in January of 1985 she booked a tour to view Algerian rock paintings dating to 8,000 B.C. To reach them required that her party first pass through the eerie, boulder-bestrewn, moon-like expanse of the Central Sahara. And she fell in love with it.

Forget the rock paintings! Learning that hardly anyone was traveling commercially to the Central Sahara, she extended her stay to perform the necessary reconnaissance and preparations, then returned to New York and formed a one-woman company to advertise and operate tours to that unique location. Today her desk is awash with bookings, and she has led multiple expeditions—of 4 to 12 passengers apiece—to both the Sahara and other virtually unvisited points of the globe.

Her name is Irma Turtle (it really is); her company is **Turtle Tours, 251 E. 51st St., New York, NY 10022 (phone 212/355-1404);** and she is representative of nearly 200 entrepreneurs scattered about the country who have formed one-person (or at best, two-person) tour operations designed to explore the most narrow of special interests or the oddest of worldwide destinations.

In the case of Irma Turtle, savings from a lucrative career permitted her to place tiny ads for her special travel offerings in *The New Yorker* and other trendy magazines, and a heavy response to those notices gave life to Turtle Tours. For other one-person companies lacking such funds, the classic advertising medium is a thick biannual magazine called the *Specialty Travel Index*. It reaches 41,000 people associated with travel agencies, but it should be on the desk or coffee table of every American avidly interested in travel. It can change your travel life.

Essentially, the *Specialty Travel Index* publishes inexpensive ads placed by 450 or so largely unknown, undersize tour operators who schedule and operate several thousands of special-interest tours. The ads appear in nearly-uniform horizontal strips in the body of the magazine, alphabetically by name, but they are preceded by indexes and cross-indexes of their subject matter and geographical emphasis.

Care to visit the Falkland Islands? Or Mauretania or Mauritius? You have only to turn to "F" or "M" in the *Index*'s geographical listings and out jump 14 tours to exactly those spots.

Longing for a tour of stamp-collecting exhibitions in northern Europe? Canoeing in Zimbabwe? Caving in Belize? Dying to discuss psychiatry with your counterparts in southern India? Simply turn to the several pages of small type in the subject-matter section of the *Specialty Travel Index* and there you'll find cross references to dozens of departures for exactly those purposes.

Merely to stab at random among those subjects is to find provocative new ideas for trips and tours. Would you believe that travel programs exist which explore "polo instruction," "porcelain china," "psychology," "public affairs," and "religion/spirituality"? Or that companies offer tours of "soccer," "solar energy," "space travel," "spectator sports," and "stress management"? Some 176 special interests or activities are listed—including "antiques," "bridge tours," "chocolate tours," "fashion tours," "holistic health tours," "llama packing," "military history," "whale watching," and "wine tasting"—and each subhead proceeds to list the programs of up to a dozen specialty-tour operators.

Though some of these are substantial companies—especially those involved in various aspects of "adventure travel"—upward of 200 are small, local firms, some composed of only a person or two, whose offerings would scarcely be known outside their immediate area if it were not for the *Specialty Travel Index*. So affirms its co-publisher, 48-year-old Steen Hanson.

To prove it, return again to the example of Irma Turtle. Though ads in *The New Yorker* launched her offerings to the moderately familiar Central Sahara (18 days for $2,850, plus air), only constant appearance in the *Specialty Travel Index* enables her to gather sufficient passengers for departures to a set of almost totally unknown destinations. As remarkable as it may seem, she is currently operating her one-woman tours to:

• The Pantanal of Brazil: World's largest wetlands, full of river networks and 600 species of tropical birds. "Every time a passenger comments that we haven't yet seen a certain species," says Ms. Turtle, "a hundred of them suddenly appear. Walt Disney couldn't do it any better."

• From Ougadougou to Timbuktu, Mali: By Land Rover, over 1,500 miles of roadless terrain. "I put these groups through one very tough trip," says Ms. Turtle, "and not only do they survive it, but they thank me at the end and say they wouldn't have missed it for the world."

• And add: the Atlas Mountains of Morocco, led by Berber guides; the Ecuadorian Amazon, among the Jivaro Indians (former headshrinkers, they now do it only to monkeys); Rajasthan, India, "where camels pull our baggage in wagons as we cross the Thar desert."

American Express she obviously isn't; a tour operator in the classic and original sense, she is. For a one-year subscription to the *Specialty Travel Index* (two issues per year), encountering the ornery, individualistic, and slightly wonderful Turtles of this world, send $8 to **Specialty Travel Index, 305 San Anselmo Ave., Suite 217, San Anselmo, CA 94960 (phone 415/459-4900).** ≈

XV ⟞ GETTING THERE THE CHEAPEST WAY

Meet America's Air Fare Bucket Shops

They've Moved Here from Britain, a Remarkable Source of Discount Tickets

Y ou've seen the ads a hundred times, and probably they confused you.

Two starkly simple, vertical columns: a list of cities, a list of prices. Nothing more.

From the East Coast: "London, $179." "Paris, $199." From the West Coast: "Singapore, $319." "Tokyo, $329." All manner of miracle air fares at nearly half the normal level. For scheduled flights.

But without a single airline name. Without, for that matter, a single recognizable name. A telephone number, of course. And a company title leaving naught to the imagination: "Travel for Peanuts, Inc." "Why Pay More, Ltd." "Don't-Be-A-Chump & Associates."

Meet the American "bucket shop"! A "discount travel agency" in more polite parlance, its counterpart has flourished in London for 20 years, but only recently taken root in the United States. Today nearly 200 are scrambling for business in big cities across the land— mainly New York, Philadelphia, Boston, Chicago, Los Angeles, San Francisco—where they are used by thousands, but shunned by tens of thousands more who feel somehow queasy, unsettled, about buying an international air ticket for less than list.

By negotiating directly with a score of major airlines, the "buckets" obtain those tickets for 35% to 50% below the normal price, and sell them to the public at discounts of 25% to 40%.

Why the term "bucket shop"? Because most are in shabby, upstairs offices crammed with ancient desks and telephones—the kind of setting remembered from stock market swindles of the 1920s. Owned very often by undercapitalized young people, they lack the colorful cardboard airline displays and racks of glossy brochures found in the traditional travel agencies. Physically, they fill you with dread.

But are they reputable? In my experience, yes. Though one of the leading New York firms was threatened with ruin only recently, it managed to squeak through; and I for one am unaware of any major scandal among them, or of any substantial number of purchasers who have failed to receive a valid ticket for money spent.

This is not to say that the "buckets" are to be trusted sight unseen. They should be visited, not simply phoned; scrutinized for proof of minimal financial resources: a typewriter or two, a desk, a junior employee. You might even protect yourself by a bit of choreography: you hold and hand over payment with your right hand while simultaneously picking up the ticket with your left. Once that's done, you'll immediately see (and sigh with relief) that you've received a totally valid ticket, issued by a real-life airline, but a ticket that's been drastically reduced in price through hard, selective bargaining by the bucket shop.

The Industry Response

Why don't traditional travel agencies engage in the same bargaining for bucket shop–type prices? Some do—but then don't advertise the fact. Eminent trade publications carry ads of "consolidators" (national bucket shops) in New York and St. Louis, offering dramatically reduced air fares to standard travel agencies (which presumably pass on the savings to their clients).

That more travel agents don't seek out these prices is, from my observations, either the result of torpor, inertia, or dullness, or of the inability of some to break away from the mind patterns formed during the recently ended era of airline regulation. Some of the agents are a stubbornly conservative lot.

Others refuse to sell at lower rates because of the claim by their trade association—the American Society of Travel Agents (A.S.T.A.)—that the practice is illegal. A number of half-forgotten treaties and long-ago laws make it arguable that certain forms of rebating in the international field are improper (although rebating of domestic air fares is clearly legal).

But even if that is the law, it is clearly, undeniably, not being enforced. In the face of the most urgent public entreaties by the chairman of A.S.T.A., the Department of Transportation has responded with massive inaction or carefully ambiguous pronouncements; its obvious refusal to turn back the clock and move against the "buckets," has led the rebate-hating *Travel Agent* magazine to write: "While rebating on

They are wholly distinct from the companies selling tickets at the last moment, known as "distress merchants"; the buckets sell their tickets many weeks ahead.

international air-fare tickets may have once been illegal, in the real world it no longer is. . . . This country has decided to let 'em rebate."

Drawbacks of the "Buckets"

So the practice is unrestrained; the bargains are there. Why, then, don't more members of the public patronize the bucket shops? Why don't the customers of discount pharmacies and grocery stores, discount record shops and bookstores, flock in the same numbers and with the same eagerness to the travel bucket shops?

The reason is, in all fairness, that the contexts aren't identical, the products aren't similar. In many instances (not all, but many), the bucket shops do not provide you with quite the same air tickets or perform other highly desirable functions of a travel agent:

• First, the "buckets" provide no travel counseling. Ask one to recommend a hotel, let alone book one, and they will fix you with a glassy stare. Theirs is a staff of order-takers selling air tickets only, and not even all tickets but only certain ones. Full-service travel agents they're not.

• They keep you guessing about the airline you've booked. Unless it is a Third World or Middle East carrier, they won't divulge its identity until you've paid in full. (The reason for the Third World and Middle East exception is that large numbers of the public are unwilling to fly on Bedouin Air or Air Village, and demand to know before they commit.) Bucket shop staff will be fired for divulging the name of any other sort of airline over the phone, thus protecting the "holier-than-thou" reputations of the more prestigious lines.

• Their tickets aren't really the full equivalent of normal ones. They are restricted tickets: nontransferable, nonendorseable, nonchangeable, noncancellable (without hefty penalties), and nonrefundable except from the bucket shop, never from the airline. And rumors persist that if a flight is overbooked, it is "you know who" that gets "bumped" the first.

• They send you, in perhaps a fifth of the cases, on distorted routings. Because the buckets rely in part on underbooked Communist-bloc, Canadian, and Third World carriers, whose route structures require them to fly first to their home cities before proceeding to where most people are going, they sometimes make you do silly things: traveling to Rome or Athens, you first fly all the way to Belgrade or Bucharest, for instance, change planes, and then "backtrack" for several hundred miles to Rome or Athens. Or you fly first to Toronto, change planes, and then use a Canadian carrier to Australia or Europe. Or you go first to Casablanca, change planes, and then fly on to Lisbon or Madrid. You inconvenience yourself and add several hours to the trip, but save hundreds and hundreds of dollars. (And in that Canadian example, the airline absorbs the cost of a flight from the U.S. to Toronto.)

• They make a heavy use of underbooked Middle East carriers to Europe (if that should bother you—and it shouldn't). Even when the itinerary is a reasonably straight line, you frequently fly on carriers you would not ordinarily select, because those carriers make European stops (at heavy discounts) on the way to their capital cities. Thus, from the U.S., Royal Jordanian Airlines (Alia) flies to Vienna or Amsterdam on its way to Amman; Egyptair stops in Paris on its way to Cairo; Kuwait Airways stops in London on the way to Kuwait. While some of these and other Middle East carriers refuse to deal with the buckets, the majority do, and a great many of the cut-rate fares to Europe result from that willingness.

But you needn't be overly edgy. In the great majority of instances, bucket shops are today using seats on the most celebrated of U.S., European, and Asian carriers. I know of only two European airlines that do *not* work on occasion with the buckets. I know of only a single U.S. carrier flying major international routes that definitely doesn't work with the buckets. Multitudes making payments to bucket shops have been pleasantly surprised to receive tickets on the most blue-blooded of airlines bearing household names.

Some Clarifications

Some other clarifications about the role of bucket shops—and a warning or two:

• Don't mistake them for "distress merchants." Note, first, that the buckets are wholly different from those celebrated clubs and firms that market unsold seats on cruises, charter flights, and tours. The latter (names like Stand-Buys, Ltd., Moment's Notice, Vacations to Go, Discount Travel International, Last Minute Cruises—bless 'em all) are known in the trade as "distress merchants," and their savings are normally greater than the buckets'. That's because the distress merchants are frantically rushing to sell products about to perish: unfilled seats and cabins on departures scheduled in the immediate days and weeks ahead. By contrast, the buckets will sell you seats many months ahead—in fact they like to do that—and obviously they're able to discount those to a lesser extent than a last-minute emergency sale would warrant.

• Beware the imitators. Recall, next, that almost all the bucket shops employ a classic and unvarying format in their ads (that's how you spot them): two vertical columns with a list of cities and a list of prices—nothing more. So successful is this approach that many standard and even stodgy retail travel agencies have taken to "aping" it, but with normal, published, nondiscounted fares appearing in their vertical column of prices. The public, thinking they've discovered a bucket shop, rushes to respond—and walks away with no bargain at all. Therefore, in using the Sunday travel sections, look first at all the air-fare ads and compare. Jot down the various prices listed to your desired destination; the cheaper offerings are those of the bucket shops.

• Cull the good from the bad. In addition to studying multiple ads, make multiple phone calls to ascertain how much the ticket really will cost—and from whom. Some bucket shops (the bad ones) will instantly disavow their printed prices in the opening moments of your phone call. "Those are for departures in January," they'll say, or "Those must be booked more than 60 days ahead." Others (the good ones) will stand behind their claims—at least to a certain extent (nearly all of them fudge a bit). I recently made four test calls to bucket shops in Chicago that had all advertised, in late summer, a round-trip fare to Rome of $499. The first

Discount travel agencies now join discount brokerages, discount pharmacies, discount record stores in bringing the benefits of free competition to the traveling public.

Their counterparts have flourished in London for nearly 20 years, but only recently taken root in the U.S. Today nearly 200 are scrambling for business in big cities across the land.

three found various excuses (I had phoned too late, I was leaving too soon, I was traveling in peak season) for offering me a far higher fare of $768; only the fourth confirmed a price as low as $599, on a routing of Chicago–Toronto–Rome. While even the $768 fare would have been a major bargain (because, on an imminent departure, the alternative would have been a much higher standard fare), the advertised rate of $499 carried no mention of advance-purchase requirements. To come as close as $599, as the last one quite definitely did, is the mark of a "good" bucket shop.

• To the Far East, every travel agency should be a bucket shop. Though many of the buckets include flights to Tokyo, Hong Kong, Bangkok, Seoul, Taipei, and Manila in their Sunday ads, such tickets should be available at nearly the same price from your own local travel agency. Nearly every such agency has access to nationwide ticket wholesalers who will pay commissions of 35% and up on flights to the hotly competitive Orient operated by nearly every major carrier. Those astonishing figures are set forth on openly circulated computer printouts mailed to thousands of agents— I'm looking at one as I write this—and obviously, when commissions are that high, they would normally be rebated to the customer, not retained as a windfall by the agent. *Warning*: The same high commissions are not widely available on flights to Australia or New Zealand, and must be sought from a limited number of bucket shops specializing in those and other locations in the South Pacific. For further information on bucket-shop fares to Asia, see the later discussion in this book.

• Beware the expensive nationwide bucket shops. In part the bucket shops achieve their bargains by frugal operations: plain offices in low-rent districts, tiny ads, limited products leaving mainly from their own home cities, local phone calls for which the customer pays. Persons who have responded to nationally advertised toll-free "800" numbers have frequently been quoted prices higher than they could have obtained from a purely local bucket shop. While there are exceptions to this rule (especially among the national wholesalers heavily engaged in selling discount tickets to travel agents and only incidentally to the public), one normally can't have it both ways. If a bucket adopts the expensive practices of the traditional retail seller, its prices must go up.

• Current market prices. It remains to be noted that with so many airlines flying the long-haul routes, the bucket shops are generally glutted with available seats and prices are low indeed. Bucket-shop proprietors with whom I've spoken are currently predicting that their transatlantic air fares for the coming winter of 1989 will drop to a one-way level of $200 or $220 from New York to London, $220–$230 to Paris, the same to Amsterdam, $260–$270 to Rome or Milan; and to a round-trip fare of only $599 to Athens. For equivalent fares from the Midwest, add about $50 each way; from the West Coast, add $85 each way. From New York to Singapore or Kuala Lumpur, some of the buckets will be charging a remarkable $850 round trip, $1,100 round trip from New York to Sydney or Melbourne in the peak-season month (to Australia) of February. To Hawaii from the West Coast, rates show signs of dropping to $275 round trip; to Mexico City, the same West Coast bucket shops will be charging only $265 round trip from Los Angeles, $293 to Acapulco. Except to Hawaii, the buckets will not be offering more than an occasional domestic seat, as winter air fares within the United States are already too low to permit further discounting.

Some Names and Addresses

In the opening section of the Appendix to this book I've set forth short descriptions and identifying information for 30 prominent bucket shops found across the country, in every major area. Although I can't vouch for any one of them, I should point out that every name listed has been in business for at least two years, and seems successful—or at least popular—in what they do.

I should also emphasize that an increasing number of traditional travel agents are now beginning to function (in part) as bucket shops by purchasing air tickets from so-called consolidators (regional or national distributors of cut-rate tickets obtained from airlines)

and reselling them to the public at bucket-shop-level prices.

Other, more traditional travel agencies continue to buck the trend, and issue stern warnings about the alleged impropriety of this form of retailing.

Like the ancient guilds seeking to halt the Industrial Revolution, like Canute vainly holding back the sea, their efforts to thwart the bucket shops are clearly foredoomed.

And isn't that all to the good? In every other economic area Americans benefit from two tiers of retail selling: full-price outlets and discount outlets. Why should travel be any different? Given a choice, numerous Americans will continue to use the full-service travel agencies, which will continue to charge full price (and perhaps an extra fee) for the wisdom of their advice, the beauty of their settings, and the ease of their itineraries. Others will opt for the buckets—the discount agencies offering no advice at all, greeting their customers in squalid lofts, sending them to adventures-in-the-air, via exotic cities and strange airlines.

And thus we enter a new era of travel pricing. Thanks to an unruly slew of scrambling entrepreneurs working out of shabby lofts—who rushed in where travel agents feared to tread—air fares now cost differing amounts depending on the retail outlets from which they are bought. Discount travel agencies now join discount brokerages, discount pharmacies, discount record stores, discount everything, in bringing the benefits of free competition to the traveling public.

As for me, I'll be flying with the "buckets"—traveling to Belgrade to go to Rome, changing planes at Casablanca to go to Lisbon. Just as I find it unnatural, even antisocial, to pay hundreds of dollars extra for a few hours in a first-class seat, so I find it impossible to pass up a saving of several hundreds of dollars gained simply by adding three or so hours to an overnight flight. If you're of a similar mind, you'll join me in a hastily composed ballad, delivered in the tempo, let's say, of Aretha Franklin:

"Singin' the air-fare blues? Prices got you down? Worried 'bout the tab? Try a bucket shop!" ≈

The Economics of a Trip to Asia

Rebating of Transpacific Air Fares Has Made a Trip to the Far East Almost as Cheap as One to Europe

Opposite page: *Far Eastern artisan*

In a sudden, sharp, and unprecedented shift of geographic preferences, Americans will be traveling by the droves this year to Asia. With the U.S. dollar languishing at almost-abysmal levels against nearly every European currency, Asia has become the destination of travel bargains.

In Bangkok, you can pay a dollar for a three-course meal. In Djakarta, the rate at modest restaurants is about the same. With the single, glaring exceptions of Japan and Taiwan, every Asian nation is at least moderately priced, and two—Indonesia and Thailand—are among the cheapest on earth.

Equally important, and fully as startling, the transportation cost of a trip to Asia can often be reduced to not much more than many are paying to cross the Atlantic. That ability—astonishing, in view of the distances involved—results from the use of so-called air-fare consolidators and travel bucket shops in the fly-to-Asia market. Travelers who know how and where to find the discounted rates can currently journey from the West Coast to the farthest reaches of the Pacific rim—as many as 15 flying hours away—for as little as $600 round trip.

A Little History

Though some traditional travel people tend to "blame" this development on others, it all comes about by deliberate, conscious decision of the airlines. However much they offer secret discounts across the Atlantic, carriers are involved to an even greater extent in "gray markets" across the Pacific. Whereas up to 20% of all U.S.-originating, transatlantic passengers were estimated to have received under-the-counter discounts in 1988 (ask any travel professional), the figure reaches 35% in the Pacific field. To many Asian nations, and in most months of the year, it is only the chump who pays full price.

The heavy discounting of transpacific air fares began at least two decades ago, and was initially concentrated in the Asian ethnic market on the West Coast. The existence of large Asian populations in Los Angeles and San Francisco proved an irresistible lure to airlines

engaged in a hotly competitive battle to fill an overabundance of empty seats. They began selling their tickets at lower-than-published rates to a select number of West Coast agencies ("consolidators") headed by persons of Asian descent, who in turn serviced an ethnic clientele eager to make frequent trips for the purpose of visiting friends and relatives. They—the airlines—made such reduced-price sales in the almost sure knowledge that the agencies or their subagents would in turn pass on ("rebate") a portion of the discount to passengers, and thus increase the frequency with which they traveled.

A similar development, on a far lesser scale, was taking place among ethnic populations on the East Coast. For years smart New Yorkers have known that if they wished to acquire discount tickets to Brazil, they had only to visit the ethnic travel agencies located on West 46th Street ("Little Rio") serving the expatriate Brazilian population of New York. If they wished cheap tickets to the Dominican Republic, they went to ethnic Dominican travel agencies on the Upper West Side of Manhattan, all of them amply and eagerly stocked with cut-rate tickets by airlines seeking to acquire a "lock" on the Dominican market.

But all such activity paled alongside the massive West Coast discounting of tickets to Asia.

And the market, in the view of some, soon grew unruly. Made giant in size by the attractive price of their merchandise, and spurred even further by deregulation of the aviation industry in 1978, the Asian consolidators began channeling their reduced-price tickets to non-ethnic travel agencies as well, which in turn began selling them to mere vacationers and not simply to Asians visiting friends and relatives.

(Incidentally, if the possessor of cut-rate tickets simply distributes them to travel agencies, it is known in the trade as a consolidator. If the travel agency then sells the ticket at lower-than-published price to the public, it is often known as a bucket shop.)

Buying from the Consolidators

Among the leading consolidators of tickets to Asia are: **C. L. Thomson Express International of San Francisco** (with smaller offices in New York, Los Angeles, and Honolulu; its president is the dynamic George Chen; phone San Francisco headquarters at 415/398-2535, or New York at 212/687-2721); **Star Tours, Inc., of Los Angeles** (with offices in Dallas, Houston, San Francisco, and New York; its executive vice-president and general manager, George Fung, was formerly a district manager for a large Asian airline; phone 213/483-5900); and **CNH International of Los Angeles** (with offices in San Diego, San Francisco, Washington, D.C., Chicago, New York, and Honolulu; its president is Patsy Ho; phone the main office at 213/387-2288). While C. L. Thomson also deals in tickets to Europe, for which it offers commissions to agents of 17% to 22%, its monthly computer printout distributed to 9,000 travel agencies lists commissions of a full 30% to 35%, and sometimes as high as 40%, on the Asian services of no fewer than 15 distinguished airlines. Asian seats are therefore discounted to a far greater degree than European ones.

Largest commissions (and thus the largest potential discounts) are to expensive Japan, where few Americans are presently vacationing. Smallest commissions are to Australia and New Zealand, both of which are enjoying a tourist boom.

According to the consolidators, if these tickets were purchased by the public at full published price, they would cost a round-trip average (to most Asian destinations) of $1,400 on a non-excursion basis, $900 if purchased 14 to 30 days in advance and with excursion restrictions. By purchasing them instead from either bucket shops or traditional retail travel agencies obtaining the tickets from consolidators, the public pays only $600 on the average, round trip from the West Coast. And they get the tickets without having to heed advance-purchase requirements.

Specifically, says one consolidator, passengers dealing with discount travel agents should be paying around $500 to $600 round trip from the West Coast to Tokyo or Seoul, as little as $550 to Hong Kong in low season, $650 in high season. To Bangkok or Singapore, figure $780; the same to Djakarta if they overnight in another Asian city en route. High season is the three summer months and part of December, when tickets are difficult to obtain.

Round-trip surcharge for East Coast departures: around $200.

The tickets obtained in this discounted fashion are, of course, valid only on the carrier issuing them; they are "non-endorseable" and thus different from usual airline tickets. Apart from that, they seem (to me, at least) hardly distinguishable from other normal tickets. Although they are good only for the dates and flights appearing on them, and also carry various cancellation penalties, so do normal advance-purchase excursion tickets issued by airlines. If purchased from a reputable travel agent or bucket shop, which in turn obtained them from a reputable consolidator, they should present you with no meaningful problem; and because they can often be obtained without lengthy advance purchase, they could be said to be more flexible than normal airline tickets in at least one respect.

But carefully check the reputation of the retail outlet from which you obtain them.

One such outlet selling discounted Asian tickets to the public is **STA Travel of Los Angeles** (with branch offices in San Francisco, Boston, New York, Chicago, Dallas, and elsewhere; although heavily in the student market, it deals with all ages, and makes a heavy use of consolidators). You can reach them by phoning their Los Angeles office (213/934-8722, or toll free 800/777-0112 outside California); or their branches in Boston (617/266-6014), Chicago (312/525-9227), New York (212/986-9470), or Dallas (214/360-0097). Another discount firm is the large **Euro-Asia Express of Millbrae, California** (near San Francisco), whose vice-president—a former prominent airline official—has advised me that his firm can frequently secure round-trip tickets from the West Coast to Bangkok on a Canadian carrier, in winter and early spring, for a price to the public of as little as $660 (otherwise, and in other seasons, for $800). Euro-Asia is at 475 El Camino Real, Suite Penthouse, Millbrae, CA 94030 (phone 415/692-9966, or toll free 800/782-9625 outside California).

If you'd rather work with a retailer in your own home city, seek out any solid travel agency that works with consolidators (ask them, point-blank, whether they do) and is willing to pass on a part of the saving to you. Many thousands of retail agencies are presently in that position.

Is it legal? That's for speculative, ivory-tower philosophers to argue: Is a massively unenforced statute still on the books? Although the rebating of international air fares would seem to violate the Federal Aviation Act of 1958, various officials of the Department of Transportation—the agency charged with enforcing the law—have repeatedly and formally announced that they have no intention of ever doing so, absent very special circumstances. This country abhors price-fixing, admires discounters, and has decided to let travel agents rebate (which many of them have been doing anyway, for their large corporate customers, for years).

By obtaining discounted tickets from retail travel agents dealing with consolidators, Americans can travel to Asia this year for not much more than they'd pay for a ticket to Europe. They can vacation, once there, at moderate cost. For the first time in travel history, average-income Americans can respond to the age-old lure of the Orient—and that's a reason to rejoice.

"For the temple bells are calling," as Kipling wrote, "and it's there that [we] would be, By the old Moulmein Pagoda, looking lazy at the sea." ≈

Floating market of Bangkok

Should Americans Use the Bucket Shops of Britain?

Though London Has the World's Greatest Array of Buckets, They Don't Always Serve the Needs of a Traveling American

The "bucket shop" was born in Britain. As early as the mid-1960s, carriers based in London made a practice of quietly assigning several seats per flight to struggling travel agencies on Earls Court Road, there to be sold at discounted rates—discreetly, without fanfare—to the ethnic and other impecunious types that clustered in that low-income section of the city.

From those beginnings emerged a flock of "discount travel agencies" (bucket shops) that still tend to be clustered on Earls Court Road or nearby. They sell reduced-price air tickets to nearly every destination of the world, on a broad variety of carriers and in giant quantities.

One such firm handles 150,000 passengers a year; it enjoys that volume simply and solely because it offers a "deal": prices lower than published rates.

Should you, an American, make use of the British buckets? The answer is rather complex.

Scarcely any British bucket shop—a notable exception is Poundsavers (see below)—will sell tickets on flights originating in U.S. cities. But even from Poundsavers, the thought of making such a purchase by transatlantic correspondence or phone call is really too daunting, expensive, or tedious to consider.

Should you, then, on long-range flights to cities well beyond London, fly first to London and purchase your onward flight on the spot from a bucket shop in London?

Not unless you truly wish to enjoy a stay in London on the way to your ultimate destination, or unless you have no access to the discounted rates offered by American bucket shops. Although you may occasionally enjoy a price saving in that fashion, over what you would have spent in a U.S. bucket shop for the same long-distance ticket, the burden of a London stop, and the uncertainty over the availability there of a discounted onward ticket, make the effort unwise.

Watch Your Step!

Thus, even if a New York–to-London ticket, combined with a London-to-Cairo ticket from a London bucket shop, costs less than a straight New York–to-

Scarcely any British bucket shop will sell tickets on flights originating in U.S. cities.

Cairo ticket, bear in mind that you may not be able to find that discounted London-to-Cairo ticket on arrival in London. Bucket-shop availabilities are notoriously fluid—here today, gone tomorrow.

However, let's assume you crave an intermediate stay in London. And are willing to take a chance. In that case, some wondrous possibilities await.

But not so wondrous as would appear in the London newspaper ads. Like most U.S. bucket shops, the British buckets are famous for headlining "low-ball" prices that aren't realistically available, or are offered only on Tuesday, or only on minor carriers.

Responding to a round-trip, bucket-shop price of, say, £57 ($97) between London and Paris, you quickly learn that the miracle rate is available only under special conditions, and that you really need to pay £73 ($124). While the latter is still an excellent price and a considerable saving over published rates, it is a sobering letdown from the euphoria occasioned by the ads (again, U.S. newspaper ads by bucket shops are often just as misleading).

What's Cheap, and What's Not

To where do the British buckets offer their best prices? To Africa and India.

To where do they offer rates no better than those available from U.S. buckets? To Australia and the Far East.

On what flights do they offer rates that are totally unavailable from U.S. bucket shops? On all intra-European flights from London to, say, Nice or Rome or Istanbul. Or to destinations that few American bucket shops serve, like Nairobi.

Some Names and Addresses

Which of the British buckets should you use? Out of 14 I've interviewed, 7 seem attractive:

Poundsavers, 254 Earls Court Rd. (phone 373-6465), is a cocky little firm that's proud to be called a bucket shop and claims to offer the city's cheapest fares to anywhere; these include an around-the-world rate of only £799 ($1,358) for the trip from London to Bangkok to Hong Kong to Taipei to Tokyo to San Francisco to New York to London. Closer in, their price is £59 ($100) for the round trip between London and Paris; £110 ($187) round trip to Munich, Rome, Madrid, or Vienna; £175 ($297) round trip to Tel Aviv; £349 ($593) round trip to New Delhi. They'll also book New York to London. A guarantee of reliability? Their nine years in business, says manager Roger Samtami.

Trailfinders, 42-48 Earls Court Rd. (phone 938-3366), in business since 1970, is the biggest of the British buckets, but doesn't like to be called one, and is a tad more expensive in its advertised rates than the others. That's because, Trailfinders says, its advertised prices are realistic ones, not unavailable "come-ons."

Whether 'tis so or not, Trailfinders' service is indisputably the finest: highly computerized and efficient, and featuring a staff of 150, an on-premises vaccination clinic and valuable travel library. Its round-trip rates are well under £102 ($173) to Berlin, Geneva, Frankfurt, or Zurich; its around-the-world fare of $1,419 a winner.

Soliman Travel, in a brightly lit, second-floor office at **233 Earls Court Rd. (phone 370-6446),** staffed by what appear to be a dozen people, specializes in fares to Spanish-speaking countries (Spain, Latin America, Puerto Rico), but claims its rates to the Middle East are also competitive with those of other shops. Round trip, London to Madrid, can go as low as £59 ($100) in low season, round-trip to Tel Aviv for only £100 to £150 ($170 to $255), low and high season.

Pan Pacific, 16A Soho Square (phone 734-3094), near the Tottenham Court Road subway station, is London's specialist to Australia and New Zealand, but charges no less from London than scheduled airlines do for the trip from U.S. cities to Australia; unless you wish to visit London first, it pays to fly directly to Australia from our own gateway cities.

London Student Travel Agency, at 52 Grosvenor Gardens a block from Victoria Station, **(phone 730-3402),** will deal with travelers of any age, despite the name, and sells cut-rate tickets to everywhere at competitive rates (London to Rome for $204 round

trip; London to New York at $472 round trip). It also operates year-round charters to Paris at the remarkable round-trip rate of £49 ($83) (these can be booked during the week of flight), and advance-purchase summer charters to Nice, Athens, and Milan (the Athens trip selling for only $168 in low season, $212 at other times, round trip, enabling a low-price London-Athens holiday).

S.T.A. ("Student Travel Agency"), at 74 Old Brompton Rd. (phone 581-1022), near the South Kensington subway stop, is another of those youth-oriented bucket shops that actually sells to all ages. A 31-year-old Australian organization with offices around the world, its rates are low but reliable, and highly touted to me by several customers I've met. Indeed, to some destinations from London, they're the lowest around: £399 ($678) round trip to Nairobi; £199 ($338) round trip to Tel Aviv; £399 ($678) round trip to Bangkok; £199 ($338) round trip from London to New York; £125 ($212) round trip to Copenhagen.

A final London source, **Topdeck Travel of 131 Earls Court Rd. (phone 373-8406),** is primarily known for its double-decker bus tours of Europe and Asia (operated for young people only), but also sells discounted air tickets to everywhere, and to everyone of any age. On trips from London to the major African capitals, it often sends you on Aeroflot via Moscow. Though that seems a bit absurd, and adds many hours to the flight, the routing saves hundreds of dollars.

In scanning the choices, Poundsavers and S.T.A. stand out if low cost is your sole consideration. If service and advice are needed as well, try Trailfinders—though possibly at a slightly higher price. But whatever the comparative merits of different firms, think hard about using a bucket if you're flying anywhere from London.

In the capital city of the bucket-shop movement, it may be that only the chump pays full price. ≈

Unscrambling the Transatlantic Air Fares

A Mystifying Assortment of Prices and Possibilities Now Confronts the Would-be Traveler to Europe—and I'm Gonna Explain It All!

Chartered or scheduled?

Once it was as simple as choosing champagne or beer, caviar or marmalade. You either flew to Europe on a scheduled flight or you went there by charter. If you opted for the latter, you saved $200. Period.

Now it's . . . uh, it's . . . uh, well, it's not that easy at all. It is, in fact, an unholy mess. A plot devised by the Marx Brothers. The charter is no longer the cheapest means of crossing the Atlantic. And at least five entirely new travel-industry concepts—"bucket shops," "distress merchants," "cheap airlines," "backhauls," and "periodic standbys"—have made an all-but-incomprehensible hash out of the normal calculation of air fares to Europe. With heart in mouth, PC Jr. at hand, I'll try to impose a bit of order—but only a bit—on the single most confusing subject in travel today.

Introducing: the "Cheap Airlines"

If there is any constant at all on the transatlantic scene, it is that two feisty carriers flying from Newark (New Jersey) International Airport—Virgin Atlantic and Continental—provide not necessarily the cheapest, but the most consistently available, all-year-round "cheap" fares to Europe. **Virgin Atlantic (phone 212/242-1330, or toll free 800/862-8621 outside New York City)** charges a maximum of $329 each way between Newark and London's Gatwick Airport, for a midweek crossing at the peak of the summer season, on a ticket purchased at least 21 days in advance (it charges considerably less—$289 and $219—in "shoulder" and "low" seasons). On tickets purchased within seven days of departure (the "LateSaver"), it reduces the rate to $289 each way (and to as little as $239 and $199 in "shoulder" and "winter" seasons). On tickets purchased on the very day of departure (a true standby) the Virgin price plummets to $259 in peak summer months, but standbys of this sort are not offered in other months.

Continental Airlines (phone toll free 800/231-0856) has no standby fare, and requires 21 days' advance booking for its lowest summer fare, but charges only $685 round trip for a midweek flight between Newark and London's Gatwick Airport at the very peak of the summer season. It then offers a much lower, 30-day advance-purchase rate in "shoulder" and "winter" seasons: $558 round trip in shoulder season, a spectacular $398 in winter.

A lesser-known but thoroughly reliable "cheap airline" known as **Tower Air (phone 718/917-8500)** flies a sleek 747 jumbo jet from JFK Airport New York to Copenhagen, Oslo, and Stockholm at round-trip rates to Copenhagen of $630 in peak summer, for only $599 starting August 15, and thereafter (in winter) for $515. Those rates are not much more than you'd pay for a charter flight to Scandinavia, and they position the "cheap airlines" as potent rivals of the charter, to which we now turn.

Those Newly Dependable Charters

Heirs to a checkered past, survivors of a cut-throat competition that has by now eliminated the thinly financed firms, closely regulated by the Department of Transportation, and often owned by celebrated international airlines, today's charter-tour operators and charter airlines are a largely respectable lot whose record of financial responsibility, physical safety, and on-time performance compares quite well with that of the scheduled carriers. Their rates are also refreshingly cheap: an average of $229 to $239 one way from New York to London in summer, $229 to $249 to Paris in the same season, $239 and up to Zurich and Munich, with proportionately higher levels from inland U.S. cities ($80 or so more each way from Los Angeles). But are these the second-cheapest levels to Europe? Fairly comparable to Continental, Virgin Atlantic, and Tower? Not always, because of—

The Rapidly Emerging "Bucket Shops"

Use a "bucket shop" and you can improve on the published prices of the charters, while sometimes using a scheduled flight all the while! And what are "the buckets"? Well (as noted earlier in this book), despite the unfortunate name, these are perfectly respectable, distressingly normal retail outlets scattered about the country who simply happen to enjoy a favored relation-

ship with one or more charter-flight operators or so-called consolidators of air tickets or international airlines; the latter use the bucket shops to dispose of a percentage of their seats at cut-rate prices—and not merely for last-minute availabilities, either. In the summer of 1988 you could, by visiting a bucket shop in Chicago, for instance, purchase scheduled seats for departures many weeks ahead at the remarkable round-trip rates of $699 between Chicago and Rome or Athens, only $599 between Chicago and London— better than most charter prices from the same city. While some traditional travel agents have angrily questioned the legality of selling international tickets through bucket shops, no official entity has yet moved against them or seems likely to do so; and if they should, it will be the bucket that's in trouble, not you the customer.

Where do you find the bucket shops? You look in the Sunday newspaper travel sections for small, one-column, two-inch ads consisting exclusively of a vertical column of European and Asian cities set next to a vertical column of round-trip prices—nothing more. The airline offering each fare is never listed, and can be ascertained only when you actually purchase your ticket. Nor is any other explanatory material included, not even a claim that these fares are, in fact, lower than official levels. Yet when you check the rates with others of which you've heard, you'll immediately notice a sharp reduction.

Warning: Some non–bucket shops have taken to imitating the classic format of the bucket shop ads, but with ordinary, nondiscounted prices appearing in them. It is important to compare the rates to similar cities in the various ads in order to pluck out the advantageous bucket shops from the ordinary offers surrounding them.

How do the airlines justify their use of bucket shops? Some claim that these discounts result from commitments made by the shops to purchase tickets in bulk. Others insist that these are "introductory fares" (whatever those may be) made available through special outlets; or else they profess ignorance that their fares are being discounted, or retort that you should "Mind your

Use a "bucket shop"—and you can improve on the published prices of the charters, while sometimes using a scheduled flight all the while.

own business." However they operate, the bucket shops seem a now-permanent fixture on the travel scene, and are increasingly used by the most cost-conscious of travelers. But do they provide the cheapest of transatlantic crossings? No, that honor goes to the—

Increasingly Prosperous "Distress Merchants"

For years, charter operators, cruise-ship companies, hotel chains, and resorts have made quiet, last-minute sales of their unsold seats, berths, and rooms at discounts of as much as 50% off published rates. In the week or so before sailings or air departures, amazing reductions are available, and the smartest of travelers actually go to the docks on the day of departure, or to the airports, and there bargain for that unsold berth or charter seat—the "distress merchandise" of travel.

Where there is merchandise, there are merchants, and at least a dozen "distress merchandise" companies (I've listed several in the Appendix to this book) now provide their subscribers with recorded listings of last-minute discounts on imminent travel departures, all via toll-free "800" numbers to be phoned on the Wednesday evening before a weekend of departures. By thus calling just a few days ahead, thousands of travelers crossed the Atlantic for as little as $179, one way, in the summer of 1988. They occupied seats on charter flights drastically reduced in price as a means of filling a few unsold places.

Bear in mind that radically discounted, eve-of-departure fares of this sort are regularly offered on charters and cruises, but only occasionally on the flights of scheduled airlines; the latter have thus far stayed aloof from the "distress merchants" (but not from the bucket shops offering lesser discounts). And distress merchandise is, of course, useful only to people with flexible work schedules, able to travel on a "moment's notice." The same brand of individual is able to use still another cheap device for crossing the Atlantic—

On-Again, Off-Again Standby Fares

Though low-cost standby air fares to London have been available for several years, the concept was only recently extended to Brussels, Amsterdam, and Vienna, though not for every month of the year. A "now-you-see-it, now-you-don't" device, valid only during certain periods, withdrawn at other times, the very existence of standby privileges must always be constantly checked in advance by phoning the various airlines. Still, for a great many months of the year, virtually all airlines flying to London offer standby fares of $269, one way from New York, a bit more from other cities. In several months of the year TWA offers a $169 standby youth fare for ages 12 to 25 to Amsterdam or Brussels from New York (higher from other cities). And Tarom Romanian Airlines, of all unlikely candidates, offers a $225 one-way standby fare from New York to Vienna on Tuesday and Friday evenings in most months.

But what can you use if your plans are to fly to the more remote European cities, for which no standby, charter flight, bucket shop, or distress merchant may be available? Ready, now, for a "weirdy"? You book the "back-haul" flights of Communist-bloc or Canadian airlines.

"Back-hauls"

I'll assume (with little chance of contradiction) that you have no interest in flying to Belgrade, Bucharest, Moscow, or Toronto, but that you'd be more than willing to pass through these cities on the way to your desired destination if the price were right. That, in essence, is the appeal of "back-haul" business. A great many Americans currently fly to Athens via Belgrade (though it's an awkward routing), or to Israel via Bucharest, or to Rome via Toronto (though this requires backtracking several hundred miles from New York or Boston first) because of the considerable price advantages offered to such passengers by airlines serving Belgrade, Bucharest, or Toronto. It is even possible to cut the London–Nairobi air fare considerably by flying there on Aeroflot, via Moscow! Though many traditional travel agents haven't the foggiest notion of how to accomplish these "back-haul" reductions, most bucket shops do, and a number of their most appealing values are based on these out-of-the-

way routings that add several hours to the flight but save several hundreds of dollars.

Why do we go to such lengths to ferret out ever-cheaper means of crossing the Atlantic? It is because a yearly trip to Europe, for many Americans, has become the almost essential requisite of a civilized life. Europe—the repository of our heritage, the mature corrective for our less-polished ways, the sophisticated teacher of arts, fashion, and cuisine—is regarded by many as too important a pleasure to be thwarted by high air costs. "Europe is worth the effort," say more than six million yearly travelers to Europe from U.S. cities, and as long as that mighty an urge exists, then bucket shops and other exotic merchandisers of travel will continue to delight us with their artful schemes and devices. ≈

Unscrambling the Domestic Air Fares Mess

By Following Several Little-Known Approaches to the Purchase of Air Tickets, You Can Heighten the Chances of Paying a Lower Fare

Though high cholesterol and triglycerides are often blamed for heart attacks, I believe that domestic air fares are far more frequently the culprit.

Picture this. You have just been told that the cheapest rate by air from Pittsburgh to Portland, Oregon, is a whopping $505, one way. "$505!" you shout, as veins contract and pulses quicken. "That's right," says the airline reservationist. "You didn't call us far enough in advance."

And, resignedly, you board the flight, troubled and a bit unhinged, but willing to accept that dozens aboard have paid only $169 for tickets purchased seven days in advance. Yet as the plane takes off, you discover that the business traveler in the next seat has paid only $280 for a ticket purchased two days later than you did. And that the matron in the seat ahead has been charged only $370 for a ticket purchased that morning. What's more, she advises, a friend traveling to Portland on a later flight that day, on a different but equally prestigious airline, will be paying only $249 for the very same journey.

And suddenly, vision blurs, the chest constricts, small stabbing pains arrive to. . . .

Who's to blame for this unsettling condition? The airlines? The now-defunct Civil Aeronautics Board (which deregulated the airlines in 1978)? Your travel agent? While deregulation is the basic cause, it is often a less-than-comprehensive computer, a less-than-diligent retail travel agent or airline reservations clerk, who can cause you to overlook the cheapest fare for your flight. As maddening as it may seem, securing advantageous air fares is frequently an art, not a science, requiring that you master a code of musical-like notes and notations—in the form of an awesome, illogical alphabet soup.

Your Airline ABCs

When deregulation occurred, a once-simple division of most domestic air fares into three basic categories—first class, coach, and "excursion"—exploded into a proliferation of fares, as many as a dozen per flight, each designated by a letter of the alphabet. When your travel agent "pulls up" an air-fare screen on a computer terminal, what comes to light is a forest of alphabetical letters next to prices. Though some letters are uniform throughout the travel industry, others are arbitrarily chosen by individual airlines. A "K"-class fare on TWA can approximate a "Q"-class fare on Eastern airlines or a "B"-class fare on United.

The *top-priced fares* are easy to understand, but irrelevant to most travelers. "P" is preferred class, for deluxe sleeperettes costing $918 from Los Angeles to New York. "F" is first class ($868 for the same), "C" and "J" are business class (on Pan Am and TWA only, transcontinental), and "Y" is that old standard, an unrestricted economy-class seat costing $560 for a one-way transcontinental flight, to use a single example.

Then come the reduced-price *advance-purchase fares*, available for the most part on a round-trip basis only, to people purchasing them several to many days ahead of departure—either 7 days in advance ("Q" class on most airlines), 14 days in advance ("M" class), 2 days in advance ("B" class on some, "H" class on others), or even 3 days in advance to a handful of cities ("K" class on several airlines). Advance-purchase fares also require, in all but isolated cases, that your stay at the destination extend over a Saturday night, but for no more than a maximum number of days; that the tickets be paid in full within 24 hours after the reservation has been made; and that you assume a penalty exposure (25% to 100% of the fare) for cancelling the transaction. By securing an advance-purchase fare, you save as much as 45% off for purchases made 14 days in advance, 25% off for those made 7 days in advance.

Next come the discount fares restricted to *Saturday* flights or other slow days of the week ("KL" class on TWA, "Q" or "B" on others). And finally, certain *unrestricted discount fares* ("B" class or "M" class, or even "K" class, according to airline) are offered to a scattered few cities—these being ultra-cheap tickets available in small quantities per flight, and sold down to the very day of departure on flights to, say, Miami or Denver or Atlanta, where heavy airline competition reigns.

It is often a less-than-comprehensive computer, a less-than-diligent retail travel agent or airline reservations clerk, who can cause you to overlook the cheapest fare for your flight.

"Capacity Controls"—the *Catch-22* of Aviation

To each of these alphabetical designations (and the discount fares they represent), the airlines allot a limited number of seats ("capacity controls"). To some popular flights they allot no discount fares whatever, regardless of whether would-be passengers have booked 30 or 14 days in advance. To others they allot a few, to some, a great many. And therein lies the rub. Not only can the number of discount seats be set at a low figure, but that figure can periodically be raised or lowered, removed or reinstated, revised on even an hourly basis by the sophisticated computers programmed to maximize the airline's revenue from a particular flight. Thus a passenger seeking on June 1 to purchase a 30-day "super-saver" leaving on October 1 can be told that no seats remain to be sold at that price. Yet a similarly situated passenger phoning the very next day may obtain a seat at super-saver levels, either because another super-saver passenger has cancelled or, infuriatingly, because the airline has simply decided to make additional super-saver seats available on a slow-selling flight. (It's as if the airline prices were written in water, or projected by flickering candlelight on the walls of a cave, as banks of ominous, faintly humming computers go about tampering with our budgets and expectations.)

In a similar fashion, the number of so-called unrestricted "M"-class or "B"-class fares for particular flights may be initially set at a fairly low level, but then raised in quantity as the departure date approaches. Which means that business traveler Richard Smith phoning on Tuesday may be unable to fly cheaply on that Thursday, but business traveler Robert Smith phoning on Wednesday gets the cut-rate Thursday seat! Or else a high level of discount seats for a particular departure may suddenly be reduced. Does any other retail industry in America experience such rapid fluctuations in price?

The Rewards of Diligence

But the system isn't perfect, and the public can fight back. The smart traveler, after purchasing a higher-priced ticket, makes a daily phone call to the airline to determine whether a discount opportunity has surfaced at a later time. You make these calls down to the last date of advance purchase (for "Q" or "M" super-savers) or down to the very day of departure (for unrestricted "B"- or "K"-class fares). While, given the low state of travel-agency commissions on domestic air fares, it probably isn't fair to ask your travel agent to make those daily calls, it pays for you to make them, and then to demand that your fare be replaced by a cheaper one when discounts materialize.

You can even attempt to "override" the computer when the airline announces that all advance-purchase seats or unrestricted "B"-class fares are gone. While a great many travel-industry professionals will vehemently deny that this can be done, I can cite occasion after occasion when determined travel agents have successfully asked to "speak with a supervisor" in the wake of a discount turndown. By then using their own special "clout" with the airline, by implying a loss of that sale to the airline, by threatening to remonstrate to a "district manager" (and sometimes doing so), by citing a particular emergency need of the passenger, they have been able to persuade an airline official in "Inventory Control" to add a discount seat or two to a flight where none is shown. To claim, as some do, that airlines will not (supposedly on principle) perform such a favor for a favored, hard-hitting travel agent is to believe in fairy tales, goblins, and sleeping princesses. Smart travelers make their choice of travel agents with just this in mind.

"Cutting Up" the Trip

Diligence also pays off in utilizing discount fares on individual segments of your journey to undercut the "through" or direct fares to your destination. As noted earlier, the airlines often offer "unrestricted" (in the sense that they need no advance purchase) but "capacity-controlled" discount fares to cities where heavy airline competition warrants it, or to cities where they are seeking to develop an efficient "hub" operation. TWA does that to St. Louis; others, to Miami or Denver. Yet although such fares appear on computer screens, their use in constructing longer flights is not always apparent to the travel agent or airline reservations clerk. Thus in the example that began this essay, a travel agent inquiring of a computer as to the cheapest last-minute seat from Pittsburgh to Portland, Oregon, may see only an American Airlines flight costing $505 each way. It is only when that agent "digs" and experiments with various possible segments for such a trip—say, Pittsburgh to Denver, then Denver to Portland—that he or she discovers the chance to combine two United Airlines flights, Pittsburgh to Denver to Portland, for a total of only $320. That's because United Airlines offers unrestricted "B"-class fares on those heavily competitive segments. Yet, surprisingly, fares for the two "B"-class segments—Pittsburgh to Denver and Denver to Portland—fail to appear on the computer screen for flights from Pittsburgh to Portland, but only on screens specifically requesting those segments.

In other words, the eagerness, inventiveness, competence, and vigor of your travel agent can make a substantial difference to your airline costs. For the airline computers are not infallible; they do not always reveal the full range of pricing possibilities—they must be jolted or caressed, pressed or pestered by human hands. The same approach can also enable not simply a travel agent but an airline reservationist to achieve an extra result for you. By testing various trip segments, by trying flights via different cities, by adding the segments into a lesser total, they can achieve savings. If you do phone the airlines directly, it's important to stress to such personnel that you may not book on their airline unless they fly you at a discount rate. "Isn't there anything cheaper?" "Isn't there anything cheaper?" should be your irksome refrain. And then: "Can you check with a supervisor?" More frequently than you'd expect, an initial turndown can then become a "Yes."

Those Short-Term Price Wars

You'll note that I have not referred to the periodic airline "price wars" that blossom in newspaper ads, announcing almost absurdly low fares for short, intensive periods of time—like the three days commencing

As maddening as it may seem, securing advantageous air fares is frequently an art, not a science, requiring that you master an awesome, illogical alphabet soup.

Not only can the number of discount seats be set at a low figure, but that figure can periodically be raised or lowered, removed or reinstated, revised on even an hourly basis by sophisticated computers.

on Thanksgiving, or in the midweeks of January—to Miami. Under deregulation, airlines can slash their prices for even a single day, and no one—not even the airline executives—can now predict whether such "seat sales" will be repeated at the same time next year. Nor have I dealt with the wonderfully low-priced, but nonrefundable, "MaxSaver" fares, whose continued existence is very much in doubt (expect them to resurface only in slow winter periods of the year). In this essay I have dealt only with the fares available throughout the year, every year.

. . . And Those "Cheap Airlines"

Nor have I written, yet, about those "cheap airlines" that price every one of their seats on every flight at low rates, without requiring advance purchase and without imposing pesky "capacity controls." Such names as Southwest Airlines, Continental, Braniff, and (to a lesser extent) Midway are among those following a firm policy of always undercutting the standard "Y"-class fares of such longer-established airlines as American, United, Delta, TWA, and Northwest. But though they offer savings, and should be mentioned in our prayers each night, the "cheap airlines" do not always provide the least expensive means of flying from city to city. Rather, a limited number of standard discount air fares are lower than even those of Continental and Braniff, although heavily ringed with restrictions on their use.

The Cheapest Air Fares Going

Currently, the cheapest air fares in all the land are those for advance-purchase seats sold more than 30 or 21 days ahead of departure (and called "MaxSavers" or "Ultra Savers" by leading airlines). Provided only that you can make such flight decisions as far in advance as that, and then adhere to those plans, you should be paying as little as $149 from New York to Los Angeles in autumn months, and a remarkably low $69 or $89 from the East Coast to Cleveland or Milwaukee on several distinguished airlines. Those rates are cheaper than the probable Continental or Braniff fares for the months ahead, and cheaper than those of any other "cheap airline," but available, again, only to those few prudent travelers who can make their fixed-in-concrete appointments so long in advance.

If you can't, then your next-cheapest level of fares is on the "cheap airlines" of the Braniff or Southwest Air ilk. Long may they survive! Thanks to these philanthropists of the air, cardio-fitness and stress-free longevity are on the rise again among America's air travelers. And let's hope that some of the approaches advised in this essay will also stave off the day when your gorge rises, and temples pound, and veins constrict . . . at the thought of a one-way domestic air fare costing $505!

Some Air-fare Tricks the Airlines Wish You Didn't Know

Shakespeare would have said they were "hoist on their own petard." So low have the airlines priced their round-trip "MaxSavers" that they have inadvertently nullified several of their high-priced one-way fares.

Let's assume that you, a New Yorker, are moving to California on a permanent basis. The airlines say you'll need to pay a one-way coach fare of $560. So what do you do? You buy a round-trip MaxSaver for $318 and then throw away, give away, or even sell the return ticket; if you can find a purchaser willing to fly under your name, you've made the trip to California free!

The same airlines have inadvertently nullified their occasional requirement that you stay for no more than 30 days at the destination when using a MaxSaver. Let's say you wish to fly from New York to California on June 1 and return on October 1. Because your stay there is for more than 30 days, the airlines (at some times of the year) refuse to sell you a MaxSaver, and require instead that you buy two one-way $560 coach tickets for a total of $1,120. So what do you do? You buy two round-trip MaxSavers. One is from New York to California on June 1, returning on the arbitrarily chosen date of June 8. The other, from California to New York on October 1, is to return on the equally fake date of October 8. You then proceed to throw away (or give away) the unnecessary halves of both tickets and fly to and fro for a total of $636 (two times

$318) instead of $1,120. And if you can sell the two unused halves, you have flown free.

Other such anomalies abound. On one domestic airline, at the time of writing it costs less to fly from New York City to Muskegon, Michigan, via Chicago ($104), than simply to fly to Chicago alone ($325). At one time it cost less to fly to Austin, Texas, via Dallas than simply to fly to Dallas. Consequently, many Chicago- and Dallas-bound passengers have saved by purchasing tickets to Muskegon or Austin but walking off the plane at Chicago or Dallas. If they had luggage other than carry-ons, they checked the bags to Chicago or Dallas at curbside, where the redcaps aren't nearly as concerned as the counter personnel would be with the fact that the passenger is "underflying."

Choosing the Right Travel Agent

Though most travel agents will make reasonable efforts to find you a better fare (by testing various flight segments; often two segments cost less than the whole), there's a limit to what can be expected of them. Twenty minutes of computer time can easily be expended in searching out all the possibilities, and how much, after all, is the agent earning for "marching that extra step"? Indeed, when the agent reduces your air fare, his or her commission income is reduced.

Be frank with your agent. If the lowest fare is always your chief consideration, it may sometimes be advisable to offer an extra fee for the extra time required to find it. With bargain fares proliferating, a fee-based system of compensation may ultimately prove far more productive and beneficial, to all concerned, than the current practice of allowing the agent a percentage of the ticket price.

Finally, take steps to ensure that your agent is competent to handle your needs. Attempt a mild form of cross-examination. Ask whether he or she is familiar with several of the air-fare "devices" described in this essay. If not, drop that agent forthwith and find another. The right one can save you a great deal of money. ≈

Under-the-Counter Discounts—the Latest Craze in Cruising

Does Only a Chump Pay Full Price for a Cruise? Yup!

Six happy passengers at a festive table on a Caribbean cruise. Four have paid $1,500 per person. Two have paid $1,100 per person. All six have purchased—and occupy—the very same category of cabin.

If the four knew about the good fortune of the two, they would flog the first officer, keelhaul the captain, string the purser to a yardarm, commit mayhem and mutiny. They'd be livid.

And yet the scene I've described is not the exception but the current rule in cruising. According to people who know—eager, tattle-tale "deep throats" among former cruise-line executives—fully a third of all cruise-ship passengers are currently sailing at substantial discounts.

The reason, as you've guessed, is a glut—an extraordinary, undeniable glut. With more than 60,000 cruise-ship berths currently marketed to the U.S. public—double the number of less than ten years ago—the industry suffers from an overcapacity of 15% to 20% at profitable price levels, or so claim my sources.

And yet there's more such capacity on the way—at least 25,000 additional berths by the start of 1991. One new behemoth—the 2,276-passenger *Sovereign of the Seas,* largest cruise ship afloat—went into service in January 1988. Another, the faintly ominous *World City Project* of Kloster Cruises, carrying a near-inconceivable 5,000 passengers (the *QE2* hauls 1,850), is currently in the planning stages.

Why the frenzied construction? Not one of my confidants can point to a rational cause. Rather, in a purely defensive and Darwinian struggle for market share, lines scramble to match the modern new ships and equipment of their competitors. Others respond to irresistible prices from desperate (and often subsidized) foreign shipyards, whose building of oil tankers has virtually ceased. Some projects have been spurred (until recently) by tax advantages promised to syndicates of investors. In this bout to the death, ultimately bound to result in economic casualties, the gap between supply and demand makes airline struggles seem like a children's game.

The Desperate Response

To beat the glut, some cruise-ship lines have thrashed about experimenting in novel marketing approaches of the most specialized sort. Some offer music cruises, investment cruises, even slimming cruises with staff of the Golden Door resort. One recently proposed the operation of Club Med–style cruises, on which unlimited drinks, beauty treatments, and daily massage would all be included in the basic charge (reportedly, to attract the younger set). From the flashy Carnival Cruise Lines we have virtual bacchanals at sea, with eight meals a day (their most recent claim) and not one, but two post-midnight buffets. We have cruises, too, of brainy content, addressed by university lecturers and operated by the distinguished Swan Hellenic organization (moderately priced) or Society Expeditions (expensive).

But mainly we have under-the-counter discounts—the classic response to oversupply—in a staggering number of instances (though not on every departure), and even on the stuffy, top-of-the-line ships. Having scanned the discount lists, I find no prominent or consistent exception to the policy of quietly releasing a portion of each ship's capacity for sale at cut-rate levels by select, discreet discounters.

The Discounts Themselves

How and from whom do you get them?

The major sources are two dozen in number, widely scattered. They rely heavily on direct mail, on word-of-mouth referrals, and occasionally on ads in limited-circulation cruise magazines in which they hint at their ability to produce the "best prices," but never quite say so. If they do advertise, they rarely list the exact ships or departures for which discounts are to be had.

For public consumption, the majority will explain these pricing feats by referring with studied vagueness to "group arrangements." One discounter caused considerable hilarity among her competitors by recently referring in a major newspaper interview to "commitments for blocs of cabins" (I'm paraphrasing) that result in discounted prices. "If I don't sell them all," she proclaimed, "I take a bath."

Another prominent firm, Cruises of Distinction, in Montclair, New Jersey, is willing to speak with greater candor—to "go public," in a sense, with what every insider already knows. "How we get these rates is a combination of several factors," explains Michael Grossman, a former marketing vice-president of the important Norwegian American Cruises. "It depends on your contacts within the industry, their confidence in you, your reputation for successfully selling the cabins for the dates they need, the effort and money you'll spend on special, discreet marketing. When all the factors are right, you receive a continuing supply of cabins for sale at substantial discounts."

That supply is especially plentiful for the coming winter season, says Grossman. "I can't remember a year when we had Thanksgiving, Christmas, and Valentine's Day departures, available at substantial discounts. But we do this year, and the situation is deteriorating rapidly."

A former director of sales for Cunard and Norwegian American explains that he left the cruise-ship lines out of a belief that "for the next five years at least, the chief opportunity is to serve as a broker for distressed inventory." He cites impressive statistics on the growing discrepancy between cruise-ship capacity and the available market for cabins.

In the East, the two most prominent sources of cruise discounts known to me are the earlier-mentioned **Cruises of Distinction, Inc., 460 Bloomfield Ave., Montclair, NJ 07042 (phone 201/744-1331, toll free 800/634-3445 outside New Jersey)**, which markets its wares all over the nation, and receives most of its calls from California (its tickets are then delivered by overnight courier service); and **White Travel Service, 342 N. Main St., West Hartford, CT 06117 (phone 203/233-2648, or toll free 800/547-4790 outside Connecticut)**. The latter is headed by the effervescent Edie White and her son, Rick, who have themselves sampled virtually every cruise ship they sell.

In the South, **Esther Grossberg Travel, Inc., 6300 W. Loop South, Bellaire, TX 77401 (phone 713/666-1761)**, long a major Sunbelt retailer, seems to have the same broad inventory of heavily discounted departures on nearly all the major lines.

In the West, two active firms offering sharply reduced rates for cabins other people are buying at list price are: **Cruise Pro, Inc., 2900 Townsgate Rd., Suite 103, Westlake Village, CA 91361 (phone 818/707-0667, or toll free 800/222-SHIP, 800/258-SHIP in California);** and **Just Cruises and Tours, Inc., 801 Portola Dr., Suite 209, San Francisco, CA 94127 (phone 415/661-SHIP, or toll free 800/331-SHIP, 800/551-SHIP in California).**

In the Southeast, **Cruise Reservations, Inc., 8975 N.E. Sixth Ave., Miami, FL 33138 (phone 305/759-8922, or toll free 800/892-9929),** does a great deal of discount advertising in cruise-ship publications, but is otherwise unknown to me.

A bit about their product: Unlike the tickets issued by airline "bucket shops," which are restricted ones, hard to change or cancel, the cruise-ship tickets obtained from discounters are indistinguishable from the full-priced variety. Because of that, a great many traditional retail travel agencies deal with the major discount firms, and you might very well ask your own preferred retailer whether they have a favorite among the group to which I've referred. Discounts are primarily available for those categories of cabins in greatest supply—those of the medium variety. (Top-priced cabins and lowest-priced cabins are usually the most heavily demanded, and therefore are less frequently discounted.)

The discounts average 20% and more—and that's no small sum. Since the great majority of cabins on most one-week cruises sell for at least $1,500 (including air fare to and from the embarkation port), the saving amounts to a hefty $300 per person, and often to considerably more than that. Currently, some knowledgeable customers of the discounters are flying to the Caribbean from as far as Los Angeles or San Francisco, enjoying an all-inclusive seven-day cruise to and among several glamorous islands, and then flying back, for a spectacular $895 per person, including both the cruise and the air fare. Even at those bargain rates, some cabins go begging—as hard as that may be to believe.

"Why," asks a vicious joke, "did God create the upper middle class?" "So that somebody would buy at retail," goes the answer. Let's hope readers of this book will "go with the market" and thus avoid that wholly unnecessary fate. ≈

Alaskan cruise

XVI ≠ THE TIME, THE RESOURCES, AND THE ATTITUDES, FOR PROPER TRAVEL

The Scandal of American Vacation Time

While Other Developed Nations Provide Their Citizens with Five Weeks and More of Paid Leave, We Squeeze Out a Meager Two—or Two and a Half

Thoughtless, at the very least. Barbaric, at worst. Inhuman, certainly. Short-sighted and ill-advised. Miserly. Unhealthy.

Depending on the depths of your passion, those are the words you may want to use to describe employer attitudes toward vacation time in the United States.

We Americans put up with the shortest, most miserably limited vacations of any advanced, prosperous nation. The result is a stunted quality of life and (if that doesn't bother you) a stunted commercial travel industry.

To gauge how bad things are, place yourself, hypothetically, into one of four national contexts:

• Imagine, first, that you are "Wilhelm Preizendorff," a young Austrian, and that you have just gone to work as an office clerk for a Viennese stationers. From the moment you enter the mailroom door, you are entitled by law to five weeks per year of paid vacation.

• Or you are "Nigel Lawson," floor manager of a small Sydney, Australia, department store. Each year, by practice of your firm, common in Australia, you receive six weeks of paid vacation. Sometimes you store up three months of vacation and take the family on an around-the-world trip.

• Or you are "Chantal Lasserre," buyer for a Paris dress shop. You are this time entitled, by minimum guarantee of French law, to five weeks' paid vacation per year. You take a month off every summer, which you then supplement with a week in winter or spring.

• And now you are "Mary Jones" or "John Smith," an American. This year you have no vacation at all; you have recently changed jobs and lost the time accrued under your former employer. Next year: one week with pay. The year after that: two. After five years of consecutive employment with the same firm, you will have three weeks per year of paid vacation—but never more than that. All your working life: three weeks per year.

Is this an exaggerated comparison? I wish it were. In numerous studies of vacation time, only a single one shows the American public enjoying as many as two and a half weeks, on the average, of vacation time.

AVERAGE NUMBER OF WEEKDAYS ENJOYED AS PAID VACATION TIME IN FOURTEEN ADVANCED NATIONS

(figures do not include public holidays)

NO. OF WEEKDAYS*

Country	No. of Weekdays
FRANCE	25
SWEDEN	25
BELGIUM	24
DENMARK	24
WEST GERMANY	24
AUSTRIA	22
ITALY	22
NETHERLANDS	21
SPAIN	21
NORWAY	20
SWITZERLAND	18
UNITED KINGDOM	18
CANADA	13
U.S.A.	9

*Five weekdays
= one week

In addition to the above vacation days, public holidays per country amount to 14 days per year in Spain, 13 days in Austria and Italy, 12 in West Germany and Sweden, 11 in France, 10 in Belgium, Canada, Norway and Switzerland, 9.5 in Denmark, and 8 in the Netherlands, United Kingdom and U.S.A.

Chart is based on statistics from International Tourism Forecasts to 1995. Published by the Economist Intelligence Unit, 1985.

We Americans put up with the shortest, most miserably limited vacations of any advanced, prosperous nation.

The two-week fling

Time for cross-cultural experience

Most other reports fix the average figure at two weeks—or even less.

Two weeks. Even two and a half weeks. Those compare with the five weeks enjoyed in numerous other advanced, industrialized nations, and with the remarkable six-week policy of Australia. Even in nations having nowhere near our own material prosperity or per-capita income—such as Britain—the average working person enjoys nearly four weeks per year of paid vacation. (My British statistics are from a 1985 survey by the respected *Economist* magazine of London.)

And it gets worse. Not only is the American average a paltry two or two-and-a-half weeks, but even that brief interlude is enjoyed under the most fragile of circumstances. Leave your job and you lose your vacation time. Painfully, patiently, you must start all over, accruing new vacation privileges from a new employer. The past counts for nothing.

No law protects the vacation. Though the United States subscribes to the Universal Declaration of Human Rights—which prescribes "the right to rest and leisure, including . . . periodic holidays with pay" as a fundamental privilege of life—not a single federal or state law, to my knowledge, guarantees a single day of paid vacation to anyone.

Either we Americans are the workaholics of the world, or we are exploited in this regard, or in our drive for improved wages, we have simply neglected to secure the time in which to enjoy the fruits of our pay.

However the neglect came about, it contributes to a serious decline in the quality of our lives. A barrier to our cultural growth. Inadequate time for study or reflection, human relationships, the eternal verities. Burn-out. Even, perhaps, worsened health.

Shouldn't we all consider whether the time for leisure is fully as important as other aspects of material prosperity? Would it not be worth a trade-off to enjoy greater respite from constant labors? A life more dignified and fulfilling? When the political pendulum of the United States begins to shift from its present rightward course, as must inevitably happen; when labor again becomes aggressive in its collective bargaining; when ordinary people once more demand improvements to their lot—shouldn't the goal of increased vacation time be high on the national agenda?

And if these quality-of-life arguments don't suffice, shouldn't we at least consider the impact of increased vacation time on our commercial travel interests?

The U.S. travel industry is also a victim of limited vacation time: it is puny in comparison with its European counterparts. Because of their enhanced vacation periods, tiny Benelux countries send as many people to winter vacation destinations in Spain and North Africa as the entire United States sends in that period to certain major islands of the Caribbean. With nearly four weeks of paid vacation available to their clientele, at least a dozen British tour operators each handle several hundreds of thousands of vacation arrangements each year, while here in the United States, with four times the population, the same companies are perhaps six in number.

Every day of vacation time added to the American average would create a need for hundreds of new hotels and resorts, tens of thousands of new jobs in leisure areas, additional airplanes, trains, and buses. The multiplier effects are dazzling.

And each such result comes about at lesser cost to employers than higher wages or other traditional fringe benefits. In service industries, and especially in those smaller economic units where vacation time is particularly meager, people take on extra tasks—work harder and in broader functions, take up the slack—when their colleagues go on vacation. The common experience of all of us confirms that increased vacation time costs less to employers than other employment benefits.

Who ideally should agitate for increased vacation time? I suggest the more than 250,000 Americans who work as travel agents. No other social change could better secure their futures, add to their opportunities, expand their industry, while at the same time performing an act for the common good. One could even argue that only travel agents and other travel professionals possess the kind of direct, compelling self-interest in the matter, and the political numbers, capable of changing American vacation policies.

But is it likely that travel agents will head such a drive? Not under their present leadership. Notoriously short-sighted, almost automatically conservative, the male officials of the American Society of Travel Agents—a profession that is 70% female—recently battled congressional efforts to secure maternity leaves for working women (it would raise their payroll costs). Imagine their reactions to proposals for additional vacation time.

Someday this may change. Someday both the men and women of America's travel agencies will realize that though they work in small storefront locations, they need not possess the souls of shopkeepers. Someday the sophistication of their travel lives will lead to a corresponding sophistication in their social outlooks, and they will champion the fight for civilized standards in vacation policies.

The way to do it? A modest, one-sentence addition to the Federal Wages and Hours Act: "All persons engaged in interstate commerce shall receive a minimum of three weeks each year of paid vacation." By bringing along those persons enjoying less than three weeks, such legislation would surely add at least half a week to the national average, setting off an explosive increase in this nation's vacation facilities and travel-related industries. What more business-like way to improve the lives of all of us!

And then we ought to work for four or five weeks of yearly vacation time. Why should Americans enjoy less than the Scandinavians, Austrians, Germans, or French? ≈

Ethical Travel: Does Tourism Cause More Harm Than Good?

Rethinking the "Rights" and "Wrongs" of Our Vacation Trips

At the bar of a tropical nightclub, on an island whose language is Dutch, two tipsy young tourists are exchanging loud comments on the "childish behavior" of the natives. "They haven't any concept of time." "They're so disorganized." "They move in slow motion." Nearby, overhearing each word, his English near perfect, a bartender stands seething with anger.

• In the marketplace of a Hindu village, a travelling couple bargain over the cost of a trinket. Though the price is that of an ice cream at home, they're determined to pick up "a steal." Resignedly, the shopkeeper reduces her quote to a marginal level, hardly enough to bring her a single rupee of real income.

• On the streets of a Mexican city, two confident visitors in costly tennis clothes go strolling in high spirits to a favorite bar. Unseeing, uncaring, they pass clusters of ragged children, who in turn stare at the elegant pair with envy and resentment.

• In the air-conditioned restaurant of a Nigerian hotel, owned by a multinational chain, guests dine on tournedos flown in from Argentina, and wash down the steak with a fine French wine. Of the monies charged for their meals, only the tiniest part remains in Nigeria.

• Onto the tarmac of the Bangkok airport steps a group of German tourists, all of them male. They have come for prostitution. Included in their "package," at no extra charge, is a young Thai farm girl for the entire week.

Does tourism involve ethics? Should tourists be trained to act responsibly? Are travel practices—and institutions—in need of reform? Each of these questions was studied last fall by a group of American church people at a conference in San Anselmo, California. Their gathering came several years after the organization of similar groups abroad.

In 1975 a conference of Asian church leaders in Penang, Malaysia, issued a broad condemnation of tourism as it was then practiced in their countries. They decried the boorish antics of tourists to Asia, the harmful role models offered to impressionable Asian children by foreign tourists, their patronizing attitudes and harsh demands, the pollution of authentic settings and communities by modern hotels, the disrespect for Asian cultures by numerous tourist groups, the heavy use of prostitution as an Asiatic tourist lure, the monetary inflation and social trauma caused by a sudden touristic influx.

But their criticism went deeper. In a dizzying outflow of bulletins, pamphlets, newsletters, and even a quarterly magazine (*Contours,* standing for "concern for tourism") occurring in the years since, the Ecumenical Coalition on Third World Tourism (ECTWT, the continuing organization) has appeared to argue that the capacity for harm is deeply ingrained in the very practice of tourism; that it brings more harm than good to poor nations; that it is, in effect, a new form of economic colonialism; that all of us should step back and rethink the methods by which tourism is conducted; and that the problem is worldwide in scope, erupting wherever the Rich visit lands of the Poor.

Think for a moment about the geographical directions of tourism. On an international level, most vacation travel consists of people from the "First World" (United States, Europe, Japan) travelling to visit islands, beaches, and picturesque towns of the "Third World" (Mexico, the Caribbean, Africa, Southeast Asia, India). Most of it occurs for the purpose of returning for a short time to a simpler way of life—to lost innocence, in settings old-fashioned and open-air.

But though we opt for the "tropical paradise," we demand that it come with all the comforts of home. So we drop glass-and-steel hotels next to peasant villages or fishermen's huts, creating luxuriant, forbidden facilities that no resident would dare enter, let alone use. We instantly separate *us* from *them.*

Within these bright new edifices, we staff all the servile posts—waiters, busboys, chambermaids—with native labor, but bring in executives from our own developed world to run the show (when, in the tropics, did you last see a native-born general manager?).

We then parade our wealth before people who can never enjoy our incomes. Though we ourselves may be only modestly well-off, we pay prices of a staggering size in local terms. Our very presence creates the most appalling contrasts.

> The capacity for harm is deeply ingrained in the very practice of tourism, which often brings more injury than good to poor nations.

Though we opt for the "tropical paradise," we demand that it come with all the comforts of home. So we drop glass-and-steel hotels next to peasant villages or fishermen's huts.

In the course of our stays, we make no use at all of the lodgings that residents use, or of their transportation or dining spots. We create our own.

We arrive without the slightest advance knowledge of their ways of life, customs, or culture. We challenge them to quickly brief us on the spot ("orientation sightseeing tours"). We demand that they pose quaintly for our Kodaks and Minoltas, dance for our amusement ("Thursday night: native entertainment"), show us their funny clothes. We care not a fig for their politics, but expect them to admire our own. Unlike the great travellers of the past—Marco Polo, Rubens, Byron—we show no real regard for their achievements and discoveries, art and literature, but expect them, in essence, to have adopted our culture, at least a bit: to speak the same language we do ("luckily, they all speak . . ."), to stock our newspapers and our books in their newsstands and shops.

In short, we pay them massive disrespect. We assault their human dignity; we necessarily imply that they are inferior to us. Some—especially the young in Third World nations—begin to believe just that.

We injure them.

But if this is the situation, what is the solution? Having read my way through a stack of the literature on ethical tourism, I intend no slight of the various Ecumenical Coalitions when I state what they would readily admit: that their work to date has defined the problem but rendered less satisfactory solutions.

Still, some solutions have emerged. They begin with a frontal, public relations attack on the most blatant exploiters of Third World people for touristic purposes: in particular, the operators of sex tours using women coerced by poverty (or physical force) into a criminal world of prostitution; the decriminalization of that activity, eliminating the exploiters, is a goal of some of the ecumenical organizations.

The solutions include political opposition to the worst excesses of tourist development: the sprawling airports and monumental hotels plopped into the midst of small villages and rural beauty.

The solutions involve encouraging the greater use of simpler, indigenous lodgings and facilities for visiting tourists; supporting and even subsidizing the operation of small guesthouses and guest-accepting private homes, pensions, and farms; promoting the sale of purely local crafts to tourists and the consumption of local food products; arranging visits by tourists to meetings of local service organizations and, indeed, to people's homes.

The solution means marketing—giving badly needed publicity to—those underfinanced travel organizations that practice "integrated tourism," placing visitors into the facilities used by local people themselves.

Finally, and perhaps most important, the solution involves educating travellers to comport themselves properly in the Third World. A recent victory of the Ecumenical Coalition was to persuade Lufthansa to show a film of advance cultural preparation and ethical conduct on its holiday flights to certain Third World nations. Another has been the widespread dissemination and increasing acceptance of a code of ethics for tourists: "Travel in a spirit of humility. . . . Be sensitively aware of [their] feelings. . . . Cultivate the habit of listening and observing. . . . Realize [they] have time concepts and thought patterns different from your own. This does not make them inferior, only different. . . . Do not expect special privileges. . . . Do not make promises [you cannot] carry through. . . ."

Once the exclusive domain of Asian and European groups, the drive for ethical travel practices is now on the march in the United States. Its "general" is Virginia T. Hadsell, her recently formed organization is the **Center for Responsible Tourism, 2 Kensington Road, San Anselmo, CA 94960 (phone 415/843-5506),** and her initial conference took place in that city (near San Rafael) in November 1986. Send her a large, self-addressed, stamped envelope, and she'll send you literature, including the interesting Code of Ethics for tourists.

Or you may make a direct contact with the **Ecumenical Coalition on Third World Tourism, P.O. Box 9-25, Bangkhen, Bangkok 10900, Thailand,** requesting a copy of the fascinating *Contours*. They'll mail it to you free, but you're invited to send a small contribution—say, $3 or so—to defray the costs.

A CODE OF ETHICS FOR TOURISTS

1. Travel in a spirit of humility and with a genuine desire to learn more about the people of your host country. Be sensitively aware of the feelings of other people, thus preventing what might be offensive behavior on your part. This applies very much to photography.

2. Cultivate the habit of listening and observing, rather than merely hearing and seeing.

3. Realize that often the people in the country you visit have time concepts and thought patterns different from your own. This does not make them inferior, only different.

4. Instead of looking for that "beach paradise," discover the enrichment of seeing a different way of life, through other eyes.

5. Acquaint yourself with local customs. What is courteous in one country may be quite the reverse in another—people will be happy to help you.

6. Instead of the Western practice of "knowing all the answers," cultivate the habit of asking questions.

7. Remember that you are only one of thousands of tourists visiting this country and do not expect special privileges.

8. If you really want your experience to be a "home away from home," it is foolish to waste money on travelling.

9. When you are shopping, remember that that "bargain" you obtained was possible only because of the low wages paid to the maker.

10. Do not make promises to people in your host country unless you can carry them through.

11. Spend time reflecting on your daily experience in an attempt to deepen your understanding. It has been said that "what enriches you may rob and violate others."

—Issued by the Ecumenical Coalition on Third World Tourism

A Plea for "Social Tourism"

Isn't It Time We Brought the Benefits of Travel to All Our Citizens?

In all the years you've read the Sunday travel sections, have you once observed a reference to "social tourism"?

Probably not. It is a concept known to every prosperous nation other than our own, to every rich continent other than North America, to every major language other than English.

"Social tourism" is tourism for the poor.

Here in America, we don't push it. Apart from various "fresh-air funds" sending underprivileged children to summer camp, not a single major program brings away-from-home vacations to low-income groups. While you and I enjoy all the widely recognized benefits of travel—the awesome beauties of an outside world, the broadening impact of foreign cultures, the mind-tingling sense of human possibilities—the same rewards are simply unavailable to persons of adult age who happen to be poor and living in the United States.

But should this be? If the ability to enjoy rest and leisure is a fundamental human right—and it certainly is—shouldn't we concern ourselves with travel opportunities for the poor? With "social tourism"?

In Europe as early as 1956, leading travel figures met to discuss the contradiction between low income and the right to travel. From those talks emerged, years later, the Bureau Internationale du Tourisme Sociale, headed today by 73-year-old Arthur Haulot of Belgium, a former chairman of the European Travel Commission.

Haulot presides over some 90-odd organizations of "social tourism" in Europe and North Africa, in South America and the Pacific Rim—but not, astonishingly, in the United States. Though their work may seem utterly basic, even a bit simple, it is of remarkable importance.

The Vacation Itself

They agitate, first, for the fundamental right to a yearly paid vacation by people of all income strata. Sounds self-evident, right? Yet in an America that mandates (in effect) the 40-hour week and the eight-

Apart from various "fresh-air funds" sending underprivileged children to summer camp, not a single major program brings away-from-home vacations to low-income groups.

hour day, no law protects the right to a paid vacation, and numerous low-income persons fail to receive one. What maid, for instance, enjoys the security of an assured, paid period of rest?

Access to the Vacation

They seek to persuade governments, owners of the railways, to provide poor persons with a free or drastically reduced round-trip rail ticket, once a year, to a vacation destination. By eliminating or lowering that transportation cost—as France, Portugal, and Switzerland have done—they bring proper vacations into the financial reach of a great many of the poor.

A Fulfilling Vacation

They attempt to eliminate the substandard, cinderblock motel and fast-food restaurant as the sole affordable facility for vacationing poor. They promote the construction and operation of dignified, low-cost "vacation villages" in seaside and mountain areas, by political parties of both the left and right, by labor unions and philanthropic societies, all receiving low-interest loans, grants, or tax rebates for the purpose, from local or national governments.

(I have visited several such "social resorts" in Europe. They permit the poor to experience nature and the finer aspects of culture, solitude, rebirth; they encourage the self-esteem of their guests; leave them replenished in energy and spirit for an assault on their own poverty. In short, they provide the poor with the same vacations that you and I enjoy—and isn't that an unarguable goal?)

Filling Unused Accommodations

They enroll farmers with large and partially underutilized homes, or educational institutions with vacated residence halls, to list those facilities for holiday use by the poor, at low rates, and then disseminate such availabilities to a low-income population, helping both the user and the provider.

A Host of Other Measures

They work for the creation of "land banks" or additions to national parks, preventing the wholesale private purchase of scenic areas, which would block their use by persons of lesser means. They develop camping facilities—the cheapest form of meaningful travel—and caravaning; issue reduced-price travel vouchers and credit facilities for travel by the poor; advocate staggered vacation schedules as the most efficient means of reducing the cost of vacations for low-income persons; and perform a multitude of other needed functions.

But now you undoubtedly have questions.

First, isn't "social tourism" a form of subsidized tourism? Of course it is—but so is "commercial tourism." When the nonpoor travel, who pays for the highways on which they drive their cars? Who funds the aviation authorities that secure the safety of their flights? Who maintains the port facilities, docks, and marinas at which they park their boats and yachts? Because the taxpayer is already so heavily supporting travel by middle-income and high-income Americans, common justice demands that at least some resources be spent on travel for the poor.

Second, don't we provide any semblance of "social tourism" in this country? Not really. Some unions maintain holiday facilities for their members—but those are not the "poor." Several hundred companies belong to the National Industrial Recreation Association, operating travel programs for their employees— but neither are those the "poor." While state and national parks are "social" in their character, their long-stay facilities (lodging, restaurants) are notoriously unsuited to the needs of the truly poor.

The "poor" of which I speak are those 50 million Americans living either below the federal poverty line or perilously close to it. At their levels of income, almost absurdly low, the road to travel and tourism is effectively blocked.

How, then, do the "poor" vacation in the United States? The overwhelming number never leave their homes. Those who do, in my experience, squeeze out a stay of three-or-so days near theme parks or casino cities, whose attractions and activities are of the basest sort—dumb and contrived, consumerist. Just as low-income groups have failed to receive adequate

low-income housing from private industry, so the American poor have been abandoned almost entirely by the commercial travel industry. They simply have no access to vacations of worth and meaning. Yet such interludes are surely the birthright of every American, the essential requisites for a civilized life.

Don't we need an Institute for Social Tourism in this country? A private body to devise, coordinate, and encourage efforts in this field? And shouldn't persons in the travel industry be the leaders of that movement?

Franklin Roosevelt said that "from those to whom much is given, much is expected." Those who earn handsome incomes from the commercial industry of travel should be the first to labor at extending the benefits of travel to those less favored.

I plan to write more on "social tourism." And I'd be grateful to have your comments and suggestions. Send them to the address listed in our introduction, and they will find their way into a subsequent edition of this book.≈

Appendix

Twenty-four Outstanding Discount Travel Agencies

Though some call them "bucket shops," they are simply discounters of air fares performing a function no less proper or respectable than the activities of discount pharmacies, discount record stores, discount clothing shops.

Primarily, they sell air fares to international destinations at discounts of as much as 30% and 40%. Because these tickets come from prestigious airlines, which make them available through selected retail outlets, the bucket shops have to possess some "standing"—a relationship with an international airline—to remain in business. And I, for one, have not yet heard of a single instance among them of blatant skullduggery, financial insolvency, or irresponsibility (stranding of passengers).

In the main text of this book, I've discussed the buckets at length, and provided the names of half a dozen. Here, now, is a more comprehensive listing of 24, out of the 100 or so that presently operate in U.S. cities.

EAST COAST

Access International, Inc.
250 West 57th Street
New York, NY 10107
(phone 212/333-7280)
Claims to be the nation's largest bucket shop, with sales of more than 150,000 seats in 1988. Its tickets are only to European destinations, at prices occasionally as low as $300, round-trip, between New York and London, $400 to Paris, $500 to Rome.

Apex Travel, Inc.
46-46 Vernon Boulevard
Long Island City, NY 11101
(phone 718/784-1111)
Wide range of sharply discounted air fares to Asia: Jakarta, Bangkok, Singapore, Taipei, Tokyo, and Hong Kong. Also, cheap China tours from Hong Kong.

European-American Travel
1522 K Street N.W.
Washington, DC 20005
(phone 202/789-2255, or toll free 800/848-6789)
Discount fares to Europe and South America, year-round. "We can waive the advance purchase requirement on excursion fares and still bring you a price lower than the excursion rate."

Getaway Travel, Inc.
1105 Ponce de Leon Boulevard
Coral Gables, FL 33134
(phone 305/446-7855, or toll free 800/334-1923)
Discounts on fares primarily to Europe: "We accommodate people planning late."

Japan Budget Travel
9 East 38th Street, Room 203
New York, NY 10016
(phone 212/686-8855)
Though nearly every employee is Japanese, with less-than-fluent abilities in English, it nevertheless pays to endure the language difficulties—their values are that good. Is primarily engaged in selling air fares to Japan at heavily discounted levels, but also has packages for sale, to both Japan and Europe. Sells Northwest and Japan Air Lines tickets to Japan at the last minute; maintains office hours Monday through Friday from 9:30 a.m. to 5:30 p.m., on Saturday from 10 a.m. to 4:30 p.m.

Maharajah Travels
518 Fifth Avenue
New York, NY 10036
(phone 212/391-0122, or toll free 800/223-6862 outside New York State)
Another prominent New York discounter (30,000 passengers in 1988), with a toll-free "800" number for out-of-state clients. Primarily to Europe, but also to Central and South America, Africa, India, Singapore, and Tokyo. Will also handle hotel reservations.

Pan Express Travel, Inc.
25 West 39th Street, Suite 705
New York, NY 10018
(phone 212/719-9292)
Has remarkable discounted air fares to islands of the Caribbean and to South America, in addition to the standard European destinations. Also offers "around-the-world specials" for as little as $1,299.

Sudo Tours
500 Fifth Avenue
New York, NY 10110
(phone 212/302-2860)
A long-established specialist to Tokyo. It will send you there for an amazing $820 (and less) round trip from the East Coast, provided you agree to go on an indirect route involving stops. "Those who know Asia, know us" is the slogan of this firm that claims to be the oldest East Coast discounter to the Far East. Use them for multiple-stop itineraries to Hong Kong, Bangkok, and Singapore as well.

Sun International Travel
6000 Dawson Boulevard
Norcross, GA 30093
(phone 404/446-3111)

Sells Japan Air Lines tickets at "wholesale rates"; in phoning, ask for "wholesale division." Best current bargain: round-trip flight between Atlanta and Tokyo for $824.

The Vacation Outlet
(in Filene's basement)
Washington Street
Boston, MA 02108
(phone 617/267-8100)
Sells tours and packages—never air fares alone—at sharply discounted prices, primarily to resort destinations. Open Monday through Friday from 9 a.m. to 6 p.m., on Saturday from 10 a.m. to 3 p.m., and claims to be the nation's only "retail travel store." Operates in a bustling, invigorating atmosphere as a result of its location in one of the busiest retail department store basements. Many packages sold are of the last-minute variety, but departures are available several weeks ahead.

MIDWEST

Japan Budget Travel (Illinois)
104 South Michigan Avenue
Suite 700
Chicago, IL 60603
(phone 312/236-9797, or toll free 800/843-0273)
Sells air tickets only, at substantial discounts, from the Midwest to the Far East. And has been doing so, reliably, for six years.

McSon Travel, Inc.
36 South State Street
Chicago, IL 60603
(phone 312/346-6272 or toll free 800/622-1421)
Discounted air fares (reduced by 15% to 35%) to Europe, the South Pacific, and the Far East.

Ryan's Regent Travel
7218 West Touhy Avenue
Chicago, IL 60648
(phone 312/774-8770)
Discounted air fares to Ireland, their main interest. Largest Irish specialist in the Midwest.

SOUTHWEST

Airvalue, Inc.
1817 So. Broadway
P.O. Box 8146
Tyler, TX 75711
(phone 214/595-4338, or toll free 800/482-8282)
Air tickets only, to Europe and Asia, often at savings as high as 30%.

Euro-Asia, Inc.
4203 East Indian School Road
Phoenix, AZ 85018
(phone 602/955-2742)
Proud to be called a "discount travel agency." Its international tickets are both transatlantic and transpacific, at considerable reductions; and they also discount tours and hotels in Asia.

WEST COAST

All Unique Travel
1030 Georgia Street
Vallejo, CA 94590
(phone 707/648-0237)
Needs three weeks' advance notice to procure you a good discount on tickets to Mexico, Hawaii, Europe, Africa, and the Middle East. Has especially good rates to Madrid. Their motto: "Why spend it here when you can spend it there?"

Community Travel Service
5237 College Avenue
Oakland, CA 94618
(phone 415/653-0990)
Particularly good discounts on air fares to the Orient, but discounts to anywhere. Best bargain for 1989: West Coast/Bangkok for $600 round-trip.

Cost Less Travel, Inc.
674 Broadway, Suite 201
San Francisco, CA 94133
(phone 415/397-6868)
Discounts of 25% to 30% on most international air fares, specializing in the Orient. Mr. Wong is the man in charge, a careful, punctilious gentleman.

Express Discount Travel
5945 Mission Gorge Road
San Diego, CA 92120
(phone 619/283-6324)
The heavyweight of the West Coast shops. Air-fare discounts of up to 50%; discounts of 20% to 30% on tour programs. Handles South America, Europe, and Asia.

Express Fun Travel, Inc.
1169 Market Street, Room 809
San Francisco, CA 94102
(phone 415/431-7152)
Sells discount tickets to the Orient, often at reductions of 30%.

International Ticketing, Inc.
2019A East Orangethorpe
Placentia, CA 92670
(phone 714/528-3366)
Sells air tickets to Europe and the South Pacific at discounts of 15% to 30% off published rates.

Sunline Express Holidays
210 Post Street
San Francisco, CA 94108
(phone 415/398-2111, or toll free 800/877-2111)
"We're the lowest on the West Coast," they claim—to Europe, Mexico, South America, Hawaii, and Australia. "Our discounts range up to 40%; our prices are sometimes cheaper than the children's fare!" Best bargain for 1989: Miami/Buenos Aires for $599 round-trip.

Transoceanic Travel
2241 Polk Street
San Francisco, CA 94109
(phone 415/673-9950)
Specializes in long-haul, cost-efficient air tickets. Can sometimes achieve 50% savings off listed rates on lengthy multistop trips.

Travel Team
4518 University Way N.E.
Seattle, WA 98105
(phone 206/632-0520)
The price leader in Seattle, primarily on tickets to Europe. Experienced agents.

Eleven Reliable "Distress Merchants" of Travel (Offering Last-Minute Discounts)

From time immemorial, travel suppliers have sold off their last-minute remaining space at distress prices. As departure dates have neared, panic has set in. Employees of cruise ships and charter operators, of tour companies and hotel chains, have leaped to the phone to call relatives and friends, offering them the chance to purchase unsold cabins or seats at drastically reduced levels. At that late stage in the travel process, any sum received for a remaining cabin or seat is better than none. It is "found money."

Some tour operators even maintained lists of people who could travel on short notice. The bulletin board in a large urban hospital would periodically blossom with notices of last-minute travel bargains for nurses and doctors. Certain preferred unions would be alerted to phone their retired members with offers of seats at such low prices as to be irresistible.

Against such a well-known practice, it is not at all surprising that commercial entrepreneurs would finally attempt to organize what had earlier been random and unplanned. What is surprising is that it took them so long. Only within the past five years have "distress merchants" or "distress travel clubs" fully caught the public's attention with bargain offers for travel departures scheduled for the very next week, or even short days ahead.

With some exceptions, the clubs charge a yearly membership fee, which enables their members to use a toll-free line to listen to recorded messages of that week's bargains. Or they receive a period-ic newsletter of bargains. Provided they have flexible work schedules and can literally leave "on a moment's notice," the members can cut their travel costs by as much as 60%.

There is nothing mysterious or arcane about it. Most travel products are totally "perishable" in nature, and must be sold for a particular date or departure, or else their value for that departure is lost forever for the producer of the product. Hence it behooves them to work with the "distress merchants" in disposing of their unsold product.

Here are 11 reliable sources of "distress travel products." My own recommendation as to which you should join: the club nearest your own city. I have the impression (and may be wrong) that each excels at departures from its own immediate vicinity.

Moment's Notice, Inc.
40 East 49th Street
New York, NY 10017
(phone 212/486-0500 or 0503)
Perhaps the oldest of the lot, Moment's Notice is a recent subsidiary of the longer-established Matterhorn Club, which for 20 years has been offering sale-priced cabins, airline seats, and tour places to its members. Its departures are mainly from the East Coast, split almost evenly between New York and Florida. Members receive access to a "hotline phone number" to hear recorded messages of what's available in the days ahead, as well as a quarterly written update, all for a yearly membership fee of $45 (valid for the member and any number of that member's travel companions). Gil Zalman is the experienced founder of the club.

The Short Notice Program
4501 Forbes Boulevard
Lanham, MD 20706
(phone toll free 800/638-8976)
An activity of American Leisure Industries' Encore Travel Club, but entirely separate from that group, and requiring an independent membership fee: $36 per year, for single travellers and travelling families alike. Upon joining, you're told a number to call for tapes updated daily (actually, on weekdays only) of travel products offered at discounts of as much as 65%—but last minute in nature. The "hotline" is a Maryland area code (301); for reservations, you're permitted to use a toll-free "800" number. Credit cards are used to book, and tickets and tour documents are either mailed or waiting for you at the airport counter or dock. A generous offer is the right to cancel with full refund within a full year of joining if services should seem unsatisfactory.

Spur-of-the-Moment Cruises, Inc.
10780 Jefferson Boulevard
Culver City, CA 90230
(phone toll free 800/343-1991)
The chief West Coast "distress merchant," it deals only with cruises, but charges no membership fee for the right to use its services. Rather, you simply dial its "hotline" number—which is 213/838-9329—and hear a six-minute tape recording of all the distinguished ships

sailing from ports all over the world that have sharply discounted cabins for sale in the two to three weeks ahead; your savings can be as much as 50%. "We're America's clearinghouse for unsold cruises," says owner Duke Butler. A recent example of their values was a departure from a Brazilian port of a ship that first stopped at Bahia and Rio, then crossed the South Atlantic to Dakar and Casablanca, and eventually went to both Barcelona and Genoa. Normal price, including air fare from Miami to Brazil, and from Genoa back to the U.S.: $2,800 (for the entire 18-day sailing). Spur-of-the-Moment's price (including air fare): a remarkable $1,689, less than $100 a day. Other similar "coups": seven days in the Caribbean, including air fare from the West Coast, $729 (reduced from $1,400); a seven-day cruise of Alaskan waters, $699 (reduced from $1,250).

Stand-Buys, Ltd.
311 West Superior Street, Suite 404
Chicago, IL 60610
(phone 312/943-5737, or toll free
800/255-1488)
In business for eight years, and therefore one of the founders of this segment of the travel industry, Stand-Buys charges $45 per household per year for access to its hotline number, announcing discounts for the purchase of unfilled space on charter flights, cruises, and tours. You also receive a quarterly newsletter, and an "International Travel Card" granting you the "second night free" at nearly 3,000 hotels. In some of its literature the organization promises a complete refund of the membership fee if you find its services unsatisfactory within 30 days of joining.

Last Minute Travel Club, Inc.
132 Brookline Avenue
Boston, MA 02215
(phone 617/267-9800)
Though some of its products depart from New York, the overwhelming number leave from Boston, and its members are heavily New England based. The $35 a

year covers you, your family, or a travel companion, and results in your receiving a monthly newsletter and access to a 24-hour hotline. David Fialkow and Joel Benard are the founders, the latter the son of a prominent tour operator. Individual memberships are available for $30. Samples of their recent values: seven nights in Jamaica, air and hotel, $299; seven nights in Aruba, air and beachfront hotel, $299.

Worldwide Discount Travel Club, Inc.
1674 Meridian Avenue
Miami Beach, FL 33139
(phone 305/534-2082)
Every third week (that's 17 times a year), it mails you a closely typed letter, front and back, listing imminent departures of tours and/or cruises leaving from Atlanta, Boston, Chicago, Los Angeles, Miami, and New York, on which seats or cabins have been radically discounted in price. You then phone a toll-free number to book the trip you desire. Membership is $40 a year for a single traveller, $50 for a family. The club has been in business for several years.

Adventures on Call, Inc.
P.O. Box 18592
BWI Airport, MD 21240
(phone 301/356-4080)
Offers last-minute availabilities on air tickets and air-plus-land packages principally from this Baltimore airport at discounts as high as 50%. Membership fee is $49 per year per household (includes two adults and children under 18 years of age). Upon joining, you receive a 24-hour hotline phone number permitting you to keep abreast of all such travel opportunities, plus a confirmed-reservation phone number to call for making bookings. Finally, at least six times a year, members are contacted to enjoy first call on special travel opportunities, again principally from BWI Airport/Baltimore.

Entertainment Hot Line Travel Club
1400 North Woodward Avenue

Birmingham, MI 48011
(phone 313/642-1406)
A subsidiary of the large, publicly owned company that publishes the famous "Entertainment" discount coupons (74 volumes dealing with the 74 largest cities of the U.S.). It purports to operate nationwide (recent departures from New York, Los Angeles, Detroit, Chicago, Philadelphia) and to bring members savings of up to 65% on last-minute travel merchandise. Membership fee is $35 per year, which includes spouse, dependent children, or a travelling companion, and the fee will be refunded in full within 30 days of joining if you are not satisfied with the club's initial services.

Discount Travel International, Inc.
Ives Building, Suite 205
Narberth, PA 19072
(phone 215/668-2182, or toll free
800/824-4000)
Claiming to be the nation's largest "distress merchant," it charges $45 a year for membership (applying to anyone living in the same household), for which members receive a toll-free, short-notice hotline phone number. By dialing, one receives word of imminent departures from one's own area, on which discounts of 35% to 70% are given. Additional benefits of membership: free membership in Quest International, entitling you to 50% discounts at nearly 1,000 hotels; a small discount coupon book (for hotels, cars, movies); a second hotline service for condos around the world; a 5% cash bonus on any domestic air fare purchased through the club; a 7% discount on any standard nondistress charters, tour packages, or cruises.

Vacations to Go, Inc.
2411 Fountain View, Suite 201
Houston, TX 77057
(phone 713/974-2121, or for general
information, or toll free 800/624-7338,
800/833-8047 in Texas)
Headquartered in Houston, it maintains telephone numbers (but not offices) in

110 cities for imparting "regionalized" information of imminent departures; usually these are departures from another major city, for which "add-on" fares for connecting flights are added to the price. Yearly membership is $29.95 (for the entire household), which brings you the special number to call from your city. You hear a hotline announcement changed two to three times a week. You also receive, for your yearly membership, a free quarterly magazine on travel, which lists future bargains and vacation values (including cruise discounts).

Vacation Hotline
1501 West Fullerton Avenue
Chicago, IL 60614
(phone 312/880-0030, or toll free
800/423-4095)
Specializes in charter flights and vacation packages based on the use of charter transportation. Is also heavily oriented to Midwest departures, and to such prominent Midwest charter-tour operators as Thomson Vacations, MTI, Hudson Holidays, and Club Med. As President Michael Dorman explains the system: "If you have the flexibility to wait until a week or two prior to departure to make reservations, we will book you with these charter operators at reduced rates. There is some risk in doing this, as not all destinations on all dates are reduced, but those people who are willing to do so can pick up remarkable savings. Whenever the charter companies do not sell all their seats and hotel rooms, they put them on sale for as much as 30% to 50% off the regular rates. . . . We advise clients to call us seven to ten days prior to planned departure dates." From the Midwest, last-minute sales are also possible.

Eight Leading "Rebators" (Discounting Every Trip)

Unlike the airline bucket shops and cruise discounters that reduce the price of certain fares or certain cruises, "rebators" reduce the price of *every* travel product, but by a smaller percentage than the other companies. They perform this feat by simply "kicking back" their commission, or a portion of it, to their clients. Some pay out the entire commission—selling the trip at their net cost to their clients—but then assess a small service charge. Others pass on a part of their commission.

Either way, travellers save a substantial amount by dealing with the rebators, but only if they are willing the forego the advice and consultation they would normally receive from a standard travel agent. The rebators limit their customers to people who have already made up their minds as to where they want to go and how. If you are firm in your plans and do not need expert travel advice—if you are willing simply to "phone in" your request

in a short call—then you spare the rebators' time and support their ability to work for less income per transaction.

Once again, bear in mind that you save far less dealing with a rebator than with an air-fare bucket shop or cruise discounter, but the latter firms offer discounts only on selected cruise sailings or air fares, whereas the rebators offer a reduction on every travel product sold: any departure, any date, to anywhere.

Though some rebators have fallen by the wayside, eight "pioneers" have survived handsomely, and do a major business:

$ave More Travel
935 Curtiss
Suite #2
Downers Grove, IL 60515
(phone 312/963-2828)
Like all the other rebators, $ave More is able to "kick back" a portion of their commission to you by dealing only with people who know exactly what they want

and will not consume $ave More's time with inquiries or requests for advice—as happens in dealings with standard travel agents. In their literature they explain the point with refreshing candor: "Most travellers have relatively simple needs: go from Point A to B and back. Due to modern, sophisticated computer systems, this is a relatively quick and easy transaction. We will book what you—and you alone—want. We're not biased. We won't try to sell you any particular airline or service. We will simply get you what you want. . . ." Specifically, $ave More rebates a flat 10% off the purchase price of tours, packages, and cruises (not air fares or simple hotel reservations) in exchange for the payment by you of a flat fee: $30 on bookings up to $599, $50 on bookings up to $1,499, $100 on bookings up to $2,999, $150 on bookings up to $4,999.

McTravel Services, Inc.
130 South Jefferson Road

Chicago, IL 60606
(phone 312/876-1116, or toll free
800/333-3335)

McTravel—an obvious takeoff on the name of the burger chain—will deal with air fares, and rebates the entire commission to their customers (usually 10% of the amount spent on domestic tickets, higher on international air fares), but then charges a flat $10 for writing domestic tickets and $20 for writing international tickets. Let's say that you have made reservations for a trip that will cost $480. You save $48, less $10, for a net saving of $38. On higher-priced tour packages or cruises, you again receive the entire 10% commission back, less a service fee of $25 to $50, depending on the price of the package or cruise. If two people book a cabin costing a total of $4,000, they'll save $400, less a $50 fee, for a net saving of $350, which isn't bad. McTravel's phone is answered seven days a week.

Pennsylvania Travel, Inc.

23 Paoli Pike
Paoli, PA 19301
(phone 215/251-9944, or toll free
800/331-0947 outside Pennsylvania)

They permit you to buy at *their* cost (in effect passing on the entire commission to you), but then charge a booking fee (per transaction, not per person) of $35 if the booking is under $700, $50 for bookings of $700 to $1,500, $100 for bookings of $1,500 to $5,000, $150 for a purchase of $5,000 to $10,000. Assume that two persons purchase a cruise for $2,200 per person, a total of $4,400. Pennsylvania Travel passes on its 10% commission ($440), and proceeds to bill you for only $3,960, plus a $100 service charge, for a total of $4,060. You save $340.

21st Century Travel, Inc.

6950 France Avenue South
Edina, MN 55435
(phone 612/929-6695)

Any trip, anytime, anywhere: 21st Century Travel will sell you the trip at their cost, but then add on a small service charge.

On charter flights, for instance, you save from 11% to 13% of your ticket price but pay a service fee of $10 (for domestic charters) or $15 (international charters). On cruises, tours, packages, and scheduled air fares, you again save 10%, but pay $30 per transaction (not per person) for purchasing up to $700, $50 for tickets or fares totaling up to $1,500, $100 up to $5,000, $150 for any sum over $5,000. Edina, Minnesota, is a suburb of Minneapolis/St. Paul.

The $mart Traveller, Inc.

3111 S.W. 27th Avenue
Miami, FL 33133
(phone 305/448-3338)

Rebates the entire commission, but then assesses a service charge of $30 for transactions up to $750, a fee of $50 for bookings between $751 and $2,000, a fee of $100 for bookings from $2,001 to $4,000, and $150 for bookings from $4,001 to $6,000. Even on a transaction of only $750, you save $45—and much more, of course, on the higher-priced transactions.

Travel Broker$

393 Broadway
New York, NY 10013
(phone 212/219-0612)

Travel Broker$ charges no fee, but only rebates a part of the commission—the exact amount varying according to a complex formula. They guarantee the following *savings:* up to $15 on a purchase of up to $400; from $10 to $50 on a purchase of $401 to $800; from $40 to $60 on a purchase of $801 to $1,000; from $50 to $100 on a purchase of $1,001 to $1,500; from $80 to $130 on a purchase of $1,501 to $2,000; from $100 to $250 on a purchase of $2,001 to $3,500; and so on. "Our program," they explain, "is based on the concept that if you furnish us with the information necessary to book your trip, we save time and money, and can pass the savings on to you." Travel Brokers is planning to open offices in Stamford, Connecticut, and Washington,

D.C., and already has a branch in Tampa, Florida (phone 813/854-2611).

Blitz Travel

8918 Manchester Road
St. Louis, MO 63144
(phone 314/961-2700)

Blitz, says founder Leroy Blitz, has been in business for nearly 40 years, handles as many as 10,000 passengers a year, and gives back the following minimum amounts (they can often do better) to customers on any transaction other than for purely domestic air tickets: $15 back on a purchase of up to $400; $20 to $50 back on purchases of up to $800; $40 to $60 back on purchases of up to $1,000; $50 to $100 back on purchases of up to $1,500; $80 to $130 back on purchases of up to $2,000; and $100 and $250 back on purchases of up to $3,500. The higher their own commission, the better Blitz can do on the rebates listed above.

All Unique Travel

1030 Georgia Street
Vallejo, CA 94590
(phone 707/648-0237)

Already heavily into the discounting of international air fares (see the discount travel agencies discussion appearing elsewhere in this Appendix), All Unique will also "give back" 10% of what you spend for cruises and tours, provided you pay a fee of $50 for bookings up to $1,000; $100 for bookings from $1,000 to $5,000; and $250 for bookings more than $5,000.

Twenty-one of the Nation's Leading Discount Cruise Agencies

These are companies that cut the cost of a cruise to almost anywhere—and not simply on imminent departures; their reductions apply to sailings many months ahead. Enjoying a special relationship with major cruise-ship lines, they have been known to sell berths and cabins for as much as 40% off published rates. Although other cruise-ship specialists may, quietly, offer the same savings—and therefore I don't mean to imply that "the 21" are your only source of discounted tickets—the firms listed below are open and unabashed about their willingness to cut the cruise-ship rates: some of them send massive mailings to potential cruise-ship passengers, while others even advertise in public periodicals that they offer cruise-ship savings.

White Travel Service, Inc.

342 North Main Street
West Hartford, CT 06117
(phone 203/233-2648, or toll free 800/547-4790)
A source of remarkable savings and discounts on cruises throughout the year, it is headed by the ebullient Edie White and her son, Rick, who have themselves personally sailed on most of the major ships in service today.

Cruises of Distinction, Inc.

460 Bloomfield Avenue
Montclair, NJ 07042
(phone 201/744-1331, or toll free 800/634-3445)
Headed by a former cruise-ship executive,

Michael Grossman (former marketing vice-president of Norwegian American Cruises), who left the industry to concentrate on discounting fares in retail sales to the public. Publishes a remarkable, quarterly catalogue of discounts far into the future.

Cruises International, Inc.

1056 South Roselle Road
Schaumburg, IL 60193
(phone 312/893-8820, or toll free 800/ALL-SHIPS)
The Chicago-area powerhouse of the cruise-ship market, selling its space at considerable reductions, in many cases, off published fares. Prepares free, custom-created "cruise profiles" for clients.

Sea & Sail, Inc.

2630 Fountainview, Suite 118
Houston, TX 77057
(phone 713/784-6006)
Owned by prominent longtime Houston travel agent Edna Leah Frosch, it offers major discounts on numerous sailings each month, and advertises their availability via a jaunty, periodic newsletter sent to a large mailing list. Write to have your name added.

Esther Grossberg Travel, Inc.

6300 West Loop South, Suite 360
Bellaire, TX 77401
(phone 713/666-1761)
Another major Sunbelt retailer, it appears to have the same broad inventory of heavily discounted departures on nearly all the major lines.

Blitz World Cruise Center, Inc.

8918 Manchester
St. Louis, MO 63144
(phone 314/961-2700)
Big in the Midwest; throws in free travel insurance, in addition to discounts ranging from 10% to 33%. Motto is: "Service plus savings."

Captain's Table

(A Division of Stowaway Travel)
703 Market Street
San Francisco, CA 94103
(phone toll free 800/247-6071, 800/527-7447 in California)
Provides discounts up to 50% on sailings of at least 14 major and prestigious lines.

Cruise Reservations, Inc.

8975 N.E. Sixth Avenue
Miami, FL 33138
(phone 305/759-8922, or toll free 800/892-9929 outside Florida)
Because of its location in the "cruise capital of the world," it claims to enjoy particularly close relationships with numerous lines, resulting in discounts of "hundreds of dollars" on air/sea programs, as much as 40% off list.

Cruisemasters, Inc.

3415 Sepulveda Boulevard, Suite 645
Los Angeles, CA 90034
(phone toll free 800/242-9444, 800/242-9000 in California)
Cites discounts of up to 50% on up to 500 cruise departures yearly; will provide informative brochures that describe ships personally sampled by staff members.

The Travel Company

333 West El Camino Real, Suite 250
Sunnyvale, CA 94087
(phone toll free 800/344-3444,
800/858-5888 in California)
In business for 20 years, and quite substantial (claims, in fact, to be the largest cruise-only agency in the world), it publishes a "1989 Discount Cruise Catalog," available free for the asking. Promises discounts "up to 40% and more" on numerous sailings.

The Cruise Market Place, Inc.

939 Laurel Street
San Carlos, CA 94070
(phone toll free 800/826-4333,
800/826-4343 in California)
Will mail information, or advise over the phone, on discount opportunities as high as 50% on a broad range of sailings. A long-established firm, it publishes a quarterly newsletter on discount possibilities.

Cruise Pro, Inc.

2900 Townsgate Road, Suite 103
Westlake Village, CA 91361
(phone toll free 800/222-SHIP,
800/258-SHIP in California)
Represents 18 cruise-ship companies, and has built a considerable reputation from its policy of major discounts on their sailings. Seven years old and therefore a pioneer in the "cruise-only" business. Ask for Mr. Seeley, an officer of the National Association of Cruise-Only Agencies, who has himself sailed on more than 60 cruises.

The Ship Shop

18675 East 39th Street, Suite P
Independence, MO 64057
(phone 816/795-0570, or toll free
800/922-5510 outside Missouri)
A discount-granting cruise club charging membership of $29.95; once a member, you enjoy expert counseling and considerable discounts. Headed and owned by Debbie Adams, dynamic president of the National Association of Cruise-Only Agencies.

Cruises, Inc.

2711 James Street
Syracuse, NY 13206
(phone 315/463-9695, or toll free
800/854-0500)
"Certified and bonded," it publishes a free 16-page newsletter detailing its special offers and discounts on cruises throughout the world. Escorts many of the groups it sends on board.

Landry & Kling, Inc.

1 Gables Water Way
1390 So. Dixie Highway #1207
Coral Gables, FL 33146
(phone 305/661-1880, or toll free
800/431-4007)
Josephine Kling and Joyce Landry are the two former cruise-ship officials making up this cruise-only travel agency, a rather elegant firm servicing an affluent clientele. Because of their heavy volume of cruise sales, they claim to obtain group space and group rates on numerous sailings, and pass on the savings to their clients. Literature is sent to their clients on a near-quarterly basis.

Bee Kalt Travel, Inc.

4628 North Woodward Avenue
Royal Oak, MI 48072
(phone 313/549-6733, or toll free
800/321-2697)
A reputable, old-line travel agency (at least 30 years old) that is nevertheless one of the largest cruise discounters in the metropolitan Detroit area. Its discounts are substantial ones.

Segale Travel Service

2321 West March Lane
Stockton, CA 95207
(phone 209/943-0911, or toll free
800/531-3734 in California,
800/341-2928 from elsewhere)
The local American Express affiliate in its area, it enjoys major sales of cruises, and often offers its cruise products at substantial discounts off published levels.

Golden Bear Travel, Inc.

2171 Francisco Boulevard
San Rafael, CA 94901
(phone 415/258-9800, or toll free
800/451-8572 in California,
800/551-1000 from elsewhere)
A standard travel agency, but one that maintains a busy "discounted cruises department"; the latter not only sells reduced-price cruises to the public, but also wholesales them to other travel agencies.

Vacations at Sea

4919 Canal Street
New Orleans, LA 70119
(phone 504/482-1572, or toll free
800/231-9966 in Louisiana,
800/247-6091 from elsewhere)
Claims to sell more cruises (at heavy discounts) than any other agency in Louisiana. Accepts credit cards without reducing the discount, pays 10% interest on customer deposits, maintains cruise video library (you pay only postage both ways).

Cruise Specialists, Inc.

500 Wall Street
Seattle, WA 98121
(phone 206/441-7447, or toll free
800/544-AHOY)
Operated by Janet Olczak, who worked as a registered nurse on ships for 10 years; she's been on 200 cruises, and now specializes in six cruise lines from which she gets very special prices—up to 50% off—for her clients.

Cruise Consultants, Inc.

100 North East Loop 410
Suite 500
San Antonio, TX 78216
(phone 512/349-7700, or toll free
800/531-9001)
Savings of up to 40%, primarily on the more exotic cruises—to the South Pacific, the Orient, and Europe. Many escorted programs; many cruises for mature and elderly travelers. Cruise Consultants is headed by Jay Silberman, a former president of the National Association of Cruise-Only Agents.

The Four Leading "Hospitality Exchanges" Available to Americans

A "hospitality exchange": in theory it's simplicity incarnate. You accommodate members of the "exchange organization" as they pass through your home city; they accommodate you when you at some time pass through their home city. Each person or couple stays free, and enjoys the pleasures and contentments of true hospitality.

In practice the activity involves a considerable amount of administration—circulation of directories, change-of-addresses, etc. Those burdens caused a number of hospitality-exchange organizations to go out of business in the 1970s; consequently, the most recent attempts at hospitality exchange are by people who (in all but one instance) charge a small sum for their services and require that you reimburse the slight out-of-pocket expenses of your host. Nevertheless, while no longer free, the hospitality exchange has probably been placed on a firmer base and has greater prospects for survival.

Please note that a hospitality exchange differs from a "vacation exchange" in that there is no simultaneous swapping of accommodations. You use the service, or provide lodgings, only when you choose, and without having to coordinate your travel plans with the simultaneous travels of someone else.

Four leading groups:

Evergreen Bed and Breakfast Club
16 Village Green, #203
Crofton, MD 21114
(phone 301/261-0180)

Offshoot and brainchild of the powerful American Bed and Breakfast Association, which limits membership in Evergreen to persons 50 and over. You pay $40 a year for single membership, $50 a year for a couple, to receive a directory of Evergreen hosts (who must also be over 50), and are then entitled to enjoy the hospitality of another member, at $10 a night for a single, $15 a night for a twin. Considering that this includes a full American breakfast, these are among the lowest bed-and-breakfast rates in all the world. Why the fee at all? Club officials think that the $10 and $15 charges, in addition to offsetting out-of-pocket costs, add a businesslike quality to normal attitudes of hospitality.

When you apply for membership, you are asked to list your own accommodations (namely, a spare room) for use by other members. But no one requires that you accept all or even most of the bookings phoned in to you. You have complete discretion in that regard. When applying for membership, or further information, send a self-addressed, stamped envelope to the above address.

INNter Lodging Co-Op
P.O. Box 7044
Tacoma, WA 98407
(phone 206/756-0343)
With several hundred members scattered across the country (most concentrated on the two coasts), INNter Lodging can provide you with instant friends (and accommodations) for an initial fee of $50 to $95 (various membership drives and

discounts account for the variance), plus $4 to $5 per person per night paid to your actual hosts for the cost of fresh linen, towels, and other usables. No minimum age for guests; children with their own sleeping bags pay only 25¢. Founder Bob Ehrenheim publishes a directory of members in May or June of each year, and requires that members agree to make their own homes available for guests at least three months a year.

Visiting Friends, Inc.
P.O. Box 231
Lake Jackson, TX 77566
(phone 409/297-7367)
Laura and Tom LaGess began this service as a hospitality organization for genealogists; as genealogists themselves, frequently traveling, they found private homes far more pleasant than motels for overnight lodgings. The organization, a so-called guestroom-exchange network, now has more than 200 members, in all but eight states, including a few in Hawaii and Alaska. The initial charge is $15 for a "lifetime membership," then a total of $20 for your stay of up to six nights at a member's home. Mr. and Mrs. LaGess centralize the reservations process, keep all addresses in their own files (not in a published directory), and thus preserve both your privacy and occasional desire to receive no inquiries at all for a number of months. Write or phone Laura or Tom at the above address.

U.S. Servas Committee
11 John Street, Suite 706

New York, NY 10038
(phone 212/267-0252)

Not really a travel organization per se—but by carrying out its avowed purpose of promoting peace by bringing together people of different backgrounds, it manages both to extend hospitality in large measure and to make travelling meaningful for its members. Members pay a fee of $45, and are interviewed by a Servas representative in their area; they are then free to receive lists of hosts at their travel destinations, who will put them up free of charge—even to the extent of letting them share the family table at meals.

The normal stay with a Servas host is three days and two nights, which may be extended at the discretion of the host and the traveller. All arrangements are made by members, and no money is ever exchanged between them. The only requirement is that members are willing to talk, to exchange ideas, to become closely involved in the life of the host family. Servas, to me, is the most exalted travel organization on earth; it not only permits you to live free as you travel throughout the world, but to realize the oneness of all mankind.

Six "Homestay" Organizations for Americans Travelling Abroad

Foreign "homestays" are radically different from bed-and-breakfast stays, mainly because the latter activity is too often just that: you occupy a bed, have breakfast, and "split."

On a homestay, you stay around. You share the daily life of your host family. You socialize and converse with them, eat at their table, perhaps accompany them on their daily rounds. That kind of sojourn, when properly arranged, is one of the great pleasures of life, introducing you to another variety of the family of mankind.

Earlier in this book I've written about several organizations that offer rather elegant homestays in Britain. Here I add several less expensive alternatives, all for areas where English is well spoken by your hosts.

DENMARK

People to People Denmark
9 Romersgade
DK-1362 Copenhagen K

Denmark
(phone 01-14-10-35 between the hours of 10 a.m. and 2 p.m., Copenhagen time)
For groups of at least ten persons, staying in as many as five homes, here is the most remarkable of all homestay programs in that it is utterly free of charge. You receive room and all three meals daily, but you enjoy those gifts as a relative would, making no payment whatever to your Danish host family. They have invited you into their homes simply for the mutual benefit of an across-the-seas friendship, without expecting anything in return (such as a reciprocal stay in your home). Why else do they do this? Because they are Danes—a remarkable people, a lesson for all of us.

Of course, as a "member of the family," it would be the gracious thing to offer to help with family chores. You ought also to adapt yourself quietly and unobtrusively to the daily patterns of the family. Since some family members will have jobs to which they must attend each day, you should also take care of your own needs and entertainment when they are away. And finally, a gesture such as a postcard or letter of thanks when you return home would be much appreciated—and a great help to the homestay idea afterward.

Some 27 people-to-people homestay committees are maintained in Denmark, all of them outside the city of Copenhagen, usually in small to middle-sized towns, most on the peninsula of Jutland. Ms. Lise Heineke is one of the administrators of the organization, and a letter to her at the above Copenhagen address will set the process in motion. Give her plenty of advance notice, and indicate the exact dates when you expect to be in Denmark.

GREAT BRITAIN

Families in Britain
Martins Cottage, Martins Lane
Birdham, Chichester
West Sussex PO20 7AU, England
(phone Birdham 0243-512-222)
This time you spend part or all of your

British holiday as a paying guest with a British family, in locations scattered all over the British Isles. Though the organization's title refers to "families," they are more than happy to accept single persons traveling alone or couples.

In their literature the company makes a great point of the fact that they specialize in introducing overseas visitors of all ages to carefully selected private families by matching ages, interests, hobbies, and backgrounds. Once placed, visitors are looked after as one of the family and are encouraged to participate in the family's cultural, social, and sporting activities. Some of the participating families have private tennis courts, swimming pools, stables, even sailing boats.

Visitors can stay with a family at any time of the year, taking either three meals a day ("full pension") or two meals a day ("half pension"). Older visitors and family groups generally prefer the latter.

Charges are remarkably low. Half pension (room and two meals) ranges from £100 ($170) to £120 ($204) per person per *week*. Full pension is £120 ($204) to £150 ($255) per person per week. An agency fee (a one-time charge of £75, $127.50) is assessed for matching you up and making the arrangements.

If you're interested, write far in advance of your arrival in Britain for a brochure and registration form (a short questionnaire), and then send it, with a registration payment of £20 ($34).

Friends in Britain
c/o Kathleen J. Johnson
Marazion
Cornwall TR17 0AZ, England
(phone 0736-710-400)
A similar organization, but this time offering hospitality for only two or three nights at a time in a wide range of private homes all over the country. Ms. Johnson also offers ten-day tours of England, Scotland, and Wales, in which she provides you with a self-drive car and a prear-

ranged itinerary of two-night and three-night stays at the homes of her clients.

Some of the hosts are professionals—archaeologists, architects, accountants, doctors, teachers, and lecturers—prescreened by Ms. Johnson and chosen for their warmth toward visitors, and their ability to represent the best of Britain.

Charges, which include Ms. Johnson's fee, differ according to the standard of the home (luxury, standard, or simple), but usually average around £35 ($59.50) per person for room, full English breakfast, and a full-scale three-course dinner (with cheese for dessert, and coffee) each night, in a medium-category home; the same charge goes down to £25 ($42.50) in a simpler accommodation.

For a descriptive brochure and application form, write to Ms. Johnson at the address set forth above.

WESTERN AUSTRALIA

Homestay of W.A.
40 Union Road
Carmel, West Australia 6076
(phone 011-61-9-293-5347)
Though they specialize in their own area, Jean and Mark Smiley of Homestay of W.A. can arrange homestays in continental Australia, as well as in New Zealand and Tasmania. Tariffs range from $25 to $35 Australian (U.S. $18.25 to $25.55) a night, including breakfast, and evening meals are by arrangement with the families in many homes. You should probably plan to rent a car, as public transport hereabouts is not highly developed.

They also provide farmstays, and a good combination might be a two-night homestay in Perth, followed by three nights or more on a farm or ranch. If you haven't time for the country portion, Jean and Mark can arrange to have you invited for an afternoon ranch stay followed by an Aussie barbecue.

Write with complete details of your visit (flight numbers, exact dates, all else) to the address set forth above.

CONTINENTAL EUROPE

Experiment in International Living
Kipling Road
Brattleboro, VT 05301
(phone toll free 800/345-2929)
For young people aged 14 to 22, the classic summer homestay program is that of the distinguished organization named above. Write for a copy of their "Summer Abroad" catalogue detailing dozens of four-week to six-week homestays with families in most European countries (including Eastern Europe), and in Brazil, Kenya, Ecuador, Mexico, Martinique, Australia, New Zealand, the USSR, Turkey, Morocco, China, and Japan.

MALAYSIA

Randco Fish Sdn. Bhd.
10 Km Jalan Pahang
35000 Tapah
Perak
Malaysia
Mr. Glenville Kingham operates this project in a typical Malay village and "orang asli" (aboriginal) settlement. Though his chief activity is farming and instructing other Malay farmers in more effective agricultural methods, he also takes visitors (up to six couples at a time) to live in Malay kampong (village) houses. Activities include participating in the daily chores of the nearby farms (if one chooses) and visiting with residents at work on their small rubber farms, cocoa and palm oil farms, fruit orchards, fish farms, butterfly farms, and the like. "We also look forward to an exchange of ideas from participants," says Kingham, "and learn from them. Our charges are $35 for a couple per night, $25 for a single person travelling alone (there is no maximum or minimum stay period), and local travelling expenses range from $1 to $6 a day, depending on how far visitors travel per day."

Five Major "Vacation Exchange" Clubs

"Vacation exchanges" are organizations that enable you to swap your home or apartment for the home or apartment of a foreign resident (or one in another part of the country) during the periods of your respective vacations.

The swap is a simultaneous one, for a period of time that the two of you have selected. Having made the arrangements through an exchange of correspondence (usually), you settle upon the date and advise the other of where the door key (and sometimes the car keys) can be found. On that date, you pass in mid-air, so to speak. You fly to Edinburgh, let's say, or to the south of France, and they fly to your home in Albuquerque. Each of you receives the lodging element of your vacation absolutely free. And each enjoys a unique vacation abroad, as a resident of a new state or foreign country and not as a mere tourist.

I've listed below five major agencies that can help you make home exchanges, either for short- or long-term stays. In each case, you're the person who handles the details: you study the directories issued by each organization, find a suitable prospect, then send letters and pictures and work out a mutually satisfactory agreement. I've also listed one agency that will do the work for you, charging a fee for the service. Specific details follow under each listing:

Vacation Exchange Club
12006 111th Avenue
Youngtown, AZ 85363
(phone 602/972-2186)
Granddaddy of all the U.S. exchange services, begun in 1960 and operating continuously ever since (something of a record in a business that is notoriously short-lived). Two directories are published yearly, the first on February 15, the second on April 15; they include some 6,000 listings in the United States and 40 countries that span the globe. A fee of $24.70 entitles you to receive both directories and be listed in one of them.

Interservice Home Exchange, Inc.
P.O. Box 387
Glen Echo, MD 20812
(phone 301/229-7567)
Ted Kobrin, a foreign service officer, founded this organization nine years ago; he has since become the East Coast representative of the Europe-based Intervac International, a federation of home-exchange companies. Together they publish three catalogues—in February, March, and May—listing 5,700 homes or apartments in 30 countries, four-fifths of them outside the United States, mainly in Europe. For a single payment of $35, you receive all three catalogues and are listed. An exceptional feature is Kobrin's willingness to refund the fee to anyone who doesn't find what they're looking for in his catalogue.

Worldwide Exchange
1344 Pacific Avenue
Suite 103
Santa Cruz, CA 95060
(phone 408/425-0531)
Their directory lists not only 1,000 homes in the U.S. and Europe available for exchange, but also several hundred bed-and-breakfast accommodations available for rental. Current (1989) printouts are available for $9.95, whereas the charge for listing a home is $19.95, $6 more if you wish to include a photograph. As with all the firms thus far described, you do all the matchmaking yourself, utilizing the leads set forth in the directory.

Loan-a-Home
2 Park Lane, Apt. 6-E
Mount Vernon, NY 10552
This is for long-term stays, suitable primarily for retired Americans or academicians (the latter comprising the bulk of Loan-a-Home's clients). Ms. Muriel Gould of Loan-a-Home publishes the only directories that specialize in such extended stays, either as exchanges or as rentals at both ends if an exchange is not feasible (her members, as noted, being mainly academics on sabbatical, or business people transferred elsewhere for a year or two). A good portion of her listings are of second homes purchased for investment purposes, and therefore presumably available even on an open-ended basis. She also has a section on vacation housing, since many of the long-term rentals are available for short periods as well.

Loan-a-Home's directory is unique in that there is no charge for a listing; but if you want your own copy of the directory and its supplements (directories are published in June and December, supplements in March and September), you pay $30 for one directory and supplement, $40 for two directories and two supplements. Ms. Gould earns her income from sales of the directory, and charges no commission on the arrangements made; the latter are your concern, in any event.

Home Exchange International
185 Park Row, Box 878
New York, NY 10038

(phone 212/349-5340)
or
22458 Ventura Boulevard
Woodland Hills, CA 91364
(phone 818/992-8990)
These are the people to contact if you crave a home exchange but don't wish to make the arrangements yourself. The or-ganization will send you questionnaires, ask for interior and exterior photos of your home, then try to match you up with someone whose lifestyle and surroundings are compatible with yours. There's a one-time registration fee of $40, then a closing fee of $150 to $525, depending on duration of the exchange and whether it is for foreign or domestic locations. Considering that this service saves you the phone calls, letters, wires, and sheer amount of time that may be involved in arranging an exchange, it's not a bad investment. Exchanges are usually for summer or holiday periods, but the group can also handle sabbaticals.

Forty-eight of America's Foremost Bed-and-Breakfast Reservations Organizations

Originally, when the movement started, each bed-and-breakfast house advertised itself—in local media—or simply hung out a "B&B" shingle on the white picket fence. That proved increasingly unsatisfactory to the out-of-state travelers seeking B&B accom-modations. Most found themselves un-able to use these fine, cheap, and unpre-tentious lodgings because they were unable to ascertain names and addresses, and were also apprehensive about staying in a home about which they knew noth-ing.

Enter the bed-and-breakfast reserva-tions organization. Regional in scope, each representing about 100 homes, these firms perform the function of prescreen-ing—inspecting each lodging to ensure its suitability for transient visitors. They also have the wherewithal to advertise (a bit), and to maintain extensive phone lines and reservations personnel.

Of the 200 or so bed-and-breakfast reservations organizations in the U.S., the following seem to be to be outstanding, based either on a perusal of their literature or on actual phone conversations with nearly three-quarters of their owners.

In booking a B&B, be sure to make a sharp distinction between "bed-and-breakfast homes" and "bed-and-break-fast inns." The first is simply a private home or apartment occupied by a family that supplements its normal income by occasionally renting out a spare room or two to overnight visitors. The second—the "inn"—is a little hotel whose propri-etors rent out multiple rooms each night and earn their living from doing so; they also specialize in touches like quiche for breakfast, or cinnamon toast, fresh flow-ers daily in a bedroom vase—you get the picture. The bed-and-breakfast inns can often be more costly than a hotel, whereas a B&B house is supposed to charge 50% less than prevailing hotel rates in its area.

It's unfortunate that this semantic overlap occurred in the bed-and-breakfast field; a different name should really be found for the bed-and-breakfast inns. When I refer to a B&B, I mean a low-priced room in a private home—the term's initial meaning.

ALASKA

Alaska Bed and Breakfast
3/6500, Suite 169
Juneau, AK 99802
(phone 907/586-2959)
Owner Steve Hamilton represents 35 Alaskan homes, including interesting "cove" houses with panoramic views. The structures tend to be large, and often the bedrooms have their own wood stoves; locations are convenient to fishing, boat-ing, and sightseeing. And rooms range in price from $40 to $65 nightly, which is cheap for Alaska. (Incidentally, the ad-dress of "3/6500" set forth above is correct!)

ARIZONA

Bed and Breakfast in Arizona
P.O. Box 8628
Scottsdale, AZ 85252
(phone 602/995-2831, or toll free in Arizona 800/822-8885)
Has 100 houses throughout the state, charging an average of $50 a night in high season. Owners Tom Thomas and Trisha

Wills stress the advantages of the locations, the comforts, hospitality, and cleanliness of the houses they offer.

CALIFORNIA

Bed and Breakfast International (San Francisco)

1181-B Solano Avenue
Albany, CA 94706
(phone 415/525-4569)

Jean Brown claims that her agency is the oldest bed-and-breakfast reservations service, offering over 300 homes in the Bay Area and throughout all other parts of California. Double rooms range from $40 to $80 a night. Homes are found in Los Angeles, Santa Barbara, the Wine Country, even in Sausalito (houseboats), and are well-described in a brochure available free for the asking (but enclose a self-addressed, stamped, #10 envelope).

America's Co-Host Bed and Breakfast

P.O. Box 9302
Whittier, CA 90608
(phone 213/699-8427)

Coleen Davis heads this dynamic organization, and prepares fascinating write-ups of the houses and proprietors she represents. Example: "California bachelor who loves to cook will prepare mouth-watering breakfasts. His interest in fishing and hunting as well as his expertise with horses will allow you to feel you've had some time away from the daily grind. Fifty dollars per night, double." Houses are found in all parts of the state, and rooms range from $40 to $60.

COLORADO

Bed and Breakfast Rocky Mountains

P.O. Box 804
Colorado Springs, CO 80901
(phone 719/630-3433)

Coordinator Kate Peterson Winters handles over 100 homes and inns in Colorado, Utah, and New Mexico. Accommodations range from budget to luxury mansions, with a heavy concentration in the ski areas. Unhosted B&Bs are also

available. Rates range from $35 to $95 per room. Hours are 9 a.m. to 5 p.m. daily from May 16 to September 14; and noon to 5 p.m. weekdays from September 15 to May 15.

CONNECTICUT

Nutmeg Bed & Breakfast

222 Girard Avenue
Hartford, CT 06105
(phone 203/236-6698 weekdays from 9 a.m. to 5 p.m.)

Nutmeg is now six years old and represents about 100 host homes ranging from simple rooms in apartments to luxurious suites in mansions. Though owner Maxine Kates is heavily involved in corporate relocation of employees (for whom she obtains temporary accommodation), she stresses her continued loyalty to the classic tourist. Her rooms are classified as "C-Conventional" (modest homes in nice neighborhoods, nonadjoining or adjoining baths, with room charges of $45 to $55 a night); "Q-Quality" (lovely homes in excellent neighborhoods, adjoining or nonadjoining baths—usually private—with room rates of $65 to $80 a night); and "D-Deluxe" (luxurious estate homes, private baths and other private entry, some with kitchenettes, all renting for $85 to $95 per room per night). Surcharge for one-night stays in high season: $10.

DELAWARE

Bed and Breakfast of Delaware

P.O. Box 177
3650 Silverside Road
Wilmington, DE 19810
(phone 302/479-9500)

Millie Alford handles period homes in the "quaint old town" of New Castle, as well as comfortable, modern homes outside Wilmington and in the Chaddsford area of Pennsylvania. Five of her properties are on the National Historic Registry, several are near museums, and others are near or on the beach. Rooms average $50 a night for singles, $65 for couples or families.

DISTRICT OF COLUMBIA

Bed and Breakfast Ltd. of D.C.

P.O. Box 12011
Washington, DC 20005
(phone 202/328-3510)

An assortment of about 60 homes in every major area of the city; some of the houses are rambling Victorian mansions featured on local house tours. Rates range, in this high-priced city, from $30 to $75 a night for singles, $10 to $20 more for each additional person.

FLORIDA

B & B Suncoast Accommodations

8690 Gulf Boulevard
St. Pete Beach Island, FL 33706
(phone 813/360-1753)

Though owner Danie Bernard specializes in Florida's west coast beach towns on the Gulf of Mexico, she also has registered host homes in and near Orlando, Delray Beach, Sarasota, Bonita Springs, Venice, Naples, Tampa, St. Petersburg, Winter Park, Clearwater, and Tarpon Springs. Standard B&B runs $40 to $50 double; better amenities, $45 to $55; "exceptional homes," $60 to $80.

B & B of the Florida Keys, Inc.

P.O. Box 1373
Marathon, FL 33050
(phone 305/743-4118)

Features 30 homes throughout the Keys. All are on the water, air-conditioned, and include a complete breakfast. Most rooms range from $40 to $55 a night.

GEORGIA

Atlanta Hospitality

2472 Lauderdale Drive N.E.
Atlanta, GA 30345
(phone 404/493-1930)

Lists 60 homes all over the Atlanta area, most on routes of public transportation. Homes are mostly modern, yet double-occupancy rooms start at $35. "Gracious hospitality—we pride ourselves on that —at a modest rate," says Erna Bryant, owner-operator of "Atlanta Hospitality."

Division of Tourism
Georgia Department of Industry and Trade
230 Peachtree Street N.W.
Atlanta, GA 30301
(phone 404/656-3590)
By writing to this address you can obtain the "Georgia Bed and Breakfast" brochure, a free pamphlet listing 85 excellent bed-and-breakfast homes in all parts of the state.

HAWAII

Bed and Breakfast Hawaii
P.O. Box 449
Kapaa, HI 96746
(phone 808/822-7771)
This firm pioneered in developing a broad network of bed-and-breakfast accommodations in Hawaii, at considerably lower nightly costs than are offered by hotels. Double rooms start at $38.50 and go up to a top of $60 in most (not all) cases.

ILLINOIS

Bed and Breakfast of Chicago, Inc.
P.O. Box 14088
Chicago, IL 60614-0088
(phone 312/951-0085)
Mary Shaw handles 60 properties, half of which are unhosted apartments with breakfast left in the refrigerator. Apartments overlook key neighborhood attractions, often with views of the Chicago skyline and Lake Michigan. Double-occupancy rooms range from $50 to $75.

INDIANA

Amish Acres
1600 Market Street West
Nappanee, IN 46550
(phone 219/773-4188)
Richard Plecther represents about 30 homes in the Nappanee area. Most are family homes in the Amish community, and houses tend to be large and comfortable; some are working farms. Rooms average $40 a night for two.

IOWA

Bed and Breakfast of Iowa

P.O. Box 430
Preston, IA 52069
(phone 319/689-4222)
Maintains an inventory of more than 40 private homes, most in rural locations. Some overlook the Mississippi River; others are old mansions filled with antiques. Travellers, it is claimed, are treated like members of the family. As owner Wilma Bloom likes to say, "You're not buying a room, you're buying a memory." Double rooms range from $35 to $65 nightly, singles from $30 to $45.

KENTUCKY

Ohio Valley Bed and Breakfast
6876 Taylor Mill Road
Independence, KY 41051
(phone 606/356-7865)
Nancy Cully represents approximately 50 rooms in Victorian mansions, rural retreats, town houses, and urban condos. Homes are located in southern Ohio, northern Kentucky, and southeastern Indiana. Rooms range from $35 to $95 a night; all are carefully inspected before being listed by the organization; and many are air-conditioned.

LOUISIANA

Southern Comfort B & B Reservations
2856 Hundred Oaks Avenue
Baton Rouge, LA 70808
(phone 504/346-1928 or 928-9815)
Operated by Susan Morris and Helen Heath. Their rates range from $37.50 for a single, $40 for a double, to $150. While reservations services are free to you upon simply phoning the firm, they'll also send you a descriptive directory of all their homes for $3.

MAINE

Bed & Breakfast Downeast, Ltd.
Box 547, Macomber Mill Road
Eastbrook, ME 04634
(phone 207/565-3517)
Represents 150 homes in rural or town locations statewide, including fourteen

working farms. Homes are situated by the ocean, on islands, mountains, and "everywhere," boasts owner Sally Godfrey. A free brochure and a $3 directory are provided on request. Doubles range from $45 to $80 a night. Belongs to the six-state consortium of New England bed-and-breakfast reservations organizations referred to elsewhere in this Appendix.

MARYLAND

Traveller in Maryland, Inc.
P.O. Box 2277
Annapolis, MD 21404
(phone 301/269-6232, or in the Washington, D.C., metropolitan area, 301/261-2233)
Disposes of more than 150 accommodations all over the state, many on or close to the water. "We shine in Annapolis, Baltimore, and the Eastern Shore," says owner Cecily Sharp-Whitehill. Rates are $55 to $75 and up per room per night; each guest is the only guest taken at a time; and all hosts are extensively interviewed before being listed. Reservations should be made by phone and are always confirmed promptly by a friendly staff. Hours are Monday through Thursday from 9 a.m. to 5 p.m., on Friday from 9 a.m. to noon.

MASSACHUSETTS

Bed and Breakfast Cambridge & Greater Boston
P.O. Box 665
Cambridge, MA 02140
(phone 617/576-1492)
Fifty homes in locations claimed to be the best in the area: Back Bay and Beacon Hill, downtown Boston and Harvard Square, M.I.T., Tufts, and Boston College, Brookline, Lexington, and surrounding towns. Rates are rather high, perhaps because of that: $42 to $69 for singles, $52 to $79 for doubles. But owner Pamela Carruthers argues that her rates have not increased, while others' have.

Bed and Breakfast Associates Bay Colony, Ltd.
P.O. Box 57166
Babson Park Branch
Boston, MA 02157-0166
(phone 617/449-5302)
Has 100 homes, both downtown and suburban, Victorian and Federalist, modern as well. Owners Arline Kardasis and Marilyn Mitchell emphasize the firm's "concerned matching" of client to host and location. Double rooms range from $65 to $85, singles from $45 to $65.

New England Bed and Breakfast
1045 Centre Street
Newton Centre, MA 02159
(phone 617/244-2112 or 617/498-9819)
Fifty generally less-expensive homes, charging $40 to $55 double, $30 to $40 single, with no extra fees or taxes—a promise. All are within 15 and 20 minutes of downtown Boston via public transportation, and always within walking distance of a subway or bus stop. Handles properties throughout the rest of the state too.

MINNESOTA

Bed and Breakfast Registry, Ltd.
P.O. Box 8174
St. Paul, MN 55108
(phone 612/646-4238)
A nationwide reservations service (which also represents limited areas in Canada, New Mexico, and the Caribbean) headed by Gary Winget. Offerings in Minnesota include homes in the Twin Cities near public transportation and downtown. Houses outside the city are in scenic locations worth visiting. Motto of the organization: "Because you're someone special, you deserve special treatment." Most rooms range from $35 to $60 a night for two persons.

MISSISSIPPI

Southern Comfort Bed and Breakfast
2856 Hundred Oaks Avenue
Baton Rouge, LA 70808
(phone 504/346-1928 or 928-9815)
This organization headquartered in Louisiana is your best source of bed-and-breakfast reservations, at pre-inspected homes, in neighboring Mississippi.

MISSOURI

River Country Bed and Breakfast, Inc.
11005 Manchester Road
St. Louis, MO 63122
(phone 314/965-4328)
Michael Warner, a woman (her first name *is* Michael), is the owner and founder of this eight-year-old firm that represents over 200 rooms in 100 locations scattered through Missouri and adjacent parts of Illinois. Most doubles here rent for $35 to $70, most singles from $20 to $60.

NEVADA

Nevada Commission on Tourism
Capital Complex
Carson City, NV 89710
Will send a free pamphlet listing each and every bed-and-breakfast accommodation in the state. Simply write to the above address.

NEW HAMPSHIRE

New Hampshire Bed and Breakfast
RFD #3, Box 53
Laconia, NH 03246
(phone 603/279-8348)
Owner Martha Dorais says she "can offer just about any type of accommodation to guests." She has 60 urban and country homes located statewide; some are on the ocean, lakes, or in the mountains. A few have swimming pools, or offer cross-country skiing out the backdoor. Rates range from $35 to $80 a night, including a full breakfast, and only personally inspected homes are taken on for representation.

NEW JERSEY

Bed and Breakfast of New Jersey, Inc.
103 Godwin Avenue, Suite 132
Midland Park, NJ 07432
(phone 201/444-7409)
Features over 500 rooms in homes ranging from modest bungalows to large country estates. Manager Aster Mould claims to have interesting accommodations scattered all over the state, including converted grist mills, stately country homes, and an artist's studio. Doubles range in most instances from $30 to $100 a night.

NEW MEXICO

Bed and Breakfast Rocky Mountains
P.O. Box 804
Colorado Springs, CO 80901
(phone 303/630-3433)
They represent around 20 properties that are concentrated in four cities—Albuquerque, Taos, Santa Fe, and Las Vegas. Rooms cost $39 to $120 double.

NEW YORK STATE

Bed and Breakfast USA, Ltd.
P.O. Box 606
Croton-on-Hudson, NY 10520
(phone 914/271-6228)
For accommodations outside New York City, in every major area of the state, this organization is unbeatable. Its 28-page directory listing hundreds of homes is a superb introduction to the world of B&B. Most rooms rent for $35 and $50 (again, outside of New York City), plus a $15 booking charge to Bed and Breakfast USA. Some Manhattan homes are also found in the directory.

NEW YORK CITY

Urban Ventures, Inc.
P.O. Box 426
New York, NY 10024
(phone 212/594-5650)
Represents a remarkable total of more than 1,000 accommodations in Manhattan, Brooklyn, Queens, and "waterfront New Jersey" (Hoboken, Jersey City, etc.), although most are in Manhattan. Their "hosted" accommodations include a continental or larger breakfast, and range in

cost from $30 to $60 a night for a single room, $40 to $80 for a double, while "unhosted" lodgings start at $60. "All homes are thoroughly screened and very clean," claims the owner of Urban Ventures, who has operated the service for nearly ten years.

Abode B & B

P.O. Box 20022
New York, NY 10028
(phone 212/472-2000)

Offers B&Bs in town houses, high-rises, walk-ups, and brownstones—most in Manhattan, a few in Brooklyn Heights—requiring a minimum of a two-night stay. Groups can be lodged in a fashion that keeps all members close to one another. The charge for hosted apartments: a rather high average of $80 per double room, but for "charming apartments decorated very attractively," according to the proprietor of Abode B & B. Unhosted apartments (they come with a refrigerator stocked with staples) start at an average of $100 a night.

City Lights Bed and Breakfast

P.O. Box 20355
Cherokee Station
New York, NY 10028
(phone 212/737-7049)

Represents 200 homes, most in Manhattan, but also in Brooklyn, Queens, and Staten Island, and charges from $65 to $80 a night for a double room, in hosted lodgings. Mrs. D. Staff-Nielsen is the proprietor; she assures that "all accommodations are personally inspected to make certain they come up to our standards. We insist that the personality of the host be reflected in the home. Our hosts are all professional people, from the theater to politics to medicine. And we obtain evaluations from every single guest. If there is a complaint, we make sure it is remedied or we no longer represent that lodging."

New World Bed & Breakfast, Ltd.

150 Fifth Avenue, Suite 711
New York, NY 10011

(phone 212/675-5600, or toll free 800/443-3800 outside New York State)
One of the largest of the New York City firms, representing 100 to 150 fully inspected Manhattan homes and apartments. The aim is to offer rates 50% less than exorbitantly high New York City hotel charges. Thus B&B prices range from $40 to $80 single occupancy, $50 to $90 double occupancy. If those seem high, wait until you inquire about rates at a hotel! Laura Tilden is president of New World.

NORTH CAROLINA

Charlotte Bed and Breakfast, Inc.

P.O. Box 220802
Charlotte, NC 28222
(phone 704/868-3762)

Ruth Hill's organization handles nearly 20 homes and 10 inns in both of the Carolinas, some of them restored, historic homes and quite remarkable. Yet double rooms rent for only $25 to $40 a night, up to $85 on the coast.

NORTH DAKOTA

The Old West Bed-and-Breakfast

P.O. Box 211
Regent, ND 58650
(phone 701/563-4542)

A limited selection of large, rural homes, including one with a swimming pool, another with a Jacuzzi. Owner Marlys Prince boasts that his hosts are hospitable and themselves well traveled, and tend to serve large ranch breakfasts. Homes are located near the scenic Badlands, good hiking, horseback riding, and fishing. Rooms average only $25 a night.

OREGON

NW Bed and Breakfast Travel Unlimited

610 S.W. Broadway
Portland, OR 97205
(phone 503/243-7616)

Represents 400 bed-and-breakfast properties in 100 communities of Oregon, including Portland and Eugene, and in

California, Washington, Hawaii, and British Columbia. Most charge $35 to $55 for a double room.

PENNSYLVANIA

Bed and Breakfast of Philadelphia

P.O. Box 630
Chester Springs, PA 19425
(phone 215/827-9650)

Offers 100 homes in the metro area and surrounding suburbs, including a dozen renovated 18th-century homes. Most locations are within walking distance of Independence Hall in the city. Highly refined in their tastes, the two women who manage B&B of Philadelphia are both careful to place their clients in a congenial and compatible setting. In most instances, double rooms range from $40 to $80 a night, singles from $30 to $60.

Pittsburgh Bed and Breakfast, Inc.

2190 Ben Franklin Drive
Pittsburgh, PA 15237
(phone 412/367-8080)

Judy Antico offers 34 private homes in the city and within a 65-mile radius of it. Clients can select from casual country homes, preserved historic landmarks, working farms, or city homes near Pittsburgh nightlife. Homes in the Laurel Highland area feature mountain climbing and both downhill and cross-country skiing. Nightly room rates for double rooms range from $34 to $65, for singles $30 to $50.

RHODE ISLAND

Bed and Breakfast of Rhode Island

P.O. Box 3291
Newport, RI 02840
(phone 401/849-1298)

Lists over 120 homes throughout Rhode Island and nearby Massachusetts. Many are historic structures from the 1700s, and a few are on the waterfront. "Of course, you're never far from the water in Rhode Island," remarks president Joy Meiser. Her hosts are mostly professionals, including oceanographers, psychologists, and antique dealers. Rooms range from $50 to $100 for a double. Belongs to Bed and Breakfast Reservation Services of New England, an association of bed-and-breakfast reservations organizations in all six New England states, enabling any member to book a continuous itinerary through Connecticut, Rhode Island, Massachusetts, New Hampshire, Vermont, and Maine.

SOUTH CAROLINA

Palmetto Bed and Breakfast, Inc.
1460 Cherokee Road
Florence, SC 29501
(phone 803/667-8956)
Mrs. Frank Yates and Mrs. Mark Buyck manage this select group of half a dozen homes in Florence, near Charleston. One is a grand, plantation-style structure, near Revolutionary War forts. Nightly rates average $40 for a single and $50 for a double.

TENNESSEE

Bed and Breakfast Host Homes of Tennessee, Inc.
P.O. Box 110227
Nashville, TN 37222
(phone 615/331-5244)
Fredda Odom takes reservations for nearly 100 homes well scattered around the state. Houses are located in every sort of region, urban and rural. Many are on the National Historic Register; and although the latter rent for as much as $110 a night, the normal bed-and-breakfast homes (not inns) start as low as $40 a night for two persons.

TEXAS

Bed & Breakfast Texas Style, Inc.
4224 West Red Bird Lane
Dallas, TX 75237
(phone 214/298-5433 or 298-8586)
Offers bed-and-breakfast homes in 51 Texas cities, from Aledo to Wimberley, from Dallas to Waxahachie, in every important location. Ruth and Don Wilson are the owner/directors, and place the biblical adage, "In this place will I give peace . . ." at the bottom of their letterhead stationery. Their rates rarely go higher than $40 to $45 for a double room, and are often lower. A top operation.

UTAH

Bed and Breakfast Rocky Mountains
P.O. Box 804
Colorado Springs, CO 80901
(phone 303/630-3433)
Represents 20 properties in the state, including three in Salt Lake City. Two in that city charge as little as $35 and $40 for a double room.

VIRGINIA

Bensonhouse of Richmond, Inc.
2036 Monument Avenue
Richmond, VA 23220
(phone 804/648-7560)
Offers 40 homes in Richmond, Williamsburg, Petersburg, Bowling Green, Fredericksburg, Orange, and the Northern Neck of Virginia; many are in historic districts. Owner Lyn M. Benson takes special care to select enthusiastic hosts who will take special pains to entertain their guests. The agency's emphasis is on older homes, and rates average $48 to $84, but with occasional "inns" going as high as $100.

WASHINGTON

Pacific Bed and Breakfast
701 N.W. 60th Street
Seattle, WA 98107
(phone 206/784-0539)
Features a wide variety of private rooms averaging $40 to $80 a night. "People are usually amazed at what I offer," says founder Irmgard Castleberry, who handles waterfront cabins, private apartments, and full-scale houses located throughout the state, and in Victoria and Vancouver, British Columbia. Her directory of lodgings is available for $7.

NW Bed and Breakfast Travel Unlimited
610 S.W. Broadway, Suite 606
Portland, OR 97205
(phone 503/243-7616)
Represents 300 to 400 properties up and down the state, and several in neighboring British Columbia, Canada, as well as Washington, California, and Hawaii. Numerous houses charge only $35 to $55 for a double room, to which you'll need to add a one-time usage charge of $5 to the organization. For a one-year membership, including receipt of their comprehensive directory, families pay $25; only $8 (including postage and handling) for the directory alone.

Thirty-eight Student Travel Agencies at Home and Abroad

The closest thing we have to an "official" student travel agency in the United States is the Council on International Educational Exchange (C.I.E.E.). An activity funded by several hundred U.S. colleges and universities, the council is our nation's representative to the International Student Travel Conference. It issues the vitally important International Student Identity Card (ISIC), which entitles students to stay and eat at student hotels and restaurants around the world, and to receive important discounts—or even free admissions—at theaters, museums, and other like facilities. It offers working vacations for American students in Britain, Ireland, France, Germany, New Zealand, and Costa Rica; operates cheap, transatlantic charter flights; and provides cheap intra-European air or rail transportation. And finally, it provides longer-term study opportunities for Americans: semester-long and full-year stints at famous universities around the world.

Usually, you secure these services simply by visiting the "student exchange" office or "travel office" on your own campus, which frequently turns out to be a representative of C.I.E.E. But a better course is to visit—if you can manage to do so—a full-scale Council Travel Office, of which there are thirty:

COUNCIL TRAVEL OFFICES
CALIFORNIA
BERKELEY

2511 Channing Way
Berkeley, CA 94704
(phone 415/848-8604)

LA JOLLA

UCSD Student Center B-023
La Jolla, CA 92093
(phone 619/452-0630)

LONG BEACH

5500 Atherton Street, Suite 212
Long Beach, CA 90815
(phone 213/598-3338)

LOS ANGELES

1093 Broxton Avenue, Suite 220
Los Angeles, CA 90024
(phone 213/208-3551)

LOS ANGELES VALLEY

14515 Ventura Boulevard, Suite 250
Sherman Oaks, CA 91403
(phone 818/905-5777)

SAN DIEGO

4429 Cass Street
San Diego, CA 92109
(phone 619/270-6401)

SAN FRANCISCO

312 Sutter Street
San Francisco, CA 94108
(phone 415/421-3473)

919 Irving Street
San Francisco, CA 94122
(phone 415/566-6222)

GEORGIA
ATLANTA

12 Park Place South
Atlanta, GA 30303
(phone 404/577-1678)

ILLINOIS
CHICAGO

29 East Delaware Place
Chicago, IL 60611
(phone 312/951-0585)

MASSACHUSETTS
AMHERST

79 South Pleasant Street
Amherst, MA 01002
(phone 413/256-1261)

BOSTON

729 Boylston Street
Boston, MA 02116
(phone 617/266-1926)

CAMBRIDGE

1384 Massachusetts Avenue
Cambridge, MA 02138
(phone 617/497-1497)

MINNESOTA
MINNEAPOLIS

1501 University Avenue SE, Room 300
Minneapolis, MN 55414
(phone 612/379-2323)

NEW YORK
NEW YORK CITY

205 East 42nd Street
New York, NY 10017
(phone 212/661-1450)

New York Student Center
356 West 34th Street
New York, NY 10001
(phone 212/695-0291)

35 West 8th Street
New York, NY 10011
(phone 212/254-2525)

OREGON
PORTLAND

715 S.W. Morrison, Suite 600
Portland, OR 97205
(phone 503/228-1900)

RHODE ISLAND
PROVIDENCE

171 Angell Street
Providence, RI 02906
(phone 401/331-5810)

TEXAS
AUSTIN

1904 Guadalupe Street
Austin, TX 78705
(phone 512/472-4931)

DALLAS

Executive Tower Office Center
3300 West Mockingbird Lane
Dallas, TX 75235
(phone 214/350-6166)

WASHINGTON
SEATTLE

1314 N.E. 43rd Street, Suite 210
Seattle, WA 98105
(phone 206/632-2448)

OVERSEAS
GERMANY
BONN

Thomas Mann Strasse 33
5300 Bonn 2
(phone 0228-659-746)

FRANCE
PARIS

31 rue St-Augustin
75002 Paris
(phone 42-66-40-94)

51 rue Dauphine
75006 Paris
(phone 43-26-79-65)

16 rue de Vaugirard
75006 Paris
(phone 46-34-02-90)

NICE

10 rue de Belgique
06000 Nice
(phone 93-87-34-96)

BORDEAUX

9 place Charles-Gruet
33000 Bordeaux
(phone 56-44-68-73)

LYON

9 rue des Remparts d'Ainay
69001 Lyon
(phone 16-78-42-99-94)

JAPAN
TOKYO

Sanno Grand Building
14-2 Nagata-Cho, 2-Chome
Chiyoda-ku
Tokyo 100
(phone 03-581-7581)

Student Travel Network

Still another source of student travel services is the Student Travel Network operated in the U.S. by the Australian-owned STA Travel Group—probably the world's largest student travel organization. Although it issues student cards and organizes student tours and exchange programs, its particular specialty is the sale of low-cost, cut-rate international air tickets on scheduled flights. Like a giant student-oriented "bucket shop," it negotiates with the world's most prestigious carriers to permit students to occupy their seats at stunning rates: as little as $489 round-trip between Los Angeles and London, $549 round-trip to Tokyo. And it provides these prices to people up to the age of 35.

STA offices in the U.S. (others are in Europe, Asia, and the South Pacific) include:

CALIFORNIA
LOS ANGELES

7204 Melrose Avenue
Los Angeles, CA 90046
(phone 213/934-8722, or toll free 800/777-0112)

SAN FRANCISCO

166 Geary Street, Suite 702
San Francisco, CA 94108
(phone 415/391-8407)

SAN DIEGO

6447 El Cajon Boulevard
San Diego, CA 92115
(phone 619/286-1322)

TEXAS
DALLAS

6609 Hillcrest Avenue
Dallas, TX 75205
(phone 214/360-0097)

HAWAII
HONOLULU

1831 South King Street, Suite 202
Honolulu, HI 96826
(phone 808/942-7755)

ILLINOIS
CHICAGO

3249 North Broadway
Chicago, IL 60657
(phone 312/525-9227)

MASSACHUSETTS
BOSTON

273 Newbury Street
Boston, MA 02116
(phone 617/266-6014)

NEW YORK
NEW YORK CITY

c/o Whole World Travel
17 East 45th Street
New York, NY 10017
(phone 212/986-9470)

Seven Major Transatlantic Charter Operators

The transatlantic charter is alive and well. Though the number of "players" is sharply diminished, and the usual period of operation (May through September) greatly reduced, the survivors are stronger than ever—better financed, more responsible and reliable. And their peak-season product is often your best means of travelling to Europe at a time when the "bucket shops" and "distress merchants" have far fewer scheduled seats to sell at reduced rates (their greatest values are had in the off- and shoulder seasons of the year).

As remarkable as it may seem, some of the charter operators are today government owned, or subsidiaries of scheduled air carriers. I've selected seven as the most enduring, best operated of the lot:

Jet Vacations, Inc.
888 Seventh Avenue
New York, NY 10106
(phone 212/247-0999, or toll free 800/JET-0999)
A subsidiary of Air France, it operates Boeing 747 charters between New York and Paris year round ($215 to $269 each way); between New York and Nice, non-stop, from June through September ($269 to $289 each way); between Boston and Paris from June through October ($229 to $269 each way); between D.C. and Paris from June through October ($249 to $289 each way); and occasionally from L.A., San Francisco, Chicago, Miami, Houston, or Philadelphia to Paris.

LTU International Airways
6033 West Century Boulevard, Suite 1000
Los Angeles, CA 90045
(phone toll free 800/888-0200)
It flies from New York to Düsseldorf or Munich ($399 round-trip); from Miami to Düsseldorf, Frankfurt, or Munich ($449 round-trip); and from Los Angeles and San Francisco to Düsseldorf, Frankfurt, or Munich ($569 round-trip). These prices are guaranteed from November 1988 to April 1989, do not include tax, but do include complimentary movies, beer, and German wine. No advance bookings needed, no minimum stay. Weekly departures or better.

Martinair Holland
1165 Northern Boulevard
Manhasset, NY 11030
(phone 516/627-8711, or toll free 800/847-6677)
A subsidiary of KLM Royal Dutch Airlines. Operates weekly charters to Amsterdam from 13 North American cities, at the following round-trip rates: Baltimore, $388; Boston, $368; Chicago, $538; Cleveland, $498; Detroit, $498; New York/JFK, $385; Los Angeles, $568; Miami, $518; Minneapolis, $538; Newark, $418; San Francisco, $568; Seattle, $548; and Toronto, $519 Canadian. Note that these are minimum round-trip prices, excluding taxes, and subject to high-season surcharges.

Condor
875 North Michigan Avenue
Chicago, IL 60611
(phone 312/951-0005)
A subsidiary of Lufthansa, it operates weekly charters to Frankfurt from Chicago, Cleveland, Denver, Detroit, Los Angeles, New York/JFK, Newark, San Francisco, Tampa, Washington/Baltimore. For reservations, phone DER Tours, Inc., toll free, at 800/782-2424, or Schwaber International at 212/432-0116.

Dollar Stretcher
11990 San Vicente Boulevard
Los Angeles, CA 90049
(phone 213/820-3535, or toll free 800/826-6547 in the western states)
or
5750 Major Boulevard
Orlando, FL 32819
(phone 305/345-0064, or toll free 800/223-5430 in Florida)
A British Airways company operating weekly charters from Los Angeles and Orlando to either London or Manchester, at round-trip rates starting at $399 (plus $13 tax).

Homeric Tours
595 Fifth Avenue
New York, NY 10017
(phone 212/753-1100, or toll free 800/223-5570)
A long-established, reputable company operating weekly Boeing 747 charters from New York to Athens, at rates starting at $299 one way, $499 round-trip. Charters generally operate during every month of the year, as many as three times a week.

Council Charters
205 East 42nd Street
New York, NY 10017
(phone 212/661-0311; or toll free 800/223-7402)
A subsidiary of C.I.E.E., it claims to be America's oldest charter company. London, Paris, and Zurich are their major destinations, from New York, Boston, and L.A. You can leave on any date, return on any date.

The Twelve Top Travel Values of 1989

Capitals of Eastern Europe

You've seen them described in earlier pages of this book. Budapest, Prague, Bucharest, Warsaw, East Berlin, Sofia, are all extraordinary values, and all except Bucharest are now receiving multitudes of Western tourists drawn there by rates of $20 and less for a double room (in modest hotels), meals for $3 and less, museum admissions for 25¢, in-city transportation for pennies. In an obvious ferment as a result of developments in the Soviet Union, they have never been as fascinating as now, and should be high on your travel list for 1989.

Turkey

The other budget stand-out of Europe, its rate structure is astonishingly low for travellers willing to make use of local facilities. Away from the Hiltons, perfectly adequate rooms are available at $15 and $20 for two, meals for $3. See the discussion elsewhere in this book

Interior Cities of Mexico

By actively avoiding the overpriced and overcrowded resorts of Mexico's Pacific and Caribbean coasts—the Acapulcos and the Puerto Vallartas, the Cancúns and the Ixtapas—and by heading instead to that diadem of 17th-century and 18th-century colonial cities surrounding Mexico City, travellers gain advantage of the distorted exchange rate for the Mexican peso. Charming hotels with posada-style courtyards (renting double rooms for $23), leisurely multicourse meals for $4 and $5, await the visitor who eschews the coast.

Costa Rica

Central America's most peaceful country is also one of its cheapest for travellers making use of unpretentious lodgings and facilities. Attending one of several Spanish-language schools in the capital city of San Jose (see our discussion elsewhere in this book), and securing your room and board through their auspices, your costs become dirt cheap though your stay remains dignified and fun.

"Extended Stays" in Spain

From November 1 through March 31, tour operators associated with Iberia Airlines send mature (over 55) Americans to vacation for at least a month on the Mediterranean Coast of Spain, at air-fare-included charges of less than $800 for thirty days. You stay in a fully-equipped studio in a modern apartment-hotel facing directly on the sea. See elsewhere in this book for all the details.

Rio and Buenos Aires

Their inflation-ravaged currencies continue to drop against the U.S. dollar, and if you purchase your "cruzados" or "australes" before leaving the U.S., or on officially tolerated "grey markets" once there (ask), you enjoy an even more remarkable rate. Even at the official exchange, men's shoes sell for $12 at good shops, women's suits for $30, "churrascuria" meals (unlimited servings) for $5 and $6, at establishments carefully chosen. And there are weekly low-cost charter flights to both destinations from several U.S. cities.

Indonesia

On the beaches of its chief touristic attraction—the island of Bali—are extremely modest facilities where you can still live, if you wish, for $5 a day! In lodgings a bit more basic, you can stay for, say, $20 a day; and the same values are had in the capital city of Jakarta and at still other locations in this vast, multi-island nation. It is an "in" area for the most canny of current travellers, now flocking to Indonesia in record numbers.

Orlando, Florida

In at least seven months of the year—that is, at all times *other* than mid-February through mid-April, July and August, Christmas and a few other dates—the area's hundreds of hotels and motels are lightly booked and a sort of price war breaks out. Then, by simply driving up and down the motel-lined highways, you'll spot signs by the score for double rooms at $19 and $20 a night. And at nearby restaurants, buffet breakfasts are selling for $2.99, all-you-can-eat chuckwagon lunches and dinners for $3.99 or $4.99. Some of the smartest of current-day tourists—people without children in tow, vacationers without the slightest intention of seeing the "Magic Kingdom" or communing with Mickey Mouse—are now flocking (in those seven magical months) to enjoy standard adult holidays of sunning and swimming, shopping, and nightlife at the lowest resort costs in the world today.

Thailand

Bangkok and Pattaya Beach, Chiang

Mai and other dream-laden spots, are the attractions of this ultra-low-cost nation, long visited by Europeans, but now increasingly popular among cost-conscious Americans. For the adventurous traveller, willing to explore and experiment, it is one of the cheapest places on earth.

Elderhostel

Though the rates of this celebrated study program for people over the age of 60 have recently risen to an average of $245 a week, that outlay brings you six nights' lodging in a university residence hall, all three meals a day for a full week, 4½ hours a day of classroom instruction by distinguished faculty members, again

for a week, and full access to university recreational facilities. It definitely qualifies among the best travel values of 1989.

Venezuela

The collapse of oil prices in 1983 caused a collapse of its currency, the once-proud "bolivar." Result: what was once among the most expensive countries on earth is now one of the cheapest. In Caracas, and in the two chief seaside resorts—the offshore island of Margarita and the beach-lined Puerto la Cruz—high-quality hotel rooms go for $50 a night, good meals for $5. Canadians were the first to spot the new-found cheapness of Venezuela, and thousands of cost-

conscious Americans will be following their lead in 1989.

Belize

The former British Honduras, at the southeast tip of the Yucatán peninsula, it is peaceful, secure, and English-speaking, and yet shunned by many tourists because of its dreaded location: Central America, near Honduras, Guatemala, Nicaragua. Visitors who overcome their apprehension find superb snorkeling and scuba, Mayan ruins, wildlife, beaches—an undiscovered travel treasure. Cheapest of all Belizean locations: Caye Caulker, with weather-beaten, ancient hotels renting double rooms for less than $20 a night, and tent space out back for $2.50!

Puerto la Cruz, Venezuela

Photo Credits

Index

About the Author

Arthur Frommer is a graduate of the Yale University Law School, where he was an editor of the Yale Law Journal, and he is a member of the New York Bar. After service with U.S. Army Intelligence at the time of the Korean War, he practiced law in New York City with the firm of the late Adlai Stevenson until the growing demands of travel writing and tour operating required his full attention. He is the author of *Europe on $5 a Day* (now in its 32nd yearly edition as *Europe on $30 a Day,* the largest selling travel guide in the United States), guidebooks to Belgium, New York, and Amsterdam, and two books dealing with legal and political subjects. In New York, he is an active trustee of the Community Service Society, the nation's largest and oldest anti-poverty organization. He writes a weekly nationally syndicated newspaper column on travel and hosts "Arthur Frommer's Almanac of Travel" on the national cable television network, The Travel Channel. He is also the founder of Arthur Frommer Holidays, Inc., one of the nation's leading international tour operators, and lectures widely on travel subjects.

FROMMER BOOKS
PRENTICE HALL PRESS
ONE GULF + WESTERN PLAZA
NEW YORK, NY 10023

Date_____

Friends:
Please send me the books checked below:

FROMMER'S™ $-A-DAY® GUIDES

(In-depth guides to sightseeing and low-cost tourist accommodations and facilities.)

☐ Europe on $30 a Day.......$14.95
☐ Australia on $30 a Day......$12.95
☐ Eastern Europe on $25 a Day .$13.95
☐ England on $40 a Day $12.95
☐ Greece on $30 a Day $12.95
☐ Hawaii on $50 a Day $13.95
☐ India on $25 a Day.........$12.95

☐ Ireland on $35 a Day $12.95
☐ Israel on $30 & $35 a Day $12.95
☐ Mexico (plus Belize & Guatemala)
    on $25 a Day $13.95
☐ New Zealand on $40 a Day ..$12.95
☐ New York on $50 a Day $12.95
☐ Scandinavia on $60 a Day $12.95

☐ Scotland and Wales on $40 a
    Day $12.95
☐ South America on $30 a Day ..$13.95
☐ Spain and Morocco (plus the Canary
    Is.) on $40 a Day $13.95
☐ Turkey on $25 a Day.........$12.95
☐ Washington, D.C., & Historic Va. on
    $40 a Day................$12.95

FROMMER'S™ DOLLARWISE® GUIDES

(Guides to sightseeing and tourist accommodations and facilities from budget to deluxe, with emphasis on the medium-priced.)

☐ Alaska................$13.95
☐ Austria & Hungary $14.95
☐ Belgium, Holland,
    Luxembourg $13.95
☐ Brazil.................$14.95
☐ Egypt.................$13.95
☐ France................$14.95
☐ England & Scotland $14.95
☐ Germany $13.95
☐ Italy $14.95
☐ Japan & Hong Kong.......$13.95

☐ Portugal, Madeira, & the
    Azores.................$13.95
☐ South Pacific $13.95
☐ Switzerland & Liechtenstein . .$13.95
☐ Bermuda & The Bahamas $13.95
☐ Canada $13.95
☐ Caribbean $13.95
☐ Cruises (incl. Alask, Carib, Mex,
    Hawaii, Panama, Canada, & US) .$14.95
☐ California & Las Vegas $14.95
☐ Florida $13.95

☐ Mid-Atlantic States $13.95
☐ New England $13.95
☐ New York State $13.95
☐ Northwest $13.95
☐ Skiing in Europe $14.95
☐ Skiing USA—East $13.95
☐ Skiing USA—West $13.95
☐ Southeast & New Orleans.....$13.95
☐ Southwest $14.95
☐ Texas $13.95
☐ USA $15.95

FROMMER'S™ TOURING GUIDES

(Color illustrated guides that include walking tours, cultural & historic sites, and other vital travel information.)

☐ Australia $9.95
☐ Egypt..................$8.95
☐ Florence $8.95

☐ London $8.95
☐ Paris $8.95

☐ Thailand................$9.95
☐ Venice $8.95

FROMMER'S™ CITY GUIDES

(Pocket-size guides to sightseeing and tourist accommodations and facilities in all price ranges.)

☐ Amsterdam/Holland.........$5.95
☐ Athens................$5.95
☐ Atlantic City/Cape May $5.95
☐ Boston................$5.95
☐ Cancún/Cozumel/Yucatán $5.95
☐ Dublin/Ireland $5.95
☐ Hawaii................$5.95
☐ Las Vegas $5.95
☐ Lisbon/Madrid/Costa del Sol ..$5.95

☐ London $5.95
☐ Los Angeles $5.95
☐ Mexico City/Acapulco $5.95
☐ Minneapolis/St. Paul $5.95
☐ Montréal/Québec City $5.95
☐ New Orleans $5.95
☐ New York...............$5.95
☐ Orlando/Disney World/EPCOT ..$5.95

☐ Paris $5.95
☐ Philadelphia $5.95
☐ Rio...................$5.95
☐ Rome..................$5.95
☐ San Francisco $5.95
☐ Santa Fe/Taos (avail. May 1989) .$5.95
☐ Sydney.................$5.95
☐ Washington, D.C............$5.95

SPECIAL EDITIONS

☐ A Shopper's Guide to the
    Caribbean $12.95
☐ Beat the High Cost of Travel . . .$6.95
☐ Bed & Breakfast—N. America .$11.95
☐ Guide to Honeymoon Destinations
    (US, Canada, Mexico, & Carib) .$12.95
☐ Manhattan's Outdoor
    Sculpture...............$15.95

☐ Motorist's Phrase Book
    (Fr/Ger/Sp) $4.95
☐ Paris Rendez-Vous.........$10.95
☐ Swap and Go (Home
    Exchanging).............$10.95
☐ The Candy Apple (NY for Kids) .$11.95
☐ Travel Diary and Record Book ..$5.95
☐ Where to Stay USA (Lodging
    from $3 to $30 a night)......$10.95

☐ Marilyn Wood's Wonderful Weekends
    (NY, Conn, Mass, RI, Vt, NH, NJ,
    Del, Pa) $11.95
☐ The New World of Travel (Annual
    sourcebook by Arthur Frommer
    previewing: new travel trends, new
    modes of travel, and the latest
    cost-cutting strategies for savvy
    travelers) $14.95

SERIOUS SHOPPER'S GUIDES

(Illustrated guides listing hundreds of stores, conveniently organized alphabetically by category)

☐ Italy..................$15.95
☐ London $15.95

☐ Los Angeles........$14.95
☐ Paris $15.95

GAULT MILLAU

(The only guides that distinguish the truly superlative from the merely overrated.)

☐ The Best of Chicago (avail. April
    1989).................$15.95
☐ The Best of France (avail. July
    1989)..................$15.95
☐ The Best of Italy (avail. July
    1989)..................$15.95

☐ The Best of Los Angeles $15.95
☐ The Best of New England
    (avail. April 1989)..........$15.95

☐ The Best of New York.......$15.95
☐ The Best of San Francisco ...$15.95
☐ The Best of Washington, D.C...$15.95

ORDER NOW!

In U.S. include $1.50 shipping UPS for 1st book; 50¢ ea. add'l book. Outside U.S. $2 and 50¢, respectively.

Allow four to six weeks for delivery in U.S., longer outside U.S.

Enclosed is my check or money order for $_____

NAME _____

ADDRESS _____

CITY _____ STATE _____ ZIP _____